Computer Structures and Software: Analysis, Integration and Verification

Computer Structures and Software: Analysis, Integration and Verification

Edited by
Alexandro Cyprus

www.willfordpress.com

Published by Willford Press,
118-35 Queens Blvd., Suite 400,
Forest Hills, NY 11375, USA

ISBN: 978-1-64728-441-1

Cataloging-in-publication Data

Computer structures and software : analysis, integration and verification / edited by Alexandro Cyprus.
   p. cm.
Includes bibliographical references and index.
ISBN 978-1-64728-441-1
1. Computer systems. 2. Computer software. 3. Cyberinfrastructure. I. Cyprus, Alexandro.
QA76 .C66 2023
004--dc23

For information on all Willford Press publications
visit our website at www.willfordpress.com

Contents

Preface VII

Chapter 1   **Controlling a Random Population** 1
             Thomas Colcombet, Nathanaël Fijalkow and Pierre Ohlmann

Chapter 2   **An Axiomatic Approach to Reversible Computation** 18
             Ivan Lanese, Iain Phillips and Irek Ulidowski

Chapter 3   **Semantical Analysis of Contextual Types** 38
             Brigitte Pientka and Ulrich Schöpp

Chapter 4   **On Well-Founded and Recursive Coalgebras** 58
             Jiří Adámek, Stefan Milius and Lawrence S. Moss

Chapter 5   **Spinal Atomic Lambda-Calculus** 78
             David Sherratt, Willem Heijltjes, Tom Gundersen and Michel Parigot

Chapter 6   **Local Local Reasoning: A BI-Hyperdoctrine for Full Ground Store** 98
             Miriam Polzer and Sergey Goncharov

Chapter 7   **The Inconsistent Labelling Problem of Stutter-Preserving
             Partial-Order Reduction** 118
             Thomas Neele, Antti Valmari and Tim A.C. Willemse

Chapter 8   **Neural Flocking: MPC-based Supervised Learning of Flocking
             Controllers** 138
             Usama Mehmood, Shouvik Roy, Radu Grosu, Scott A. Smolka,
             Scott D. Stoller and Ashish Tiwari

Chapter 9   **Quantum Programming with Inductive Datatypes: Causality and
             Affine Type Theory** 154
             Romain Péchoux, Simon Perdrix, Mathys Rennela and
             Vladimir Zamdzhiev

Chapter 10   **Timed Negotiations** 174
             S. Akshay, Blaise Genest, Loïc Hélouët and Sharvik Mital

Chapter 11   **Ambiguity, Weakness and Regularity in Probabilistic Büchi
             Automata** 193
             Christof Löding and Anton Pirogov

Chapter 12   **The Polynomial Complexity of Vector Addition Systems with States**...213
Florian Zuleger

Permissions

List of Contributors

Index

Preface

This book has been an outcome of determined endeavour from a group of educationists in the field. The primary objective was to involve a broad spectrum of professionals from diverse cultural background involved in the field for developing new researches. The book not only targets students but also scholars pursuing higher research for further enhancement of the theoretical and practical applications of the subject.

Computer structure refers to the various parts of the computer, which are organized in such a way that makes it possible to communicate with the computer. It can be categorized into five main parts, including input devices, memory, output devices, central processing unit, and input and output ports. Input devices take command from the user and enter data in the system, whereas output devices display results after processing data in forms such as hard copy, soft copy, and video or voice. Central processing unit regulates the functioning of the computer using arithmetic logic unit, register and control unit. Memory is the storage medium, and input and output ports are connectors controlled by the processor for managing input and output actions. Verification is the process of determining whether or not a software system meets the required specifications and standards and serves its intended purpose. This book provides comprehensive insights into analysis, integration and verification of computer structures and software. It is a resource guide for experts as well as students.

It was an honour to edit such a profound book and also a challenging task to compile and examine all the relevant data for accuracy and originality. I wish to acknowledge the efforts of the contributors for submitting such brilliant and diverse chapters in the field and for endlessly working for the completion of the book. Last, but not the least; I thank my family for being a constant source of support in all my research endeavours.

Editor

Controlling a Random Population⋆

Thomas Colcombet[1], Nathanaël Fijalkow[2,3](✉), and Pierre Ohlmann[1]

[1] Université de Paris, IRIF, CNRS, Paris, France
{thomas.colcombet,pierre.ohlmann}@irif.fr
[2] CNRS, LaBRI, Bordeaux, France
nathanael.fijalkow@labri.fr
[3] The Alan Turing Institute of data science, London, United Kingdom

Abstract. Bertrand et al. introduced a model of parameterised systems, where each agent is represented by a finite state system, and studied the following control problem: for any number of agents, does there exist a controller able to bring all agents to a target state? They showed that the problem is decidable and **EXPTIME**-complete in the adversarial setting, and posed as an open problem the stochastic setting, where the agent is represented by a Markov decision process. In this paper, we show that the stochastic control problem is decidable. Our solution makes significant uses of well quasi orders, of the max-flow min-cut theorem, and of the theory of regular cost functions.

1 Introduction

The control problem for populations of identical agents. The model we study was introduced in [3] (see also the journal version [4]): a population of agents are controlled uniformly, meaning that the controller applies the same action to every agent. The agents are represented by a finite state system, the same for every agent. The key difficulty is that there is an arbitrary large number of agents: the control problem is whether for every $n \in \mathbb{N}$, there exists a controller able to bring all n agents synchronously to a target state.

The technical contribution of [3,4] is to prove that in the adversarial setting where an opponent chooses the evolution of the agents, the (adversarial) control problem is **EXPTIME**-complete.

In this paper, we study the stochastic setting, where each agent evolves independently according to a probabilistic distribution, *i.e.* the finite state system modelling an agent is a Markov decision process. The control problem becomes whether for every $n \in \mathbb{N}$, there exists a controller able to bring all n agents synchronously to a target state with probability one.

Our main technical result is that the stochastic control problem is decidable. In the next paragraphs we discuss four motivations for studying this problem: control of biological systems, parameterised verification and control, distributed computing, and automata theory.

Modelling biological systems. The original motivation for studying this model was for controlling population of yeasts ([21]). In this application, the concentration of some molecule is monitored through fluorescence level. Controlling the frequency and duration of injections of a sorbitol solution influences the concentration of the target molecule, triggering different chemical reactions which can be modelled by a finite state system. The objective is to control the population to reach a predetermined fluorescence state. As discussed in the conclusions of [3,4], the stochastic semantics is more satisfactory than the adversarial one for representing the behaviours of the chemical reactions, so our decidability result is a step towards a better understanding of the modelling of biological systems as populations of arbitrarily many agents represented by finite state systems.

From parameterised verification to parameterised control. Parameterised verification was introduced in [12]: it is the verification of a system composed of an arbitrary number of identical components. The control problem we study here and introduced in [3,4] is the first step towards *parameterised control*: the goal is control a system composed of many identical components in order to ensure a given property. To the best of our knowledge, the contributions of [3,4] are the first results on parameterised control; by extension, we present the first results on parameterised control in a stochastic setting.

Distributed computing. Our model resembles two models introduced for the study of distributed computing. The first and most widely studied is population protocols, introduced in [2]: the agents are modelled by finite state systems and interact by pairs drawn at random. The mode of interaction is the key difference with the model we study here: in a time step, all of our agents perform simultaneously and independently the same action. This brings us closer to broadcast protocols as studied for instance in [8], in which one action involves an arbitrary number of agents. As explained in [3,4], our model can be seen as a subclass of (stochastic) broadcast protocols, but key differences exist in the semantics, making the two bodies of work technically independent.

The focus of the distributed computing community when studying population or broadcast protocols is to construct the most efficient protocols for a given task, such as (prominently) electing a leader. A growing literature from the verification community focusses on checking the correctness of a given protocol against a given specification; we refer to the recent survey [7] for an overview. We concentrate on the control problem, which can then be seen as a first result in the control of distributed systems in a stochastic setting.

Alternative semantics for probabilistic automata. It is very tempting to consider the limit case of infinitely many agents: the parameterised control question becomes the value 1 problem for probabilistic automata, which was proved undecidable in [13], and even in very restricted cases ([10]). Hence abstracting continuous distributions by a discrete population of arbitrary size can be seen as an approximation technique for probabilistic automata. Using n agents correponds to using numerical approximation up to 2^{-n} with random rounding; in this sense the control problem considers arbitrarily fine approximations. The plague of undecidability results on probabilistic automata (see *e.g.* [9]) is nicely contrasted by our positive result, which is one of the few decidability results on probabilistic automata not making structural assumptions on the underlying graph.

Our results. We prove decidability of the stochastic control problem. The first insight is given by the theory of well quasi orders, which motivates the introduction of a new problem called the sequential flow problem. The first step of our solution is to reduce the stochastic control problem to (many instances of) the sequential flow problem. The second insight comes from the theory of regular cost functions, providing us with a set of tools for addressing the key difficulty of the problem, namely the fact that there are arbitarily many agents. Our key technical contribution is to show the computability of the sequential flow problem by reducing it to a boundedness question expressed in the cost monadic second order logic using the max-flow min-cut theorem.

Related work. The notion of decisive Markov chains was introduced in [1] as a unifying property for studying infinite-state Markov chains with finite-like properties. A typical example of decisive Markov chains is lossy channel systems where tokens can be lost anytime inducing monotonicity properties. Our situation is the exact opposite as we are considering (using the Petri nets terminology) safe Petri nets where the number of tokens along a run is constant. So it is not clear whether the underlying argument in both cases can be unified using decisiveness.

Organisation of the paper. We define the stochastic control problem in Section 2, and the sequential flow problem in Section 3. We construct a reduction from the former to (many instances of) the latter in Section 4, and show the decidability of the sequential flow problem in Section 5.

2 The stochastic control problem

Definition 1. *A* Markov decision process *(MDP for short) consists of*

- *a finite set of* states $\mathcal{Q}$,
- *a finite set of* actions $\mathcal{A}$,
- *a stochastic* transition table $\rho : \mathcal{Q} \times \mathcal{A} \to \mathcal{D}(\mathcal{Q})$.

The interpretation of the transition table is that from the state p under action a, the probability to transition to q is $\rho(p, a)(q)$. The *transition relation* Δ is defined by

$$\Delta = \{(p, a, q) \in \mathcal{Q} \times \mathcal{A} \times \mathcal{Q} : \rho(p, a)(q) > 0\}\,.$$

We also use Δ_a given by $\{(p, q) \in Q \times Q : (p, a, q) \in \Delta\}$.

We refer to [17] for the usual notions related to MDPs; it turns out that very little probability theory will be needed in this paper, so we restrict ourselves to mentioning only the relevant objects. In an MDP $\mathcal{M}$, a strategy is a function $\sigma : \mathcal{Q} \to \mathcal{A}$; note that we consider only pure and positional strategies, as they will be sufficient for our purposes.

Given a *source* $s \in \mathcal{Q}$ and a *target* $t \in \mathcal{Q}$, we say that the strategy σ *almost surely* reaches t if the probability that a path starting from s and consistent with σ eventually leads to t is 1. As we shall recall in Section 4, whether there exists a strategy ensuring to reach t almost surely from s, called the *almost sure reachability problem* for MDP can be reduced to solving a two player Büchi game, and in particular does not depend upon the exact probabilities. In other words, the only relevant information for each $(p, a, q) \in \mathcal{Q} \times \mathcal{A} \times \mathcal{Q}$ is whether $\rho(p, a)(q) > 0$ or not. Since the same will be true for the stochastic control problem we study in this paper, in our examples we do not specify the exact probabilities, and an edge from p to q labelled a means that $\rho(p, a)(q) > 0$.

Let us now fix an MDP $\mathcal{M}$ and consider a population of n *tokens* (we use tokens to represent the agents). Each token evolves in an independent copy of the MDP $\mathcal{M}$. The controller acts through a *strategy* $\sigma : \mathcal{Q}^n \to \mathcal{A}$, meaning that given the state each of the n tokens is in, the controller chooses *one* action to be performed by all tokens independently. Formally, we are considering the product MDP $\mathcal{M}^n$ whose set of states is $\mathcal{Q}^n$, set of actions is $\mathcal{A}$, and transition table is $\rho^n(u, a)(v) = \prod_{i=1}^n \rho(u_i, a)(v_i)$, where $u, v \in \mathcal{Q}^n$ and u_i, v_i are the ith components of u and v.

Let $s, t \in \mathcal{Q}$ be the source and target states, we write s^n and t^n for the constant n-tuples where all components are s and t. For a fixed value of n, whether there exists a strategy ensuring to reach t^n almost surely from s^n can be reduced to solving a two player Büchi game in the same way as above for a single MDP, replacing $\mathcal{M}$ by $\mathcal{M}^n$. The stochastic control problem asks whether this is true for arbitrary values of n:

Problem 1 (Stochastic control problem). The inputs are an MDP $\mathcal{M}$, a source state $s \in \mathcal{Q}$ and a target state $t \in \mathcal{Q}$. The question is whether for all $n \in \mathbb{N}$, there exists a strategy ensuring to reach t^n almost surely from s^n.

Our main result is the following.

Theorem 1. *The stochastic control problem is decidable.*

The fact that the problem is co-recursively enumerable is easy to see: if the answer is "no", there exists $n \in \mathbb{N}$ such that there exist no strategy ensuring to reach t^n almost surely from s^n. Enumerating the values of n and solving the almost sure reachability problem for $\mathcal{M}^n$ eventually finds this out. However, it is not clear whether one can place an upper bound on such a witness n, which would yield a simple (yet inefficient!) algorithm. As a corollary of our analysis we can indeed derive such an upper bound, but it is non elementary in the size of the MDP.

In the remainder of this section we present a few interesting examples.

Example 1 Let us consider the MDP represented in Figure 1. We show that for this MDP, for any $n \in \mathbb{N}$, the controller has an almost sure strategy to reach t^n from s^n. Starting with n tokens on s, we iterate the following strategy:

- Repeatedly play action a until all tokens are in q;
- Play action b.

The first step is eventually successful with probability one, since at each iteration there is a positive probability that the number of tokens in state q increases. In the second step, with non zero probability at least one token goes to t, while the rest go back to s. It follows that each iteration of this strategy increases with non zero probability the number of tokens in t. Hence, all tokens are eventually transferred to t^n almost surely.

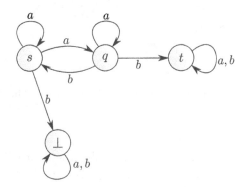

Fig. 1. The controller can almost surely reach t^n from s^n, for any $n \in \mathbb{N}$.

Example 2 We now consider the MDP represented in Figure 2. By convention, if from a state some action does not have any outgoing transition (for instance the action u from s), then it goes to the sink state $\perp$.

We show that there exists a controller ensuring to transfer seven tokens from s to t, but that the same does not hold for eight tokens. For the first assertion, we present the following strategy:

- Play a. One of the states $q_1^{i_1}$ for $i_1 \in \{u, d\}$ receives at least 4 tokens.
- Play $i_1 \in \{u, d\}$. At least 4 tokens go to t while at most 3 go to q_1.
- Play a. One of the states $q_2^{i_2}$ for $i_2 \in \{u, d\}$ receives at least 2 tokens.
- Play $i_2 \in \{u, d\}$. At least 2 tokens go to t while at most 1 token goes to q_2.
- Play a. The token (if any) goes to q_3^i for $i_3 \in \{u, d\}$.

– Play $i_3 \in \{u, d\}$. The remaining token (if any) goes to t.

Now assume that there are 8 tokens or more on s. The only choices for a strategy are to play u or d on the second, fourth, and sixth move. First, with non zero probability at least 4 tokens are in each of q_1^i for $i \in \{u, d\}$. Then, whatever the choice of action $i \in \{u, d\}$, there are at least 4 tokens in q_1 after the next step. Proceeding likewise, there are at least 2 tokens in q_2 with non zero probability two steps later. Then again two steps later, at least 1 token falls in the sink with non zero probability.

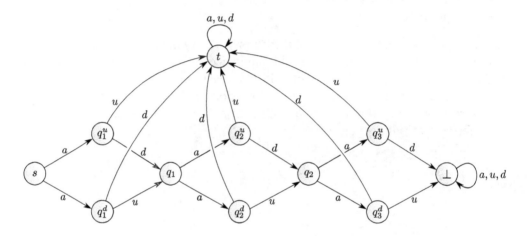

Fig. 2. The controller can synchronise up to 7 tokens on the target state t almost surely, but not more.

Generalising this example shows that if the answer to the stochastic control problem is "no", the smallest number of tokens n for which there exist no almost surely strategy for reaching t^n from s^n may be exponential in $|\mathcal{Q}|$. This can further extended to show a doubly exponential in $\mathcal{Q}$ lower bound, as done in [3,4]; the example produced there holds for both the adversarial and the stochastic setting. Interestingly, for the adversarial setting this doubly exponential lower bound is tight. Our proof for the stochastic setting yields a non-elementary bound, leaving a very large gap.

Example 3 We consider the MDP represented in Figure 3. For any $n \in \mathbb{N}$, there exists a strategy almost surely reaching t^n from s^n. However, this strategy has to pass tokens one by one through q_1. We iterate the following strategy:

– Repeatedly play action a until exactly 1 token is in q_1.
– Play action b. The token goes to q_i for some $i \in \{l, r\}$.
– Play action $i \in \{l, r\}$, which moves the token to t.

Note that the first step may take a very long time (the expectation of the number of as to be played until this happens is exponential in the number of tokens), but it is eventually successful with probability one. This very slow strategy is necessary: if q_1 contains at least two tokens, then action b should not be played: with non zero probability, at least one token ends up in each of q_l, q_r, so at the next step some token ends up in $\bot$. It follows that any strategy almost surely reaching t^n has to be able to detect the presence of at most 1 token in q_1. This is a key example for understanding the difficulty of the stochastic control problem.

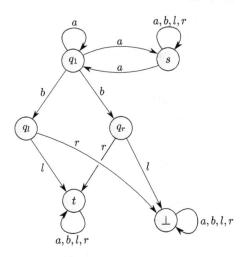

Fig. 3. The controller can synchronise any number of tokens almost surely on the target state t, but they have to go one by one.

3 The sequential flow problem

We let $\mathcal{Q}$ be a finite set of states. We call *configuration* an element of $\mathbb{N}^{\mathcal{Q}}$ and *flow* an element of $f \in \mathbb{N}^{\mathcal{Q} \times \mathcal{Q}}$. A flow f induces two configurations $\mathrm{pre}(f)$ and $\mathrm{post}(f)$ defined by

$$\mathrm{pre}(f)(p) = \sum_{q \in \mathcal{Q}} f(p, q) \qquad \text{and} \qquad \mathrm{post}(f)(q) = \sum_{p \in \mathcal{Q}} f(p, q).$$

Given c, c' two configurations and f a flow, we say that c *goes to* c' using f and write $c \rightarrow^f c'$, if $c = \mathrm{pre}(f)$ and $c' = \mathrm{post}(f)$.

A *flow word* is $f = f_1 \ldots f_\ell$ where each f_i is a flow. We write $c \leadsto^f c'$ if there exists a sequence of configurations $c = c_0, c_1, \ldots, c_\ell = c'$ such that $c_{i-1} \rightarrow^{f_i} c_i$ for all $i \in \{1, \ldots, \ell\}$. In this case, we say that c goes to c' using the flow word f.

We now recall some classical definitions related to well quasi orders ([15,16], see [19] for an exposition of recent results). Let $(E, \leqslant)$ be a quasi ordered set (*i.e.* $\leqslant$ is reflexive and transitive), it is a *well quasi ordered set* (WQO) if any infinite sequence contains an increasing pair. We say that $S \subseteq E$ is *downward closed* if for any $x \in S$, if $y \leqslant x$ then $y \in S$. An *ideal* is a non-empty downward closed set $I \subseteq E$ such that for all $x, y \in I$, there exists some $z \in I$ satisfying both $x \leqslant z$ and $y \leqslant z$.

Lemma 1.

- *Any infinite sequence of decreasing downward closed sets in a WQO is eventually constant.*
- *A subset is downward closed if and only if it is a finite union of incomparable ideals. We call it its* decomposition into ideals *(or simply, its* decomposition*), which is unique (up to permutation).*
- *An ideal is included in a downward closed set if and only if it is included in one of the ideals of its decomposition.*

We equip the set of configurations $\mathbb{N}^{\mathcal{Q}}$ and the set of flows $\mathbb{N}^{\mathcal{Q} \times \mathcal{Q}}$ with the quasi order $\leqslant$ defined component wise, yielding thanks to Dickson's Lemma [6] two WQOs.

Lemma 2. *Let X be a finite set. A subset of $\mathbb{N}^X$ is an ideal if and only if it is of the form*

$$a{\downarrow} = \{c \in \mathbb{N}^X \mid c \leqslant a\},$$

for some $a \in (\mathbb{N} \cup \{\omega\})^X$ (in which ω is larger than all integers).

We represent downward closed sets of configurations and flows using their decomposition into finitely many ideals of the form $a{\downarrow}$ for $a \in (\mathbb{N} \cup \{\omega\})^{\mathcal{Q}}$ or $a \in (\mathbb{N} \cup \{\omega\})^{\mathcal{Q} \times \mathcal{Q}}$.

Problem 2 (Sequential flow problem). Let $\mathcal{Q}$ be a finite set of states. Given a downward closed set of flows $Flows \subseteq \mathbb{N}^{\mathcal{Q} \times \mathcal{Q}}$ and a downward closed set of final configurations $F \subseteq \mathbb{N}^{\mathcal{Q}}$, compute the downward closed set

$$\mathrm{Pre}^*(Flows, F) = \{c \in \mathbb{N}^{\mathcal{Q}} \mid c \rightsquigarrow^f c' \in F, \ f \in Flows^*\},$$

i.e. the configurations from which one may reach F using only flows from *Flows*.

4   Reduction of the stochastic control problem to the sequential flow problem

Let us consider an MDP $\mathcal{M}$ and a target $t \in \mathcal{Q}$. We first recall a folklore result reducing the almost sure reachability question for MDPs to solving a two player Büchi game (we refer to [14] for the definitions and notations of Büchi games). The Büchi game is played between *Eve* and *Adam* as follows. From a state p:

1. Eve chooses an action a and a transition $(p, q) \in \Delta_a$;
2. Adam can either choose to
   agree and the game continues from q, or
   interrupt and choose another transition $(p, q') \in \Delta_a$, the game continues from q'.

The Büchi objective is satisfied (meaning Eve wins) if either the target state t is reached or Adam interrupts infinitely many times.

Lemma 3. *There exists a strategy ensuring almost surely to reach t from s if and only if Eve has a winning strategy from s in the above Büchi game.*

We now explain how this reduction can be extended to the stochastic control problem. Let us consider an MDP $\mathcal{M}$ and a target $t \in \mathcal{Q}$. We now define an infinite Büchi game $\mathcal{G}_{\mathcal{M}}$. The set of vertices is the set of configurations $\mathbb{N}^{\mathcal{Q}}$. For a flow f, we write $\mathrm{supp}(f) = \{(p,q) \in \mathcal{Q}^2 : f(p,q) > 0\}$. The game is played as follows from a configuration c:

1. Eve chooses an action a and a flow f such that $\mathrm{pre}(f) = c$ and $\mathrm{supp}(f) \subseteq \Delta_a$.
2. Adam can either choose to

   agree and the game continues from $c' = \mathrm{post}(f)$

   interrupt and choose a flow f' such that $\mathrm{pre}(f') = c$ and $\mathrm{supp}(f') \subseteq \Delta_a$, and the game continues from $c'' = \mathrm{post}(f')$.

Note that Eve choosing a flow f is equivalent to choosing for each token a transition $(p,q) \in \Delta_a$, inducing the configuration c', and simiarly for Adam should he decide to interrupt.

Eve wins if either all tokens are in the target state, or if Adam interrupts infinitely many times.

Note that although the game is infinite, it is actually a disjoint union of finite games. Indeed, along a play the number of tokens is fixed, so each play is included in $\mathcal{Q}^n$ for some $n \in \mathbb{N}$.

Lemma 4. *Let c be a configuration with n tokens in total, the following are equivalent:*

- *There exists a strategy almost surely reaching t^n from c,*
- *Eve has a winning strategy in the Büchi game $\mathcal{G}_{\mathcal{M}}$ starting from c.*

Lemma 4 follows from applying Lemma 3 on the product MDP $\mathcal{M}^n$.

We also consider the game $\mathcal{G}_{\mathcal{M}}^{(i)}$ for $i \in \mathbb{N}$, which is defined just as $\mathcal{G}_{\mathcal{M}}$ except for the winning objective: Eve wins in $\mathcal{G}_{\mathcal{M}}^{(i)}$ if either all tokens are in the target state, or if Adam interrupts more than i times. It is clear that if Eve has a winning strategy in $\mathcal{G}_{\mathcal{M}}$ then she has a winning strategy in $\mathcal{G}_{\mathcal{M}}^{(i)}$. Conversely, the following result states that $\mathcal{G}_{\mathcal{M}}^{(i)}$ is equivalent to $\mathcal{G}_{\mathcal{M}}$ for some i.

Lemma 5. *There exists $i \in \mathbb{N}$ such that from any configuration $c \in \mathbb{N}^{\mathcal{Q}}$, Eve has a winning strategy in $\mathcal{G}_{\mathcal{M}}$ if and only if Eve has a winning strategy in $\mathcal{G}_{\mathcal{M}}^{(i)}$.*

Proof: Let $X^{(i)} \subseteq \mathbb{N}^{\mathcal{Q}}$ be the winning region for Eve in $\mathcal{G}_{\mathcal{M}}^{(i)}$. We first argue that $X = \bigcap_i X^{(i)}$ is the winning region in $\mathcal{G}_{\mathcal{M}}$. It is clear that X is contained in the winning region: if Eve has a strategy to ensure that either all tokens are in the target state, or that Adam interrupts infinitely many times, then it particular this is true for Adam interrupting more than i times for any i. The converse inclusion holds because $\mathcal{G}_{\mathcal{M}}$ is a disjoint union of finite Büchi games. Indeed, in a finite Büchi game, since Adam can restrict himself to playing a memoryless winning strategy, if Eve can ensure that he interrupts a certain number of times (larger than the size of the game), then by a simple pumping argument this implies that Adam will interrupt infinitely many times.

To conclude, we note that each $X^{(i)}$ is downward closed: indeed, a winning strategy from a configuration c can be used from a configuration c' where there are fewer tokens in each state. It follows that $(X^{(i)})_{i \geq 0}$ is a decreasing sequence of downward closed sets in $\mathbb{N}^{\mathcal{Q}}$, hence it stabilises thanks to Lemma 1, *i.e.* there exists $i_0 \in \mathbb{N}$ such that $X^{(i_0)} = \bigcap_i X^{(i)}$, which concludes. $\qquad\square$

Note that Lemma 4 and Lemma 5 substantiate the claims made in Section 2: pure positional strategies are enough and the answer to the stochastic control problem does not depend upon the exact probabilities in the MDP. Indeed, the construction of the Büchi games do not depend on them, and the answer to the former is equivalent to determining whether Eve has a winning strategy in each of them.

We are now fully equipped to show that a solution to the sequential flow problem yields the decidability of the stochastic control problem.

Let F be the set of configurations for which all tokens are in state t. we let $X^{(i)} \subseteq \mathbb{N}^{\mathcal{Q}}$ denote the winning region for Eve in the game $\mathcal{G}_{\mathcal{M}}^{(i)}$. Note first that $X^{(0)} = \mathrm{Pre}^*(Flows^0, F)$ where

$$Flows^0 = \{f \in \mathbb{N}^{\mathcal{Q} \times \mathcal{Q}} : \exists a \in \mathcal{A}, \; \mathrm{supp}(f) \subseteq \Delta_a\}.$$

Indeed, in the game $\mathcal{G}_{\mathcal{M}}^{(0)}$ Adam cannot interrupt as this would make him lose immediately. Hence, the winning region for Eve in $\mathcal{G}_{\mathcal{M}}^{(0)}$ is $\mathrm{Pre}^*(Flows^0, F)$.

We generalise this by setting $Flows^i$ for all $i > 0$ to be the set of flows $f \in \mathbb{N}^{\mathcal{Q} \times \mathcal{Q}}$ such that for some action $a \in \mathcal{A}$,

- $\mathrm{supp}(f) \subseteq \Delta_a$, and
- for f' with $\mathrm{pre}(f') = \mathrm{pre}(f)$ and $\mathrm{supp}(f') \subseteq \Delta_a$, we have $\mathrm{post}(f') \in X^{(i-1)}$.

Equivalently, this is the set of flows for which, when played in the game $\mathcal{G}_{\mathcal{M}}$ by Eve, Adam cannot use an interrupt move and force the configuration outside of $X^{(i-1)}$.

We now claim that

$$X^{(i)} = \mathrm{Pre}^*(Flows^i, F)$$

for all $i \geq 0$.

We note that this means that for each i computing $X^{(i)}$ reduces to solving one instance of the sequential flow problem. This induces an algorithm for solving the stochastic control problem: compute the sequence $(X^{(i)})_{i \geq 0}$ until it stabilises, which is ensured by Lemma 5 and yields the winning region of $\mathcal{G}_\mathcal{M}$. The answer to the stochastic control problem is then whether the initial configuration where all tokens are in s belongs to the winning region of $\mathcal{G}_\mathcal{M}$.

Let us prove the claim by induction on i.

Let c be a configuration in $\mathrm{Pre}^*(\mathit{Flows}^i, F)$. This means that there exists a flow word $f = f_1 \cdots f_\ell$ such that $f_k \in \mathit{Flows}^i$ for all k, and $c \rightsquigarrow^f c' \in F$. Expanding the definition, there exist $c_0 = c, \ldots, c_\ell = c'$ such that $c_{k-1} \to^{f_k} c_k$ for all k.

Let us now describe a strategy for Eve in $\mathcal{G}_\mathcal{M}^{(i)}$ starting from c. As long as Adam agrees, Eve successively chooses the sequence of flows $f_1, f_2, \ldots$ and the corresponding configurations $c_1, c_2, \ldots$. If Adam never interrupts, then the game reaches the configuration $c' \in F$, and Eve wins. Otherwise, as soon as Adam interrupts, by definition of Flows^i, we reach a configuration $d \in X^{(i-1)}$. By induction hypothesis, Eve has a strategy which ensures from d to either reach F or that Adam interrupts at least $i - 1$ times. In the latter case, adding the interrupt move leading to d yields i interrupts, so this is a winning strategy for Eve in $\mathcal{G}_\mathcal{M}^{(i)}$, witnessing that $c \in X^{(i)}$.

Conversely, assume that there is a winning strategy σ of Eve in $\mathcal{G}_\mathcal{M}^{(i)}$ from a configuration c. Consider a play consistent with σ, it either reaches F or Adam interrupts. Let us denote by $f = f_1, f_2, \ldots, f_\ell$ the sequence of flows until then. We argue that $f_k \in \mathit{Flows}^i$ for $k \in \{1, \ldots, \ell\}$. Let $f = f_k$ for some k, by definition of the game $\mathrm{supp}(f) \subseteq \Delta_a$ for some action a. Let f' such that $\mathrm{pre}(f') = \mathrm{pre}(f)$ and $\mathrm{supp}(f') \subseteq \Delta_a$. In the game $\mathcal{G}_\mathcal{M}$ after Eve played f_k, Adam has the possibility to interrupt and choose f'. From this configuration onward the strategy σ is winning in $\mathcal{G}_\mathcal{M}^{(i-1)}$, implying that $f \in \mathit{Flows}^i$. Thus $f = f_1 f_2 \ldots f_\ell$ is a witness that $c \in X^{(i)}$.

5 Computability of the sequential flow problem

Let $\mathcal{Q}$ be a finite set of states, $\mathit{Flows} \subseteq \mathbb{N}^{\mathcal{Q} \times \mathcal{Q}}$ a downward closed set of flows and $F \subseteq \mathbb{N}^\mathcal{Q}$ a downward closed set of configurations, the sequential flow problem is to compute the downward closed set Pre^* defined by

$$\mathrm{Pre}^*(\mathit{Flows}, F) = \{c \in \mathbb{N}^\mathcal{Q} \mid c \rightsquigarrow^f c' \in F, \ f \in \mathit{Flows}^*\},$$

i.e. the configurations from which one may reach F using only flows from Flows.

The following classical result of [22] allows us to further reduce our problem.

Lemma 6. *The task of computing a downward closed set can be reduced to the task of deciding whether a given ideal is included in a downward closed set.*

Thanks to Lemma 6, it is sufficient for solving the sequential flow problem to establish the following result.

Lemma 7. *Let I be an ideal of the form $a{\downarrow}$ for $a \in (\mathbb{N} \cup \{\omega\})^{\mathcal{Q}}$, and Flows $\subseteq$ $\mathbb{N}^{\mathcal{Q} \times \mathcal{Q}}$ be a downward closed set of flows. It is decidable whether F can be reached from all configurations of I using only flows from Flows.*

We call a vector $a \in (\mathbb{N} \cup \{\omega\})^{\mathcal{Q} \times \mathcal{Q}}$ a *capacity*. A *capacity word* is a finite sequence of capacities. For two capacity words w, w' of the same length, we write $w \le w'$ to mean that $w_i \le w'_i$ for each i. Since flows are particular cases of capacities, we can compare flows with capacities in the same way.

Before proving Lemma 7 let us give an example and some notations.

Given a state q, we write $q \in \mathbb{N}^{\mathcal{Q}}$ for the vector which has value 1 on the q component and 0 elsewhere. More generally we let αq for $\alpha \in \mathbb{N} \cup \{\omega\}$ denote the vector with value α on the q component and 0 elsewhere. We use similar notations for flows. For instance, $\omega q_1 + q_2$ has value ω in the q_1 component, 1 in the q_2 component, and 0 elsewhere.

In the instance of the sequential flow problem represented in Figure 4, we ask the following question: can F be reached from any configuration of $I = (\omega q_2){\downarrow}$? The answer is yes: the capacity word $w = (ac^{n-1}b)^n$ is such that $nq_2 \rightsquigarrow^f nq_4 \in F$ for a flow word $f \le w$, the begining of which is described in Figure 5.

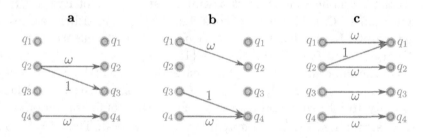

Fig. 4. An instance of the sequential flow problem. We let *Flows* $= a{\downarrow} \cup b{\downarrow} \cup c{\downarrow}$ where $a = \omega(q_2, q_2) + (q_2, q_3) + \omega(q_4, q_4)$, $b = \omega(q_1, q_2) + (q_3, q_4) + \omega(q_4, q_4)$, and $c = \omega(q_1, q_1) + (q_2, q_1) + \omega(q_2, q_2) + \omega(q_3, q_3) + \omega(q_4, q_4)$. Set also $F = (\omega q_4){\downarrow}$.

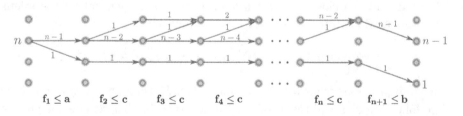

Fig. 5. A flow word $f = f_1 f_2 \ldots f_{n+1} \le ac^{n-1}b$ such that nq_2 goes to $(n-1)q_1 + q_4$ using f. This construction can be extended to $f \le w$ such that nq_2 goes to nq_4 using f.

We write $a[\omega \leftarrow n]$ for the configuration obtained from a by replacing all ωs by n.

The key idea for solving the sequential flow problem is to rephrase it using *regular cost functions* (a set of tools for solving boundedness questions). Indeed, whether F can be reached from all configurations of $I = a{\downarrow}$ using only flows from *Flows* can be equivalently phrased as a boundedness question, as follows:

does there exist a bound on the values of $n \in \mathbb{N}$ such that $a[\omega \leftarrow n] \leadsto^f c$ for some $c \in F$ and $f \in Flows^*$?

We show that this boundedness question can be formulated as a boundedness question for a formula of *cost monadic logic*, a formalism that we introduce now. We assume that the reader is familiar with *monadic second order logic* (MSO) over finite words, and refer to [20] for the definitions. The syntax of cost monadic logic (cost MSO for short) extends MSO with the construct $|X| \leq N$, where X is a second order variable and N is a bounding variable. The semantics is defined as usual: $w, n \models \varphi$ for a word $w \in A^*$, with $n \in \mathbb{N}$ specifying the bound N. We assume that there is at most one bounding variable, and that the construct $|X| \leq N$ appears positively, *i.e.* under an even number of negations. This ensures that the larger N, the more true the formula is: if $w, n \models \varphi$, then $w, n' \models \varphi$ for all $n' \geq n$. The semantics of a formula φ of cost MSO induces a function $A^* \to \mathbb{N} \cup \{\infty\}$ defined by $\varphi(w) = \inf \{n \in \mathbb{N} \mid w, n \models \varphi\}$.

The *boundedness problem* for cost monadic logic is the following problem: given a cost MSO formula φ over A^*, is it true that the function $A^* \to \mathbb{N} \cup \{\infty\}$ is bounded, *i.e.*:

$$\exists n \in \mathbb{N}, \ \forall w \in A^*, \ w, n \models \varphi?$$

The decidability of the boundedness problem is a central result in the theory of regular cost functions ([5]). Since in the theory of regular cost functions, when considering functions we are only interested in whether they are bounded or not, we will consider functions "up to boundedness properties". Concretely, this means that a *cost function* is an equivalence class of functions $A^* \to \mathbb{N} \cup \{\infty\}$, with the equivalence being $f \approx g$ if there exists $\alpha : \mathbb{N} \to \mathbb{N}$ such that $f(w)$ is finite if and only if $g(w)$ is finite, and in this case, $f(w) \leqslant \alpha(g(w))$ and $g(w) \leqslant \alpha(f(w))$. This is equivalent to stating that for all $X \subseteq A^*$, if f is bounded over X if and only if g is bounded over X.

Let us now establish Lemma 7.

Proof: Let $T = \{q \in \mathcal{Q} \mid a(q) = \omega\}$. Note that for n sufficiently large, we have $a[\omega \leftarrow n]{\downarrow} = I \cap \{0, 1, \ldots, n\}$. We let $\mathscr{C} \subseteq (\mathbb{N} \cup \{\omega\})^{\mathcal{Q} \times \mathcal{Q}}$ be the decomposition of *Flows* into ideals, that is, $\mathscr{C}$ is the minimal finite set such that

$$Flows = \bigcup_{b \in \mathscr{C}} b{\downarrow} \ .$$

We let k denote the largest finite value that appears in the definition of $\mathscr{C}$, that is, $k = \max\{b(q, q') : b \in \mathscr{C}, q, q' \in \mathcal{Q}, b(q, q') \neq \omega\}$.

Let us define the function

$$\Phi : \mathscr{C}^* \longrightarrow \mathbb{N} \cup \{\omega\}$$
$$w \longmapsto \sup\{n \in \mathbb{N} : \exists f \leqslant w, a[\omega \leftarrow n] \leadsto^f F\}.$$

By definition Φ is unbounded if and only if F can be reached from all configurations of I. Since boundedness of cost MSO is decidable, it suffices to construct a formula in cost monadic logic for Φ to obtain the decidability of our problem. Our approach will be to additively decompose the capacity word w into a finitary part $w^{(\text{fin})}$ (which is handled using a regular language), and several unbounded parts $w^{(s)}$ for each $s \in T$. The unbounded parts require a more careful analysis which notably goes through the use of the max-flow min-cut theorem.

Note that $a[\omega \leftarrow n]$ decomposes as the sum of its finite part $a_{\text{fin}} = a[\omega \leftarrow 0]$ and $\sum_{s \in T} ns$. Since flows are additive, it holds that $f \leqslant w = w_1 \ldots w_l$ is a flow from c_n to F if and only if the capacity word w may be decomposed into $(w^{(s)})_{s \in T} = (w_1^{(s)} \ldots w_l^{(s)})_{s \in T}$ and $w^{(\text{fin})} = w_1^{(\text{fin})} \ldots w_l^{(\text{fin})}$ such that

- all the numbers appearing in the $w_i^{(s)}$ capacities are bounded by k,
- for all $i \in \{1, \ldots, l\}$, $w_i = \sum_{s \in T \cup \{fin\}} w_i^{(s)}$,
- for all $s \in T$, $ns \rightsquigarrow^f F$ for some flow word $f \leqslant w^{(s)}$,
- and $a_{\text{fin}} \rightsquigarrow^f F$ for some flow word $f \leqslant w^{(\text{fin})}$.

In order to encode such capacity words in cost MSO we use monadic variables $W_{q,q',p}^{(s)}$ where $q, q' \in \mathcal{Q}$, $p \in \{0, \ldots, k, \omega\}$ and $s \in T \cup \{\text{fin}\}$. They are meant to satisfy that $i \in W_{q,q',p,s}^{(s)}$ if and only if $w_i^{(s)}(q, q') = p$. We use bold $\boldsymbol{W}$ to denote the tuple $(W_{q,q',p,s}^{(s)})_{q,q',p,s}$, and $\boldsymbol{W}^{(s)}$ for $(W_{q,q',p}^{(s)})_{q,q',p}$ when $s \in T \cup \{\omega\}$ is fixed. The MSO formula $\texttt{IsDecomp}(\boldsymbol{W}, w)$ states that a decomposition $(w^{(s)})_{s \in T \cup \{\omega\}}$ is semantically valid and sums to w:

$$\forall i, \quad \left[\bigwedge\nolimits_{q,q',s} \bigvee\nolimits_{p \in \{0,\ldots,k,\omega\}} \left(i \in W_{q,q',p}^{(s)} \wedge \bigwedge\nolimits_{p' \neq p} i \notin W_{q,q',p}^{(s)} \right) \right]$$
$$\wedge \left[\left(\bigwedge\nolimits_{q,q'p} w_i(q,q') = p \right) \implies \bigvee\nolimits_{\substack{(p_s)_{s \in T \cup \{\text{fin}\}} \\ \sum p_s = p}} \bigwedge\nolimits_{s \in T \cup \{\text{fin}\}} i \in W_{q,q',p_s}^{(s)} \right]$$

For $s \in T$, we now consider the function

$$\Psi^{(s)} : \left(\{0, 1, \ldots, k, \omega\}^{\mathcal{Q} \times \mathcal{Q}} \right)^* \longrightarrow \mathbb{N} \cup \{\omega\}$$
$$w^{(s)} \longmapsto \sup\{n \in \mathbb{N} \mid \exists f \leqslant w^{(s)}, \ ns \xrightarrow{f} F\}.$$

We also define $\Psi^{(\text{fin})} \subseteq (\{0, \ldots, k, \omega\})^{\mathcal{Q} \times \mathcal{Q}}$ to be the language of capacity words $w^{(\text{fin})}$ such that there exists a flow $f \leqslant w^{(\text{fin})}$ with $a_{\text{fin}} \rightsquigarrow^f F$. Note that $\Psi^{(\text{fin})}$ is a regular language since it is recognized by a finite automaton over $\{0, 1, \ldots, k|Q|\}^{\mathcal{Q}}$ that may update the current bounded configuration only with flows smaller than the current letter of $w^{(\text{fin})}$.

We have

$$\Phi(w) = \sup_n \left[\exists \boldsymbol{W}, \texttt{IsDecomp}(\boldsymbol{W}, w) \wedge \left(\bigwedge_{s \in T} \Psi^{(s)}(\boldsymbol{W}^{(s)}) \geq n \right) \wedge \boldsymbol{W}^{(\text{fin})} \in \Psi^{(\text{fin})} \right].$$

Hence, it is sufficient to prove that for each $s \in T$, $\Psi^{(s)}$ is definable in cost MSO.

Let us fix s and a capacity word $w \in \{0, \ldots, k, \omega\}^{\mathcal{Q} \times \mathcal{Q}}$ of length $|w| = \ell$. Consider the finite graph G with vertex set $\mathcal{Q} \times \{0, 1, \ldots, \ell\}$ and for all $i \geq 1$, an edge from $(q, i-1)$ to (q', i) labelled by $w_i(q, q')$. Then $\Psi^{(s)}(w)$ is the maximal flow from $(s, 0)$ to (t, ℓ) in G. We recall that a *cut* in a graph with distinguished source s and target t is a set of edges such that removing them disconnects s and t. The *cost of a cut* is the sum of the weight of its edges. The *max-flow min-cut theorem* states that the maximal flow in a graph is exactly the minimal cost of a cut ([11]).

We now define a cost MSO formula $\tilde{\Psi}^{(s)}$ which is equivalent (in terms of cost functions) to the minimal cost of cut in the previous graph G and thus to $\Psi^{(s)}$. In the following formula, $\boldsymbol{X} = (X_{q,q'})_{q,q' \in \mathcal{Q}}$ represents a cut in the graph: $i \in X_{q,q'}$ means that edge $((q, i-1), (q', i))$ belongs to the cut. Likewise, $\boldsymbol{P} = (P_{q,q'})_{q,q' \in \mathcal{Q}}$ represents paths in the graph. Let $\tilde{\Psi}^{(s)}(w)$ be defined by

$$\inf_n \left\{ \exists \boldsymbol{X} \left[\bigwedge_{q,q'} n \geq |X_{q,q'}| \right] \wedge \left(\forall i, i \in X_{q,q'} \implies w_i(q, q') < \omega \right) \wedge \mathrm{Disc}_{s,t}(\boldsymbol{X}, w) \right\},$$

where $\mathrm{Disc}_{s,t}(\boldsymbol{X}, w)$ expresses that $\boldsymbol{X}$ disconnects $(s, 0)$ and (t, ℓ) in G. For instance $\mathrm{Disc}_{s,t}(\boldsymbol{X}, w)$ is defined by

$$\forall \boldsymbol{P}, \left[\left(\forall i, \bigwedge_{q,q'} i \in P_{q,q'} \implies w_i(q, q') > 0 \right) \wedge \left(\bigvee_{q'} 0 \in P_{s,q'} \right) \wedge \left(\bigvee_q \ell \in P_{q,t} \right) \wedge \right.$$

$$\left. \forall i \geq 1, \bigwedge_{q,q'} i \in P_{q,q'} \implies \left(\bigvee_{q''} i - 1 \in P_{q'',q} \right) \right] \implies \exists i, \bigvee_{q,q'} (i \in X_{q,q'} \wedge i \in P_{q,q'}).$$

Now $\tilde{\Psi}^{(s)}(w)$ does not exactly define the minimal total weight $\Phi^{(s)}(w)$ of a cut, but rather the minimal value over all cuts of the minimum over $(q, q') \in \mathcal{Q}^2$ of how many edges are of the form $((q, i-1), (q', i))$. This is good enough for our purposes since these two values are related by

$$\tilde{\Psi}^{(s)}(w) \leqslant \Phi^{(s)}(w) \leqslant k|Q|^2 \tilde{\Psi}^{(s)}(w),$$

implying that the functions $\tilde{\Psi}^{(s)}$ and $\Phi^{(s)}$ define the same cost function. In particular, $\Phi^{(s)}$ is definable in cost MSO. $\square$

6   Conclusions

We showed the decidability of the stochastic control problem. Our approach uses well quasi orders and the sequential flow problem, which is then solved using the theory of regular cost functions.

Together with the original result of [3,4] in the adversarial setting, our result contributes to the theoretical foundations of parameterised control. We return to the first application of this model, control of biological systems. As we discussed the stochastic setting is perhaps more satisfactory than the adversarial one, although as we saw very complicated behaviours emerge in the stochastic setting involving single agents, which are arguably not pertinent for modelling biological systems.

We thus pose two open questions. The first is to settle the complexity status of the stochastic control problem. Very recently [18] proved the **EXPTIME**-hardness of the problem, which is interesting because the underlying phenomena involved in this hardness result are specific to the stochastic setting (and do not apply to the adversarial setting). Our algorithm does not even yield elementary upper bounds, leaving a very large complexity gap. The second question is towards more accurately modelling biological systems: can we refine the stochastic control problem by taking into account the synchronising time of the controller, and restrict it to reasonable bounds?

Acknowledgements

We thank Nathalie Bertrand and Blaise Genest for introducing us to this fascinating problem, and the preliminary discussions at the Simons Institute for the Theory of Computing in Fall 2015.

References

1. Abdulla, P.A., Henda, N.B., Mayr, R.: Decisive Markov chains. Logical Methods in Computer Science **3**(4) (2007). https://doi.org/10.2168/LMCS-3(4:7)2007
2. Angluin, D., Aspnes, J., Diamadi, Z., Fischer, M.J., Peralta, R.: Computation in networks of passively mobile finite-state sensors. Distributed Computing **18**(4), 235–253 (2006). https://doi.org/10.1007/s00446-005-0138-3
3. Bertrand, N., Dewaskar, M., Genest, B., Gimbert, H.: Controlling a population. In: CONCUR. pp. 12:1–12:16 (2017). https://doi.org/10.4230/LIPIcs.CONCUR.2017.12
4. Bertrand, N., Dewaskar, M., Genest, B., Gimbert, H., Godbole, A.A.: Controlling a population. Logical Methods in Computer Science **15**(3) (2019), https://lmcs.episciences.org/5647
5. Colcombet, T.: Regular cost functions, part I: logic and algebra over words. Logical Methods in Computer Science **9**(3) (2013). https://doi.org/10.2168/LMCS-9(3:3)2013
6. Dickson, L.E.: Finiteness of the odd perfect and primitive abundant numbers with n distinct prime factors. American Journal of Mathematics **35**(4), 413–422 (1913), http://www.jstor.org/stable/2370405
7. Esparza, J.: Parameterized verification of crowds of anonymous processes. In: Dependable Software Systems Engineering, pp. 59–71. IOS Press (2016). https://doi.org/10.3233/978-1-61499-627-9-59
8. Esparza, J., Finkel, A., Mayr, R.: On the verification of broadcast protocols. In: LICS. pp. 352–359 (1999). https://doi.org/10.1109/LICS.1999.782630
9. Fijalkow, N.: Undecidability results for probabilistic automata. SIGLOG News **4**(4), 10–17 (2017), https://dl.acm.org/citation.cfm?id=3157833

10. Fijalkow, N., Gimbert, H., Horn, F., Oualhadj, Y.: Two recursively insep-
    arable problems for probabilistic automata. In: MFCS. pp. 267–278 (2014).
    https://doi.org/10.1007/978-3-662-44522-8_23
11. Ford, L.R., Fulkerson, D.R.: Maximal flow through a network. Canadian Journal
    of Mathematics 8, 399–404 (1956). https://doi.org/10.4153/CJM-1956-045-5
12. German, S.M., Sistla, A.P.: Reasoning about systems with many processes. Journal
    of the ACM 39(3), 675–735 (1992)
13. Gimbert, H., Oualhadj, Y.: Probabilistic automata on finite words: De-
    cidable and undecidable problems. In: ICALP. pp. 527–538 (2010).
    https://doi.org/10.1007/978-3-642-14162-1_44
14. Grädel, E., Thomas, W., Wilke, T. (eds.): Automata, Logics, and Infinite Games,
    LNCS, vol. 2500. Springer (2002)
15. Higman, G.: Ordering by divisibility in abstract algebras. Proceed-
    ings of the London Mathematical Society s3-2(1), 326–336 (1952).
    https://doi.org/10.1112/plms/s3-2.1.326
16. Kruskal, J.B.: The theory of well-quasi-ordering: A frequently discovered concept.
    J. Comb. Theory, Ser. A 13(3), 297–305 (1972). https://doi.org/10.1016/0097-
    3165(72)90063-5
17. Kučera, A.: Turn-Based Stochastic Games. Lectures in Game Theory for Computer
    Scientists, Cambridge University Press (2011)
18. Mascle, C., Shirmohammadi, M., Totzke, P.: Controlling a random population is
    EXPTIME-hard. CoRR (2019), http://arxiv.org/abs/1909.06420
19. Schmitz, S.: Algorithmic Complexity of Well-Quasi-Orders. Habilitation à diriger
    des recherches, École normale supérieure Paris-Saclay (Nov 2017), https://tel.
    archives-ouvertes.fr/tel-01663266
20. Thomas, W.: Languages, automata, and logic. In: Handbook of Formal Language
    Theory, vol. III, pp. 389–455. Springer (1997)
21. Uhlendorf, J., Miermont, A., Delaveau, T., Charvin, G., Fages, F., Bottani, S.,
    Hersen, P., Batt, G.: In silico control of biomolecular processes. Computational
    Methods in Synthetic Biology 13, 277–285 (2015)
22. Valk, R., Jantzen, M.: The residue of vector sets with applications to de-
    cidability problems in Petri nets. Acta Informatica 21, 643–674 (03 1985).
    https://doi.org/10.1007/BF00289715

An Axiomatic Approach to Reversible Computation⋆

Ivan Lanese[1] (✉), Iain Phillips[2], and Irek Ulidowski[3]

[1] Focus Team, University of Bologna/INRIA, Italy ivan.lanese@gmail.com
[2] Imperial College London, England i.phillips@imperial.ac.uk
[3] University of Leicester, England i.ulidowski@leicester.ac.uk

Abstract. Undoing computations of a concurrent system is beneficial in many situations, e.g., in reversible debugging of multi-threaded programs and in recovery from errors due to optimistic execution in parallel discrete event simulation. A number of approaches have been proposed for how to reverse formal models of concurrent computation including process calculi such as CCS, languages like Erlang, prime event structures and occurrence nets. However it has not been settled what properties a reversible system should enjoy, nor how the various properties that have been suggested, such as the parabolic lemma and the causal-consistency property, are related. We contribute to a solution to these issues by using a generic labelled transition system equipped with a relation capturing whether transitions are independent to explore the implications between these properties. In particular, we show how they are derivable from a set of axioms. Our intention is that when establishing properties of some formalism it will be easier to verify the axioms rather than proving properties such as the parabolic lemma directly. We also introduce two new notions related to causal consistent reversibility, namely causal safety and causal liveness, and show that they are derivable from our axioms.

Keywords: Reversible Computation, Labelled Transition System with Independence, Causal Safety, Causal Liveness

1 Introduction

Reversible computing studies computations which can proceed both in the standard, forward direction, and backward, going back to past states. Reversible computation has attracted interest due to its applications in areas as different as low-power computing [15], simulation [4], robotics [21], biological modelling [31] and debugging [23].

There is widespread agreement in the literature about what properties characterise reversible computation in the sequential setting. Thus in reversible finite state automata [32], reversible cellular automata [13], reversible Turing machines [2] and reversible programming languages such as Janus [35] the main point is that the mapping from inputs to outputs is injective, and the reverse computation is deterministic.

Matters are less clear when it comes to reversible computation in the concurrent setting. Indeed, various reversible concurrent models have been studied, most notably in the areas of process calculi [6,29,18], event structures [34], Petri nets [1,25] and programming languages such as Erlang [20].

A main result of this line of research is that the notion of reversibility most suited for concurrent systems is *causal-consistent reversibility* (other notions are also used, e.g., to model biological systems [31]). According to an informal account of causal-consistent reversibility, any action can be undone provided that its consequences, if any, are undone beforehand. Following [6] this account is formalised using the notion of causal equivalent traces: two traces are causal equivalent if and only if they only differ for swapping independent actions, and inserting or removing pairs of an action and its reverse. According to [6, Section 3]

> Backtracking an event is possible when and only when a causally equivalent trace would have brought this event as the last one

which is then formalised as the so called causal consistency (CC) [6, Theorem 1], stating that coinitial computations are causal equivalent if and only if they are cofinal. Our new proof of CC (Proposition 3.6) shows that it holds in essentially any reversible formalism satisfying the Loop Lemma and the Parabolic Lemma, and we believe that CC is insufficient on its own to capture the informal notion.

A formalisation closer to the informal statement above is provided in [20, Corollary 22], stating that a forward transition t can be undone after a derivation iff all its consequences, if any, are undone beforehand. We are not aware of other discussions trying to formalise such a notion, except for [30], in the setting of reversible event structures. In [30], a reversible event structure is *cause-respecting* if an event cannot be reversed until all events it has caused have also been reversed; it is *causal* if it is cause-respecting and a reversible event can be reversed if all events it has caused have been reversed [30, Definition 3.34].

We provide (Section 4) a novel definition of the idea above, composed by:

Causal Safety (CS): an action cannot be reversed until any actions caused by it have been reversed;

Causal Liveness (CL): we should allow actions to reverse in any order compatible with CS, not necessarily the exact inverse of the forward order.

We shall see that CC does not capture the same property as CS+CL (Examples 4.15, 4.37), and that there are slightly different versions of CS and CL, which can all be proved under a small set of reasonable assumptions.

The main aim of this paper is to take an abstract model, namely labelled transition systems with independence equipped with reverse transitions (Section 2), and to show that the properties above (as well as others) can be derived

Acronym	Name	Defined in	Proved in	using
SP	Square Property	Def. 3.1	Axiom	-
BTI	Backward Transitions are Independent	Def. 3.1	Axiom	-
WF	Well-Founded	Def. 3.1	Axiom	-
CPI	Coinitial Propagation of Independence	Def. 4.2	Axiom	-
IRE	Independence Respects Events	Def. 4.12	Axiom	-
CIRE	Coinitial Independence Respects Events	Def. 4.29	Axiom	implied by IRE
IEC	Independence of Events is Coinitial	Def. 4.16	Axiom	-
PL	Parabolic Lemma	Def. 3.3	Prop. 3.4	BTI, SP
CC	Causal Consistency	Def. 3.5	Prop. 3.6	WF, PL
UT	Unique Transition	Def. 3.7	Cor. 3.8	CC
ID	Independence of Diamonds	Def. 4.6	Prop. 4.7	BTI, CPI
RPI	Reversing Preserves Independence	Def. 4.17	Prop. 4.18	SP, CPI, IRE, IEC
CS	Causal Safety	Def. 4.11	Thm. 4.13	SP, BTI, WF, CPI, IRE
CL	Causal Liveness	Def. 4.11	Thm. 4.14	SP, BTI, WF, CPI, IRE
$CS_<$	ordered Causal Safety	Def. 4.24	Prop. 4.39	SP, BTI, WF, CPI, NRE
$CL_<$	ordered Causal Liveness	Def. 4.24	Prop. 4.39	SP, BTI, WF, CPI, CIRE
CS_{ci}	coinitial Causal Safety	Def. 4.27	Thm. 4.28	SP, BTI, WF, CPI
CL_{ci}	coinitial Causal Liveness	Def. 4.27	Thm. 4.30	SP, BTI, WF, CPI, CIRE
NRE	No Repeated Events	Def. 4.35	Prop. 4.42	SP, BTI, WF, CPI, CIRE
RED	Reverse Event Determinism	Def. 4.40	Prop. 4.41	SP, BTI, WF, CPI, NRE

Table 1. Axioms and properties for causal reversibility.

from a small set of simple axioms (Sections 3, 4, 5). This is in sharp contrast with the large part of works in the literature, which consider specific frameworks such as CCS [6], CCS with broadcast [26], CCB [14], π-calculus [5], higher-order π [18], Klaim [11], Petri nets [25], μOz [22] and Erlang [20], and all give similar but formally unrelated proofs of the same main results. Such proofs will become instances of our general results. More precisely, our axioms will:

- exclude behaviours which are not compatible with causal-consistent reversibility (as we will discuss shortly);
- allow us to derive the main properties of reversible calculi which have been studied in the literature, such as CC (Proposition 3.6);
- hold for a number of reversible calculi which have been proposed, such as RCCS [6] and reversible Erlang [20] (Section 6).

Thus, when defining a new reversible formalism, one just has to check whether the axioms hold, and get for free the proofs of the most relevant properties. Notably, the axioms are normally easier to prove than the properties, hence the assessment of a reversible calculus gets much simpler.

As a reference, Table 1 lists the axioms and properties used in this paper.

In order to understand which kinds of behaviours are incompatible with a causal-consistent reversible setting, consider the following LTSs in CCS:

$a.\mathbf{0} \xrightarrow{a} \mathbf{0}, b.\mathbf{0} \xrightarrow{b} \mathbf{0}$: from state $\mathbf{0}$ one does not know whether to go back to $a.\mathbf{0}$ or to $b.\mathbf{0}$;

$a.0 + b.0 \xrightarrow{a} 0$, $a.0 + b.0 \xrightarrow{b} 0$: as above, but starting from the same process, hence showing that it is not enough to remember the initial configuration;

$P \xrightarrow{a} P$ **where** $P = a.P$: one can go back forever, against the idea that a state models a process reachable after a finite computation.

We remark that all such behaviours are perfectly reasonable in CCS, and they are dealt with in the reversible setting by adding history information about past actions. For example, in the first case one could remember the initial state, in the second case both the initial state and the action taken, and in the last case the number of iterations that have been performed.

Due to space constraints, some proofs and additional results can only be found in the companion technical report [16].

2   Labelled Transition Systems with Independence

We want to study reversibility in a setting as general as possible. Thus, we base on the core of the notion of *labelled transition system with independence* (LTSI) [33, Definition 3.7]. However, while [33] requires a number of axioms on LTSI, we take the basic definition and explore what can be done by adding or not adding various axioms. Also, we extend LTSI with reverse transitions, since we study reversible systems. We define first labelled transition systems (LTSs).

We consider the LTS of the entire set of processes in a calculus, rather than the transition graph of a particular process and its derivatives, hence we do not fix an initial state.

Definition 2.1. *A* labelled transition system (LTS) *is a* structure (Proc, Lab, →), *where* Proc *is the set of states (or processes),* Lab *is the set of action labels and* → ⊆ Proc × Lab × Proc *is a* transition relation.

We let $P, Q, \ldots$ range over processes, $a, b, c, \ldots$ range over labels, and $t, u, v, \ldots$ range over transitions. We can write $t : P \xrightarrow{a} Q$ to denote that $t = (P, a, Q)$. We call a-transition a transition with label a.

Definition 2.2 (LTS with independence). *We say that* (Proc, Lab, →, ι) *is an* LTS with independence *(LTSI) if* (Proc, Lab, →) *is an LTS and* ι *is an ir-reflexive symmetric binary relation on transitions.*

In many cases (see Section 6), the notion of independence coincides with the notion of concurrency. However, this is not always the case. Indeed, concurrency implies that transitions are independent since they happen in different processses, but transitions taken by the same process can be independent as well. Think, for instance, of a reactive process that may react in any order to two events arriving at the same time, and the final result does not depend on the order of reactions.

We shall assume that all transitions are reversible, so that the Loop Lemma [6, Lemma 6] holds. This does not hold in models of reversibility with control mechanisms such as irreversible actions [6,7] or a rollback operator [17]. Nevertheless, when showing properties of models with controlled reversibility it has proved sensible to first consider the underlying models where all transitions are reversible, and then study how control mechanisms change the picture [11,20]. The present work helps with the first step.

Definition 2.3. *Given* $(\mathsf{Proc}, \mathsf{Lab}, \to)$, *let the* reverse LTS *be* $(\mathsf{Proc}, \mathsf{Lab}, \rightsquigarrow)$, *where* $P \overset{a}{\rightsquigarrow} Q$ *iff* $Q \overset{a}{\to} P$. *It is convenient to combine the two LTSs (forward and reverse): let the reverse labels be* $\underline{\mathsf{Lab}} = \{\underline{a} : a \in \mathsf{Lab}\}$, *and define the combined LTS to be* $\to \subseteq \mathsf{Proc} \times (\mathsf{Lab} \cup \underline{\mathsf{Lab}}) \times \mathsf{Proc}$ *by* $P \overset{a}{\to} Q$ *iff* $P \overset{a}{\to} Q$ *and* $P \overset{\underline{a}}{\to} Q$ *iff* $P \overset{a}{\rightsquigarrow} Q$.

We stipulate that the union $\mathsf{Lab} \cup \underline{\mathsf{Lab}}$ is disjoint. We let $\alpha, \dots$ range over $\mathsf{Lab} \cup \underline{\mathsf{Lab}}$. For $\alpha \in \mathsf{Lab} \cup \underline{\mathsf{Lab}}$, the *underlying* action label $\mathsf{und}(\alpha)$ is defined as $\mathsf{und}(a) = a$ and $\mathsf{und}(\underline{a}) = a$. Let $\underline{\underline{a}} = a$ for $a \in \mathsf{Lab}$. Given $t : P \overset{\alpha}{\to} Q$, let $\underline{t} : Q \overset{\underline{\alpha}}{\to} P$ be the transition which reverses t.

We let $\rho, \sigma, \dots$ range over finite sequences $\alpha_1 \dots \alpha_n$, with ε_P representing the empty sequence starting and ending at P. We shall write ε when P is understood. Given an LTS, a *path* is a sequence of forward or reverse transitions of the form $P_0 \overset{\alpha_1}{\to} P_1 \cdots \overset{\alpha_n}{\to} P_n$. We let $r, s, \dots$ range over paths. We may write $r : P \overset{\rho}{\to}_* Q$ where the intermediate states are understood. On occasion we may refer to a path simply by its sequence of labels ρ. Given a path $r : P \overset{\rho}{\to}_* Q$, the inverse path is $\underline{r} : Q \overset{\underline{\rho}}{\to}_* P$ where $\underline{\varepsilon} = \varepsilon$ and $\underline{\alpha\rho} = \underline{\rho}\, \underline{\alpha}$. The length of a path r (notated $|r|$) is the number of transitions in the path. Paths $r : P \overset{\rho}{\to}_* Q$ and $R \overset{\sigma}{\to}_* S$ are *coinitial* if $P = R$ and *cofinal* if $Q = S$. We say that a path is *forward-only* if it contains no reverse transitions.

Let $(\mathsf{Proc}, \mathsf{Lab}, \to)$ be an LTS. The irreversible processes in $(\mathsf{Proc}, \mathsf{Lab}, \to)$ are $\mathsf{Irr} = \{P \in \mathsf{Proc} : P \not\rightsquigarrow\}$. A *rooted path* is a path $r : P \overset{\rho}{\to}_* Q$ such that $P \in \mathsf{Irr}$.

In the following we will consider LTSIs obtained by adding a notion of independence to combined LTSs as above. We will call the result a *combined LTSI*.

3 Basic Properties

In this section we show that most of the properties in the reversibility literature (see, e.g., [6,29,18,20]), in particular the parabolic lemma and causal consistency, can be proved under minimal assumptions on the combined LTSI under analysis.

We formalise the minimal assumptions using three axioms, described below.

Definition 3.1 (Basic axioms). *Let* $\mathcal{L} = (\mathsf{Proc}, \mathsf{Lab}, \to, \iota)$ *be a combined LTSI. We say* $\mathcal{L}$ *satisfies:*

Square Property (SP) *if whenever* $t : P \overset{\alpha}{\to} Q$, $u : P \overset{\beta}{\to} R$ *with* $t \iota u$ *then there are cofinal transitions* $u' : Q \overset{\beta}{\to} S$ *and* $t' : R \overset{\alpha}{\to} S$;

Backward Transitions are Independent (BTI) *if whenever* $t : P \overset{a}{\rightsquigarrow} Q$ *and* $t' : P \overset{b}{\rightsquigarrow} Q'$ *and* $t \neq t'$ *then* $t \iota t'$;

Well-Foundedness (WF) *if there is no infinite reverse computation, i.e. we do not have P_i (not necessarily distinct) such that $P_{i+1} \xrightarrow{a_i} P_i$ for all $i = 0, 1, \ldots$.*

WF can alternatively be formulated using backward transitions, but the current formulation makes sense also in non-reversible calculi (e.g., CCS), which can be used as a comparison. Let us discuss the intuition behind these axioms. SP takes its name from the Square Lemma, where it is proved for concrete calculi and languages in [6,18,20], and captures the idea that independent transitions can be executed in any order, that is they form commuting diamonds. SP can be seen as a sanity check on the chosen notion of independence. BTI generalises the key notion of backward determinism used in sequential reversibility (see, e.g., [32] for finite state automata and [35] for the imperative language Janus) to a concurrent setting. Backward determinism can be spelled as "two coinitial backward transitions do coincide". This can be generalised to "two coinitial backward transitions are independent". Finally, WF means that we consider systems which have a finite past. That is, we consider systems starting from some initial state and then moving forward and back.

Axioms SP and BTI are related to properties which are part of the definition of (occurrence) transition systems with independence in [33, Definitions 3.7, 4.1]. WF was used as an axiom in [28].

Using the minimal assumptions above we can prove relevant results from the literature. We first define causal equivalence, equating computations differing only for swaps of independent transitions and simplification of a transition with its reverse.

Definition 3.2 (cf. [6]). *Let* $(\mathsf{Proc}, \mathsf{Lab}, \rightarrow, \iota)$ *be an LTSI satisfying SP. Let* $\approx$ *be the smallest equivalence relation on paths closed under composition and satisfying:*

1. *if* $t : P \xrightarrow{\alpha} Q$, $u : P \xrightarrow{\beta} R$ *are independent, and* $u' : Q \xrightarrow{\beta} S$, $t' : R \xrightarrow{\alpha} S$ *(which exist by SP) then* $tu' \approx ut'$;
2. $t\underline{t} \approx \varepsilon$ *and* $\underline{t}t \approx \varepsilon$.

We first consider the Parabolic Lemma ([6, Lemma 10]), which states that each path is causal equivalent to a backward path followed by a forward path.

Definition 3.3. Parabolic Lemma (PL): *for any path r there are forward-only paths s, s' such that $r \approx \underline{s}s'$ and $|s| + |s'| \leq |r|$.*

Proposition 3.4. *Suppose an LTSI satisfies BTI and SP. Then PL holds.*

The proof of Proposition 3.4 (available in [16]) is very similar to that of [6, Lemma 10] except that in the latter BTI is shown directly as part of the proof.

A corollary of PL is that if a process is reachable from an irreversible process, then it is also forwards reachable from it. In other words, making a system reversible does not introduce new reachable states but only allows one to explore differently forwards reachable states. This is relevant in reversible debugging of concurrent systems [10,20], where one wants to find bugs that actually occur in forward-only computations. See the companion technical report [16, Corollary A.1]. We now move to causal consistency [6, Theorem 1].

Definition 3.5. Causal Consistency (CC): *if r and s are coinitial and cofinal then $r \approx s$.*

Essentially, causal consistency states that history information allows one to distinguish computations which are not causal equivalent, indeed, if two computations are cofinal, that is they reach the same final state (which includes the stored history information) then they need to be causal equivalent.

Causal consistency frequently includes the other direction, namely that coinitial causal equivalent computations are cofinal, meaning that there is no way to distinguish causal equivalent computations. This second direction follows easily from the definition of causal equivalence.

Notably, our proof of CC below is very much shorter than existing proofs.

Proposition 3.6. *Suppose an LTSI satisfies WF and PL. Then CC holds.*

Proof. Let $r : P \xrightarrow{\rho}_* Q$ and $r' : P \xrightarrow{\rho'}_* Q$. Using WF, let I, s be such that $s : I \xrightarrow{\sigma}_* P$, $I \in \mathsf{Irr}$. Now $sr\underline{sr'}$ is a path from I to I, and so by PL there are r_1, r_2 forward-only such that $r_1 r_2 \approx sr\underline{sr'}$. But $I \in \mathsf{Irr}$ and so $r_1 = \varepsilon$ and $r_2 = \varepsilon$. Thus $\varepsilon \approx sr\underline{sr'}$, so that $sr \approx sr'$ and $r \approx r'$ as required. $\qquad\square$

Causal consistency implies the unique transition property.

Definition 3.7. *An LTSI* $(\mathsf{Proc}, \mathsf{Lab}, \rightarrow, \iota)$ *satisfies* **Unique Transition (UT)** *if $P \xrightarrow{a} Q$ and $P \xrightarrow{b} Q$ imply $a = b$.*

Corollary 3.8. *If an LTSI satisfies CC then it satisfies UT.*

UT was shown in the forward-only setting of occurrence TSIs in [33, Corollary 4.4]; it was taken as an axiom in [28].

Example 3.9 (PL alone does not imply WF or CC). Consider the LTSI with states P_i for $i = 0, 1, \ldots$ and transitions $t_i : P_{i+1} \xrightarrow{a} P_i$, $u_i : P_{i+1} \xrightarrow{b} P_i$ with $a \neq b$ and $t_i \iota u_i$. BTI and SP hold. Hence PL holds by Proposition 3.4. However clearly WF fails. Also t_i and u_i are coinitial and cofinal, and $a \neq b$, so that UT fails, and hence CC fails using Corollary 3.8. Note that the ab diamonds here have the same side states so are degenerate (cf. Lemma 4.4).

4   Causal Safety and Causal Liveness

In the literature, causal consistent reversibility is frequently informally described by saying that "a transition can be undone if and only if each of its consequences, if any, has been undone". In this section we study this property, where the two implications will be referred to as causal safety and causal liveness. We provide three different versions of such properties, based on independence of transitions (Section 4.2), ordering of events (Section 4.3), and independence of events (Section 4.4), and study their relationships. In order to define such properties we need the concept of event.

4.1   Events

Definition 4.1 (Event, general definition). *Let* $(\mathsf{Proc}, \mathsf{Lab}, \rightarrow, \iota)$ *be an LTSI.* *Let* $\sim$ *be the smallest equivalence relation satisfying: if* $t : P \xrightarrow{\alpha} Q$, $u : P \xrightarrow{\beta} R$, $u' : Q \xrightarrow{\beta} S$, $t' : R \xrightarrow{\alpha} S$, *and* $t \, \iota \, u$, $\underline{u} \, \iota \, t'$, $\underline{t'} \, \iota \, \underline{u'}$, $u' \, \iota \, \underline{t}$, *and*

- $Q \neq R$ *if* α *and* β *are both forwards or both backwards;*
- $P \neq S$ *otherwise;*

then $t \sim t'$. *The equivalence classes of forward transitions, written* $[P, a, Q]$, *are the* events. *The equivalence classes of reverse transitions, written* $[P, \underline{a}, Q]$, *are the* reverse events. *Define a labelling function* ℓ *from* $\rightarrow / \sim$ *to* Lab *by setting* $\ell([P, \alpha, Q]) = \alpha$.

Events are introduced as a derived notion in an LTS with independence in [33], in the context of forward-only computation. We have changed their definition by using coinitial independence at all corners of the diamond, yielding rotational symmetry. This reflects our view that forward and backward transitions have equal status.

Our definition can be simplified if the LTSI, and independence in particular, · are well-behaved. Thus, we now add a further axiom related to independence.

Definition 4.2 (Coinitial Propagation of Independence (CPI)). *If* $t : P \xrightarrow{\alpha} Q$, $u : P \xrightarrow{\beta} R$, $u' : Q \xrightarrow{\beta} S$ *and* $t' : R \xrightarrow{\alpha} S$ *with* $t \, \iota \, u$, *then* $u' \, \iota \, \underline{t}$.

CPI states that independence is a property of commuting diamonds more than of their specific pairs of edges. Indeed, it allows independence to propagate around a commuting diamond.

Definition 4.3. *If a combined LTSI satisfies axioms SP, BTI, WF and CPI, we say that it is* pre-reversible.

The name 'pre-reversible' indicates that we expect to require further axioms, but the present four are enough to ensure that LTSIs are well-behaved, with events compatible with causal equivalence. Pre-reversible axioms are separated from further axioms by a dashed line in Table 1.

The following non-degeneracy property was shown for occurrence transition systems with independence in [33, page 312], which have forward transitions only. We have to cope with backwards as well as forward transitions.

Lemma 4.4. *Suppose that an LTSI is pre-reversible. If we have a diamond* $t : P \xrightarrow{\alpha} Q$, $u : P \xrightarrow{\beta} R$ *with* $t \, \iota \, u$ *together with cofinal transitions* $u' : Q \xrightarrow{\beta} S$ *and* $t' : R \xrightarrow{\alpha} S$, *then the diamond is* non-degenerate, *meaning that* P, Q, R, S *are distinct states.*

If an LTSI is pre-reversible then by Lemma 4.4 and the use of CPI we can simplify the statement of Definition 4.1 to:

Definition 4.5 (Event, simplified definition). *Let* $(\mathsf{Proc}, \mathsf{Lab}, \rightarrow, \iota)$ *be a pre-reversible LTSI. Let* $\sim$ *be the smallest equivalence relation satisfying: if* $t : P \xrightarrow{\alpha} Q$, $u : P \xrightarrow{\beta} R$, $u' : Q \xrightarrow{\beta} S$, $t' : R \xrightarrow{\alpha} S$, *and* $t \iota u$, *then* $t \sim t'$.

We are now able to show independence of diamonds (ID), which can be seen as dual of SP.

Definition 4.6 (Independence of Diamonds (ID)). *An LTSI satisfies the Independence of Diamonds property (ID) if whenever we have a diamond* $t : P \xrightarrow{\alpha} Q$, $u : P \xrightarrow{\beta} R$, $u' : Q \xrightarrow{\beta} S$ *and* $t' : R \xrightarrow{\alpha} S$, *with*

- $Q \neq R$ *if* α *and* β *are both forwards or both backwards;*
- $P \neq S$ *otherwise;*

then $t \iota u$.

Proposition 4.7. *If an LTSI satisfies BTI and CPI then it satisfies ID.*

We now consider the interaction between events and causal equivalence. We need some notation first.

Definition 4.8. *Let* r *be a path in an LTSI* $\mathcal{L}$ *and let* e *be an event of* $\mathcal{L}$. *Let* $\sharp(r, e)$ *be the number of occurrences of transitions* t *in* r *such that* $t \in e$, *minus the number of occurrences of transitions* t *in* r *such that* $t \in \underline{e}$.

We now show that $\sharp(r, e)$ is invariant under causal equivalent traces.

Lemma 4.9. *Let* $\mathcal{L}$ *be a pre-reversible LTSI. Let* $r \approx s$. *Then for each event* e *we have that* $\sharp(r, e) = \sharp(s, e)$.

Lemma 4.9 generalises what was shown for the forward-only setting in [33, Corollary 4.3].

Proposition 4.10. *If an LTSI is pre-reversible, then for any rooted path* r *and any forward event* e *we have* $\sharp(r, e) \geq 0$.

4.2 CS and CL via Independence of Transitions

We first define causal safety and liveness using the independence relation.

Definition 4.11. *Let* $\mathcal{L} = (\mathsf{Proc}, \mathsf{Lab}, \rightarrow, \iota)$ *be a pre-reversible LTSI.*

1. *We say that* $\mathcal{L}$ *is* causally safe (CS) *if whenever* $P \xrightarrow{a} Q$, $r : Q \xrightarrow{\rho}_* R$, $\sharp(r, [P, a, Q]) = 0$ *and* $S \xrightarrow{a} R$ *with* $(P, a, Q) \sim (S, a, R)$, *then* $(P, a, Q) \iota t$ *for all* t *in* r *such that* $\sharp(r, [t]) > 0$.
2. *We say that* $\mathcal{L}$ *is* causally live (CL) *if whenever* $P \xrightarrow{a} Q$, $r : Q \xrightarrow{\rho}_* R$ *and* $\sharp(r, [P, a, Q]) = 0$ *and* $(P, a, Q) \iota t$, *for all* t *in* r *such that* $\sharp(r, [t]) > 0$, *then we have* $S \xrightarrow{a} R$ *with* $(P, a, Q) \sim (S, a, R)$.

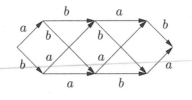

Fig. 1.

We may wish to close the independence relation over this axiom:

Definition 4.12 (Independence Respects Events (IRE)). *Whenever $t \sim t' \iota u$ we have $t \iota u$.*

IRE is one of the conditions in the definition of transition systems with independence [33, Definition 3.7]. Together with the axioms for pre-reversibility, it is enough to show both causal safety and causal liveness.

Theorem 4.13. *Let a pre-reversible LTSI satisfy IRE. Then it satisfies CS.*

Theorem 4.14. *Let a pre-reversible LTSI satisfy IRE. Then it satisfies CL.*

CS and CL are not derivable from CC; we give an example LTSI which satisfies CC but not CS and not CL.

Example 4.15. Consider the LTS in Figure 1. Independence is mostly coinitial and given by closing under BTI and CPI. Additionally we make the leftmost a-transition independent with all b-transitions. Note that all a-transitions belong to the same event, and all b-transitions belong to the same event. Also SP and WF hold, so that the LTSI is pre-reversible, and CC holds. However IRE does not hold. Furthermore CS fails using Definition 4.11. Indeed, consider any path $\stackrel{bab}{\to}_*$ from the start. CS would imply that the first b is independent with the a but this is not the case (we do have $\underline{b} \iota a$).

Also CL fails using Definition 4.11. Indeed, consider any path $\stackrel{abb}{\to}_*$ from the start. Since the leftmost a-transition is independent with all b-transitions, we should be able to reverse a at the end of the path, but this is not possible.

The next axiom states that independence is fully determined by its restriction to coinitial transitions. This is related to axiom (E) of [33, page 325], but here we allow reverse as well as forward transitions.

Definition 4.16 (Independence of Events is Coinitial (IEC)). *If $t_1 \iota t_2$ then there are $t_1' \sim t_1$, $t_2' \sim t_2$ such that t_1' and t_2' are coinitial and $t_1' \iota t_2'$.*

Thanks to previous axioms, independence behaves well w.r.t. reversing.

Definition 4.17 (Reversing Preserves Independence (RPI)). *If $t \iota t'$ then $\underline{t} \iota t'$.*

Proposition 4.18. *If an LTSI satisfies SP, CPI, IRE, IEC then it also satisfies RPI.*

All the axioms that we have introduced are independent, i.e. none is derivable from the remaining axioms.

Proposition 4.19. *SP, BTI, WF, CPI, IRE, IEC are independent of each other.*

4.3   CS and CL via Ordering of Events

To define CS and CL via ordering of events, we define the causality relation $\leq$ on events.

Definition 4.20. *Let $\mathcal{L} = (\mathsf{Proc}, \mathsf{Lab}, \to, \iota)$ be an LTSI. Let e, e' be events of $\mathcal{L}$. Let $e \leq e'$ iff for all rooted paths r, if $\sharp(r, e') > 0$ then $\sharp(r, e) > 0$. As usual $e < e'$ means $e \leq e'$ and $e \neq e'$. If $e < e'$ we say that e is a* cause *of e'.*

Lemma 4.21. *If an LTSI satisfies SP, BTI, WF and CPI then $\leq$ is a partial ordering on events.*

Previously, orderings on events have been defined using forward-only rooted paths; in fact, the definitions coincide for pre-reversible LTSIs.

Definition 4.22 ([12,28]). *Let $\mathcal{L} = (\mathsf{Proc}, \mathsf{Lab}, \to, \iota)$ be an LTSI. Let e, e' be events of $\mathcal{L}$. Let $e \leq_{\mathsf{f}} e'$ iff for all rooted forward-only paths r, if r contains a representative of e' then r also contains a representative of e.*

Lemma 4.23. *For any LTSI, $e \leq e'$ implies $e \leq_{\mathsf{f}} e'$. If an LTSI satisfies SP, BTI, WF and CPI then $e \leq_{\mathsf{f}} e'$ implies $e \leq e'$.*

Proof. Straightforward using PL and Lemma 4.9.   □

We now give definitions of causal safety and causal liveness using ordering on events.

Definition 4.24. *Let $\mathcal{L} = (\mathsf{Proc}, \mathsf{Lab}, \to, \iota)$ be an LTSI.*

1. *We say that $\mathcal{L}$ is* ordered causally safe *(CS$_<$) if whenever $P \xrightarrow{a} Q$, $r : Q \xrightarrow{\rho}_* R$, $\sharp(r, [P, a, Q]) = 0$ and $S \xrightarrow{a} R$ with $(P, a, Q) \sim (S, a, R)$, then $[P, a, Q] \not< e'$ for all e' such that $\sharp(r, e') > 0$.*

2. *We say that $\mathcal{L}$ is* ordered causally live *(CL$_<$) if whenever $P \xrightarrow{a} Q$, $r : Q \xrightarrow{\rho}_* R$ and $\sharp(r, [P, a, Q]) = 0$ and $[P, a, Q] \not< e'$ for all e' such that $\sharp(r, e') > 0$ then we have $S \xrightarrow{a} R$ with $(P, a, Q) \sim (S, a, R)$.*

We postpone giving proofs of CS$_<$ and CL$_<$ until we have introduced a further definition of causal safety and liveness using independence of events.

4.4   CS and CL via Independent Events

We now introduce a third version of causal safety and liveness, which uses independence like CS and CL, but on events rather than on transitions. First we lift independence from transitions to events.

Definition 4.25 (Coinitially independent events). *Let events e, e' be (coinitially) independent, written e ci e', iff there are coinitial transitions t, t' such that $[t] = e$, $[t'] = e'$ and $t \iota t'$.*

Lemma 4.26. *If an LTSI is pre-reversible, then if e ci e' we have also $\underline{e}$ ci e'.*

Thus in pre-reversible LTSIs, ci is fully determined just considering forward events. By Lemma 4.26, if we know e ci e' then we know $\mathsf{und}(e)$ ci $\mathsf{und}(e')$.

We can give a third formulation of causal safety and liveness using ci:

Definition 4.27. *Let $\mathcal{L} = (\mathsf{Proc}, \mathsf{Lab}, \rightarrow, \iota)$ be a pre-reversible LTSI.*

1. *We say that $\mathcal{L}$ is coinitially causally safe (CS_{ci}) if whenever $P \xrightarrow{a} Q$, $r : Q \xrightarrow{\rho}_* R$, $\sharp(r, [P, a, Q]) = 0$ and $S \xrightarrow{a} R$ with $(P, a, Q) \sim (S, a, R)$, then $[P, a, Q]$ ci e for all forward events e such that $\sharp(r, e) > 0$.*

2. *We say that $\mathcal{L}$ is coinitially causally live (CL_{ci}) if whenever $P \xrightarrow{a} Q$, $r : Q \xrightarrow{\rho}_* R$ and $\sharp(r, [P, a, Q]) = 0$ and $[P, a, Q]$ ci e, for all forward events e such that $\sharp(r, e) > 0$, then we have $S \xrightarrow{a} R$ with $(P, a, Q) \sim (S, a, R)$.*

Note that in Definition 4.27 we operate at the level of events, rather than at the level of transitions as in Definition 4.11.

Theorem 4.28. *If an LTSI is pre-reversible then it satisfies CS_{ci}.*

We now introduce a weaker version of axiom IRE (Definition 4.12).

Definition 4.29 (Coinitial IRE (CIRE)). *If $[t]$ ci $[u]$ and t, u are coinitial then $t \iota u$.*

Theorem 4.30. *If a pre-reversible LTSI satisfies CIRE then it satisfies CL_{ci}.*

We next give an example where CC holds but not CS_{ci} (and not CPI).

Example 4.31. Consider the cube with transitions a, b, c on the left in Figure 2, where the forward direction is from left to right. We add independence as given by BTI. So SP, BTI, WF hold, but not CPI. From the start we have an a-transition followed by a path $r = bc$ followed by $\underline{a}$. For CS_{ci} to hold, we want $\underline{a}$ to be the reverse of the same event as the first a. They are connected by a ladder with sides cb. We add independence for all corners on the two faces of the ladder (ab and ac). Then we get $bc \approx cb$ (independence at a single corner is enough). However the bs are not the same event since the bc face does not have independence at each corner. Therefore we do not get $[a]$ ci $[b]$, and CS_{ci} fails.

We next give an example where CS_{ci} and CL_{ci} hold but not CC.

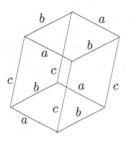 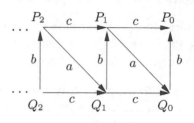

Fig. 2.

Example 4.32. Consider the LTSI with $Q_i \xrightarrow{b} P_i$, $P_{i+1} \xrightarrow{c} P_i$, $Q_{i+1} \xrightarrow{c} Q_i$, $P_{i+1} \xrightarrow{a} Q_i$ for $i = 0, 1, \ldots$. This is shown on the right in Figure 2. Clearly WF does not hold. We add coinitial independence to make BTI and CPI hold. Then also SP and CIRE hold. However, CC fails since, for example $P_1 \xrightarrow{a} Q_0 \xrightarrow{b} P_0$ and $P_1 \xrightarrow{c} P_0$ are coinitial and cofinal but not causally equivalent. Note that there are just three events a, b, c with a ci c, b ci c but not a ci b. CS_{ci} and CL_{ci} hold. Indeed, c is independent from every other action, and it can always be undone, while a and b are independent from c only and they can be undone after any path composed by c and no others.

4.5   Polychotomy

In this section we relate our three versions of causal safety and liveness, with the help of what we call *polychotomy*, which states that if events do not cause each other and are not in conflict, then they must be independent. We start by defining a conflict relation on events.

Definition 4.33. *Two forward events e, e' are in* conflict, *written $e \# e'$, if there is no rooted path r such that $\sharp(r, e) > 0$ and $\sharp(r, e') > 0$.*

Much as for orderings, conflict on events has been defined previously using forward-only rooted paths [12,28]; in fact, the definitions coincide for pre-reversible LTSIs. We omit the details.

Definition 4.34 (Polychotomy). *Let $\mathcal{L}$ be a pre-reversible LTSI. We say that $\mathcal{L}$ satisfies* polychotomy *if whenever e, e' are forward events, then exactly one of the following holds: 1. $e = e'$;   2. $e < e'$;   3. $e' < e$;   4. $e \# e'$; or   5. e ci e'.*

Property NRE below is related to polychotomy.

Definition 4.35 (No Repeated Events (NRE)). *In any rooted path r, for any forward event e we have $\sharp(r, e) \leq 1$.*

Lemma 4.36 (Polychotomy).   *Suppose that a pre-reversible LTSI satisfies NRE. Then polychotomy holds.*

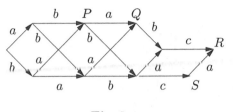

Fig. 3.

Example 4.37. Consider the LTSI in Figure 3. We add independence to make BTI and CPI hold. Both SP and WF hold. Hence, CC holds as well. There are three events, labelled with a, b, c. Clearly NRE fails for both a and b. We see that $a < c$ but also a ci c, so that polychotomy fails. CS_{ci} holds by Theorem 4.28. However $CS_<$ fails: consider the transition $P \xrightarrow{a} Q$ together with the path $r :$ $Q \xrightarrow{bc}_* R$ and $S \xrightarrow{a} R$, and note that $a < c$.

The next lemma allows us to connect ordered safety and liveness with coinitial safety and liveness.

Lemma 4.38. *Suppose that a pre-reversible LTSI satisfies NRE. Suppose $P \xrightarrow{a}$ Q, $e = [P, a, Q]$, $r : Q \xrightarrow{\rho}_* R$ and $\sharp(r, e') > 0$ where e' is a forward event. Then exactly one of e ci e' and $e < e'$ holds.*

Proposition 4.39. *Suppose that a pre-reversible LTSI $\mathcal{L}$ satisfies NRE. Then*

1. *$\mathcal{L}$ satisfies $CS_<$.*
2. *$\mathcal{L}$ satisfies CL_{ci} iff $\mathcal{L}$ satisfies $CL_<$.*

Property RED below is also related to NRE and polychotomy.

Definition 4.40. *An LTSI satisfies **Reverse Event Determinism (RED)** if whenever t, t' are backward coinitial transitions and $t \sim t'$ then $t = t'$.*

Proposition 4.41. *If a LTSI $\mathcal{L}$ is pre-reversible then the following are equivalent: 1. $\mathcal{L}$ satisfies NRE; 2. $\mathcal{L}$ satisfies RED; 3. independence ci is irreflexive on events; and 4. polychotomy holds.*

Proposition 4.42. *Suppose that a pre-reversible LTSI satisfies CIRE. Then it also satisfies NRE.*

NRE was shown in the forward-only setting of occurrence transition systems with independence in [33, Corollary 4.6]. It was also shown in the reversible setting without independence in [28, Proposition 2.10].

Example 4.43. Consider the LTSI in Figure 4. Independence is given by closing under BTI and CPI. There are three events, labelled a, b, c, which are all independent of each other. We see that NRE holds but not CIRE. Also CL_{ci} and $CL_<$ fail: consider $P \xrightarrow{a} Q \xrightarrow{b} R$, where a cannot be reversed at R.

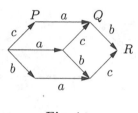

Fig. 4.

Proposition 4.44. *Let $\mathcal{L}$ be a pre-reversible LTSI.*

1. *If IEC holds then CL_{ci} implies CL.*
2. *If IEC and NRE hold then $CL_<$ implies CL.*

5   Coinitial Independence

In this section we consider coinitial LTSIs, defined as follows, and their relationship with LTSIs in general.

Definition 5.1. *Let $\mathcal{L} = (\mathsf{Proc}, \mathsf{Lab}, \to, \iota)$ be a combined LTSI. Then ι is coinitial if for all transitions t, u, if $t \,\iota\, u$ then t and u are coinitial. We say that $\mathcal{L}$ is coinitial if ι is coinitial.*

We define a mapping c restricting general independence to coinitial transitions and a mapping g extending independence along events.

Definition 5.2. *Given an LTSI $(\mathsf{Proc}, \mathsf{Lab}, \to, \iota)$, define $t \, g(\iota) \, u$ iff $t \sim t' \, \iota \, u' \sim u$ for some t', u'. Furthermore, define $t \, c(\iota) \, u$ iff $t \, \iota \, u$ and t, u are coinitial.*

Proposition 5.3. *Let $\mathcal{L} = (\mathsf{Proc}, \mathsf{Lab}, \to, \iota)$ be a pre-reversible LTSI.*

1. *If $\mathcal{L}$ is coinitial and satisfies CIRE then $\mathcal{L}' = (\mathsf{Proc}, \mathsf{Lab}, \to, g(\iota))$ is a pre-reversible LTSI and satisfies IRE and IEC.*
2. *if $\mathcal{L}$ satisfies IRE then $\mathcal{L}' = (\mathsf{Proc}, \mathsf{Lab}, \to, c(\iota))$ is a pre-reversible coinitial LTSI and satisfies CIRE.*

Thanks to Proposition 5.3, we can extend a coinitial pre-reversible LTSI satisfying CIRE in a canonical way to a pre-reversible LTSI satisfying IRE and IEC.

In some reversible calculi (such as RCCS) independence of coinitial transitions is defined purely by reference to the labels. If this is the case it is a simple matter to verify the axioms CPI and CIRE.

Proposition 5.4. *Let $\mathcal{L} = (\mathsf{Proc}, \mathsf{Lab}, \to, \iota)$ be a coinitial combined LTSI. Suppose that I is a binary relation on Lab such that for any coinitial transitions $t : P \xrightarrow{\alpha} Q$ and $u : P \xrightarrow{\beta} R$ we have $t \, \iota \, u$ iff $I(a,b)$, where a and b are the underlying labels $a = \mathsf{und}(\alpha)$, $b = \mathsf{und}(\beta)$. Then $\mathcal{L}$ satisfies CPI and CIRE.*

Proof. Straightforward, noting that labels on opposite sides of a diamond of transitions must be equal. □

Note that I must be irreflexive, since ι is irreflexive.

If we have a coinitial pre-reversible LTSI satisfying CIRE then $CS_<$ and $CL_<$ hold (using Proposition 4.42 and Proposition 4.39). Applying mapping g we get a general pre-reversible LTSI satisfying IRE and IEC by Proposition 5.3. This will satisfy CS and CL as a result of applying Theorem 4.13 and Theorem 4.14 respectively. It will also satisfy $CS_<$ and $CL_<$. Conversely, if we have a general pre-reversible LTSI satisfying IRE then CS and CL hold by Theorem 4.13 and Theorem 4.14 respectively. Applying mapping c we get a coinitial pre-reversible LTSI satisfying CIRE. This will satisfy $CS_<$ and $CL_<$.

6 Case Studies

We look at whether our axioms hold in various reversible formalisms. Remarkably, all the works below provide proofs of the Loop Lemma.

RCCS We consider here the semantics of RCCS in [6], and restrict the attention to coherent processes [6, Definition 2]. In RCCS, transitions $P \xrightarrow{\mu:\varsigma} Q$ and $P \xrightarrow{\mu':\varsigma'} Q'$ are concurrent if $\mu \cap \mu' = \emptyset$ [6, Definition 7]. This allows us to define coinitial independence as $t \iota u$ iff t and u are concurrent. We now argue that the resulting coinitial LTSI is pre-reversible and also satisfies CIRE. SP was shown in [6, Lemma 8]. BTI was shown in the proof of [6, Lemma 10]. WF is straightforward, noting that backward transitions decrease memory size. Hence, we obtain a very much simplified proof of CC. For CPI and CIRE we note that independence is defined on the underlying labels and thus Proposition 5.4 applies. Therefore $CS_<$ and $CL_<$ hold. Using Proposition 5.3, we can get an LTSI with general independence satisfying IRE and IEC, and therefore CS and CL. This is the first time these causal properties have been proved for RCCS.

HOπ We consider here the uncontrolled reversible semantics for HOπ [18]. We restrict our attention to reachable processes, called there consistent. The semantics is a reduction semantics; hence there are no labels (or, equivalently, all the labels coincide). To have more informative labels we can consider the transitions defined in [18, Section 3.1], where labels are composed of memory information and a flag denoting whether the transition is forward or backward. The notion of independence would be given by the concurrency relation on coinitial transitions [18, Definition 9]. All pre-reversible LTSI axioms hold, as well as CIRE which is needed for causal safety and liveness. Specifically, SP is proved in [18, Lemma 9]. BTI holds since distinct memories have disjoint sets of keys [18, Definition 3 and Lemma 3] and by the definition of concurrency [18, Definition 9]. WF holds as each backward step consumes a memory, which is finite to start with. Finally, CPI and CIRE are valid since the notion of concurrency is defined on the annotated labels and using our Proposition 5.4.

As a result we obtain a very much simplified proof of CC. Moreover, using CPI and CIRE, we get the $CS_<$ and $CL_<$ safety and liveness properties and, applying mapping g from Section 5, we get a general pre-reversible LTSI satisfying IRE and IEC, hence CS and CL are satisfied. This is the first time that causal properties have been shown for HOπ.

Rπ We consider the (uncontrolled) reversible semantics for π-calculus defined in [5]. We restrict the attention to reachable processes. The semantics is an LTS semantics. Independence is given as concurrency which is defined for consecutive transitions [5, Definition 4.1]. CC holds [5, Theorem 4.5].

Our results are not directly applicable to Rπ, since SP holds up to label equivalence of transitions on opposite sides of the diamond, rather than equality of labels as in our approach. We would need to extend axiom SP and the definition of causal equivalence to allow for label equivalence in order to handle Rπ using our axiomatic method.

Erlang We consider the uncontrolled reversible (reduction) semantics for Erlang in [20]. We restrict our attention to reachable processes. In order to have more informative labels we can consider the annotations defined in [20, Section 4.1]. We then can define coinitial transitions to be independent if they are concurrent [20, Definition 12].

We next discuss the validity of our axioms in reversible Erlang. SP is proved in [20, Lemma 13] and BTI is trivial from the definition of concurrency [20, Definition 12]. WF holds since the pairs of integers (total number of elements in memories, total number of messages queued) ordered under lexicographic order are always positive and decrease at each backward step. Intuitively, each step but the ones derived using the rule for reverse sched (see [20, Figure 11]) consumes an item of memory, and each step derived using rule reverse sched removes a message from a process queue. Finally, CPI and CIRE hold since the notion of concurrency is defined on the annotated labels, and by Proposition 5.4.

Since this the setting is very similar to the one of HOπ (both calculi have a reduction semantics and a coinitial notion of independence defined on enriched labels), we get the same results as for HOπ, including CC, and CS and CL.

Reversible occurrence nets Reversible occurrence nets [25,24] are traditional occurrence nets (safe and with no backward conflicts) extended with a reverse transition for each forward transition. They give rise to an LTS where states are pairis (N, m) with N a net and m a marking. A computation that represents firing a transition t in (N, m) and resulting in (N, m') is given by a firing relation $(N, m) \xrightarrow{t} (N, m')$. The notion of independence is the concurrency relation [25, Section 3] which is defined between arbitrary firings (transitions). Hence, we get a general LTSI. The CC property is shown by following the traditional approach in [6]. SP and PL are shown as well. PL and CC require several pages of proofs [24]. The causal safety and causal liveness properties are not considered in [25,24].

We can obtain CC, and additionally CS and CL, as follows. SP and BTI are proved for reversible occurrence nets in [24] as Lemma 4.3 and Lemma 3.3

respectively. WF holds because there are no forward cycles of firings in occurrence nets, hence no infinite reverse paths. In order to have CS and CL, we need to show CPI and IRE. Lemma 3.4 in [24] gives CPI. Events can be defined on firings as in our Definition 4.5, and then IRE holds as the concurrency relation preserves such events.

7   Conclusion, Related and Future Work

The literature on causal-consistent reversibility (see, for example the early survey [19]) has a number of proofs of results such as the parabolic lemma (PL) and the causal consistency property (CC), all of which are instantiated to a specific calculus, language or formalism. We have taken here a complementary approach, analysing the properties of interest in an abstract and language-independent setting. In particular, we have shown how to prove the most relevant of these properties from a small number of axioms.

Our approach builds upon [28], where a set of axioms for reverse LTSs was given and several interesting properties were shown. While the idea is similar, the development is rather different since we consider more basic axioms (we only share WF, while many of the axioms in [28], such as UT, follow from ours), and since the two papers focus on different properties. We focus on CC and various forms of CS and CL, while [28] considers correspondence with prime event structures and reversible bisimulations. Moreover, LTSs in [28] do not have a notion of independence.

In other related work, we may particularly mention [8], which like ours takes an abstract view, though based on category theory. However, its results concern irreversible actions, and do not provide insights in our setting, where all actions are reversible. The only other work which takes a general perspective is [3], which concentrates on how to derive a reversible extension of a given formalism. However, proofs concern a limited number of properties (essentially our CC), and hold only for extensions built using the technique proposed there. Also [27,29] are general, since they propose how to reverse a calculus that can be defined in a general format of SOS rules. However, the format has its syntactic constraints while our approach abstracts from them. Finally, [9] presents a number of properties such as, for example, backward confluence, which arise in the context of reversing of steps of executed transitions in Place/Transition nets.

The approach proposed in this paper opens a number of new possibilities. Firstly, when devising a new reversible formalism, our results provide a rich toolbox to prove (or disprove) relevant properties in a simple way. This is particularly relevant since causal-consistent reversibility is getting applied to more and more complex languages, such as Erlang [20], where direct proofs become cumbersome and error-prone. Secondly, our abstract proofs are relatively easy to formalise in a proof-assistant, which is even more relevant given that this will certify the correctness of the results for many possible instances. Another possible extension of our work concerns integrating into our framework irreversible actions [7]. In order to do that we could take inspiration from the above-mentioned [8].

References

1. Barylska, K., Koutny, M., Mikulski, Ł., Piątkowski, M.: Reversible computation vs. reversibility in Petri nets. Science of Computer Programming **151**, 48–60 (2018)
2. Bennett, C.H.: Logical reversibility of computation. IBM Journal of Research and Development **17**(6), 525–532 (1973)
3. Bernadet, A., Lanese, I.: A modular formalization of reversibility for concurrent models and languages. In: Bartoletti, M., Henrio, L., Knight, S., Vieira, H.T. (eds.) ICE. EPTCS, vol. 223, pp. 98–112 (2016)
4. Carothers, C.D., Perumalla, K.S., Fujimoto, R.: Efficient optimistic parallel simulations using reverse computation. ACM Transactions on Modeling and Computer Simulation **9**(3), 224–253 (1999)
5. Cristescu, I., Krivine, J., Varacca, D.: A compositional semantics for the reversible pi-calculus. In: LICS. pp. 388–397. IEEE Computer Society (2013)
6. Danos, V., Krivine, J.: Reversible communicating systems. In: Gardner, P., Yoshida, N. (eds.) CONCUR. LNCS, vol. 3170, pp. 292–307. Springer (2004)
7. Danos, V., Krivine, J.: Transactions in RCCS. In: Abadi, M., de Alfaro, L. (eds.) CONCUR. LNCS, vol. 3653, pp. 398–412. Springer (2005)
8. Danos, V., Krivine, J., Sobociński, P.: General reversibility. In: Amadio, R.M., Phillips, I. (eds.) EXPRESS. ENTCS, vol. 175(3), pp. 75–86. Elsevier (2006)
9. de Frutos Escrig, D., Koutny, M., Mikulski, Ł.: Reversing steps in Petri nets. In: Donelli, S., Haar, S. (eds.) Petri Nets. LNCS, vol. 11522. Springer (2019)
10. Giachino, E., Lanese, I., Mezzina, C.A.: Causal-consistent reversible debugging. In: Gnesi, S., Rensink, A. (eds.) FASE. LNCS, vol. 8411, pp. 370–384. Springer (2014)
11. Giachino, E., Lanese, I., Mezzina, C.A., Tiezzi, F.: Causal-consistent rollback in a tuple-based language. Journal of Logical and Algebraic Methods in Programming **88**, 99–120 (2017)
12. van Glabbeek, R., Vaandrager, F.: The difference between splitting in n and $n+1$. Information and Computation **136**(2), 109–142 (1997)
13. Kari, J.: Reversible cellular automata: From fundamental classical results to recent developments. New Generation Computing **36**(3), 145–172 (2018)
14. Kuhn, S., Ulidowski, I.: Local reversibility in a Calculus of Covalent Bonding. Science of Computer Programming **151**, 18–47 (2018)
15. Landauer, R.: Irreversibility and heat generated in the computing process. IBM Journal of Research and Development **5**, 183 –191 (1961)
16. Lanese, I., Phillips, I., Ulidowski, I.: An axiomatic approach to reversible computation (TR) (2020), http://www.cs.unibo.it/~lanese/work/axrev-TR.pdf
17. Lanese, I., Mezzina, C.A., Schmitt, A., Stefani, J.: Controlling reversibility in higher-order pi. In: Katoen, J., König, B. (eds.) CONCUR. LNCS, vol. 6901, pp. 297–311. Springer (2011)
18. Lanese, I., Mezzina, C.A., Stefani, J.: Reversibility in the higher-order π-calculus. Theoretical Computer Science **625**, 25–84 (2016)
19. Lanese, I., Mezzina, C.A., Tiezzi, F.: Causal-consistent reversibility. Bulletin of the EATCS **114** (2014)
20. Lanese, I., Nishida, N., Palacios, A., Vidal, G.: A theory of reversibility for Erlang. Journal of Logical and Algebraic Methods in Programming **100**, 71–97 (2018)
21. Laursen, J.S., Schultz, U.P., Ellekilde, L.: Automatic error recovery in robot assembly operations using reverse execution. In: IROS. pp. 1785–1792. IEEE (2015)
22. Lienhardt, M., Lanese, I., Mezzina, C.A., Stefani, J.: A reversible abstract machine and its space overhead. In: Giese, H., Rosu, G. (eds.) FMOODS/FORTE. LNCS, vol. 7273, pp. 1–17. Springer (2012)

23. McNellis, J., Mola, J., Sykes, K.: Time travel debugging: Root causing bugs in commercial scale software. CppCon talk, https://www.youtube.com/watch?v=l1YJTg_A914 (2017)
24. Melgratti, H.C., Mezzina, C.A., Ulidowski, I.: Reversing Place Transition nets. arXiv **1910.04266** (2019)
25. Melgratti, H.C., Mezzina, C.A., Ulidowski, I.: Reversing P/T nets. In: Nielson, H.R., Tuosto, E. (eds.) COORDINATION. LNCS, vol. 11533, pp. 19–36. Springer (2019)
26. Mezzina, C.A.: On reversibility and broadcast. In: Kari, J., Ulidowski, I. (eds.) RC 2018. LNCS, vol. 11106, pp. 67–83. Springer (2018)
27. Phillips, I., Ulidowski, I.: Reversing algebraic process calculi. In: Aceto, L., Ingólfsdóttir, A. (eds.) FoSSaCS. LNCS, vol. 3921, pp. 246–260. Springer (2006)
28. Phillips, I., Ulidowski, I.: Reversibility and models for concurrency. In: Hennessy, M., van Glabbeek, R. (eds.) SOS. ENTCS, vol. 192(1), pp. 93–108. Elsevier (2007)
29. Phillips, I., Ulidowski, I.: Reversing algebraic process calculi. Journal of Logic and Algebraic Programming **73**(1-2), 70–96 (2007)
30. Phillips, I., Ulidowski, I.: Reversibility and asymmetric conflict in event structures. Journal of Logical and Algebraic Methods in Programming **84**, 781–805 (2015)
31. Phillips, I., Ulidowski, I., Yuen, S.: A reversible process calculus and the modelling of the ERK signalling pathway. In: Glück, R., Yokoyama, T. (eds.) RC. LNCS, vol. 7581, pp. 218–232. Springer (2012)
32. Pin, J.: On the language accepted by finite reversible automata. In: Ottmann, T. (ed.) ICALP. LNCS, vol. 267, pp. 237–249. Springer (1987)
33. Sassone, V., Nielsen, M., Winskel, G.: Models of concurrency: Towards a classification. Theoretical Computer Science **170**(1-2), 297–348 (1996)
34. Ulidowski, I., Phillips, I., Yuen, S.: Reversing event structures. New Generation Computing **36**(3), 281–306 (2018)
35. Yokoyama, T., Glück, R.: A reversible programming language and its invertible self-interpreter. In: Ramalingam, G., Visser, E. (eds.) ACM SIGPLAN PEMP. pp. 144–153. ACM (2007)

3

Semantical Analysis of Contextual Types

Brigitte Pientka[1] and Ulrich Schöpp[2](✉)

[1] McGill University, Montreal, Canada, bpientka@cs.mcgill.ca
[2] fortiss GmbH, Munich, Germany, schoepp@fortiss.org

Abstract. We describe a category-theoretic semantics for a simply typed variant of Cocon, a contextual modal type theory where the box modality mediates between the weak function space that is used to represent higher-order abstract syntax (HOAS) trees and the strong function space that describes (recursive) computations about them. What makes Cocon different from standard type theories is the presence of first-class contexts and contextual objects to describe syntax trees that are closed with respect to a given context of assumptions. Following M. Hofmann's work, we use a presheaf model to characterise HOAS trees. Surprisingly, this model already provides the necessary structure to also model Cocon. In particular, we can capture the contextual objects of Cocon using a comonad ♭ that restricts presheaves to their closed elements. This gives a simple semantic characterisation of the invariants of contextual types (e.g. substitution invariance) and identifies Cocon as a type-theoretic syntax of presheaf models. We express our category-theoretic constructions by using a modal internal type theory that is implemented in Agda-Flat.

1 Introduction

A fundamental question when defining, implementing, and working with languages and logics is: How do we represent and analyse syntactic structures? Higher-order abstract syntax [19] (or lambda-tree syntax [17]) provides a deceptively simple answer to this question. The basic idea to represent syntactic structures is to map uniformly binding structures in our object language (OL) to the function space in a meta-language thereby inheriting α-renaming and capture-avoiding substitution. In the logical framework LF [10], for example, we can define a small functional programming language consisting of functions, function application, and let-expressions using a type tm as follows:

```
lam : (tm → tm) → tm.          letv: tm → (tm → tm) → tm.
app : tm → tm → tm.
```

The object-language term (lam x. lam y. let $w = x\ y$ in $w\ y$) is then encoded as lam λx.lam λy.letv (app x y) λw.app w y using the LF abstractions to model binding. Object-level substitution is modelled through LF application; for instance, the fact that ((lam $x.M$) N) reduces to $[N/x]M$ in our object language is expressed as (app (lam M) N) reducing to (M N).

This approach is elegant and can offer substantial benefits: we can treat objects equivalent modulo renaming and do not need to define object-level substitution.

However, we not only want to just construct HOAS trees, but also to analyse them and to select sub-trees. This is challenging, as sub-trees are context sensitive. For example, the term letv (app x y) λw.app w y only makes sense in a context x:tm,y:tm. Moreover, one cannot simply extend LF to allow syntax analysis. If one simply added a recursion combinator to LF, then it could be used to define many functions M: tm → tm for which lam M would not represent an object-level syntax term [12].

Contextual types [18,20] offer a type-theoretic solution to these problems by reifying the typing judgement, i.e. that letv (app x y) λw.app w y has type tm in the context x:tm,y:tm, as a *contextual type* ⌈x:tm, y:tm ⊢ tm⌉. The contextual type ⌈x:tm, y:tm ⊢ tm⌉ describes a set of terms of type tm that may contain variables x and y. In particular, the contextual object ⌈x, y ⊢ letv (app x y) λw.app w y⌉ has the given contextual type. By abstracting over contexts and treating contexts as first-class, we can now recursively analyse HOAS trees [20,25,21]. Recently, [23] further generalised these ideas and presented a contextual modal type theory, Cocon, where we can mix HOAS trees and computations, i.e. we can use (recursive) computations to analyse and traverse (contextual) HOAS trees and we can embed computations within HOAS trees. This line of work provides a syntactic perspective to the question of how to represent and analyse syntactic structures with binders, as it focuses on decidability of type checking and normalisation. However, its semantics remains not well-understood. What is the semantic meaning of a contextual type? Can we semantically justify the given induction principles? What is the semantics of a first-class context?

While a number of closely related categorical models of abstract syntax with bindings [12,8,9] were proposed around 2000, the relationship of these models to concrete type-theoretic languages for computing with HOAS structures was teneous. In this paper, we give a category-theoretic semantics for Cocon (for simply-typed HOAS). This provides semantic perspective of contextual types and first-class contexts. Maybe surprisingly, the presheaf model introduced by Hofmann [12] already provides the necessary structure to also model contextual modal type theory. Besides the standard structure of this model, we only need two additional concepts: a ♭-modality and a cartesian closed universe of representables. For simplicity and lack of space, we focus on the special case of Cocon where the HOAS trees are simply-typed. Concentrating on the simply-typed setting allows us to introduce the main idea without the additional complexity that type dependencies bring with them. We outline the dependently-typed case in Sec. 6.

Our work provides a semantic foundation to Cocon and can serve as a starting point to investigate connections to similar work. First, our work connects Cocon to other work on internal languages for presheaf categories with a ♭-modality, such as spatial type theory [27] or crisp type theory [16]. Second, it may help to understand the relations of Cocon to type theories that use a modality for metaprogramming and intensional recursion, such as [15]. While Cocon is built on the same general ideas, a main difference seems to be that Cocon distinguishes between HOAS trees and computations, even though it allows mixed use of them. We hope to clarify the relation by providing a semantical perspective.

2   Presheaves for Higher-Order Abstract Syntax

Our work begins with the presheaf models for HOAS of [12,8]. The key idea of those approaches is to integrate substitution-invariance in the computational universe in a controlled way. For the representation of abstract syntax, one wants to allow only substitution-invariant constructions. For example, `lam M` represents an object-level abstraction if and only if `M` is a function that uses its argument in a substitution-invariant way. For computation with abstract syntax, on the other hand, one wants to allow non-substitution-invariant constructions too. Presheaf categories allow one to choose the desired amount of substitution-invariance.

Let $\mathbb{D}$ be a small category. The presheaf category $\widehat{\mathbb{D}}$ is defined to be the category $\mathrm{Set}^{\mathbb{D}^{\mathrm{op}}}$. Its objects are functors $F \colon \mathbb{D}^{\mathrm{op}} \to \mathrm{Set}$, which are also called *presheaves*. Such a functor F is given by a set $F(\Psi)$ for each object Ψ of $\mathbb{D}$ together with a function $F(\sigma) \colon F(\Phi) \to F(\Psi)$ for any object Φ and $\sigma \colon \Psi \to \Phi$ in $\mathbb{D}$, subject to the functor laws. The intuition is that F defines sets of elements in various $\mathbb{D}$-contexts, together with a $\mathbb{D}$-substitution action. A morphism $f \colon F \to G$ is a natural transformation, which is a family of functions $f_\Psi \colon F(\Psi) \to G(\Psi)$ for any Ψ. This family of functions must be natural, i.e. commute with substitution $f_\Psi \circ F(\sigma) = F(\sigma) \circ f_\Phi$.

For the purposes of modelling higher-order abstract syntax, $\mathbb{D}$ will typically be the term model of some domain-level lambda-calculus. By domain-level, we mean the calculus that serves as the meta-level for object-language encodings. It is the calculus that contains constants like `lam` and `app` from the Introduction. We call it domain-level to avoid possible confusion between different meta-levels later. For simplicity, let us for now use a simply-typed lambda-calculus with functions and products as the domain language. It is sufficient to encode the example from the Introduction and allows us to explain the main idea underlying our approach.

The term model of the simply-typed domain-level lambda-calculus forms a cartesian closed category $\mathbb{D}$. The objects of $\mathbb{D}$ are contexts $x_1 \colon A_1, \ldots, x_n \colon A_n$ of simple types. We use Φ and Ψ to range over such contexts. A morphism from $x_1 \colon A_1, \ldots, x_n \colon A_n$ to $x_1 \colon B_1, \ldots, x_m \colon B_m$ is a tuple $(t_1, \ldots, t_m)$ of terms $x_1 \colon A_1, \ldots, x_n \colon A_n \vdash t_i \colon B_i$ for $i = 1, \ldots, m$. A morphism of type $\Psi \to \Phi$ in $\mathbb{D}$ thus amounts to a (domain-level) substitution that provides a (domain-level) term in context Ψ for each of the variables in Φ. Terms are identified up to $\alpha\beta\eta$-equality. One may achieve this by using a de Bruijn encoding, for example, but the specific encoding is not important for this paper. The terminal object is the empty context, which we denote by 1, and the product $\Phi \times \Psi$ is defined by context concatenation. It is not hard to see that any object $x_1 \colon A_1, \ldots, x_n \colon A_n$ is isomorphic to an object that is given by a context with a single variable, namely $x_1 \colon (A_1 \times \cdots \times A_n)$. This is to say that contexts can be identified with product types. In view of this isomorphism, we shall allow ourselves to consider the objects of $\mathbb{D}$ also as types and vice versa. The category $\mathbb{D}$ is cartesian closed, the exponential of Φ and Ψ being given by the function type $\Phi \to \Psi$ (where the objects are considered as types).

The presheaf category $\widehat{\mathbb{D}}$ is a computational universe that both embeds the term model $\mathbb{D}$ and that can represent computations about it. Note that we cannot just enrich $\mathbb{D}$ with terms for computations if we want to use HOAS. In a simply-typed lambda-calculus with just the constant terms app: tm → tm → tm and lam: (tm → tm) → tm, each term of type tm represents an object-level term. This would not be the true anymore, if we were to allow computations in the domain language, since one could define M to be something like (λx. if x represents an object-level application then M1 else M2) for distinct M1 and M2. In this case, lam M would not represent an object-level term anymore. If we want to preserve a bijection between the object-level terms and their representations in the domain-language, we cannot allow case-distinction over whether a term represents an object-level an application.

The category $\widehat{\mathbb{D}}$ unites syntax with computations by allowing one to enforce various degrees of substitution-invariance. By choosing objects with different substitution actions, one can control the required amount of substitution-invariance.

In one extreme, a set S can be represented by the constant presheaf ΔS with $\Delta S(\Psi) = S$ and $\Delta S(\sigma) = \mathsf{id}$ for all Ψ and σ. The substitution action is trivial. As a consequence, a morphism $\Delta S \to \Delta T$ amounts to a function from set S to set T, since the trivial choice of the substitution action makes the naturality condition vacuous.

The Yoneda embedding represents the other extreme. For any object Φ of $\mathbb{D}$, the presheaf $\mathsf{y}(\Phi)\colon \mathbb{D}^{\mathrm{op}} \to \mathrm{Set}$ is defined by $\mathsf{y}(\Phi)(\Psi) = \mathbb{D}(\Psi, \Phi)$, which is the set of morphisms from Ψ to Φ in $\mathbb{D}$. The functor action is pre-composition. The presheaf $\mathsf{y}(\Phi)$ should be understood as the type of all domain-level substitutions with codomain Φ. An important example is $\mathrm{Tm} := y(\mathrm{tm})$. In this case, $\mathrm{Tm}(\Psi)$ is the set of all morphisms of type $\Psi \to \mathrm{tm}$ in $\mathbb{D}$. By the definition of $\mathbb{D}$, these correspond to domain-level terms of type tm in context Ψ. In this way, the presheaf Tm represents the domain-level terms of type tm.

The Yoneda embedding does in fact embed $\mathbb{D}$ into $\widehat{\mathbb{D}}$ fully and faithfully. The Yoneda embedding becomes a functor $\mathsf{y}\colon \mathbb{D} \to \widehat{\mathbb{D}}$ if one defines the morphism action to be post-composition. This means that y maps a morphism $\sigma\colon \Psi \to \Phi$ in $\mathbb{D}$ to the natural transformation $\mathsf{y}(\sigma)\colon \mathsf{y}(\Psi) \to \mathsf{y}(\Phi)$ that is defined by post-composing with σ. This definition makes y into a functor $\mathsf{y}\colon \mathbb{D} \to \widehat{\mathbb{D}}$ that is moreover full and faithful: its action on morphisms is a bijection from $\mathbb{D}(\Psi, \Phi)$ to $\widehat{\mathbb{D}}(\mathsf{y}(\Psi), \mathsf{y}(\Phi))$ for any Ψ and Φ. This is because a natural transformation $f\colon \mathsf{y}(\Psi) \to \mathsf{y}(\Phi)$ is, by naturality, uniquely determined by $f_\Psi(\mathsf{id})$, where $\mathsf{id} \in \mathbb{D}(\Psi, \Psi) = \mathsf{y}(\Psi)(\Psi)$, and $f_\Psi(\mathsf{id})$ is an element of $y(\Phi)(\Psi) = \mathbb{D}(\Psi, \Phi)$.

Since $\mathbb{D}$ embeds into $\widehat{\mathbb{D}}$ fully and faithfully, the term model of the domain language is available in $\widehat{\mathbb{D}}$. Consider for example $\mathrm{Tm} = y(\mathrm{tm})$. Since y is full and faithful, the morphisms from Tm to Tm in $\widehat{\mathbb{D}}$ are in one-to-one correspondence with the morphisms from tm to tm in $\mathbb{D}$. These, in turn, are defined to be substitutions and correspond to simply-typed (domain-level) lambda terms with one free variable. This shows that substitution invariance cuts down the morphisms from Tm to Tm in $\widehat{\mathbb{D}}$ just as much as one would like for HOAS encodings.

But $\widehat{\mathbb{D}}$ contains not just a term model of the domain language. It can also represent computations about the domain-level syntax and computations that are not substitution-invariant. For example, arbitrary functions on terms can be represented as morphisms from the constant presheaf $\Delta(\mathtt{Tm}(1))$ to $\mathtt{Tm}$. Recall that 1 is the empty context, so that $\mathtt{Tm}(1)$ is the set $\mathbb{D}(1, \mathtt{tm})$, by definition, which is isomorphic to the set of closed domain-level terms of type $\mathtt{tm}$. The morphisms from $\Delta(\mathtt{Tm}(1))$ to $\mathtt{Tm}$ in $\widehat{\mathbb{D}}$ correspond to arbitrary functions from closed terms to closed terms, without any restriction of substitution invariance.

The restriction to the constant presheaf of closed terms can be generalised to arbitrary presheaves. Define a functor $\flat \colon \widehat{\mathbb{D}} \to \widehat{\mathbb{D}}$ by letting $\flat F$ be the constant presheaf $\Delta(F(1))$, i.e. $\flat F(\Psi) = F(1)$ and $\flat F(\sigma) = \mathrm{id}$. Thus, $\flat$ restricts any presheaf to the set of its closed elements. The functor $\flat$ defines a comonad where the counit $\varepsilon_F \colon \flat F \to F$ is the obvious inclusion and the comultiplication $\nu_F \colon \flat F \to \flat\flat F$ is the identity. The latter means that the comonad $\flat$ is idempotent.

3   Internal Language

To explain how $\widehat{\mathbb{D}}$ models higher-order abstract syntax and contextual types, we need to expose more of its structure. Most of this structure is standard. Defining it directly in terms of functors and natural transformations is somewhat laborious and the technical details may obscure the basic idea of our approach.

We therefore use the internal type theory of $\widehat{\mathbb{D}}$ as a meta-language for working with its structure. The structure of $\widehat{\mathbb{D}}$ furnishes a model of a dependent type theory that supports dependent products, dependent sums and extensional identity types, among others, in a standard way [11]. We use Agda notation for the types and terms of this internal type theory. We write $(x \colon S) \to T$ for a dependent function type and write $\lambda x \colon S.m$ and $m\ n$ for the associated lambda-abstractions and applications. As usual, we will sometimes also write $S \to T$ for $(x \colon S) \to T$ if x does not appear in T. However, to make it easier to distinguish the function spaces at various levels, we will write $(x \colon S) \to T$ by default even when x does not appear in T. We use $\mathtt{let}\ x = m\ \mathtt{in}\ n$ as an abbreviation for $(\lambda x \colon T.n)\ m$, as usual. For two terms $m \colon T$ and $n \colon T$, we write $m =_T n$ or just $m = n$ for the associated identity type. Our notation is similar to Agda's, since the internal type theory can be seen as a fragment of Agda's type theory. Agda has been useful as a tool for type-checking our constructions in the internal type theory [1].

In the spirit of Martin-Löf type theory, we will define basic types and terms successively as they are needed. In the Agda development this corresponds to postulating constants that are justified by the interpretation in $\widehat{\mathbb{D}}$. In the following sections, we will expose the structure of $\widehat{\mathbb{D}}$ step by step until we have enough to interpret contextual types.

While much of the structure of $\widehat{\mathbb{D}}$ can be captured by adding rules and constants to standard Martin-Löf type theory, for the comonad $\flat$ such a formulation would not be very satisfactory. The issues are discussed by Shulman [27, p.7], for example. To obtain a more satisfactory syntax for the comonad, we refine the internal type theory into a modal type theory in which $\flat$ appears as a necessity modality. This approach goes back to [3,4,6] and is also used by recent work of Shulman [27], Licata et al. [16] and others on working with the $\flat$-modality in type theory. Agda has recently gained support for such a $\flat$-modality [29].

We summarise here the typing rules for the $\flat$-modality which we will rely on. To control the modality, one uses two kinds of variables. In addition to standard variables $x\colon T$, one has a second kind of so-called *crisp* variables $x\colon\colon T$. Typing judgements have the form $\Delta \mid \Theta \vdash m\colon T$, where Δ collects the crisp variables and Θ collects the ordinary variables. In essence, a crisp variable $x\colon\colon T$ represents an assumption of the form $x\colon \flat T$. The syntactic distinction is useful, since it leads to a type theory that is well-behaved with respect to substitution, see [6,27].

The typing rules are closely related to those in modal type systems [6,18], where Δ is the typing context for modal (global) assumptions and Θ for (local) assumptions, and type systems for linear logic [4], where Δ is the typing context for non-linear assumptions and Θ for linear assumptions.

$$\frac{}{\Delta, u\colon\colon T, \Delta' \mid \Theta \vdash u\colon T} \qquad \frac{}{\Delta \mid \Theta, x\colon T, \Theta' \vdash x\colon T}$$

$$\frac{\Delta \mid \cdot \vdash m\colon T}{\Delta \mid \Theta \vdash \mathsf{box}\ m\colon \flat T} \qquad \frac{\Delta \mid \Theta \vdash m\colon \flat T \quad \Delta, x\colon\colon T \mid \Theta \vdash n\colon S}{\Delta \mid \Theta \vdash \mathsf{let\ box}\ x = m\ \mathsf{in}\ n\colon S}$$

Given any term $m\colon T$ which only depends on modal variable context Δ, we can form the term $\mathsf{box}\ m\colon \flat T$. We have a let-term $\mathsf{let\ box}\ x = m\ \mathsf{in}\ n$ that takes a term $m\colon \flat T$ and binds it to a variable $x\colon\colon T$. The rules maintain the invariant that the free variables in a type $\flat T$ or a term $\mathsf{box}\ m$ are all crisp variables from the crisp context Δ.

The other typing rules do not modify the crisp context. For examples, the rules for dependent products are:

$$\frac{\Delta \mid \Theta, x\colon T \vdash m\colon S}{\Delta \mid \Theta \vdash \lambda x\colon T.m\colon (x\colon T) \to S} \qquad \frac{\Delta \mid \Theta \vdash m\colon (y\colon T) \to S \quad \Delta \mid \Theta \vdash n\colon T}{\Delta \mid \Theta \vdash m\ n\colon [n/y]S}$$

When Δ is empty, we shall write just $\Theta \vdash m\colon T$ for $\Delta \mid \Theta \vdash m\colon T$.

4 From Presheaves to Contextual Types

Armed with the internal type theory, we can now explore the structure of $\widehat{\mathbb{D}}$.

4.1 A Universe of Representables

For our purposes, the main feature of $\widehat{\mathbb{D}}$ is that it embeds $\mathbb{D}$ fully and faithfully via the Yoneda embedding. In the type theory for $\widehat{\mathbb{D}}$, we may capture this embedding by means of a Tarski-style universe. Such a universe is defined by a type of codes for types together with a decoding function that maps codes to actual types.

The type of codes Obj represents the set of objects of $\mathbb{D}$ in the internal type theory of $\widehat{\mathbb{D}}$. We have seen above that any set can be represented as a presheaf with trivial substitution action, and Obj is one such example. Particular objects of $\mathbb{D}$ then appear as terms of type Obj. The cartesian closed structure of $\mathbb{D}$ gives us terms unit, times, arrow for the terminal object 1, finite products $\times$ and the exponential (function type). We also have a term for the domain-level type tm.

$$\vdash \mathsf{Obj}\ \mathrm{type} \qquad \vdash \mathsf{tm}\colon \mathsf{Obj} \qquad \vdash \mathsf{times}\colon (a\colon\mathsf{Obj}) \to (b\colon\mathsf{Obj}) \to \mathsf{Obj}$$
$$\vdash \mathsf{unit}\colon \mathsf{Obj} \qquad \vdash \mathsf{arrow}\colon (a\colon\mathsf{Obj}) \to (b\colon\mathsf{Obj}) \to \mathsf{Obj}$$

Subsequently, we sometimes talk about objects of $\mathbb{D}$ when we intend to describe terms of type `Obj` (and vice versa).

The morphisms of $\mathbb{D}$ could similarly be encoded as a constant presheaf with many term constants, but this is in fact not necessary. Instead, we can use the Yoneda embedding as a function that decodes elements of `Obj` into actual types.

$$x\colon \mathtt{Obj} \vdash \mathtt{El}\, x \text{ type}$$

The function `El` is almost direct syntax for the Yoneda embedding. The interpretation in $\widehat{\mathbb{D}}$ is such that, for any object A of $\mathbb{D}$, the type $\mathtt{El}\, A$ is interpreted by the presheaf $\mathrm{y}(A)$. Such a presheaf is called *representable*. One can think of $\mathtt{El}\, A$ as the type of all morphisms of type $\Psi \to A$ in $\mathbb{D}$ for arbitrary Ψ. Recall from above that a morphism of type $\Psi \to A$ in $\mathbb{D}$ amounts to a domain-level term of type A that may refer to variables in Ψ. In this sense, one should think of $\mathtt{El}\, A$ as a type of domain-level terms of type A, both closed and open ones.

We get all morphisms of $\mathbb{D}$, and no more, in this way, since the Yoneda embedding is full and faithful, recall Sec. 2. In our case, this means that the type $(x\colon \mathtt{El}\, A) \to \mathtt{El}\, B$ represents the morphisms of type $A \to B$ in $\mathbb{D}$. Any closed term of type $(x : \mathtt{El}\, A) \to \mathtt{El}\, B$ corresponds to such a morphism and vice versa. This is because the naturality requirements in $\widehat{\mathbb{D}}$ enforce substitution-invariance, as outlined in Sec. 2. The type $(x : \mathtt{El}\, A) \to \mathtt{El}\, B$ thus does not represent arbitrary functions from terms of type A to terms of type B, but only substitution-invariant ones. If a function of this type maps a domain-level variable $x\colon A$ (encoded as an element of $\mathtt{El}\, A$) to some term $M\colon B$ (encoded as an element of $\mathtt{El}\, B$), then it must map any other $N\colon A$ to $[N/x]M$.

We note that the type dependency in `El` is easy to work with. A term of type $(a\colon \mathtt{Obj}) \to (b\colon \mathtt{Obj}) \to (x\colon \mathtt{El}\, a) \to \mathtt{El}\, b$ corresponds to a family of terms $(x\colon \mathtt{El}\, A) \to \mathtt{El}\, B$ indexed by objects A and B in $\mathbb{D}$. This is because `Obj` is just a set, so that the naturality constraints of $\widehat{\mathbb{D}}$ are vacuous for functions out of `Obj`.

To summarise, we get access to $\mathbb{D}$ in the internal type theory of $\widehat{\mathbb{D}}$ simply by considering the Yoneda embedding as the decoding function `El` of a universe á la Tarski. Since is consists of the representable presheaves, we call it the *universe of representables*. The following lemmas state that the embedding preserves terminal object, binary products and the exponential.

Lemma 1. *The internal type theory of $\widehat{\mathbb{D}}$ has a term $\vdash$ `terminal`$\colon \mathtt{El}\,\mathtt{unit}$, such that $x = $ `terminal` holds for any $x\colon \mathtt{El}\,\mathtt{unit}$.*

Lemma 2. *The internal type theory of $\widehat{\mathbb{D}}$ justifies the terms below, such that $\mathit{fst}\,(\mathit{pair}\,x\,y) = x$, $\mathit{snd}\,(\mathit{pair}\,x\,y) = y$, $z = \mathit{pair}\,(\mathit{fst}\,z)\,(\mathit{snd}\,z)$ for all x, y, z.*

> $c\colon \mathtt{Obj},\, d\colon \mathtt{Obj} \vdash \mathit{fst}\colon (z : \mathtt{El}\,(\mathit{times}\,c\,d)) \to \mathtt{El}\,c$
>
> $c\colon \mathtt{Obj},\, d\colon \mathtt{Obj} \vdash \mathit{snd}\colon (z : \mathtt{El}\,(\mathit{times}\,c\,d)) \to \mathtt{El}\,d$
>
> $c\colon \mathtt{Obj},\, d\colon \mathtt{Obj} \vdash \mathit{pair}\colon (x : \mathtt{El}\,c) \to (y : \mathtt{El}\,d) \to \mathtt{El}\,(\mathit{times}\,c\,d)$

Lemma 3. *The internal type theory of $\widehat{\mathbb{D}}$ justifies the terms below such that $\mathit{arrow\text{-}i}\,(\mathit{arrow\text{-}e}\,f) = f$ and $\mathit{arrow\text{-}e}\,(\mathit{arrow\text{-}i}\,g) = g$ for all f, g.*

> $c\colon \mathtt{Obj},\, d\colon \mathtt{Obj} \vdash \mathit{arrow\text{-}e}\colon (x\colon \mathtt{El}\,(\mathit{arrow}\,c\,d)) \to (y\colon \mathtt{El}\,c) \to \mathtt{El}\,d$
>
> $c\colon \mathtt{Obj},\, d\colon \mathtt{Obj} \vdash \mathit{arrow\text{-}i}\colon (y\colon (\mathtt{El}\,c \to \mathtt{El}\,d)) \to \mathtt{El}\,(\mathit{arrow}\,c\,d)$

4.2 Higher-Order Abstract Syntax

The last lemma in the previous section states that $\mathtt{El}\,A \to \mathtt{El}\,B$ is isomorphic to $\mathtt{El}\,(\mathtt{arrow}\ A\ B)$. This is particularly useful to lift HOAS-encodings from $\mathbb{D}$ to $\widehat{\mathbb{D}}$. For instance, the domain-level term constant $\mathtt{lam}\colon (\mathtt{tm} \to \mathtt{tm}) \to \mathtt{tm}$ gives rise to an element of $\mathtt{El}\,(\mathtt{arrow}\ (\mathtt{arrow}\ \mathtt{tm}\ \mathtt{tm})\ \mathtt{tm})$. But this type is isomorphic to $(\mathtt{El}\,\mathtt{tm} \to \mathtt{El}\,\mathtt{tm}) \to \mathtt{El}\,\mathtt{tm}$, by the lemma.

This means that the higher-order abstract syntax constants lift to $\widehat{\mathbb{D}}$:

$$\mathtt{app}\colon (m\colon \mathtt{El}\,\mathtt{tm}) \to (n\colon \mathtt{El}\,\mathtt{tm}) \to \mathtt{El}\,\mathtt{tm} \quad \mathtt{lam}\colon (m\colon (\mathtt{El}\,\mathtt{tm} \to \mathtt{El}\,\mathtt{tm})) \to \mathtt{El}\,\mathtt{tm}$$

Once one recognises $\mathtt{El}\,A$ as $\mathrm{y}(A)$, the adequacy of this higher-order abstract syntax encoding lifts from $\mathbb{D}$ to $\widehat{\mathbb{D}}$ as in [12]. For example, an argument M to $\mathtt{lam}$ has type $\mathtt{El}\,\mathtt{tm} \to \mathtt{El}\,\mathtt{tm}$, which is isomorphic to $\mathtt{El}\,(\mathtt{arrow}\ \mathtt{tm}\ \mathtt{tm})$. But this type represents (open) domain-level terms $t\colon \mathtt{tm} \to \mathtt{tm}$. The term $\mathtt{lam}\,M\colon \mathtt{El}\,\mathtt{tm}$ then represents the domain-level term $\mathtt{lam}\,t\colon \mathtt{tm}$, so it just lifts the domain-level.

4.3 Closed Objects

One should think of $\flat T$ as the type of 'closed' elements of T. In particular, $\flat(\mathtt{El}\,A)$ represents morphisms of type $1 \to A$ in $\mathbb{D}$, recall the definition of $\flat$ from Sec. 2 and that $\mathtt{El}\,A$ corresponds to $\mathrm{y}A$. In the term model $\mathbb{D}$, the morphisms $1 \to A$ correspond to closed domain-language terms of type A. Thus, while $\mathtt{El}\,A$ represents both open and closed domain-level terms, $\flat(\mathtt{El}\,A)$ represents only the closed ones.

This applies also to the type $\mathtt{El}\,A \to \mathtt{El}\,B$. We have seen above that $\mathtt{El}\,A \to \mathtt{El}\,B$ is isomorphic to $\mathtt{El}\,(\mathtt{arrow}\ A\ B)$ and may therefore be thought of as containing the terms of type B with a distinguished variable of type A. But, these terms may contain other free domain language variables. The type $\flat(\mathtt{El}\,A \to \mathtt{El}\,B)$, on the other hand, contains only terms of type B that may contain (at most) one variable of type A.

Restricting to closed object with the modality is useful because it disables substitution-invariance. For example, the internal type theory for $\widehat{\mathbb{D}}$ justifies a function $\mathtt{is\text{-}lam}\colon (x\colon\flat(\mathtt{El}\,\mathtt{tm})) \to \mathtt{bool}$ that returns $\mathtt{true}$ if and only if the argument represents a domain language lambda abstraction. We shall define it in the next section. Such a function cannot be defined with type $\mathtt{El}\,\mathtt{tm} \to \mathtt{bool}$, since it would not be invariant under substitution. Its argument ranges over terms that may be open; which particularly includes domain-level variables. The function would have to return $\mathtt{false}$ for them, since a domain-level variable is not a lambda-abstraction. But after substituting a lambda-abstraction for the variable, it would have to return $\mathtt{true}$, so it could not be substitution-invariant.

We note that the type $\mathtt{Obj}$ consists only of closed elements and that $\mathtt{Obj}$ and $\flat\mathtt{Obj}$ happen to be definitionally equal types (an isomorphism would suffice, but equality is more convenient).

4.4   Contextual Objects

Using function types and the modality, it is now possible to work with contextual objects that represent domain level terms in a certain context, much like in [20,21]. A contextual type $\lceil \Psi \vdash A \rceil$ is a boxed function type of the form $\flat(\text{El}\,\Psi \to \text{El}\,A)$. It represents domain-level terms of type A with variables from Ψ. Here, we consider the domain-level context Ψ as a term that encodes it. The interpretation will make this precise.

For example, domain-level terms with up to two free variables now appear as terms of type $\flat(\text{El}\,((\text{times}\,(\text{times}\,\text{unit}\,\text{tm})\,\text{tm}) \to \text{El}\,\text{tm})$, as the following example illustrates.

$$\text{box}\,(\lambda u{:}\,\text{El}\,((\text{times}\,(\text{times}\,\text{unit}\,\text{tm})\,\text{tm}).\,\text{let}\ x_1 = \text{snd}\,(\text{fst}\,u)\ \text{in}$$
$$\text{let}\ x_2 = \text{snd}\,u\ \text{in}$$
$$\text{app}\,(\text{lam}\,(\lambda x{:}\,\text{El}\,\text{tm}.\,\text{app}\,x_1\,x))\,x_2\,)$$

The context variables x_1 and x_2 are bound at the meta level.

This representation integrates substitution as usual. For example, given crisp variables $m{::}\text{El}\,(\text{times}\,c\,\text{tm}) \to \text{tm}$ and $n{::}\text{El}\,c \to \text{tm}$ for contextual terms, the term $\text{box}\,(\lambda u{:}\,\text{El}\,c.\,m\,(\text{pair}\,u\,(n\,u)))$ represents substitution of n for the last variable in the context of m.

For working with contextual objects, it is convenient to lift the constants app and lam to contextual types.

$$c{:}\,\text{Obj} \vdash \text{app}'{:}\,\flat(\text{El}\,c \to \text{El}\,\text{tm}) \to \flat(\text{El}\,c \to \text{El}\,\text{tm}) \to \flat(\text{El}\,c \to \text{tm})$$
$$c{:}\text{Obj} \vdash \text{lam}'{:}\,\flat(\text{El}\,(\text{times}\,c\,\text{tm}) \to \text{El}\,\text{tm}) \to \flat(\text{El}\,c \to \text{El}\,\text{tm})$$

These terms are defined by:

$$\text{app}' := \lambda m, n.\,\text{let box}\ m' = m\ \text{in let box}\ n' = n\ \text{in}$$
$$\text{box}\,(\lambda u{:}\,\text{El}\,c.\,\text{app}\,(m'\,u)\,(n'\,u))$$
$$\text{lam}' := \lambda m.\,\text{let box}\ m' = m\ \text{in box}\,(\lambda u{:}\,\text{El}\,c.\,\text{lam}\,(\lambda x{:}\,\text{El}\,\text{tm}.\,m'\,(\text{pair}\,u\,x)))$$

A contextual type for domain-level variables (as opposed to arbitrary terms) can be defined by restricting the function space in $\flat(\text{El}\,\Psi \to \text{El}\,A)$ to consist only of projections. Projections are functions of the form $\text{snd} \circ \text{fst}_k$, where we write fst_k for the k-fold iteration $\text{fst} \circ \cdots \circ \text{fst}$. Let us write $S \to_v T$ for the subtype of $S \to T$ consisting only of projections. The contextual type $\flat(\text{El}\,\Psi \to_v \text{El}\,A)$ is then a subtype of $\flat(\text{El}\,\Psi \to \text{El}\,A)$.

With these definitions, we can express a primitive recursion scheme for contextual types. We write it in its general form where the result type A can possibly depend on x. This is only relevant for the dependently typed case; in the simply typed case, the only dependency is on c.

Lemma 4. *Let* $c{:}\,\text{Obj},\ x{:}\,\flat(\text{El}\,c \to \text{El}\,\text{tm}) \vdash A\,c\,x$ *type and define:*

$$X_{var} := (c{:}\,\text{Obj}) \to (x{:}\,\flat(\text{El}\,c \to_v \text{El}\,\text{tm})) \to A\,c\,x$$
$$X_{app} := (c{:}\,\text{Obj}) \to (x,y{:}\,\flat(\text{El}\,c \to \text{El}\,\text{tm})) \to A\,c\,x \to A\,c\,y \to A\,c\,(\text{app}'\,x\ y)$$
$$X_{lam} := (c{:}\,\text{Obj}) \to (x{:}\,\flat(\text{El}\,(\text{times}\,c\,\text{tm}) \to \text{El}\,\text{tm})) \to A\,(\text{times}\,c\,\text{tm})\,x \to A\,c\,(\text{lam}'\,x)$$

Then, $\widehat{\mathbb{D}}$ justifies a term

$$\vdash \mathtt{rec} \colon X_{var} \to X_{app} \to X_{lam} \to (c \colon \mathit{Obj}) \to (x \colon \flat(\mathit{El}\, c \to \mathit{El}\, \mathtt{tm})) \to A\ c\ x$$

such that the following equations are valid.

$$
\begin{aligned}
\mathtt{rec}\ t_{var}\ t_{app}\ t_{lam}\ c\ x && = t_{var}\ c\ x \qquad && \text{if } x \colon \flat(\mathit{El}\, c \to_v \mathit{El}\, \mathtt{tm}) \\
\mathtt{rec}\ t_{var}\ t_{app}\ t_{lam}\ c\ (app'\ s\ t) &= t_{app}\ c\ s\ t \\
\mathtt{rec}\ t_{var}\ t_{app}\ t_{lam}\ c\ (lam'\ s) &= t_{lam}\ c\ s
\end{aligned}
$$

Proof (outline). To outline the proof idea, note first that a function of type $(c \colon \mathtt{Obj}) \to (x \colon \flat(\mathtt{El}\, c \to \mathtt{El}\, \mathtt{tm})) \to A\ c\ x$ in $\widehat{\mathbb{D}}$, corresponds to an inhabitant of $A\ \Phi\ t$ for each concrete object Φ of $\mathbb{D}$ and each inhabitant $t \colon \flat(\mathtt{El}\, \Phi \to \mathtt{El}\, \mathtt{tm})$. This is because naturality constraints for boxed types are vacuous (and $\mathtt{Obj} = \flat\mathtt{Obj}$). Next, note that inhabitants of $\flat(\mathtt{El}\, \Phi \to \mathtt{El}\, \mathtt{tm})$ correspond to domain-level terms of type $\mathtt{tm}$ in context Φ up to $\alpha\beta\eta$-equality. We can perform a case-distinction on whether it is a variable, abstraction or application and depending on the result use t_{var}, t_{app} or t_{lam} to define the required inhabitant of $A\ \Phi\ t$.

As a simple example for $\mathtt{rec}$, we can define the function $\mathtt{is\text{-}lam}$ discussed above by $\mathtt{rec}\ (\lambda c, x.\, \mathtt{false})\ (\lambda c, x, y, r_x, r_y.\, \mathtt{false})\ (\lambda c, x, r_x.\, \mathtt{true})$.

5   Simple Contextual Modal Type Theory

We have outlined informally how the internal dependent type theory of $\widehat{\mathbb{D}}$ can model contextual types. In this section, we make this precise by giving the interpretation of Cocon [23], a contextual modal type theory where we can work with contextual HOAS trees and computations about them, into $\widehat{\mathbb{D}}$. We will focus here on a simply-typed version of Cocon where we use a simply-typed domain-language with constants app and lam and also only allow computations about HOAS trees, but do not consider, for example, universes. Concentrating on a stripped down, simply-typed version of Cocon allows us to focus on the essential aspects, namely how to interpret domain-level contexts and domain-level contextual objects and types semantically. The generalisation to a dependently typed domain-level such as LF in Sec. 6 will be conceptually straightforward, although more technical. Handling universes is an orthogonal issue (see also [16]).

We first define our simply-typed domain-level with the type tm the term constants lam and app (see Fig. 1). Following Cocon, we allow computations to be embedded into domain-level terms via unboxing. The intuition is that if a program t promises to compute a value of type $\lceil x{:}\mathtt{tm}, y{:}\mathtt{tm} \vdash \mathtt{tm} \rceil$, then we can embed t directly into a domain-level object writing $\mathtt{lam}\ \lambda x.\mathtt{lam}\ \lambda y.\mathtt{app}\ \lfloor t \rfloor\ x$, unboxing t. Domain-level objects (resp. types) can be packaged together with their domain-level context to form a contextual object (resp. type). Domain-level contexts are formed as usual, but may contain context variables to describe a yet unknown prefix. Last, we include domain-level substitutions that allow us to move between domain-level contexts. The compound substitution σ, M extends the substitution σ with domain $\widehat{\Psi}$ to a substitution with domain $\widehat{\Psi}, x$, where M replaces x. Following [18,23], we do not store the domain (like $\widehat{\Psi}$) in the

Domain-level types	A, B	$::= \mathsf{tm} \mid A \to B$
Domain-level terms	M, N	$::= \lambda x.M \mid M\,N \mid x \mid \mathsf{lam} \mid \mathsf{app} \mid \lfloor t \rfloor_\sigma$
Domain-level contexts	Ψ, Φ	$::= \cdot \mid \psi \mid \Psi, x{:}A$
Domain-level context (erased)	$\widehat{\Psi}, \widehat{\Phi}$	$::= \cdot \mid \psi \mid \widehat{\Psi}, x$
Domain-level substitutions	σ	$::= \cdot \mid \mathsf{wk}_{\widehat{\Psi}} \mid \sigma, M$
Contextual types	T	$::= \Psi \vdash A \mid \Psi \vdash_v A$
Contextual objects	C	$::= \widehat{\Psi} \vdash M$
Domain of discourse	$\check{\tau}$	$::= \tau \mid \mathsf{ctx}$
Types and Terms	$\tau, \mathcal{I}$	$::= \lceil T \rceil \mid (y : \check{\tau}_1) \Rightarrow \tau_2$
	t, s	$::= y \mid \lceil C \rceil \mid \mathsf{rec}^{\mathcal{I}}\,\mathcal{B}\,\Psi\,t \mid \mathsf{fn}\,y \Rightarrow t \mid t_1\,t_2$
Branches	$\mathcal{B}$	$::= \Gamma \mapsto t$
Contexts	Γ	$::= \cdot \mid \Gamma, y : \check{\tau}$

Fig. 1. Syntax of COCON with a fixed simply-typed domain tm

substitution, it can always be recovered before applying the substitution. We also include *weakening substitution*, written as $\mathsf{wk}_{\widehat{\Psi}}$, to describe the weakening of the domain Ψ to $\Psi, \overrightarrow{x{:}A}$. Weakening substitutions are necessary, as they allow us to express the weakening of a context variable ψ. Identity is a special form of the $\mathsf{wk}_{\widehat{\Psi}}$ substitution, which follows immediately from the typing rule of $\mathsf{wk}_{\widehat{\Psi}}$. Composition is admissible.

We summarise the typing rules for domain-level terms and types in Fig. 2. We also include typing rules for domain-level contexts. Note that since we restrict ourselves to a simply-typed domain-level, we simply check that A is a well-formed type. We defer the reduction and expansion rules to the appendix and only remark here that equality for domain-level terms and substitution is modulo $\beta\eta$. In particular, $\lfloor \lceil \widehat{\Phi} \vdash N \rceil \rfloor_\sigma$ reduces to $[\sigma]N$.

In our grammar, we distinguish between the contextual type $\Psi \vdash A$ and the more restricted contextual type $\Phi \vdash_v A$ which characterises only variables of type A from the domain-level context Φ. We give here two sample typing rules for $\Phi \vdash_v A$ which are the ones used most in practice to illustrate the main idea. We embed contextual objects into computations via the modality. Computation-level types include boxed contextual types, $\lceil \Phi \vdash A \rceil$, and function types, written as $(y : \check{\tau}_1) \Rightarrow \tau_2$. We overload the function space and allow as domain of discourse both computation-level types and the schema ctx of domain-level context, although only in the latter case y can occur in τ_2. We use $\mathsf{fn}\,y \Rightarrow t$ to introduce functions of both kinds. We also overload function application $t\,s$ to eliminate function types $(y : \tau_1) \Rightarrow \tau_2$ and $(y : \mathsf{ctx}) \Rightarrow \tau_2$, although in the latter case s stands for a domain-level context. We separate domain-level contexts from contextual objects, as we do not allow functions that return a domain-level context.

The recursor is written as $\mathsf{rec}^{\mathcal{I}}\,\mathcal{B}\,\Psi\,t$. Here, t describes a term of type $\lceil \Psi \vdash \mathsf{tm} \rceil$ that we recurse over and $\mathcal{B}$ describes the different branches that we can take

$\boxed{\Gamma; \Psi \vdash M : A}$ Term M has type A in domain-level context Ψ and context Γ

$$\frac{\Gamma \vdash \Psi : \mathsf{ctx} \quad x{:}A \in \Psi}{\Gamma; \Psi \vdash x : A} \qquad \frac{\Gamma \vdash \Psi : \mathsf{ctx}}{\Gamma; \Psi \vdash \mathsf{lam} : (\mathsf{tm} \to \mathsf{tm}) \to \mathsf{tm}} \quad \frac{\Gamma \vdash \Psi : \mathsf{ctx}}{\Gamma; \Psi \vdash \mathsf{app} : \mathsf{tm} \to \mathsf{tm} \to \mathsf{tm}}$$

$$\frac{\Gamma; \Psi \vdash M : A \to B \quad \Gamma; \Psi \vdash N : A}{\Gamma; \Psi \vdash M \; N : B} \qquad \frac{\Gamma; \Psi, x{:}A \vdash M : B}{\Gamma; \Psi \vdash \lambda x.M : A \to B}$$

$$\frac{\Gamma \vdash t : \lceil \Phi \vdash A \rceil \quad \Gamma; \Psi \vdash \sigma : \Phi}{\Gamma; \Psi \vdash \lfloor t \rfloor_\sigma : A}$$

$\boxed{\Gamma; \Phi \vdash \sigma : \Psi}$ Substitution σ provides a mapping from the (domain) context Ψ to Φ

$$\frac{\Gamma \vdash \Psi, x{:}\vec{A} : \mathsf{ctx}}{\Gamma; \Psi, x{:}\vec{A} \vdash \mathsf{wk}_{\widehat{\Psi}} : \Psi} \quad \frac{\Gamma \vdash \Phi : \mathsf{ctx}}{\Gamma; \Phi \vdash \cdot : \cdot} \quad \frac{\Gamma; \Phi \vdash \sigma : \Psi \quad \Gamma; \Phi \vdash M : A}{\Gamma; \Phi \vdash \sigma, M : \Psi, x{:}A}$$

$\boxed{\Gamma \vdash \Psi : \mathsf{ctx}}$ Domain-level context Ψ is a well-formed

$$\frac{}{\Gamma \vdash \cdot : \mathsf{ctx}} \quad \frac{\Gamma(y) = \mathsf{ctx}}{\Gamma \vdash y : \mathsf{ctx}} \quad \frac{\Gamma \vdash \Psi : \mathsf{ctx}}{\Gamma \vdash \Psi, x{:}A : \mathsf{ctx}}$$

Fig. 2. Typing Rules for Domain-level Terms, Substitutions, Contexts

depending on the value computed by t. As is common when we have dependencies, we annotate the recursor with the typing invariant $\mathcal{I}$. Here, we consider only the recursor over domain-level terms of type tm. Hence, we annotate it with $\mathcal{I} = (\psi : \mathsf{ctx}) \Rightarrow (y : \lceil \psi \vdash \mathsf{tm} \rceil) \Rightarrow \tau$. To check that the recursor $\mathsf{rec}^{\mathcal{I}} \, \mathcal{B} \, \Psi \, t$ has type $[\Psi/\psi]\tau$, we check that each of the three branches has the specified type $\mathcal{I}$. In the base case, we may assume in addition to $\psi : \mathsf{ctx}$ that we have a variable $p : \lceil \psi \vdash_v \mathsf{tm} \rceil$ and check that the body has the appropriate type. If we encounter a contextual object built with the domain-level constant app, then we choose the branch b_{app}. We assume $\psi{:}\mathsf{ctx}$, $m{:}\lceil \psi \vdash \mathsf{tm} \rceil$, $n{:}\lceil \psi \vdash \mathsf{tm} \rceil$, as well as f_n and f_m which stand for the recursive calls on m and n respectively. We then check that the body t_{app} is well-typed. If we encounter a domain object built with the domain-level constant lam, then we choose the branch b_{lam}. We assume $\psi{:}\mathsf{ctx}$ and $m{:}\lceil \psi, x{:}\mathsf{tm} \vdash \mathsf{tm} \rceil$ together with the recursive call f_m on m in the extended LF context $\psi, x{:}\mathsf{tm}$. We then check that the body t_{lam} is well-typed. The typing rules for computations are given in Fig. 3. We omit the reduction rules here and refer the interested reader to the appendix.

5.1 Interpretation

We now give an interpretation of simply-typed Cocon in a presheaf model with a cartesian closed universe of representables. Let us first extend the internal dependent type theory with the constant tm for modelling the domain-level type constant tm and with the constants $\mathsf{app} : \mathsf{El} \, \mathsf{tm} \to \mathsf{El} \, \mathsf{tm} \to \mathsf{El} \, \mathsf{tm}$ and

$\boxed{\Gamma \vdash C : T}$ Contextual object C has contextual type T

$$\frac{\Gamma; \Psi \vdash M : A}{\Gamma \vdash (\widehat{\Psi} \vdash M) : (\Psi \vdash A)} \qquad \frac{\Gamma \vdash \Psi : \mathsf{ctx} \quad x{:}A \in \Psi}{\Gamma \vdash (\widehat{\Psi} \vdash x) : (\Psi \vdash_{\overline{v}} A)} \qquad \frac{x{:}\lceil \Phi \vdash_{\overline{v}} A \rceil \in \Gamma \quad \Gamma; \Psi \vdash \mathsf{wk}_{\widehat{\Psi}} : \Phi}{\Gamma \vdash (\widehat{\Psi} \vdash \lfloor x \rfloor_{\mathsf{wk}_{\widehat{\Psi}}}) : (\Psi \vdash_{\overline{v}} A)}$$

$\boxed{\Gamma \vdash t : \tau}$ Term t has computation type τ
$$\frac{y : \check{\tau} \in \Gamma}{\Gamma \vdash y : \check{\tau}} \qquad \frac{\Gamma \vdash C : T}{\Gamma \vdash \lceil C \rceil : \lceil T \rceil}$$

$$\frac{\Gamma \vdash t : (y : \check{\tau}_1) \Rightarrow \tau_2 \quad \Gamma \vdash s : \check{\tau}_1}{\Gamma \vdash t \; s : [s/y]\tau_2} \qquad \frac{\Gamma, y : \check{\tau}_1 \vdash t : \tau_2 \quad \Gamma \vdash (y : \check{\tau}_1) \Rightarrow \tau_2 : \mathsf{type}}{\Gamma \vdash \mathsf{fn}\; y \Rightarrow t : (y : \check{\tau}_1) \Rightarrow \tau_2}$$

Recursor over domain-level terms $\mathcal{I} = (\psi : \mathsf{ctx}) \Rightarrow (y : \lceil \psi \vdash \mathsf{tm} \rceil) \Rightarrow \tau$

$$\frac{\Gamma \vdash t : \lceil \Psi \vdash \mathsf{tm} \rceil \quad \Gamma \vdash \mathcal{I} : u \quad \Gamma \vdash b_v : \mathcal{I} \quad \Gamma \vdash b_{\mathsf{app}} : \mathcal{I} \quad \Gamma \vdash b_{\mathsf{lam}} : \mathcal{I}}{\Gamma \vdash \mathsf{rec}^{\mathcal{I}}(b_v \mid b_{\mathsf{app}} \mid b_{\mathsf{lam}}) \; \Psi \; t : [\Psi/\psi]\tau}$$

Branch for Variable $\qquad \dfrac{\Gamma, \psi : \mathsf{ctx}, p : \lceil \psi \vdash_{\overline{v}} \mathsf{tm} \rceil \vdash t_v : \tau}{\Gamma \vdash (\psi, p \mapsto t_v) : \mathcal{I}}$

Branch for Application app $\qquad \dfrac{\Gamma, \psi : \mathsf{ctx}, m{:}\lceil \psi \vdash \mathsf{tm} \rceil, n{:}\lceil \psi \vdash \mathsf{tm} \rceil, f_m{:}\tau, f_n{:}\tau \vdash t_{\mathsf{app}} : \tau}{\Gamma \vdash (\psi, m, n, f_n, f_m \mapsto t_{\mathsf{app}}) : \mathcal{I}}$

Branch for Function lam $\qquad \dfrac{\Gamma, \phi : \mathsf{ctx}, m{:}\lceil \phi, x{:}\mathsf{tm} \vdash \mathsf{tm} \rceil, f_m{:}[(\phi, x{:}\mathsf{tm})/\psi]\tau \vdash t_{\mathsf{lam}} : [\phi/\psi]\tau}{\Gamma \vdash \psi, m, f_m \mapsto t_{\mathsf{lam}} : \mathcal{I}}$

Fig. 3. Typing Rules for Contextual Objects and Computations

$\mathsf{lam}: (\mathtt{El\,tm} \to \mathtt{El\,tm}) \to \mathtt{El\,tm}$ to model the corresponding domain-level constants app and lam.

We can now translate domain-level and computation-level types of Cocon into the internal dependent type theory for $\widehat{\mathbb{D}}$. We do so by interpreting the domain-level terms, types, substitutions, and contexts (see Fig. 4). All translations are on well-typed terms and types. Domain-level types are interpreted as the terms of type $\mathtt{Obj}$ in the internal dependent type theory that represent them. Domain-level contexts are also interpreted as terms of type $\mathtt{Obj}$ by $[\![\Gamma \vdash \Psi : \mathsf{ctx}]\!]$. For example, a domain-level context $x{:}\mathsf{tm}, y{:}\mathsf{tm}$ is interpreted as $\mathtt{times\ (times\ unit\ tm)\ tm}$: $\mathtt{Obj}$. A domain-level substitution with domain Ψ and codomain Φ becomes a term of type $\mathtt{El}\, e'$ that is parameterised by an element $u{:}\mathtt{El}\, e$, where $e = [\![\Gamma \vdash \Phi : \mathsf{ctx}]\!]$ and $e' = [\![\Gamma \vdash \Psi : \mathsf{ctx}]\!]$. As e' is some product, for example $\mathtt{times\ (times\ unit\ tm)\ tm}$, the domain-level substitution is translated into an n-ary tuple. A weakening substitution $\Gamma; \Psi, x{:}\mathsf{tm} \vdash \mathsf{wk}_\Psi : \Psi$ is interpreted as $\mathtt{fst}\, u$ where $u{:}\mathtt{El\,(times}\, e\, \mathtt{tm)}$ and $e = [\![\Gamma \vdash \Psi : \mathsf{ctx}]\!]$. More generally, when we weaken a context Ψ by n declarations, i.e. $\overrightarrow{x{:}A}$, we interpret wk_Ψ as $\mathtt{fst}_n\, u$.

A well-typed domain-level term, $\Gamma; \Psi \vdash M : A$, is mapped to an object of type $\mathtt{El}\, [\![A]\!]$ that depends on $u{:}\mathtt{El}\, [\![\Gamma \vdash \Psi : \mathsf{ctx}]\!]$.

Hence the translation of a well-typed domain-level term is indexed by u that stands for the term-level interpretation of a domain-level context Φ. Initially, u

Interpretation of domain-level types

$\llbracket \mathtt{tm} \rrbracket \qquad\qquad\qquad = \mathtt{tm}$

$\llbracket A \to B \rrbracket \qquad\qquad\quad = \mathtt{arrow}\ \llbracket A \rrbracket\ \llbracket B \rrbracket$

Interpretation of domain-level contexts

$\llbracket \Gamma \vdash \psi : \mathtt{ctx} \rrbracket \qquad\qquad = \psi$

$\llbracket \Gamma \vdash \cdot : \mathtt{ctx} \rrbracket \qquad\qquad = \mathtt{unit}$

$\llbracket \Gamma \vdash (\Psi, x{:}A) : \mathtt{ctx} \rrbracket \quad = \mathtt{times}\ e\ \llbracket A \rrbracket \qquad\qquad\qquad$ where $\llbracket \Gamma \vdash \Psi : \mathtt{ctx} \rrbracket = e$

Interpretation of domain-level terms where $u{:}\mathtt{El}\ e$ and $\llbracket \Gamma \vdash \Psi : \mathtt{ctx} \rrbracket = e$

$\llbracket \Gamma; \Psi \vdash x : A \rrbracket_u \qquad\quad = \mathtt{snd}\ (\mathtt{fst}_k\ u) \qquad$ where $\Psi = \Psi_0, x{:}A, y_k{:}A_k, \ldots, y_1{:}A_1$

$\llbracket \Gamma; \Psi \vdash \lambda x.\, M : A \to B \rrbracket_u = \mathtt{arrow\text{-}i}\ (\lambda x{:}\mathtt{El}\ \llbracket A \rrbracket.\ e)$
$\qquad\qquad\qquad\qquad\qquad\qquad$ where $\llbracket \Gamma; \Psi, x{:}A \vdash M : B \rrbracket_{(\mathtt{pair}\ u\ x)} = e$

$\llbracket \Gamma; \Psi \vdash M\ N : B \rrbracket_u \qquad = \mathtt{arrow\text{-}e}\ e_1\ e_2 \qquad$ where $\llbracket \Gamma; \Psi \vdash M : A \to B \rrbracket_u = e_1$
$\qquad\qquad\qquad\qquad\qquad\qquad\qquad\qquad\quad$ and $\quad \llbracket \Gamma; \Psi \vdash N : A \rrbracket_u = e_2$

$\llbracket \Gamma; \Psi \vdash \lfloor t \rfloor_\sigma : A \rrbracket_u \quad = \mathtt{let\ box}\ x = e_1\ \mathtt{in}\ x\ e_2$ where $\llbracket \Gamma \vdash t : \lceil \Phi \vdash A \rceil \rrbracket = e_1$
$\qquad\qquad\qquad\qquad\qquad\qquad\qquad\qquad\quad$ and $\quad \llbracket \Gamma; \Psi \vdash \sigma : \Phi \rrbracket_u = e_2$

$\llbracket \Gamma; \Psi \vdash \mathtt{app} : \mathtt{tm} \to \mathtt{tm} \to \mathtt{tm} \rrbracket_u = \mathtt{arrow\text{-}i}(\lambda x{:}\mathtt{El}\ \mathtt{tm}.\ \mathtt{arrow\text{-}i}\ (\lambda y{:}\mathtt{El}\ \mathtt{tm}.\ \mathtt{app}\ x\ y))$

$\llbracket \Gamma; \Psi \vdash \mathtt{lam} : (\mathtt{tm} \to \mathtt{tm}) \to \mathtt{tm} \rrbracket_u = \mathtt{arrow\text{-}i}(\lambda f{:}\mathtt{El}\ (\mathtt{arrow}\ \mathtt{tm}\ \mathtt{tm}).$
$\qquad\qquad\qquad\qquad\qquad\qquad\qquad\qquad\qquad\quad \mathtt{lam}\ (\lambda x{:}\mathtt{El}\ \mathtt{tm}.\ \mathtt{arrow\text{-}e}\ f\ x))$

Interpretation of domain-level substitutions where $u{:}\mathtt{El}\ e$ and $\llbracket \Gamma \vdash \Phi : \mathtt{ctx} \rrbracket = e$

$\llbracket \Gamma; \Psi \vdash \cdot : \cdot \rrbracket_u \qquad\quad = \mathtt{terminal}$

$\llbracket \Gamma; \Psi \vdash (\sigma, M) : \Phi, x{:}A \rrbracket_u = \mathtt{pair}\ e_1\ e_2 \qquad\qquad$ where $\llbracket \Gamma; \Psi \vdash \sigma : \Phi \rrbracket_u = e_1$
$\qquad\qquad\qquad\qquad\qquad\qquad\qquad\qquad\qquad$ and $\llbracket \Gamma; \Psi \vdash M : A \rrbracket_u = e_2$

$\llbracket \Gamma; \Psi, \overrightarrow{x{:}A} \vdash \mathtt{wk}_{\widehat{\Phi}} : \Phi \rrbracket_u \quad = \mathtt{fst}_n\ u \qquad\qquad$ where $n = |\overrightarrow{x{:}A}|$

Fig. 4. Interpretation of Domain-level Types and Terms

is simply a variable. However, when we translate $\Gamma; \Phi \vdash \lambda x.M : A \to B$ given $u{:}\mathtt{El}\ e$ where $\llbracket \Gamma \vdash \Psi : \mathtt{ctx} \rrbracket = e$, we need to recursively translate M in the extended domain-level context $\Psi, x{:}A$ and hence we also need to build a term $\mathtt{pair}\ u\ x$ that inhabits $\mathtt{El}\,(\mathtt{times}\ e\ \llbracket A \rrbracket)$. The translation of $\Gamma; \Phi, x{:}A \vdash M : A$ will return a term e that may contain x. However, note that x will eventually be bound in $\mathtt{arrow\text{-}i}\ (\lambda x{:}\mathtt{El}\ \llbracket A \rrbracket.\ e)$ When we translate a variable x where $\Phi = \Phi_0, x{:}A, y_k{:}A_k, \ldots, y_1{:}A_1$, we return $\mathtt{fst}_k\ (\mathtt{snd}\ u)$. We translate $\Gamma; \Phi \vdash \lfloor t \rfloor_\sigma : A$ directly using $\mathtt{let\ box}$-construct where the domain-level substitution σ is simply translated into a pair. As the computation t has the contextual type $\lceil \Psi \vdash \mathtt{tm} \rceil$ its translation will be of type $\flat(\mathtt{El}\ e \to \mathtt{El}\ \mathtt{tm})$ where $e = \llbracket \Gamma \vdash \Psi : \mathtt{ctx} \rrbracket$. Hence we simply can extract a function $x{:}(\mathtt{El}\ e \to \mathtt{El}\ \mathtt{tm})$ using $\mathtt{let\ box}$ construct and pass to it the interpretation of σ. The translation of domain-level applications and domain-level constants $\mathtt{app}$ and $\mathtt{lam}$ is straightforward.

The interpretation of a contextual types $\lceil \Psi \vdash A \rceil$ makes explicit the fact that they correspond to functions $\mathtt{El}\ e \to \mathtt{El}\ \llbracket A \rrbracket$ where $e = \llbracket \Gamma \vdash \Psi : \mathtt{ctx} \rrbracket$ (see Fig. 5). Consequently, the corresponding contextual object $(\widehat{\Phi} \vdash M)$ is interpreted as a

Interpretation of contextual objects (C)

$$[\![\Gamma \vdash (\widehat{\varPhi} \vdash M) : (\varPhi \vdash A)]\!] = \lambda u\!:\! \text{El}\, e.\, e' \qquad \text{where } [\![\Gamma \vdash \varPhi : \text{ctx}]\!] = e$$
$$\text{and } [\![\Gamma; \varPhi \vdash M : A]\!]_u = e'$$

$$[\![\Gamma \vdash (\widehat{\varPhi} \vdash M) : (\varPhi \overset{\shortmid}{\vdash}_{\bar{v}} A)]\!] = \lambda u\!:\! \text{El}\, e.\, e' \qquad \text{where } [\![\Gamma \vdash \varPhi : \text{ctx}]\!] = e$$
$$\text{and } [\![\Gamma; \varPhi \vdash M : A]\!]_u = e'$$

Interpretation of contextual types (T)

$$[\![\Gamma \vdash (\varPhi \vdash A)]\!] \qquad = (u\!:\!\text{El}\, e) \to \text{El}\, [\![A]\!] \quad \text{where } [\![\Gamma \vdash \varPhi : \text{ctx}]\!] = e$$
$$[\![\Gamma \vdash (\varPhi \overset{\shortmid}{\vdash}_{\bar{v}} A)]\!] \qquad = (u\!:\!\text{El}\, e) \to_v \text{El}\, [\![A]\!] \quad \text{where } [\![\Gamma \vdash \varPhi : \text{ctx}]\!] = e$$

Fig. 5. Interpretation of Contextual Objects and Types

Interpretation of computation-level types $(\breve{\tau})$

$$[\![\ulcorner T \urcorner]\!] \qquad\qquad = \flat [\![T]\!]$$
$$[\![(x\!:\!\breve{\tau}_1) \Rightarrow \tau_2]\!] \qquad = (x\!:\![\![\breve{\tau}_1]\!]) \to [\![\tau_2]\!]$$
$$[\![\text{ctx}]\!] \qquad\qquad\quad = \text{Obj}$$

Computation-level typing contexts (Γ)

$$[\![\cdot]\!] \qquad\qquad\qquad = \cdot$$
$$[\![\Gamma, x\!:\!\breve{\tau}]\!] \qquad\qquad = [\![\Gamma]\!],\, x\!:\![\![\breve{\tau}]\!]$$

Interpretation of computations $(\Gamma \vdash t : \tau;$ without recursor)

$$[\![\Gamma \vdash \ulcorner C \urcorner : \ulcorner T \urcorner]\!] \qquad = \text{box}\, e \qquad\qquad \text{where } [\![\Gamma \vdash C : T]\!] = e$$
$$[\![\Gamma \vdash t_1\, t_2 : \tau]\!] \qquad\quad = e_1\, e_2 \qquad\qquad \text{where } [\![\Gamma \vdash t_1 : (x\!:\!\breve{\tau}_2) \Rightarrow \tau]\!] = e_1$$
$$\text{and } [\![\Gamma \vdash t_2 : \breve{\tau}_2]\!] = e_2$$
$$[\![\Gamma \vdash \text{fn}\, x \Rightarrow t : (x\!:\!\breve{\tau}_1) \Rightarrow \tau_2]\!] = \lambda x\!:\![\![\breve{\tau}_1]\!].\, e \qquad \text{where } [\![\Gamma, x\!:\!\breve{\tau}_1 \vdash t : \tau_2]\!] = e$$
$$[\![\Gamma \vdash x : \tau]\!] \qquad\qquad = x$$

Fig. 6. Interpretation of Computation-level Types and Terms – without recursor

function. Similarly, $\ulcorner \varPsi \overset{\shortmid}{\vdash}_{\bar{v}} A \urcorner$ is mapped to the restricted function space denoted by $\to_v$, which describes functions with bodies that only contain projections.

Last, we give the interpretation of computation-level types, contexts and terms (see Fig. 6). It is mostly straightforward, as we simply map $\ulcorner T \urcorner$ to $\flat [\![T]\!]$ and $\ulcorner C \urcorner$ is simply interpreted as boxed term.

The interpretation of the recursor is also straightforward now (see Fig. 7). In Lemma 4, we expressed a primitive recursion scheme in our internal type theory and defined a term **rec** together with its type. We now interpret every branch of our recursor in the computation-level as a function of the required type in our internal type theory. While this is somewhat tedious, it is straightforward.

We can now show that all well-typed domain-level and computation-level objects are translated into well-typed constructions in our internal type theory. As a consequence, we can show that equality in Cocon is equivalent to the corresponding equivalence in our internal type theoretic interpretation.

Interpretation of recursor for $\mathcal{I} = (\psi : \mathsf{ctx}) \Rightarrow (y : \ulcorner \psi \vdash \mathsf{tm} \urcorner) \Rightarrow \tau$:

$[\![\Gamma \vdash \mathsf{rec}^{\mathcal{I}}(b_v \mid b_{\mathsf{app}} \mid b_{\mathsf{lam}}) \ \Psi \ t : [\Psi/\psi, \ t/y]\tau]\!] = \mathsf{rec} \ e_v \ e_{\mathsf{app}} \ e_{\mathsf{lam}} \ e_c \ e$

    where $[\![\Gamma \vdash b_v : \mathcal{I}]\!] = e_v, [\![\Gamma \vdash b_{\mathsf{app}} : \mathcal{I}]\!] = e_{\mathsf{app}}, [\![\Gamma \vdash b_{\mathsf{lam}} : \mathcal{I}]\!] = e_{\mathsf{lam}},$

        $[\![\Gamma \vdash \Psi : \mathsf{ctx}]\!] = e_c$ and $[\![\Gamma \vdash t : \ulcorner \Psi \vdash \mathsf{tm} \urcorner]\!] = e$

Interpretation of Variable Branch

$[\![\Gamma \vdash (\psi, x \mapsto t_v) : \mathcal{I}]\!] \hspace{3.5cm} = \lambda \psi : \mathsf{Obj}. \ \lambda \ x : \flat(\mathsf{El} \ \psi \rightarrow_v \mathsf{El} \ \mathsf{tm}). \ e$

    where $[\![\Gamma, \psi : \mathsf{ctx}, x : \ulcorner \psi \vdash_v \mathsf{tm} \urcorner \vdash t_v : [x/y]\tau]\!] = e$

Interpretation of Application Branch

$[\![\Gamma \vdash (\psi, m, n, f_n, f_m \mapsto t_{\mathsf{app}}) : \mathcal{I}]\!] = \lambda \psi : \mathsf{Obj}. \ \lambda \ m, n : \flat(\mathsf{El} \ \psi \rightarrow \mathsf{El} \ \mathsf{tm}).$
$$\lambda f_m : [\![m/y]\tau]\!]. \ \lambda \ f_n : [\![n/y]\tau]\!]. \ e$$

    where $[\![\Gamma, \psi : \mathsf{ctx}, m : \ulcorner \psi \vdash \mathsf{tm} \urcorner, n : \ulcorner \psi \vdash \mathsf{tm} \urcorner \vdash t_{\mathsf{app}} : [\ulcorner \psi \vdash \mathsf{app} \ \lfloor m \rfloor \ \lfloor n \rfloor \urcorner / y]\tau]\!] = e$

Interpretation of Lambda-Abstraction Branch

$[\![\Gamma \vdash (\psi, m, f_m \mapsto t_{\mathsf{lam}}) : \mathcal{I}]\!] \hspace{2cm} = \lambda \psi : \mathsf{Obj}. \lambda \ m : \flat(\mathsf{El} \ (\mathsf{times} \ \psi \ \mathsf{tm}) \rightarrow \mathsf{El} \ \mathsf{tm}).$
$$\lambda f_m : \tau_m . e$$

    where $[\![[(\psi, x : \mathsf{tm})/\psi, \ m/y]\tau]\!] = \tau_m,$
        $[\![\Gamma, \psi : \mathsf{ctx}, m : \ulcorner \psi, x : \mathsf{tm} \vdash \mathsf{tm} \urcorner \vdash t_{\mathsf{app}} : [\ulcorner \psi \vdash \mathsf{lam} \ \lambda x. \lfloor m \rfloor \urcorner / y]\tau]\!] = e$

Fig. 7. Interpretation of Recursor

Lemma 5. *The interpretation maintains the following typing invariants:*

- *If $\Gamma \vdash \Psi : \mathsf{ctx}$ then $[\![\Gamma \vdash \Psi : \mathsf{ctx}]\!] : \mathsf{Obj}$.*
- *If $\Gamma; \Psi \vdash M : A$ then $[\![\Gamma]\!], u : \mathsf{El} \ [\![\Gamma \vdash \Psi : \mathsf{ctx}]\!] \vdash [\![\Gamma; \Psi \vdash M : A]\!]_u : \mathsf{El} \ [\![A]\!]$.*
- *If $\Gamma; \Psi \vdash \sigma : \Psi$ then $[\![\Gamma]\!], u : \mathsf{El} \ [\![\Gamma \vdash \Psi : \mathsf{ctx}]\!] \vdash [\![\Gamma; \Psi \vdash \sigma : \Psi]\!]_u : \mathsf{El} \ [\![\Psi]\!]$.*
- *If $\Gamma \vdash C : T$ then $[\![\Gamma]\!] \vdash [\![\Gamma \vdash C : T]\!] : [\![T]\!]$.*
- *If $\Gamma \vdash t : \tau$ then $[\![\Gamma]\!] \vdash [\![\Gamma \vdash t : \tau]\!] : [\![\tau]\!]$.*

The proof goes by induction on derivations.

Proposition 1 (Soundness). *The following are true.*

- *If $\Gamma; \Psi \vdash M \equiv N : A$ then*
  $[\![\Gamma]\!], u : \mathsf{El} \ [\![\Psi]\!] \vdash [\![\Gamma; \Psi \vdash M : A]\!]_u = [\![\Gamma; \Psi \vdash N : A]\!]_u : \mathsf{El} \ [\![A]\!]$.
- *If $\Gamma; \Psi \vdash \sigma \equiv \sigma' : \Phi$ then*
  $[\![\Gamma]\!], u : \mathsf{El} \ [\![\Psi]\!] \vdash [\![\Gamma; \Psi \vdash \sigma : \Phi]\!]_u = [\![\Gamma; \Psi \vdash \sigma' : \Phi]\!]_u : \mathsf{El} \ [\![\Phi]\!]$.
- *If $\Gamma \vdash t_1 \equiv t_2 : \tau$ then $[\![\Gamma]\!] \vdash [\![\Gamma \vdash t_1 : \tau]\!] = [\![\Gamma \vdash t_2 : \tau]\!] : [\![\tau]\!]$.*

6 Presheaves on a Small Category with Attributes

To explain the core of our approach as simply as possible, we have concentrated on a simply-typed domain language. In the remaining space, we outline how our approach generalises to dependent domain languages like LF.

    We follow the same approach as above. We start from a term model $\mathbb{D}$ of the domain language and then interpret contextual types in the presheaf category $\widehat{\mathbb{D}}$. In the simply-typed case above, $\mathbb{D}$ was a small cartesian closed category. In the dependent case, $\mathbb{D}$ is a small *Category with Attributes*. Categories with attributes (CwAs) [11] are a general notion of model for dependent type theories that is suitable for modelling dependent domain languages like LF.

With this change, we follow essentially the same approach as above. The main difference is that the universe of representables now makes available the CwA-structure of $\mathbb{D}$ instead of the cartesian closed structure. The following section outlines this in analogy to Sec. 4.1.

6.1   Yoneda CwA

In a Yoneda CwA we again have a type for the objects of $\mathbb{D}$, which we now denote `Ctx`. In the term model for LF, these would be the LF contexts. The type `Ty` c represents (possibly dependent) LF types in context c. Contexts can be built with the constants `nil` and `cons`.

$$\vdash \texttt{Ctx type} \qquad \vdash \texttt{nil: Ctx}$$
$$c\colon \texttt{Ctx} \vdash \texttt{Ty}\, c \text{ type} \qquad \vdash \texttt{cons}\colon (c\colon \texttt{Ctx}) \to (a\colon \texttt{Ty}\, c) \to \texttt{Ctx}$$

Both `Ctx` and `Ty` c are constant presheaves, i.e. $\flat\texttt{Ctx} = \texttt{Ctx}$ and $\flat(\texttt{Ty}\, c) = \texttt{Ty}\, c$.

As in Sec. 4.1, we consider the contexts as codes of a universe.

$$c\colon \texttt{Ctx} \vdash \texttt{El}\, c \text{ type}$$

The type `El` c has the same interpretation as before and is essentially just the Yoneda embedding. The morphisms $c \to d$ of the CwA $\mathbb{D}$ thus appear as functions of type `El` $c \to$ `El` d.

The axioms of a CwA can be stated using terms and equations in the internal language of $\widehat{\mathbb{D}}$. For example, substitution on types and context projection morphisms are given by the following constants.

$$c, d\colon \texttt{Ctx} \vdash \texttt{sub}\colon (a\colon \texttt{Ty}\, d) \to (f\colon \texttt{El}\, c \to \texttt{El}\, d) \to \texttt{Ty}\, c$$
$$c\colon \texttt{Ctx},\, a\colon \texttt{Ty}\, c \vdash p\colon \texttt{El}\ (\texttt{cons}\, c\, a) \to \texttt{El}\, c$$

The other components of a CwA are added similarly and the CwA-axioms [11] are expressed in terms of equations for these constants.

The inhabitants of a type can then be captured by the dependent type

$$c\colon \texttt{Ctx},\, a\colon \texttt{Ty}\, c,\, u\colon \texttt{El}\, c \vdash \texttt{I}\, a\, u \text{ type}$$

defined by $\texttt{I}\, a\, u := \Sigma v\colon \texttt{El}\ (\texttt{cons}\, c\, a).\, (p\, v) = u$. This type contains all values in `El` $(\texttt{cons}\, c\, a)$ whose first projection is u. If one considers $u\colon \texttt{El}\, c$ as a dependent tuple of LF terms (one term for each variable in the context represented by c), then $\texttt{I}\, a\, u$ represents all the terms that can be appended to this tuple to make it into one of type `El` $(\texttt{cons}\, c\, a)$. Indeed, one can define a pairing operation by $\texttt{pair} := \lambda u.\, \lambda\langle v, p\rangle.\, v$.

$$c\colon \texttt{Ctx},\, a\colon (\texttt{Ty}\, c) \vdash \texttt{pair}\colon (u\colon \texttt{El}\, c) \to \texttt{I}\, a\, u \to \texttt{El}\ (\texttt{cons}\, c\, a)$$

With these definitions, we can represent dependent contextual types much like the simply-typed ones. Recall that we had interpreted $\Phi \vdash A$ by $\text{El} \llbracket \Phi \rrbracket \to \text{El} \llbracket A \rrbracket$ where both $\llbracket \Phi \rrbracket$ and $\llbracket A \rrbracket$ were terms of type Obj. In the dependent case, A may depend on Φ. The interpretation of Φ is a term $\llbracket \Phi \rrbracket \colon \text{Ctx}$, much as before. The interpretation of A takes the dependency into account: $u \colon \text{El} \llbracket \Phi \rrbracket \vdash \llbracket A \rrbracket_u \colon \text{Ty } u$. The interpretation of the contextual type $\Phi \vdash A$ will then be:

$$(u \colon \text{El} \llbracket \Phi \rrbracket) \to \text{I} \llbracket A \rrbracket_u \, u$$

It may be interesting to note that $(u \colon \text{El } c) \to \text{I } a \, u$ is isomorphic to the type of sections of $p \colon \text{El} (\text{cons } c \, a) \to \text{El } c$.

Object-level term constants in LF can be lifted using I. Consider, for example, an encoding of the simply-typed lambda-calculus in LF. It represents only well-typed terms by means of the constants $\text{app} \colon \Pi a, b \colon \text{ty. tm } (\text{arr } a \, b) \to \text{tm } a \to \text{tm } b$ and $\text{lam} \colon \Pi a, b \colon \text{ty. } (\text{tm } a \to \text{tm } b) \to \text{tm } (\text{arr } a \, b)$. Therein, the type tm of object-level terms is dependent on an object-level type ty, which may be built using a constant $\text{o} \colon \text{ty}$ for a base type and a constant $\text{arr} \colon \text{ty} \to \text{ty} \to \text{ty}$ for function types. This encoding lifts to the Yoneda CwA as in simply-typed case:

$$
\begin{array}{ll}
c \colon \text{Ctx} \vdash \text{ty} \colon \text{Ty } c & \Gamma \vdash \text{o} \colon \text{I ty } u \\
c \colon \text{Ctx} \vdash \text{tm} \colon \text{Ty } (\text{cons } c \text{ ty}) & \Gamma \vdash \text{arr} \colon \text{I ty } u \to \text{I ty } u \to \text{I ty } u
\end{array}
$$

$$\Delta \vdash \text{app} \colon \text{I tm } (\text{pair } u \, (\text{arr } a \, b)) \to \text{I tm } (\text{pair } u \, a) \to \text{I tm } (\text{pair } u \, b)$$
$$\vdash \text{lam} \colon (\text{I tm } (\text{pair } u \, a) \to \text{I tm } (\text{pair } u \, b)) \to \text{I tm } (\text{pair } u \, (\text{arr } a \, b))$$

Here, Γ abbreviates $c \colon \text{Ctx}, u \colon (\text{El } c)$ and Δ abbreviates $\Gamma, a, b \colon (\text{I ty } u)$. Notice how lam uses higher-order abstract syntax at the meta level.

With these definitions, the interpretation of Cocon is essentially just as before. For working with the dependencies in a Yoneda CwA, we found it very useful to type-check our definitions in Agda, see our sources [1].

7 Conclusion

We have given a rational reconstruction of contextual type theory in presheaf models of higher-order abstract syntax. This provides a semantical way of understanding the invariants of contextual types independently of the algorithmic details of type checking. At the same time, we identify the contextual modal type theory, Cocon, which is known to be normalising, as a syntax for presheaf models of HOAS. By accounting for the Yoneda embedding with a universe á la Tarski, we obtain a manageable way of constructing contextual types in the model, especially in the dependent case. While various forms of universes are being studied in the context of functor categories, e.g. [2,16], we are not aware of previous uses of presheaves over CwAs or similar.

In future work, one may consider using the model as a way of compiling contextual types, by implementing the semantics. In another direction, it may be interesting to apply the syntax of contextual types to other presheaf categories. We also hope that the model will help to guide the further development of Cocon.

Acknowledgements. We thank the anonymous reviewers for helpful feedback.

References

1. The Agda sources for this paper are available from: http://github.com/uelis/contextual.

2. Guillaume Allais, Robert Atkey, James Chapman, Conor McBride, and James McKinna. A type and scope safe universe of syntaxes with binding: Their semantics and proofs. *Proc. ACM Program. Lang.*, 2(ICFP):90:1–90:30, July 2018.

3. Benton, P.N., Bierman, G.M., de Paiva, V., Hyland, M.: A term calculus for intuitionistic linear logic. In: Bezem, M., Groote, J.F. (eds.) Typed Lambda Calculi and Applications, International Conference on Typed Lambda Calculi and Applications, TLCA '93, Utrecht, The Netherlands, March 16-18, 1993, Proceedings. vol. 664, pp. 75–90. Springer (1993)

4. Andrew Barber and Gordon Plotkin. Dual intuitionistic linear logic. Technical Report, LFCS, University of Edinburgh, 1997.

5. John Cartmell. Generalised algebraic theories and contextual categories. *Annals of Pure and Applied Logic*, 32:209 – 243, 1986.

6. Rowan Davies and Frank Pfenning. A modal analysis of staged computation. *Journal of the ACM*, 48(3):555–604, 2001.

7. Peter Dybjer. Internal type theory. In *Types for Proofs and Programs (TYPES'95)*, pages 120–134, 1995.

8. M. Fiore, G. D. Plotkin, and D. Turi. Abstract syntax and variable binding. In *Logic in Computer Science (LICS'99)*, pages 193–202. IEEE Press, 1999.

9. Murdoch Gabbay and Andrew Pitts. A new approach to abstract syntax involving binders. In *Logic in Computer Science (LICS'99)*, pages 214–224. IEEE Press, 1999.

10. Robert Harper, Furio Honsell, and Gordon Plotkin. A framework for defining logics. *Journal of the ACM*, 40(1):143–184, January 1993.

11. Martin Hofmann. *Syntax and Semantics of Dependent Types*, page 79–130. Publications of the Newton Institute. Cambridge University Press, 1997.

12. Martin Hofmann. Semantical analysis of higher-order abstract syntax. In *Logic in Computer Science (LICS'99)*, pages 204–213. IEEE Press, 1999.

13. Furio Honsell, Marino Miculan, and Ivan Scagnetto. An axiomatic approach to metareasoning on nominal algebras in HOAS. In *International Colloquium on Automata, Languages and Programming (ICALP'01)*, LNCS 2076, pages 963–978. Springer, 2001.

14. Bart Jacobs. Comprehension categories and the semantics of type dependency. *Theor. Comput. Sci.*, 107(2):169–207, 1993.

15. Kavvos, G.A.: Intensionality, intensional recursion, and the Gödel-Löb axiom. CoRR **abs/1703.01288** (2017), http://arxiv.org/abs/1703.01288

16. Daniel R. Licata, Ian Orton, Andrew M. Pitts, and Bas Spitters. Internal universes in models of homotopy type theory. In *Formal Structures for Computation and Deduction (FSCD'18)*, pages 22:1–22:17, 2018.

17. Dale Miller and Catuscia Palamidessi. Foundational aspects of syntax. *ACM Comput. Surv.*, 31(3es), 1999.

18. Aleksandar Nanevski, Frank Pfenning, and Brigitte Pientka. Contextual modal type theory. *ACM Transactions on Computational Logic*, 9(3):1–49, 2008.

19. Frank Pfenning and Conal Elliott. Higher-order abstract syntax. In *Symposium on Language Design and Implementation (PLDI'88)*, pages 199–208, June 1988.

20. Brigitte Pientka. A type-theoretic foundation for programming with higher-order abstract syntax and first-class substitutions. In *Principles of Programming Languages (POPL'08)*, pages 371–382. ACM Press, 2008.

21. Brigitte Pientka and Andreas Abel. Well-founded recursion over contextual objects. In *Typed Lambda Calculi and Applications (TLCA'15)*, pages 273–287, 2015.
22. Brigitte Pientka, Andreas Abel, Francisco Ferreira, David Thibodeau, and Rébecca Zucchini. Cocon: Computation in contextual type theory. *CoRR*, abs/1901.03378, 2019.
23. Brigitte Pientka, Andreas Abel, Francisco Ferreira, David Thibodeau, and Rebecca Zucchini. A type theory for defining logics and proofs. In *34th IEEE/ ACM Symposium on Logic in Computer Science (LICS'19)*, pages 1–13, IEEE Computer Society, 2019.
24. Brigitte Pientka and Andrew Cave. Inductive Beluga: Programming Proofs (System Description). In *Conference on Automated Deduction (CADE-25)*, LNCS 9195, pages 272–281. Springer, 2015.
25. Brigitte Pientka and Joshua Dunfield. Programming with proofs and explicit contexts. In *Principles and Practice of Declarative Programming (PPDP'08)*, pages 163–173, 2008.
26. Brigitte Pientka and Joshua Dunfield. Beluga: a framework for programming and reasoning with deductive systems (System Description). In *International Joint Conference on Automated Reasoning (IJCAR'10)*, LNAI 6173, pages 15–21. Springer, 2010.
27. Shulman, M.: Brouwer's fixed-point theorem in real-cohesive homotopy type theory. Mathematical Structures in Computer Science **28**(6), 856–941 (2018)
28. Thomas Streicher. *Semantics of Type Theory*. Birkhäuser, 1991.
29. Andrea Vezzosi. Agda with a flat modality. Available from https://github.com/agda/agda/tree/flat, 2018.

4

On Well-Founded and Recursive Coalgebras[*]

Jiří Adámek[1],[**], Stefan Milius[2],[***],[(✉)] (iD), and Lawrence S. Moss[3],[†]

[1] Czech Technical University, Prague, Czech Republic
j.adamek@tu-braunschweig.de
[2] Friedrich-Alexander-Universität Erlangen-Nürnberg, Germany
mail@stefan-milius.eu
[3] Indiana University, Bloomington, IN, USA
lmoss@indiana.edu

Abstract This paper studies fundamental questions concerning category-theoretic models of induction and recursion. We are concerned with the relationship between well-founded and recursive coalgebras for an endofunctor. For monomorphism preserving endofunctors on complete and well-powered categories every coalgebra has a well-founded part, and we provide a new, shorter proof that this is the coreflection in the category of all well-founded coalgebras. We present a new more general proof of Taylor's General Recursion Theorem that every well-founded coalgebra is recursive, and we study conditions which imply the converse. In addition, we present a new equivalent characterization of well-foundedness: a coalgebra is well-founded iff it admits a coalgebra-to-algebra morphism to the initial algebra.

Keywords: Well-founded · Recursive · Coalgebra · Initial Algebra · General Recursion Theorem

1 Introduction

What is induction? What is recursion? In areas of theoretical computer science, the most common answers are related to *initial algebras*. Indeed, the dominant trend in abstract data types is initial algebra semantics (see e.g. [19]), and this approach has spread to other semantically-inclined areas of the subject. The approach in broad slogans is that, for an endofunctor F describing the type of algebraic operations of interest, the initial algebra μF has the property that for every F-algebra A, there is a unique homomorphism $\mu F \to A$, and this *is* recursion. Perhaps the primary example is *recursion on* $\mathbb{N}$, *the natural numbers*. Recall that $\mathbb{N}$ is the initial algebra for the set functor $FX = X + 1$. If A is any set, and $a \in A$ and $\alpha \colon A \to A + 1$ are given, then initiality tells us that there is a unique $f \colon \mathbb{N} \to A$ such that for all $n \in \mathbb{N}$,

$$f(0) = a \qquad f(n+1) = \alpha(f(n)). \tag{1.1}$$

Then the first additional problem coming with this approach is that of how to "recognize" initial algebras: Given an algebra, how do we really know if it is initial? The answer – again in slogans – is that initial algebras are the ones with "no junk and no confusion."

Although initiality captures some important aspects of recursion, it cannot be a fully satisfactory approach. One big missing piece concerns recursive definitions based on well-founded relations. For example, the whole study of termination of rewriting systems depends on well-orders, the primary example of *recursion on a well-founded order*. Let (X, R) be a well-founded relation, i.e. one with no infinite sequences $\cdots x_2 \, R \, x_1 \, R \, x_0$. Let A be any set, and let $\alpha \colon \mathscr{P}A \to A$. (Here and below, $\mathscr{P}$ is the power set functor, taking a set to the set of its subsets.) Then there is a unique $f \colon X \to A$ such that for all $x \in X$,

$$f(x) = \alpha(\{f(y) : y \, R \, x\}). \qquad (1.2)$$

The main goal of this paper is the study of concepts that allow one to extend the algebraic spirit behind initiality in (1.1) to the setting of recursion arising from well-foundedness as we find it in (1.2). The corresponding concepts are those of well-founded and recursive coalgebras for an endofunctor, which first appear in work by Osius [22] and Taylor [23, 24], respectively. In his work on categorical set theory, Osius [22] first studied the notions of well-founded and recursive coalgebras (for the power-set functor on sets and, more generally, the power-object functor on an elementary topos). He defined recursive coalgebras as those coalgebras $\alpha \colon A \to \mathscr{P}A$ which have a unique coalgebra-to-algebra homomorphism into every algebra (see Definition 3.2).

Taylor [23, 24] took Osius' ideas much further. He introduced well-founded coalgebras for a general endofunctor, capturing the notion of a well-founded relation categorically, and considered recursive coalgebras under the name 'coalgebras obeying the recursion scheme'. He then proved the General Recursion Theorem that all well-founded coalgebras are recursive, for every endofunctor on sets (and on more general categories) preserving inverse images. Recursive coalgebras were also investigated by Eppendahl [12], who called them algebra-initial coalgebras. Capretta, Uustalu, and Vene [10] further studied recursive coalgebras, and they showed how to construct new ones from given ones by using comonads. They also explained nicely how recursive coalgebras allow for the semantic treatment of (functional) divide-and-conquer programs. More recently, Jeannin et al. [15] proved the General Recursion Theorem for polynomial functors on the category of many-sorted sets; they also provide many interesting examples of recursive coalgebras arising in programming.

Our contributions in this paper are as follows. We start by recalling some preliminaries in Section 2 and the definition of (parametrically) recursive coalgebras in Section 3 and of well-founded coalgebras in Section 4 (using a formulation based on Jacobs' next time operator [14], which we extend from Kripke polynomial set functors to arbitrary functors). We show that every coalgebra for a monomorphism preserving functor on a complete and well-powered category has a well-founded part, and provide a new proof that this is the coreflection in the category of well-founded coalgebras (Proposition 4.19), shortening our previous proof [6]. Next we provide a new proof of Taylor's General Recursion Theorem (Theorem 5.1), generalizing this to endofunctors preserving monomorphisms on a complete and well-powered category having smooth monomorphisms (see Definition 2.8). For the category of sets, this implies that "well-founded $\Rightarrow$ recursive" holds for all endofunctors, strengthening Taylor's result. We then discuss the converse: is every recursive coalgebra well-founded? Here the assumption that F preserves inverse images cannot be lifted, and one needs additional assumptions. In fact, we present two results: one assumes universally smooth monomorphisms and that the functor has a pre-fixed point (see Theorem 5.5). Under these assumptions we also give a new equivalent characterization of recursiveness and well-foundedness: a coalgebra is recursive if it has a coalgebra-to-algebra morphism into the initial algebra (which exists under our assumptions), see Corollary 5.6. This characterization was previously established for finitary functors on sets [3]. The other converse of the above implication is due to Taylor using the concept of a subobject classifier (Theorem 5.8). It implies that 'recursive' and 'well-founded' are equivalent concepts for all set functors preserving inverse images. We also prove that a similar result holds for the category of vector spaces over a fixed field (Theorem 5.12).

Finally, we show in Section 6 that well-founded coalgebras are closed under coproducts, quotients and, assuming mild assumptions, under subcoalgebras.

2   Preliminaries

We start by recalling some background material. Except for the definitions of *algebra* and *coalgebra* in Subsection 2.1, the subsections below may be read as needed. We assume that readers are familiar with notions of basic category theory; see e.g. [2] for everything which we do not detail. We indicate monomorphisms by writing $\rightarrowtail$ and strong epimorphisms by $\twoheadrightarrow$.

2.1   Algebras and Coalgebras.   We are concerned throughout this paper with *algebras* and *coalgebras* for an endofunctor. This means that we have an underlying category, usually written $\mathscr{A}$; frequently it is the category of sets or of vector spaces over a fixed field, and that a functor $F\colon \mathscr{A} \to \mathscr{A}$ is given. An *F-algebra* is a pair (A, α), where $\alpha\colon FA \to A$. An *F-coalgebra* is a pair (A, α), where $\alpha\colon A \to FA$. We usually drop the functor F. Given two algebras (A, α) and (B, β), an *algebra homomorphism* from the first to the second is $h\colon A \to B$ in $\mathscr{A}$ such that $h \cdot \alpha = \beta \cdot Fh$. Similarly, a *coalgebra homomorphism* satisfies $\beta \cdot h = Fh \cdot \alpha$. We denote by $\mathsf{Coalg}\, F$ the category of all coalgebras for F.

Example 2.1.   (1) The power set functor $\mathscr{P}\colon \mathsf{Set} \to \mathsf{Set}$ takes a set X to the set $\mathscr{P}X$ of all subsets of it; for a morphism $f\colon X \to Y$, $\mathscr{P}f\colon \mathscr{P}X \to \mathscr{P}Y$ takes a subset $S \subseteq X$ to its direct image $f[S]$. Coalgebras $\alpha\colon X \to \mathscr{P}X$ may be identified with directed graphs on the set X of vertices, and the coalgebra structure α describes the edges: $b \in \alpha(a)$ means that there is an edge $a \to b$ in the graph.

(2) Let Σ be a signature, i.e. a set of operation symbols, each with a finite arity. The *polynomial functor* H_Σ associated to Σ assigns to a set X the set

$$H_\Sigma X = \coprod_{n \in \mathbb{N}} \Sigma_n \times X^n,$$

where Σ_n is the set of operation symbols of arity n. This may be identified with the set of all terms $\sigma(x_1, \ldots, x_n)$, for $\sigma \in \Sigma_n$, and $x_1, \ldots, x_n \in X$. Algebras for H_Σ are the usual Σ-algebras.

(3) Deterministic automata over an input alphabet Σ are coalgebras for the functor $FX = \{0,1\} \times X^\Sigma$. Indeed, given a set S of states, a next-state map $S \times \Sigma \to S$ may be curried to $\delta\colon S \to S^\Sigma$. The set of final states yields the acceptance predicate $a\colon S \to \{0,1\}$. So an automaton may be regarded as a coalgebra $\langle a, \delta \rangle\colon S \to \{0,1\} \times S^\Sigma$.

(4) Labelled transitions systems are coalgebras for $FX = \mathcal{P}(\Sigma \times X)$.

(5) To describe linear weighted automata, i.e. weighted automata over the input alphabet Σ with weights in a field K, as coalgebras, one works with the category Vec_K of vector spaces over K. A linear weighted automaton is then a coalgebra for $FX = K \times X^\Sigma$.

2.2 Preservation Properties. Recall that an intersection of two subobjects $s_i\colon S_i \rightarrowtail A$ $(i = 1, 2)$ of a given object A is given by their pullback. Analogously, (general) intersections are given by wide pullbacks. Furthermore, the inverse image of a subobject $s\colon S \rightarrowtail B$ under a morphism $f\colon A \to B$ is the subobject $t\colon T \rightarrowtail A$ obtained by a pullback of s along f.

All of the 'usual' set functors preserve intersections and inverse images:

Example 2.2. (1) Every polynomial functor preserves intersections and inverse images.

(2) The power-set functor $\mathcal{P}$ preserves intersections and inverse images.

(3) Intersection-preserving set functors are closed under taking coproducts, products and composition. Similarly, for inverse images.

(4) Consider next the set functor R defined by $RX = \{(x, y) \in X \times X \colon x \neq y\} + \{d\}$ for sets X. For a function $f\colon X \to Y$ put $Rf(x, y) = (f(x), f(y))$ if $f(x) \neq f(y)$, and d otherwise. R preserves intersections but not inverse images.

Proposition 2.3 [27]. *For every set functor F there exists an essentially unique set functor $\bar{F}$ which coincides with F on nonempty sets and functions and preserves finite intersections (whence monomorphisms).*

Remark 2.4. (1) In fact, Trnková gave a construction of $\bar{F}$: she defined $\bar{F}\emptyset$ as the set of all natural transformations $C_{01} \to F$, where C_{01} is the set functor with $C_{01}\emptyset = \emptyset$ and $C_{01}X = 1$ for all nonempty sets X. For the empty map $e\colon \emptyset \to X$ with $X \neq \emptyset$, $\bar{F}e$ maps a natural transformation $\tau\colon C_{01} \to F$ to the element given by $\tau_X\colon 1 \to FX$.

(2) The above functor $\bar{F}$ is called the *Trnková hull* of F. It allows us to achieve preservation of intersections for all *finitary* set functors. Intuitively, a functor on

sets is finitary if its behavior is completely determined by its action on *finite* sets and functions. For a general functor, this intuition is captured by requiring that the functor preserves filtered colimits [8]. For a set functor F this is equivalent to being *finitely bounded*, which is the following condition: for each element $x \in FX$ there exists a finite subset $M \subseteq X$ such that $x \in Fi[FM]$, where $i: M \hookrightarrow X$ is the inclusion map [7, Rem. 3.14].

Proposition 2.5 [4, p. 66]. *The Trnková hull of a finitary set functor preserves all intersections.*

2.3 Factorizations. Recall that an epimorphism $e: A \to B$ is called *strong* if it satisfies the following *diagonal fill-in property*: given a monomorphism $m: C \rightarrowtail D$ and morphisms $f: A \to C$ and $g: B \to D$ such that $m \cdot f = g \cdot e$ then there exists a unique $d: B \to C$ such that $f = d \cdot e$ and $g = m \cdot d$.

Every complete and well-powered category has factorizations of morphisms: every morphism f may be written as $f = m \cdot e$, where e is a strong epimorphism and m is a monomorphism [9, Prop. 4.4.3]. We call the subobject m the *image* of f. It follows from a result in Kurz' thesis [16, Prop. 1.3.6] that factorizations of morphisms lift to coalgebras:

Proposition 2.6 (Coalg F inherits factorizations from $\mathscr{A}$). *Suppose that F preserves monomorphisms. Then the category Coalg F has factorizations of homomorphisms f as $f = m \cdot e$, where e is carried by a strong epimorphism and m by a monomorphism in $\mathscr{A}$. The diagonal fill-in property holds in Coalg F.*

Remark 2.7. By a *subcoalgebra* of a coalgebra (A, α) we mean a subobject in Coalg F represented by a homomorphism $m: (B, \beta) \rightarrowtail (A, \alpha)$, where m is monic in $\mathscr{A}$. Similarly, by a *strong quotient* of a coalgebra (A, α) we mean one represented by a homomorphism $e: (A, \alpha) \twoheadrightarrow (C, \gamma)$ with e strongly epic in $\mathscr{A}$.

2.4 Chains. By a *transfinite chain* in a category $\mathscr{A}$ we understand a functor from the ordered class Ord of all ordinals into $\mathscr{A}$. Moreover, for an ordinal λ, a λ-*chain* in $\mathscr{A}$ is a functor from λ to $\mathscr{A}$. A category *has colimits of chains* if for every ordinal λ it has a colimit of every λ-chain. This includes the initial object 0 (the case $\lambda = 0$).

Definition 2.8. (1) A category $\mathscr{A}$ has *smooth monomorphisms* if for every λ-chain C of monomorphisms a colimit exists, its colimit cocone is formed by monomorphisms, and for every cone of C formed by monomorphisms, the factorizing morphism from $\operatorname{colim} C$ is monic. In particuar, every morphism from 0 is monic.

(2) $\mathscr{A}$ has *universally smooth monomorphisms* if $\mathscr{A}$ also has pullbacks, and for every morphism $f: X \to \operatorname{colim} C$, the functor $\mathscr{A} / \operatorname{colim} C \to \mathscr{A}/X$ forming pullbacks along f preserves the colimit of C. This implies that initial object 0 is *strict*, i.e. every morphism $f: X \to 0$ is an isomorphism. Indeed, consider the empty chain ($\lambda = 0$).

Example 2.9. (1) Set has universally smooth monomorphisms.

(2) Vec_K has smooth monomorphisms, but not universally so because the initial object is not strict.

(3) Categories in which colimits of chains and pullbacks are formed "set-like" have universally smooth monomorphisms. These include the categories of posets, graphs, topological spaces, presheaf categories, and many varieties, such as monoids, groups, and unary algebras.

(4) Every locally finitely presentable category $\mathscr{A}$ with a strict initial object (see Remark 2.12(1)) has smooth monomorphisms. This follows from [8, Prop. 1.62]. Moreover, since pullbacks commute with colimits of chains, it is easy to prove that colimits of chains are universal using the strictness of 0.

(5) The category CPO of complete partial orders does not have smooth monomorphisms. Indeed, consider the ω-chain of linearly ordered sets $A_n = \{0, \ldots, n\} + \{\top\}$ ($\top$ a top element) with inclusion maps $A_n \to A_{n+1}$. Its colimit is the linearly ordered set $\mathbb{N} + \{\top, \top'\}$ of natural numbers with two added top elements $\top' < \top$. For the sub-cpo $\mathbb{N} + \{\top\}$, the inclusions of A_n are monic and form a cocone. But the unique factorizing morphism from the colimit is not monic.

Notation 2.10. For every object A we denote by $\mathsf{Sub}(A)$ the poset of all subobjects of A (represented by monomorphisms $s\colon S \rightarrowtail A$), where $s \leq s'$ if there exists i with $s = s' \cdot i$. If $\mathscr{A}$ has pullbacks we have, for every morphism $f\colon A \to B$, the *inverse image operator*, viz. the monotone map $\overleftarrow{f}\colon \mathsf{Sub}(B) \to \mathsf{Sub}(A)$ assigning to a subobject $s\colon S \rightarrowtail A$ the subobject of B obtained by forming the inverse image of s under f, i.e. the pullback of s along f.

Lemma 2.11. *If $\mathscr{A}$ is complete and well-powered, then $\overleftarrow{f}$ has a left adjoint given by the (direct) image operator $\overrightarrow{f}\colon \mathsf{Sub}(A) \to \mathsf{Sub}(B)$. It maps a subobject $t\colon T \rightarrowtail B$ to the subobject of A given by the image of $f \cdot t$; in symbols we have $\overrightarrow{f}(t) \leq s$ iff $t \leq \overleftarrow{f}(s)$.*

Remark 2.12. If $\mathscr{A}$ is a complete and well-powered category, then $\mathsf{Sub}(A)$ is a complete lattice. Now suppose that $\mathscr{A}$ has smooth monomorphisms.

(1) In this setting, the unique morphism $\perp_A\colon 0 \to A$ is a monomorphism and therefore is the bottom element of the poset $\mathsf{Sub}(A)$.

(2) Furthermore, a join of a chain in $\mathsf{Sub}(A)$ is obtained by forming a colimit, in the obvious way.

(3) If $\mathscr{A}$ has universally smooth monomorphisms, then for every morphism $f\colon A \to B$, the operator $\overleftarrow{f}\colon \mathsf{Sub}(B) \to \mathsf{Sub}(A)$ preserves unions of chains.

Remark 2.13. Recall [1] that every endofunctor F yields the *initial-algebra chain*, viz. a transfinite chain formed by the objects $F^i 0$ of $\mathscr{A}$, as follows: $F^0 0 = 0$, the initial object; $F^{i+1} 0 = F(F^i 0)$, and for a limit ordinal i we take the colimit of the chain $(F^j 0)_{j<i}$. The connecting morphisms $w_{i,j}\colon F^i 0 \to F^j 0$ are defined by a similar transfinite recursion.

3   Recursive Coalgebras

Assumption 3.1. We work with a standard set theory (e.g. Zermelo-Fraenkel), assuming the Axiom of Choice. In particular, we use transfinite induction on several occasions. (We are not concerned with constructive foundations in this paper.)

Throughout this paper we assume that $\mathscr{A}$ is a complete and well-powered category $\mathscr{A}$ and that $F\colon \mathscr{A} \to \mathscr{A}$ preserves monomorphisms.

For $\mathscr{A} = \mathsf{Set}$ the condition that F preserves monomorphisms may be dropped. In fact, preservation of non-empty monomorphism is sufficient in general (for a suitable notion of non-empty monomorphism) [21, Lemma 2.5], and this holds for every set functor.

The following definition of recursive coalgebras was first given by Osius [22]. Taylor [24] speaks of *coalgebras obeying the recursion scheme*. Capretta et al. [10] extended the concept to *parametrically recursive* coalgebra by dualizing completely iterative algebras [20].

Definition 3.2. A coalgebra $\alpha\colon A \to FA$ is called *recursive* if for every algebra $e\colon FX \to X$ there exists a unique coalgebra-to-algebra morphism $e^\dagger\colon A \to X$, i.e. a unique morphism such that the square on the left below commutes:

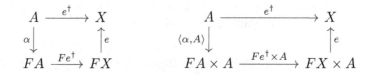

(A, α) is called *parametrically recursive* if for every morphism $e\colon FX \times A \to X$ there is a unique morphism $e^\dagger\colon A \to X$ such that the square on the right above commutes.

Example 3.3. (1) A graph regarded as a coalgebra for $\mathscr{P}$ is recursive iff it has no infinite path. This is an immediate consequence of the General Recursion Theorem (see Corollary 5.6 and Example 4.5(2)).

(2) Let $\iota\colon F(\mu F) \to \mu F$ be an initial algebra. By Lambek's Lemma, ι is an isomorphism. So we have a coalgebra $\iota^{-1}\colon \mu F \to F(\mu F)$. This algebra is (parametrically) recursive. By [20, Thm. 2.8], in dual form, this is precisely the same as the terminal parametrically recursive coalgebra (see also [10, Prop. 7]).

(3) The initial coalgebra $0 \to F0$ is recursive.

(4) If (C, γ) is recursive so is $(FC, F\gamma)$, see [10, Prop. 6].

(5) Colimits of recursive coalgebras in $\mathsf{Coalg}\,F$ are recursive. This is easy to prove, using that colimits of coalgebras are formed on the level of the underlying category.

(6) It follows from items (3)–(5) that in the initial-algebra chain from Remark 2.13 all coalgebras $w_{i,i+1}\colon F^i0 \to F^{i+1}0$, $i \in \mathsf{Ord}$, are recursive.

(7) Every parametrically recursive coalgebra is recursive. (To see this, form for a given $e\colon FX \to X$ the morphism $e' = e \cdot \pi$, where $\pi\colon FX \times A \to FX$ is the projection.) In Corollaries 5.6 and 5.9 we will see that the converse often holds.

Here is an example where the converse fails [3]. Let $R\colon \mathsf{Set} \to \mathsf{Set}$ be the functor defined in Example 2.2(4). Also, let $C = \{0, 1\}$, and define $\gamma\colon C \to RC$ by $\gamma(0) = \gamma(1) = (0, 1)$. Then (C, γ) is a recursive coalgebra. Indeed, for every algebra $\alpha\colon RA \to A$ the constant map $h\colon C \to A$ with $h(0) = h(1) = \alpha(d)$ is the unique coalgebra-to-algebra morphism.

However, (C, γ) is not parametrically recursive. To see this, consider any morphism $e\colon RX \times \{0, 1\} \to X$ such that RX contains more than one pair (x_0, x_1), $x_0 \neq x_1$ with $e((x_0, x_1), i) = x_i$ for $i = 0, 1$. Then each such pair yields $h\colon C \to X$ with $h(i) = x_i$ making the appropriate square commutative. Thus, (C, γ) is not parametrically recursive.

(8) Capretta et al. [11] showed that recursivity semantically models divide-and-conquer programs, as demonstrated by the example of Quicksort. For every linearly ordered set A (of data elements), Quicksort is usually defined as the recursive function $q\colon A^* \to A^*$ given by

$$q(\varepsilon) = \varepsilon \qquad \text{and} \qquad q(aw) = q(w_{\leq a}) \star (aq(w_{>a})),$$

where A^* is the set of all lists on A, ε is the empty list, $\star$ is the concatenation of lists and $w_{\leq a}$ denotes the list of those elements of w which are less than or equal than a; analogously for $w_{>a}$.

Now consider the functor $FX = 1 + A \times X \times X$ on Set, where $1 = \{\bullet\}$, and form the coalgebra $s\colon A^* \to 1 + A \times A^* \times A^*$ given by

$$s(\varepsilon) = \bullet \qquad \text{and} \qquad s(aw) = (a, w_{\leq a}, w_{>a}) \qquad \text{for } a \in A \text{ and } w \in A^*.$$

We shall see that this coalgebra is recursive in Example 5.3. Thus, for the F-algebra $m : 1 + A \times A^* \times A^* \to A^*$ given by

$$m(\bullet) = \varepsilon \qquad \text{and} \qquad m(a, w, v) = w \star (av)$$

there exists a unique function q on A^* such that $q = m \cdot Fq \cdot s$. Notice that the last equation reflects the idea that Quicksort is a divide-and-conquer algorithm. The coalgebra structure s divides a list into two parts $w_{\leq a}$ and $w_{>a}$. Then Fq sorts these two smaller lists, and finally in the combine- (or conquer-) step, the algebra structure m merges the two sorted parts to obtain the desired whole sorted list.

Jeannin et al. [15, Sec. 4] provide a number of recursive functions arising in programming that are determined by recursivity of a coalgebra, e.g. the gcd of integers, the Ackermann function, and the Towers of Hanoi.

4 The Next Time Operator and Well-Founded Coalgebras

As we have mentioned in the Introduction, the main issue of this paper is the relationship between two concepts pertaining to coalgebras: recursiveness and well-foundedness. The concept of well-foundedness is well-known for directed graphs $(G, \rightarrow)$: it means that there are no infinite directed paths $g_0 \rightarrow g_1 \rightarrow \cdots$. For a set X with a relation R, well-foundedness means that there are no *backwards* sequences $\cdots R\, x_2\, R\, x_1\, R\, x_0$, i.e. the converse of the relation is well-founded as a graph. Taylor [24, Def. 6.2.3] gave a more general category theoretic formulation of well-foundedness. We observe here that his definition can be presented in a compact way, by using an operator that generalizes the way one thinks of the semantics of the 'next time' operator of temporal logics for non-deterministic (or even probabilistic) automata and transitions systems. It is also strongly related to the algebraic semantics of modal logic, where one passes from a graph G to a function on $\mathscr{P}G$. Jacobs [14] defined and studied the 'next time' operator on coalgebras for Kripke polynomial set functors. This can be generalized to arbitrary functors as follows.

Recall that $\mathsf{Sub}(A)$ denotes the complete lattice of subobjects of A.

Definition 4.1 [4, Def. 8.9]. Every coalgebra $\alpha \colon A \rightarrow FA$ induces an endofunction on $\mathsf{Sub}(A)$, called the *next time operator*

$$\bigcirc \colon \mathsf{Sub}(A) \rightarrow \mathsf{Sub}(A), \qquad \bigcirc(s) = \overleftarrow{\alpha}(Fs) \quad \text{for } s \in \mathsf{Sub}(A).$$

In more detail: we define $\bigcirc s$ and $\alpha(s)$ by the pullback in (4.1). (Being a pullback is indicated by the "corner" symbol.) In words, $\bigcirc$ assigns to each subobject $s \colon S \rightarrowtail A$ the inverse image of Fs under α. Since Fs is a monomorphism, $\bigcirc s$ is a monomorphism and $\alpha(s)$ is (for every representation $\bigcirc s$ of that subobject of A) uniquely determined.

$$\begin{array}{ccc} \bigcirc S & \xrightarrow{\ \alpha(s)\ } & FS \\ {\scriptstyle \bigcirc s}\downarrow & \lrcorner & \downarrow{\scriptstyle Fs} \\ A & \xrightarrow{\ \alpha\ } & FA \end{array} \quad (4.1)$$

Example 4.2. (1) Let A be a graph, considered as a coalgebra for $\mathscr{P} \colon \mathsf{Set} \rightarrow \mathsf{Set}$. If $S \subseteq A$ is a set of vertices, then $\bigcirc S$ is the set of vertices all of whose successors belong to S.

(2) For the set functor $FX = \mathscr{P}(\Sigma \times X)$ expressing labelled transition systems the operator $\bigcirc$ for a coalgebra $\alpha \colon A \rightarrow \mathscr{P}(\Sigma \times A)$ is the semantic counterpart of the next time operator of classical linear temporal logic, see e.g. Manna and Pnüeli [18]. In fact, for a subset $S \hookrightarrow A$ we have that $\bigcirc S$ consists of those states all of whose next states lie in S, in symbols:

$$\bigcirc S = \big\{ x \in A \mid (s, y) \in \alpha(x) \text{ implies } y \in S, \text{ for all } s \in \Sigma \big\}.$$

The next time operator allows a compact definition of well-foundedness as characterized by Taylor [24, Exercise VI.17] (see also [6, Corollary 2.19]):

Definition 4.3. A coalgebra is *well-founded* if id_A is the only fixed point of its next time operator.

Remark 4.4. (1) Let us call a subcoalgebra $m \colon (B, \beta) \rightarrowtail (A, \alpha)$ *cartesian* provided that the square (4.2) is a pullback. Then (A, α) is well-founded iff it has no proper cartesian subcoalgebra. That is, if $m \colon (B, \beta) \rightarrowtail (A, \alpha)$ is a cartesian subcoalgebra, then m is an isomorphism. Indeed, the fixed points of next time are precisely the

$$\begin{array}{ccc} B & \xrightarrow{\ \beta\ } & FB \\ {\scriptstyle m}\downarrow & \lrcorner & \downarrow{\scriptstyle Fm} \\ A & \xrightarrow{\ \alpha\ } & FA \end{array} \quad (4.2)$$

cartesian subcoalgebras.

(2) A coalgebra is well-founded iff $\bigcirc$ has a unique pre-fixed point $\bigcirc m \leq m$. Indeed, since $\mathsf{Sub}(A)$ is a complete lattice, the least fixed point of a monotone map is its least pre-fixed point. Taylor's definition [24, Def. 6.3.2] uses that property: he calls a coalgebra well-founded iff $\bigcirc$ has no proper subobject as a pre-fixed point.

Example 4.5. (1) Consider a graph as a coalgebra $\alpha \colon A \to \mathscr{P}A$ for the power-set functor (see Example 2.1). A subcoalgebra is a subset $m \colon B \hookrightarrow A$ such that with every vertex v it contains all neighbors of v. The coalgebra structure $\beta \colon B \to \mathscr{P}B$ is then the domain-codomain restriction of α. To say that B is a cartesian subcoalgebra means that whenever a vertex of A has all neighbors in B, it also lies in B. It follows that (A, α) is well-founded iff it has no infinite directed path, see [24, Example 6.3.3].

(2) If μF exists, then as a coalgebra it is well-founded. Indeed, in every pull-back (4.2), since ι^{-1} (as α) is invertible, so is β. The unique algebra homomorphism from μF to the algebra $\beta^{-1} \colon FB \to B$ is clearly inverse to m.

(3) If a set functor F fulfils $F\emptyset = \emptyset$, then the only well-founded coalgebra is the empty one. Indeed, this follows from the fact that the empty coalgebra is a fixed point of $\bigcirc$. For example, a deterministic automaton over the input alphabet Σ, as a coalgebra for $FX = \{0, 1\} \times X^{\Sigma}$, is well-founded iff it is empty.

(4) A non-deterministic automaton may be considered as a coalgebra for the set functor $FX = \{0, 1\} \times (\mathscr{P}X)^{\Sigma}$. It is well-founded iff the state transition graph is well-founded (i.e. has no infinite path). This follows from Corollary 4.10 below.

(5) A linear weighted automaton, i.e. a coalgebra for $FX = K \times X^{\Sigma}$ on Vec_K, is well-founded iff every path in its state transition graph eventually leads to 0. This means that every path starting in a given state leads to the state 0 after finitely many steps (where it stays).

Notation 4.6. Given a set functor F, we define for every set X the map $\tau_X \colon FX \to \mathscr{P}X$ assigning to every element $x \in FX$ the intersection of all subsets $m \colon M \hookrightarrow X$ such that x lies in the image of Fm:

$$\tau_X(x) = \bigcap \{m \mid m \colon M \hookrightarrow X \text{ satisfies } x \in Fm[FM]\}. \tag{4.3}$$

Recall that a functor *preserves intersections* if it preserves (wide) pullbacks of families of monomorphisms.

Gumm [13, Thm. 7.3] observed that for a set functor preserving intersections, the maps $\tau_X \colon FX \to \mathscr{P}X$ in (4.3) form a "subnatural" transformation from F to the power-set functor $\mathscr{P}$. Subnaturality means that (although these maps do not form a natural transformation in general) for every monomorphism $i \colon X \to Y$ we have a commutative square:

$$\begin{array}{ccc} FX & \xrightarrow{\tau_X} & \mathscr{P}X \\ {\scriptstyle Fi} \uparrow & & \uparrow {\scriptstyle \mathscr{P}i} \\ FY & \xrightarrow{\tau_Y} & \mathscr{P}Y \end{array} \tag{4.4}$$

Remark 4.7. As shown in [13, Thm. 7.4] and [23, Prop. 7.5], a set functor F preserves intersections iff the squares in (4.4) above are pullbacks. Moreover, *loc. cit.* and [13, Thm. 8.1] prove that $\tau \colon F \to \mathscr{P}$ is a natural transformation, provided F preserves inverse images and intersections.

Definition 4.8. Let F be a set functor. For every coalgebra $\alpha \colon A \to FA$ its *canonical graph* is the following coalgebra for $\mathscr{P} \colon A \xrightarrow{\alpha} FA \xrightarrow{\tau_A} \mathscr{P}A$.

Thanks to the subnaturality of τ one obtains the following results.

Proposition 4.9. *For every set functor F preserving intersections, the next time operator of a coalgebra (A, α) coincides with that of its canonical graph.*

Corollary 4.10 [24, Rem. 6.3.4]. *A coalgebra for a set functor preserving intersections is well-founded iff its canonical graph is well-founded.*

Example 4.11. (1) For a (deterministic or non-deterministic) automaton, the canonical graph has an edge from s to t iff there is a transition from s to t for some input letter. Thus, we obtain the characterization of well-foundedness as stated in Example 4.5(3) and (4).

(2) Every polynomial functor $H_\Sigma \colon \mathsf{Set} \to \mathsf{Set}$ preserves intersections. Thus, a coalgebra (A, α) is well-founded if there are no infinite paths in its canonical graph. The canonical graph of A has an edge from a to b if $\alpha(a)$ is of the form $\sigma(c_1, \ldots, c_n)$ for some $\sigma \in \Sigma_n$ and if b is one of the c_i's.

(3) Thus, for the functor $FX = 1 + A \times X \times X$, the coalgebra (A^*, s) of Example 3.3(8) is easily seen to be well-founded via its canonical graph. Indeed, this graph has for every list w one outgoing edge to the list $w_{\leq a}$ and one to $w_{>a}$ for every $a \in A$. Hence, this is a well-founded graph.

Lemma 4.12. *The next time operator is monotone: if $m \leq n$, then $\bigcirc m \leq \bigcirc n$.*

Lemma 4.13. *Let $\alpha \colon A \to FA$ be a coalgebra and $m \colon B \rightarrowtail A$ a subobject.*

(1) *There is a coalgebra structure $\beta \colon B \to FB$ for which m gives a subcoalgebra of (A, α) iff $m \leq \bigcirc m$.*

(2) *There is a coalgebra structure $\beta \colon B \to FB$ for which m gives a cartesian subcoalgebra of (A, α) iff $m = \bigcirc m$.*

Lemma 4.14. *For every coalgebra homomorphism $f \colon (B, \beta) \to (A, \alpha)$ we have*

$$\bigcirc_\beta \cdot \overleftarrow{f} \leq \overleftarrow{f} \cdot \bigcirc_\alpha,$$

where $\bigcirc_\alpha$ and $\bigcirc_\beta$ denote the next time operators of the coalgebras (A, α) and (B, β), respectively, and $\leq$ is the pointwise order.

Corollary 4.15. *For every coalgebra homomorphism $f \colon (B, \beta) \to (A, \alpha)$ we have $\bigcirc_\beta \cdot \overleftarrow{f} = \overleftarrow{f} \cdot \bigcirc_\alpha$, provided that either*

(1) f is a monomorphism in $\mathscr{A}$ and F preserves finite intersections, or

(2) F preserves inverse images.

Definition 4.16 [4]. The *well-founded part* of a coalgebra is its largest well-founded subcoalgebra.

The well-founded part of a coalgebra always exists and is the coreflection in the category of well-founded coalgebras [6, Prop. 2.27]. We provide a new, shorter proof of this fact. The well-founded part is obtained by the following:

Construction 4.17 [6, Not. 2.22]. Let $\alpha\colon A \to FA$ be a coalgebra. We know that $\mathsf{Sub}(A)$ is a complete lattice and that the next time operator $\bigcirc$ is monotone (see Lemma 4.12). Hence, by the Knaster-Tarski fixed point theorem, $\bigcirc$ has a least fixed point, which we denote by $a^*\colon A^* \rightarrowtail A$.

By Lemma 4.13(2), we know that there is a coalgebra structure $\alpha^*\colon A^* \to FA^*$ so that $a^*\colon (A^*, \alpha^*) \rightarrowtail (A, \alpha)$ is the smallest cartesian subcoalgebra of (A, α).

Proposition 4.18. *For every coalgebra* (A, α), *the coalgebra* (A^*, α^*) *is well-founded.*

Proof. Let $m\colon (B, \beta) \rightarrowtail (A^*, \alpha^*)$ be a cartesian subcoalgebra. By Lemma 4.13, $a^* \cdot m\colon B \to A$ is a fixed point of $\bigcirc$. Since a^* is the least fixed point, we have $a^* \leq a^* \cdot m$, i.e. $a^* = a^* \cdot m \cdot x$ for some $x\colon A^* \rightarrowtail B$. Since a^* is monic, we thus have $m \cdot x = id_{A^*}$. So m is a monomorphism and a split epimorphism, whence an isomorphism. $\square$

Proposition 4.19. *The full subcategory of* $\mathsf{Coalg}\, F$ *given by well-founded coalgebras is coreflective. In fact, the well-founded coreflection of a coalgebra* (A, α) *is its well-founded part* $a^*\colon (A^*, \alpha^*) \rightarrowtail (A, \alpha)$.

Proof. We are to prove that for every coalgebra homomorphism $f\colon (B, \beta) \to (A, \alpha)$, where (B, β) is well-founded, there exists a coalgebra homomorphism $f^\sharp\colon (B, \beta) \to (A^*, \alpha^*)$ such that $a^* \cdot f^\sharp = f$. The uniqueness is easy.

For the existence of $f^\sharp$, we first observe that $\overleftarrow{f}(a^*)$ is a pre-fixed point of $\bigcirc_\beta$: indeed, using Lemma 4.14 we have $\bigcirc_\beta(\overleftarrow{f}(a^*)) \leq \overleftarrow{f}(\bigcirc_\alpha(a^*)) = \overleftarrow{f}(a^*)$. By Remark 4.4(2), we therefore have $id_B = b^* \leq \overleftarrow{f}(a^*)$ in $\mathsf{Sub}(B)$. Using the adjunction of Lemma 2.11, we have $\overrightarrow{f}(id_B) \leq a^*$ in $\mathsf{Sub}(A)$. Now factorize f as $B \xrightarrow{e} C \xrightarrow{m} A$. We have $\overrightarrow{f}(id_B) = m$, and we then obtain $m = \overrightarrow{f}(id_B) \leq a^*$, i.e. there exists a morphism $h\colon C \rightarrowtail A^*$ such that $a^* \cdot h = m$. Thus, $f^\sharp = h \cdot e\colon B \to A^*$ is a morphism satisfying $a^* \cdot f^\sharp = a^* \cdot h \cdot e = m \cdot e = f$. It follows that $f^\sharp$ is a coalgebra homomorphism from (B, β) to (A^*, α^*) since f and a^* are and F preserves monomorphisms. $\square$

Construction 4.20 [6, Not. 2.22]. Let (A, α) be a coalgebra. We obtain a^*, the least fixed point of $\bigcirc$, as the join of the following transfinite chain of subobjects $a_i\colon A_i \rightarrowtail A$, $i \in \mathsf{Ord}$. First, put $a_0 = \bot_A$, the least subobject of A. Given $a_i\colon A_i \rightarrowtail A$, put $a_{i+1} = \bigcirc a_i\colon A_{i+1} = \bigcirc A_i \rightarrowtail A$. For every limit ordinal j, put $a_j = \bigvee_{i<j} a_i$. Since $\mathsf{Sub}(A)$ is a set, there exists an ordinal i such that $a_i = a^*\colon A^* \rightarrowtail A$.

Remark 4.21. Note that, whenever monomorphisms are smooth, we have $A_0 = 0$ and the above join a_j is obtained as the colimit of the chain of the subobject $a_i \colon A_i \rightarrowtail A$, $i < j$ (see Remark 2.12).

If F is a finitary functor on a locally finitely presentable category, then the least ordinal i with $a^* = a_i$ is at most ω, but in general one needs transfinite iteration to reach a fixed point.

Example 4.22. Let (A, α) be a graph regarded as a coalgebra for $\mathscr{P}$ (see Example 2.1). Then $A_0 = \emptyset$, A_1 is formed by all leaves; i.e. those nodes with no neighbors, A_2 by all leaves and all nodes such that every neighbor is a leaf, etc. We see that a node x lies in A_{i+1} iff every path starting in x has length at most i. Hence $A^* = A_\omega$ is the set of all nodes from which no infinite paths start.

We close with a general fact on well-founded parts of *fixed points* (i.e. (co)algebras whose structure is invertible). The following result generalizes [15, Cor. 3.4], and it also appeared before for functors preserving finite intersections [4, Theorem 8.16 and Remark 8.18]. Here we lift the latter assumption (see [5, Theorem 7.6] for the new proof):

Theorem 4.23. *Let $\mathscr{A}$ be a complete and well-powered category with smooth monomorphisms. For F preserving monomorphisms, the well-founded part of every fixed point is an initial algebra. In particular, the only well-founded fixed point is the initial algebra.*

Example 4.24. We illustrate that for a set functor F preserving monomorphisms, the well-founded part of the terminal coalgebra is the initial algebra. Consider $FX = A \times X + 1$. The terminal coalgebra is the set $A^\infty \cup A^*$ of finite and infinite sequences from the set A. The initial algebra is A^*. It is easy to check that A^* is the well-founded part of $A^\infty \cup A^*$.

5   The General Recursion Theorem and its Converse

The main consequence of well-foundedness is parametric recursivity. This is Taylor's General Recursion Theorem [24, Theorem 6.3.13]. Taylor assumed that F preserves inverse images. We present a new proof for which it is sufficient that F preserves monomorphisms, assuming those are smooth.

Theorem 5.1 (General Recursion Theorem). *Let $\mathscr{A}$ be a complete and wellpowered category with smooth monomorphisms. For $F\colon \mathscr{A} \to \mathscr{A}$ preserving monomorphisms, every well-founded coalgebra is parametrically recursive.*

Proof sketch. (1) Let (A, α) be well-founded. We first prove that it is recursive. We use the subobjects $a_i \colon A_i \rightarrowtail A$ of Construction 4.20[4], the corresponding

---

[4] One might object to this use of transfinite recursion, since Theorem 5.1 itself could be used as a justification for transfinite recursion. Let us emphasize that we are not presenting Theorem 5.1 as a foundational contribution. We are building on the classical theory of transfinite recursion.

morphisms $\alpha(a_i)\colon A_{i+1} = \bigcirc A_i \to FA_i$ (cf. Definition 4.3), and the recursive coalgebras $(F^i 0, w_{i,i+1})$ of Example 3.3(6). We obtain a natural transformation h from the chain (A_i) in Construction 4.20 to the initial-algebra chain $(F^i 0)$ (see Remark 2.13) by transfinite recursion.

Now for every algebra $e\colon FX \to X$, we obtain a unique coalgebra-to-algebra morphism $f_i\colon F^i 0 \to X$, i.e. we have that $f_i = e \cdot Ff_i \cdot w_{i,i+1}$. Since (A, α) is well-founded, we know that $\alpha = \alpha^* = \alpha(a_i)$ for some i. From this it is not difficult to prove that $f_i \cdot h_i$ is a coalgebra-to-algebra morphism from (A, α) to (X, e).

In order to prove uniqueness, we prove by transfinite induction that for any given coalgebra-to-algebra homomorphism $e^\dagger$, one has $e^\dagger \cdot a_j = f_j \cdot h_j \cdot a_j$ for every ordinal number j. Then for the above ordinal number i with $a_i = id_A$, we have $e^\dagger = f_i \cdot h_i$, as desired. This shows that (A, α) is recursive.

(2) We prove that (A, α) is parametrically recursive. Consider the coalgebra $\langle \alpha, id_A \rangle \colon A \to FA \times A$ for $F(-) \times A$. This functor preserves monomorphisms since F does and monomorphisms are closed under products. The next time operator $\bigcirc$ on $\mathsf{Sub}(A)$ is the same for both coalgebras since the square (4.1) is a pullback if and only if the square on the right below is one.

Since id_A is the unique fixed point of $\bigcirc$ w.r.t. F (see Definition 4.3), it is also the unique fixed point of $\bigcirc$ w.r.t. $F(-) \times A$. Thus, $(A, \langle \alpha, id_A \rangle)$ is a well-founded coalgebra for $F(-) \times A$. By the previous argument, this coalgebra is thus recursive for

$$
\begin{array}{ccc}
\bigcirc S & \xrightarrow{\langle \alpha(m), \bigcirc m \rangle} & FS \times A \\
{\scriptstyle \bigcirc m} \downarrow \quad {\scriptstyle \lrcorner} & & \downarrow {\scriptstyle Fm \times A} \\
A & \xrightarrow{\langle \alpha, A \rangle} & FA \times A
\end{array}
$$

$F(-) \times A$; equivalently, (A, α) is parametrically recursive for F. $\qquad \square$

Theorem 5.2. *For every endofunctor on* Set *or* Vec_K *(vector spaces and linear maps), every well-founded coalgebra is parametrically recursive.*

Proof sketch. For Set, we apply Theorem 5.1 to the Trnková hull $\bar{F}$ (see Proposition 2.3), noting that F and $\bar{F}$ have the same (non-empty) coalgebras. Moreover, one can show that every well-founded (or recursive) F-coalgebra is a well-founded (recursive, resp.) $\bar{F}$-coalgebra. For Vec_K, observe that monomorphisms split and are therefore preserved by every endofunctor F. $\qquad \square$

Example 5.3. We saw in Example 4.11(3) that for $FX = 1 + A \times X \times X$ the coalgebra (A, s) from Example 3.3(8) is well-founded, and therefore it is (parametrically) recursive.

Example 5.4. Well-founded coalgebras need not be recursive when F does not preserve monomorphisms. We take $\mathscr{A}$ to be the category of *sets with a predicate*, i.e. pairs (X, A), where $A \subseteq X$. Morphisms $f\colon (X, A) \to (Y, B)$ satisfy $f[A] \subseteq B$. Denote by $\mathbb{1}$ the terminal object $(1, 1)$. We define an endofunctor F by $F(X, \emptyset) = (X + 1, \emptyset)$, and for $A \neq \emptyset$, $F(X, A) = \mathbb{1}$. For a morphism $f\colon (X, A) \to (Y, B)$, put $Ff = f + id$ if $A = \emptyset$; if $A \neq \emptyset$, then also $B \neq \emptyset$ and Ff is $id\colon \mathbb{1} \to \mathbb{1}$.

The terminal coalgebra is $id: \mathbb{1} \to \mathbb{1}$, and it is easy to see that it is well-founded. But it is not recursive: there are no coalgebra-to-algebra morphisms into an algebra of the form $F(X, \emptyset) \to (X, \emptyset)$.

We next prove a converse to Theorem 5.1: "recursive $\implies$ well-founded". Related results appear in Taylor [23, 24], Adámek et al. [3] and Jeannin et al. [15].

Recall universally smooth monomorphisms from Definition 2.8(2). A *pre-fixed point* of F is a monic algebra $\alpha: FA \rightarrowtail A$.

Theorem 5.5. *Let $\mathscr{A}$ be a complete and wellpowered category with universally smooth monomorphisms, and suppose that $F: \mathscr{A} \to \mathscr{A}$ preserves inverse images and has a pre-fixed point. Then every recursive coalgebra is well-founded.*

Proof. (1) We first observe that an initial algebra exists. This follows from results by Trnková et al. [25] as we now briefly recall. Recall the initial-algebra chain from Remark 2.13. Let $\beta: FB \rightarrowtail B$ be a pre-fixed point. Then there is a unique cocone $\beta_i: F^i 0 \to B$ satisfying $\beta_{i+1} = \beta \cdot F\beta_i$. Moreover, each β_i is monomorphic. Since B has only a set of subobjects, there is some λ such that for every $i > \lambda$, all of the morphisms β_i represent the same subobject of B. Consequently, $w_{\lambda, \lambda+1}$ of Remark 2.13 is an isomorphism, due to $\beta_\lambda = \beta_{\lambda+1} \cdot w_{\lambda, \lambda+1}$. Then $\mu F = F^\lambda 0$ with the structure $\iota = w_{\lambda, \lambda+1}^{-1}: F(\mu F) \to \mu F$ is an initial algebra.

(2) Now suppose that (A, α) is a recursive coalgebra. Then there exists a unique coalgebra homomorphism $h: (A, \alpha) \to (\mu F, \iota^{-1})$. Let us abbreviate $w_{i\lambda}$ by $c_i: F^i 0 \rightarrowtail \mu F$, and recall the subobjects $a_i: A_i \rightarrowtail A$ from Construction 4.20. We will prove by transfinite induction that a_i is the inverse image of c_i under h; in symbols: $a_i = \overleftarrow{h}(c_i)$ for all ordinals i. Then it follows that a_λ is an isomorphism, since so is c_λ, whence (A, α) is well-founded.

In the base case $i = 0$ this is clear since $A_0 = W_0 = 0$ is a strict initial object.

For the isolated step we compute the pullback of $c_{i+1}: W_{i+1} \to \mu F$ along h using the following diagram:

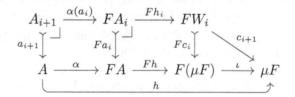

By the induction hypothesis and since F preserves inverse images, the middle square above is a pullback. Since the structure map ι of the initial algebra is an isomorphism, it follows that the middle square pasted with the right-hand triangle is also a pullback. Finally, the left-hand square is a pullback by the definition of a_{i+1}. Thus, the outside of the above diagram is a pullback, as required.

For a limit ordinal j, we know that $a_j = \bigvee_{i<j} a_i$ and similarly, $c_j = \bigvee_{i<j} c_i$ since $W_j = \text{colim}_{i<j} W_j$ and monomorphisms are smooth (see Remark 2.12(2)). Using Remark 2.12(3) and the induction hypothesis we thus obtain $\overleftarrow{h}(c_j) = \overleftarrow{h}\left(\bigvee_{i<j} c_i\right) = \bigvee_{i<j} \overleftarrow{h}(c_i) = \bigvee_{i<j} a_i = a_j$. $\qquad\square$

Corollary 5.6. *Let $\mathscr{A}$ and F satisfy the assumptions of Theorem 5.5. Then the following properties of a coalgebra are equivalent:*

(1) *well-foundedness,*

(2) *parametric recursiveness,*

(3) *recursiveness,*

(4) *existence of a homomorphism into $(\mu F, \iota^{-1})$,*

(5) *existence of a homomorphism into a well-founded coalgebra.*

Proof sketch. We already know $(1) \Rightarrow (2) \Rightarrow (3)$. Since F has an initial algebra (as proved in Theorem 5.5), the implication $(3) \Rightarrow (4)$ follows from Example 3.3(2). In Theorem 5.5 we also proved $(4) \Rightarrow (1)$. The implication $(4) \Rightarrow (5)$ follows from Example 4.5(2). Finally, it follows from [6, Remark 2.40] that $(\mu F, \iota^{-1})$ is a terminal well-founded coalgebra, whence $(5) \Rightarrow (4)$. □

Example 5.7. (1) The category of many-sorted sets satisfies the assumptions of Theorem 5.5, and polynomial endofunctors on that category preserve inverse images. Thus, we obtain Jeannin et al.'s result [15, Thm. 3.3] that (1)–(4) in Corollary 5.6 are equivalent as a special instance.

(2) The implication $(4) \Rightarrow (3)$ in Corollary 5.6 does not hold for vector spaces. In fact, for the identity functor on Vec_K we have $\mu Id = (0, id)$. Hence, every coalgebra has a homomorphism into μId. However, not every coalgebra is recursive, e.g. the coalgebra (K, id) admits many coalgebra-to-algebra morphisms to the algebra (K, id). Similarly, the implication $(4) \Rightarrow (1)$ does not hold.

We also wish to mention a result due to Taylor [23, Rem. 3.8]. It uses the concept of a *subobject classifier* originating in [17] and prominent in topos theory. This is an object Ω with a subobject $t \colon 1 \rightarrowtail \Omega$ such that for every subobject $b \colon B \rightarrowtail A$ there is a unique $\hat{b} \colon A \to \Omega$ such that b is the inverse image of t under $\hat{b}$. By definition, every elementary topos has a subobject classifier, in particular every category $\mathsf{Set}^{\mathscr{C}}$ with $\mathscr{C}$ small.

Our standing assumption that $\mathscr{A}$ is a complete and well-powered category is not needed for the next result: finite limits are sufficient.

Theorem 5.8 (Taylor [23]). *Let F be an endofunctor preserving inverse images on a finitely complete category with a subobject classifier. Then every recursive coalgebra is well-founded.*

Corollary 5.9. *For every set functor preserving inverse images, the following properties of a coalgebra are equivalent:*

$$\text{well-foundedness} \iff \text{parametric recursiveness} \iff \text{recursiveness}.$$

Example 5.10. The hypothesis in Theorems 5.5 and 5.8 that the functor preserves inverse images cannot be lifted. In order to see this, we consider the functor $R \colon \mathsf{Set} \to \mathsf{Set}$ of Example 2.2(4). It preserves monomorphisms but not inverse images. The coalgebra $A = \{0, 1\}$ with the structure α constant to $(0, 1)$ is recursive: given an algebra $\beta \colon RB \to B$, the unique coalgebra-to-algebra homomorphism $h\colon \{0,1\} \to B$ is given by $h(0) = h(1) = \beta(d)$. But A is not well-founded: $\emptyset$ is a cartesian subcoalgebra.

Recall that an initial algebra $(\mu F, \iota)$ is also considered as a coalgebra $(\mu F, \iota^{-1})$. Taylor [23, Cor. 9.9] showed that, for functors preserving inverse images, the terminal well-founded coalgebra is the initial algebra. Surprisingly, this result is true for *all* set functors.

Theorem 5.11 [6, Thm. 2.46]. *For every set functor, a terminal well-founded coalgebra is precisely an initial algebra.*

Theorem 5.12. *For every functor on* Vec_K *preserving inverse images, the following properties of a coalgebra are equivalent:*

$$\text{well-foundedness} \iff \text{parametric recursiveness} \iff \text{recursiveness}.$$

6   Closure Properties of Well-founded Coalgebras

In this section we will see that strong quotients and subcoalgebras (see Remark 2.7) of well-founded coalgebras are well-founded again. We mention the following corollary to Proposition 4.19. For endofunctors on sets preserving inverse images this was stated by Taylor [24, Exercise VI.16]:

Proposition 6.1. *The subcategory of* $\mathsf{Coalg}\, F$ *formed by all well-founded coalgebras is closed under strong quotients and coproducts in* $\mathsf{Coalg}\, F$.

This follows from a general result on coreflective subcategories [2, Thm. 16.8]: the category $\mathsf{Coalg}\, F$ has the factorization system of Proposition 2.6, and its full subcategory of well-founded coalgebras is coreflective with monomorphic coreflections (see Proposition 4.19). Consequently, it is closed under strong quotients and colimits.

We prove next that, for an endofunctor preserving finite intersections, well-founded coalgebras are closed under subcoalgebras provided that the complete lattice $\mathsf{Sub}(A)$ is a *frame*. This means that for every subobject $m\colon B \rightarrowtail A$ and every family m_i $(i \in I)$ of subobjects of A we have $m \wedge \bigvee_{i \in I} m_i = \bigvee_{i \in I}(m \wedge m_i)$. Equivalently, $\overleftarrow{m}\colon \mathsf{Sub}(A) \to \mathsf{Sub}(B)$ (see Notation 2.10) has a right adjoint $m_*\colon \mathsf{Sub}(B) \to \mathsf{Sub}(A)$.

This property holds for Set as well as for the categories of posets, graphs, topological spaces, and presheaf categories $\mathsf{Set}^{\mathscr{C}}$, $\mathscr{C}$ small. Moreover, it holds for every Grothendieck topos. The categories of complete partial orders and Vec_K do not satisfy this requirement.

Proposition 6.2. *Suppose that F preserves finite intersections, and let (A, α) be a well-founded coalgebra such that $\mathsf{Sub}(A)$ a frame. Then every subcoalgebra of (A, α) is well-founded.*

Proof. Let $m\colon (B,\beta) \rightarrowtail (A,\alpha)$ be a subcoalgebra. We will show that the only pre-fixed point of $\bigcirc_\beta$ is id_B (cf. Remark 4.4(2)). Suppose $s\colon S \rightarrowtail B$ fulfils $\bigcirc_\beta(s) \leq s$. Since F preserves finite intersections, we have $\overleftarrow{m} \cdot \bigcirc_\alpha = \bigcirc_\beta \cdot \overleftarrow{m}$ by Corollary 4.15(1). The counit of the above adjunction $\overleftarrow{m} \dashv m_*$ yields $\overleftarrow{m}(m_*(s)) \leq s$, so that we obtain $\overleftarrow{m}(\bigcirc_\alpha(m_*(s))) = \bigcirc_\beta(\overleftarrow{m}(m_*(s))) \leq \bigcirc_\beta(s) \leq s$. Using again the adjunction $\overleftarrow{m} \dashv m_*$, we have equivalently that $\bigcirc_\alpha(m_*(s)) \leq m_*(s)$; i.e. $m_*(s)$ is a pre-fixed point of $\bigcirc_\alpha$. Since (A,α) is well-founded, Corollary 4.15(1) implies that $m_*(s) = id_A$. Since $\overleftarrow{m}$ is also a right adjoint and therefore preserves the top element of $\mathsf{Sub}(B)$, we thus obtain $id_B = \overleftarrow{m}(id_A) = \overleftarrow{m}(m_*(s)) \leq s$. $\quad\square$

Remark 6.3. Given a set functor F preserving inverse images, a much better result was proved by Taylor [24, Corollary 6.3.6]: for every coalgebra homomorphism $f\colon (B,\beta) \to (A,\alpha)$ with (A,α) well-founded so is (B,β). In fact, our proof above is essentially Taylor's.

Corollary 6.4. *If a set functor preserves finite intersections, then subcoalgebras of well-founded coalgebras are well-founded.*

Trnková [26] proved that every set functor preserves all *nonempty* finite intersections. However, this does not suffice for Corollary 6.4:

Example 6.5. A well-founded coalgebra for a set functor can have non-well-founded subcoalgebras. Let $F\emptyset = 1$ and $FX = 1+1$ for all nonempty sets X, and let $Ff = \mathsf{inl}\colon 1 \to 1+1$ be the left-hand injection for all maps $f\colon \emptyset \to X$ with X nonempty. The coalgebra $\mathsf{inr}\colon 1 \to F1$ is not well-founded because its empty subcoalgebra is cartesian. However, this is a subcoalgebra of $id\colon 1+1 \to 1+1$ (via the embedding inr), and the latter is well-founded.

The fact that subcoalgebras of a well-founded coalgebra are well-founded does not necessarily need the assumption that $\mathsf{Sub}(A)$ is a frame. Instead, one may assume that the class of morphisms is universally smooth:

Theorem 6.6. *If $\mathscr{A}$ has universally smooth monomorphisms and F preserves finite intersections, every subcoalgebra of a well-founded coalgebra is well-founded.*

7 Conclusions

Well-founded coalgebras introduced by Taylor [24] have a compact definition based on an extension of Jacobs' 'next time' operator. Our main contribution is a new proof of Taylor's General Recursion Theorem that every well-founded coalgebra is recursive, generalizing this result to all endofunctors preserving monomorphisms on a complete and well-powered category with smooth monomorphisms. For functors preserving inverse images, we also have seen two variants of the converse implication "recursive $\Rightarrow$ well-founded", under additional hypothesis: one due to Taylor for categories with a subobject classifier, and the second one provided that the category has universally smooth monomorphisms and the functor has a pre-fixed point. Various counterexamples demonstrate that all our hypotheses are necessary.

References

1. Adámek, J.: Free algebras and automata realizations in the language of categories. Comment. Math. Univ. Carolin. 15, 589–602 (1974)
2. Adámek, J., Herrlich, H., Strecker, G.E.: Abstract and Concrete Categories: The Joy of Cats. Dover Publications, 3rd edn. (2009)
3. Adámek, J., Lücke, D., Milius, S.: Recursive coalgebras of finitary functors. Theor. Inform. Appl. 41(4), 447–462 (2007)
4. Adámek, J., Milius, S., Moss, L.S.: Fixed points of functors. J. Log. Algebr. Methods Program. 95, 41–81 (2018)
5. Adámek, J., Milius, S., Moss, L.S.: On well-founded and recursive coalgebras (2019), full version; available online at http://arxiv.org/abs/1910.09401
6. Adámek, J., Milius, S., Moss, L.S., Sousa, L.: Well-pointed coalgebras. Log. Methods Comput. Sci. 9(2), 1–51 (2014)
7. Adámek, J., Milius, S., Sousa, L., Wißmann, T.: On finitary functors. Theor. Appl. Categ. 34, 1134–1164 (2019). available online at https://arxiv.org/abs/1902.05788
8. Adámek, J., Rosický, J.: Locally Presentable and Accessible Categories. Cambridge University Press (1994)
9. Borceux, F.: Handbook of Categorical Algebra: Volume 1, Basic Category Theory. Encyclopedia of Mathematics and its Applications, Cambridge University Press (1994)
10. Capretta, V., Uustalu, T., Vene, V.: Recursive coalgebras from comonads. Inform. and Comput. 204, 437–468 (2006)
11. Capretta, V., Uustalu, T., Vene, V.: Corecursive algebras: A study of general structured corecursion. In: Oliveira, M., Woodcock, J. (eds.) Formal Methods: Foundations and Applications, Lecture Notes in Computer Science, vol. 5902, pp. 84–100. Springer Berlin Heidelberg (2009)
12. Eppendahl, A.: Coalgebra-to-algebra morphisms. In: Proc. Category Theory and Computer Science (CTCS). Electron. Notes Theor. Comput. Sci., vol. 29, pp. 42–49 (1999)
13. Gumm, H.: From T-coalgebras to filter structures and transition systems. In: Fiadeiro, J.L., Harman, N., Roggenbach, M., Rutten, J. (eds.) Algebra and Coalgebra in Computer Science, Lecture Notes in Computer Science, vol. 3629, pp. 194–212. Springer Berlin Heidelberg (2005)
14. Jacobs, B.: The temporal logic of coalgebras via Galois algebras. Math. Structures Comput. Sci. 12(6), 875–903 (2002)
15. Jeannin, J.B., Kozen, D., Silva, A.: Well-founded coalgebras, revisited. Math. Structures Comput. Sci. 27, 1111–1131 (2017)
16. Kurz, A.: Logics for Coalgebras and Applications to Computer Science. Ph.D. thesis, Ludwig-Maximilians-Universität München (2000)
17. Lawvere, W.F.: Quantifiers and sheaves. Actes Congès Intern. Math. 1, 329–334 (1970)
18. Manna, Z., Pnüeli, A.: The Temporal Logic of Reactive and Concurrent Systems: Specification. Springer-Verlag (1992)
19. Meseguer, J., Goguen, J.A.: Initiality, induction, and computability. In: Algebraic methods in semantics (Fontainebleau, 1982), pp. 459–541. Cambridge Univ. Press, Cambridge (1985)
20. Milius, S.: Completely iterative algebras and completely iterative monads. Inform. and Comput. 196, 1–41 (2005)

21. Milius, S., Pattinson, D., Wißmann, T.: A new foundation for finitary corecursion and iterative algebras. Inform. and Comput. 217 (2020), available online at https://doi.org/10.1016/j.ic.2019.104456.

22. Osius, G.: Categorical set theory: a characterization of the category of sets. J. Pure Appl. Algebra 4(79–119) (1974)

23. Taylor, P.: Towards a unified treatment of induction I: the general recursion theorem (1995–6), preprint, available at www.paultaylor.eu/ordinals/#towuti

24. Taylor, P.: Practical Foundations of Mathematics. Cambridge University Press (1999)

25. Trnková, V., Adámek, J., Koubek, V., Reiterman, J.: Free algebras, input processes and free monads. Comment. Math. Univ. Carolin. 16, 339–351 (1975)

26. Trnková, V.: Some properties of set functors. Comment. Math. Univ. Carolin. 10, 323–352 (1969)

27. Trnková, V.: On a descriptive classification of set functors I. Comment. Math. Univ. Carolin. 12, 143–174 (1971)

5

Spinal Atomic Lambda-Calculus

David Sherratt[1] (✉), Willem Heijltjes[2], Tom Gundersen[3], and Michel Parigot[4]

[1] Friedrich-Schiller-Universität Jena, Germany.
david.rhys.sherratt@uni-jena.de
[2] University of Bath, United Kingdom.
w.b.heijltjes@bath.ac.uk
[3] Red Hat, Inc. Norway.
teg@jklm.no
[4] Institut de Recherche en Informatique Fondamentale, CNRS, Université de Paris. France.
parigot@irif.fr

Abstract. We present the spinal atomic λ-calculus, a typed λ-calculus with explicit sharing and atomic duplication that achieves spinal full laziness: duplicating only the direct paths between a binder and bound variables is enough for beta reduction to proceed. We show this calculus is the result of a Curry–Howard style interpretation of a deep-inference proof system, and prove that it has natural properties with respect to the λ-calculus: confluence and preservation of strong normalisation.

Keywords: Lambda-Calculus · Full laziness · Deep inference · Curry–Howard

1 Introduction

In the λ-calculus, a main source of efficiency is *sharing*: multiple use of a single subterm, commonly expressed through graph reduction [27] or explicit substitution [1]. This work, and the *atomic λ-calculus* [16] on which it builds, is an investigation into sharing as it occurs naturally in intuitionistic *deep-inference* proof theory [26]. The atomic λ-calculus arose as a Curry–Howard interpretation of a deep-inference proof system, in particular of the *distribution* rule given below left, a variant of the characteristic *medial* rule [10, 26]. In the term calculus, the corresponding *distributor* enables duplication to proceed *atomically*, on individual constructors, in the style of sharing graphs [21]. As a consequence, the natural reduction strategy in the atomic λ-calculus is *fully lazy* [27, 4]: it duplicates only the minimal part of a term, the *skeleton*, that can be obtained by lifting out subterms as explicit substitutions. (While duplication is atomic *locally*, a duplicated abstraction does not form a redex until also its bound variables have been duplicated; hence duplication becomes fully lazy *globally*.)

Distribution: $\dfrac{A \to (B \wedge C)}{(A \to B) \wedge (A \to C)} d$ \qquad Switch: $\dfrac{(A \to B) \wedge C}{A \to (B \wedge C)} s$

We investigate the computational interpretation of another characteristic deep-inference proof rule: the *switch* rule above right [26].[5] Our result is the *spinal atomic λ-calculus*, a λ-calculus with a refined form of full laziness, *spine duplication*. In the terminology of [4], this strategy duplicates only the *spine* of an abstraction: the paths to its bound variables in the syntax tree of the term.[6]

We illustrate these notions in Figure 1, for the example $\lambda x.\lambda y.((\lambda z.z)y)x$. The *scope* of the abstraction λx is the entire subterm, $\lambda y.((\lambda z.z)y)x$ (which may or may not be taken to include λx itself). Note that with explicit substitution, the scope may grow or shrink by lifting explicit substitutions in or out. The *skeleton* is the term $\lambda x.\lambda y.(wy)x$ where the subterm $\lambda z.z$ is lifted out as an (explicit) substitution $[\lambda z.z/w]$. The *spine* of a term, indicated in the second image, cannot naturally be expressed with explicit substitution, though one can get an impression with *capturing* substitutions: it would be $\lambda x.\lambda y.wx$, with the subterm $(\lambda z.z)y$ extracted by a capturing substitution $[(\lambda z.z)y/w]$. Observe that the skeleton can be described as the *iterated spine*: it is the smallest subgraph of the syntax tree closed under taking the spine of each abstraction, i.e. that contains the spine of every abstraction it contains.

These notions give rise to four natural duplication regimes. For a shared abstraction to become available as the function in a β-redex: *laziness* duplicates its *scope* [22]; *Full laziness* duplicates its *skeleton* [27]; *Spinal full laziness* duplicates its *spine* [8]; *optimal reduction* duplicates only the abstraction λx and its bound variables x [21, 3].[7]

While each of these duplication strategies has been expressed in graphs and labelled calculi, the atomic λ-calculus is the first term calculus with Curry–Howard corresponding proof system to naturally describe full laziness. Likewise, the spinal atomic λ-calculus presented here is the first term calculus with Curry–Howard corresponding proof system to naturally describe spinal full laziness.

Switch and Spine. One way to describe the skeleton or the spine of an abstraction within a λ-term is through explicit end-of-scope markers, as explored by Berkling and Fehr [7], and more recently by Hendriks and Van Oostrom [18]. We use their *adbmal* ($\curlywedge$) to illustrate the idea: the constructor $\curlywedge x.N$ indicates that the subterm N does not contain occurrences of x (or that any that do occur are

---

[5] The switch rule is an intuitionistic variant of *weak* or *linear distributivity* [12] for multiplicative linear logic.

[6] There is a clash of (existing) terminology: the *spine of an abstraction*, as we use here, is a different notion from the *spine of a λ-term*, which is the path from the root to the leftmost variable, as used e.g. in head reduction and abstract machines.

[7] Interestingly, Balabonski [5] shows that for *weak* reduction (where one does not reduce under an abstraction) full laziness and spinal full laziness are both optimal (in the number of beta-steps required to reach a normal form).

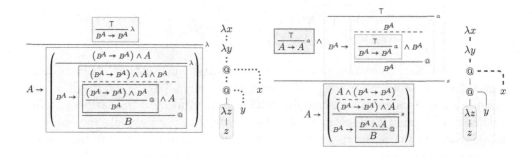

Fig. 1: Balanced and unbalanced typing derivations for $\lambda x.\lambda y.((\lambda z.z)y)x$, with corresponding graphical representations of the term. The variable x has type A and y, z type $A \to B$, shortened to B^A. The left derivation isolates the skeleton of λx, and the right derivation its spine, both by the subderivations in braces.

not available to a binder λx outside $\lambda x.N$). The scope of an abstraction thus becomes explicitly indicated in the term. This opens up a distinction between *balanced* and *unbalanced* scopes: whether scopes must be properly nested, or not; for example, in $\lambda x.\lambda y.N$, a subterm $\lambda y.\lambda x.M$ is balanced, but $\lambda x.\lambda y.M$ is not. With balanced scope, one can indicate the skeleton of an abstraction; with unbalanced scope (which Hendriks and Van Oostrom dismiss) one can indicate the spine. We do so for our example term $\lambda x.\lambda y.((\lambda z.z)y)x$ below.

Balanced scope/skeleton: $\lambda x.\lambda y.(\lambda y.(\lambda x.\lambda z.z)y)(\lambda y.x)$

Unbalanced scope/spine: $\lambda x.\lambda y.(\lambda x.(\lambda y.\lambda z.z)y)(\lambda y.x)$

A closely related approach is *director strings*, introduced by Kennaway and Sleep [19] for combinator reduction and generalized to any reduction strategy by Fernández, Mackie, and Sinot in [13]. The idea is to use nameless abstractions identified by their nesting (as with De Bruijn indices), and make the paths to bound variables explicit by annotating each constructor with a string of *directors*, that outline the paths. The primary aim of these approaches is to eliminate α-conversion and to streamline substitution. Consequently, while they can *identify* the spine, they do not readily isolate it for duplication.

The present work starts from our observation that the *switch* rule of open deduction functions as a proof-theoretic end-of-scope construction (see [25] for details). However, it does so in a *structural* way: it forces a deconstruction of a proof into readily duplicable parts, which together may form the spine of an abstraction. The derivations in Figure 1 demonstrate this, as we will now explain—see the next section for how they are formally constructed.

The abstraction λx corresponds in the proof system to the implication $A\to$, explicitly scoping over its right-hand side. On the left, with the *abstraction* rule (λ), scopes must be balanced, and the proof system may identify the *skeleton*; here, that of λx as the largest blue box. Decomposing the abstraction (λ) into *axiom* (a) and *switch* (s), on the right the proof system may express unbalanced scope. It does so by separating the scope of an abstraction into multiple parts; here, that of λx is captured as the two top-level red boxes. Each box is ready to be duplicated; in this way, one may duplicate the spine of an abstraction only.

These two derivations correspond to terms in our calculus. The subterms not part of the skeleton (i.e. $\lambda z.z$) remain shared and we are able to duplicate the skeleton alone. This is also possible in [16]. In our calculus we are also able to duplicate just the spine by using a *distributor*. We require this construct as otherwise we break the binding of the y-abstraction. The distributor manages and maintains these bindings. The y-abstraction in the spine $(y\langle a\rangle)$ is a *phantom-abstraction*, because it is not real and we cannot perform β-reduction on it. However, it may become real during reduction. It can be seen as a placeholder for the abstraction. The variables in the *cover* (a) represent subterms that both remain shared and are found in the distributor.

$$\text{Skeleton:} \qquad \underline{\lambda x.\lambda y.(a\,y)\,x}\,[a \leftarrow \lambda z.z]$$

$$\text{Spine:} \qquad \underline{\lambda x.y\langle a\rangle.(a)\,x}\,[y\langle a\rangle\,|\,\lambda y.\,[a \leftarrow (\lambda z.z)y]]$$

Our investigation is then focused on the interaction of switch and distribution (later observed in the rewrite rule l_5). The use of the distribution rule allows us to perform duplication atomically, and thus provides a natural strategy for spinal full laziness. In Figure 1 on the right, this means duplicating the two top-level red boxes can be done independently from duplicating the yellow box.

2 Typing a λ-calculus in open deduction

We work in *open deduction* [15], a formalism of deep-inference proof theory, using the following proof system for (conjunction–implication) intuitionistic logic. A *derivation* from a *premise* formula X to a *conclusion* formula Z is constructed inductively as in Figure 2a, with from left to right: a propositional atom a, where $X = Z = a$; *horizontal composition* with a connective $\rightarrow$, where $X = Y \rightarrow X_2$ and $Z = Y \rightarrow Z_2$; *horizontal composition* with a connective $\wedge$, where $X = X_1 \wedge X_2$ and $Z = Z_1 \wedge Z_2$; and *rule composition*, where r is an inference rule (Figure 2b) from Y_1 to Y_2. The boxes serve as parentheses (since derivations extend in two dimensions) and may be omitted. Derivations are considered up to associativity of rule composition. One may consider formulas as derivations that omit rule composition. We work modulo associativity, symmetry, and unitality of conjunction, justifying the n-ary contraction, and may omit $\top$ from the axiom rule. A 0-ary contraction, with conclusion $\top$, is a *weakening*. Figure 2b: the abstraction rule (λ) is derived from axiom and switch. *Vertical composition* of a derivation from X to Y and one from Y to Z, depicted by a dashed line, is a defined operation, given in Figure 2c, where $* \in \{\wedge, \rightarrow\}$.

2.1 The Sharing Calculus

Our starting point is the *sharing calculus* (Λ^S), a calculus with an explicit sharing construct, similar to explicit substitution.

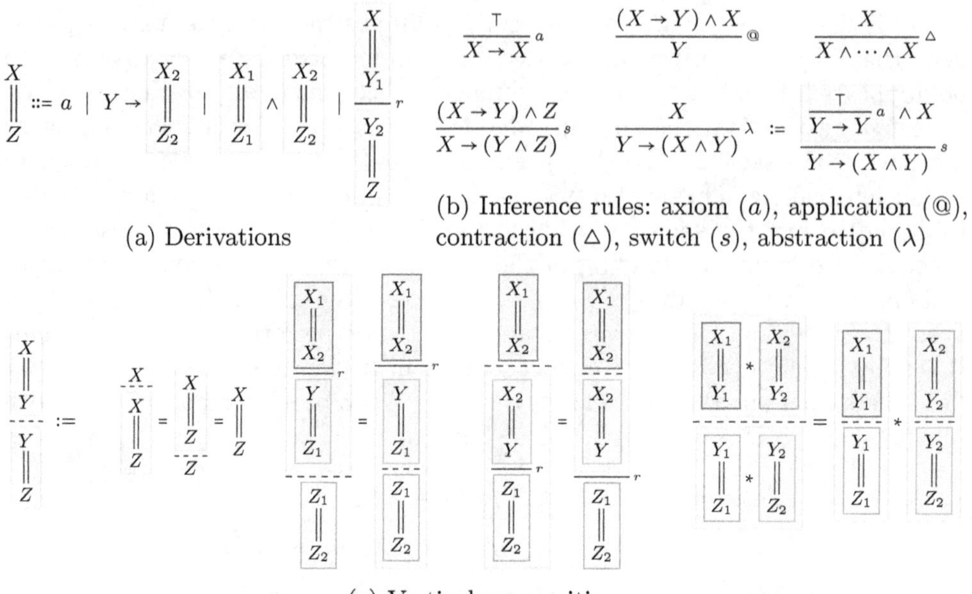

(a) Derivations

(b) Inference rules: axiom (a), application $(@)$, contraction $(\triangle)$, switch (s), abstraction (λ)

(c) Vertical composition

Fig. 2: Intuitionistic proof system in open deduction

Definition 1. *The **pre-terms** r, s, t, u and **sharings** $[\Gamma]$ of the Λ^S are defined by:*

$$s, t ::= x \mid \lambda x.t \mid s\,t \mid t[\Gamma] \qquad [\Gamma] ::= [x_1, \ldots, x_n \leftarrow s]$$

*with from left to right: a **variable**; an **abstraction**, where x occurs free in t and becomes bound; an **application**, where s and t use distinct variable names; and a **closure**; in $t[\vec{x} \leftarrow s]$ the variables in the vector $\vec{x} = x_1, \ldots, x_n$ all occur in t and become bound, and s and t use distinct variable names. **Terms** are pre-terms modulo **permutation** equivalence $(\sim)$:*

$$t[\vec{x} \leftarrow s][\vec{y} \leftarrow r] \sim t[\vec{y} \leftarrow r][\vec{x} \leftarrow s] \qquad (\{\vec{y}\} \cap (s)_{fv} = \{\})$$

*A term is in **sharing normal form** if all sharings occur as $[\vec{x} \leftarrow x]$ either at the top level or directly under a binding abstraction, as $\lambda x.t[\vec{x} \leftarrow x]$.*

Note that variables are *linear*: variables occur at most once, and bound variables must occur. A vector $\vec{x}$ has length $|\vec{x}|$ and consist of the variables $x_1, \ldots, x_{|\vec{x}|}$. An **environment** is a sequence of sharings $\overline{[\Gamma]} = [\Gamma_1] \ldots [\Gamma_n]$. Substitution is written $\{t/x\}$, and $\{t_1/x_1\} \ldots \{t_n/x_n\}$ may be abbreviated to $\{t_i/x_i\}_{i \in [n]}$.

Definition 2. *The **interpretation** $[\![-]\!] : \Lambda \to \Lambda^S$ is defined below.*

$$[\![x]\!] = x \quad [\![\lambda x.t]\!] = \lambda x.[\![t]\!] \quad [\![s\,t]\!] = [\![s]\!]\,[\![t]\!] \quad [\![t[\vec{x} \leftarrow s]]\!] = [\![t]\!]\{[\![s]\!]/x_i\}_{i \in [n]}$$

The **translation** $(\!|N|\!)$ of a λ-term N is the unique sharing-normal term t such that $N = [\![t]\!]$. A term t will be typed by a derivation with restricted types,

Basic Types: $A, B, C := a \mid A \to B$ Context Types: $\Gamma, \Delta, \Omega := A \mid \top \mid \Gamma \wedge \Delta$

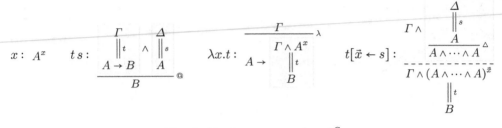

Fig. 3: Typing system for Λ^S

as shown below, where the *context type* $\Gamma = A_1 \wedge \cdots \wedge A_n$ will have an A_i for each free variable x_i of t. We connect free variables to their premises by writing A^x and $\Gamma^{\vec{x}}$. The Λ^S is then typed as in Figure 3.

3   The Spinal Atomic λ-Calculus

We now formally introduce the syntax of the spinal atomic λ-calculus (Λ_a^S), by extending the definition of the sharing calculus in Definition 1 with a *distributor* construct that allows for atomic duplication of terms.

Definition 3 (Pre-Terms). *The **pre-terms** r, s, t, **closures** $[\Gamma]$, and **environments** $\overline{[\Gamma]}$ of the Λ_a^S are defined by:*

$$t \quad ::= \quad x \quad \mid \quad st \quad \mid \quad x\langle\vec{y}\rangle.t \quad \mid \quad t[\Gamma] \qquad \overline{[\Gamma]} \quad ::= \quad [\Gamma] \quad \mid \quad \overline{[\Gamma]}[\Gamma]$$

$$[\Gamma] \quad ::= \quad [\vec{x} \leftarrow t] \quad \mid \quad [\vec{x} \mid y\langle\vec{z}\rangle \, \overline{[\Gamma]}]$$

Our generalized abstraction $x\langle\vec{y}\rangle.t$ is a **phantom-abstraction**, where x a **phantom-variable** and the **cover** $\vec{y}$ will be a subset of the free variables of t. It can be thought of as a "delayed" abstraction: x is a binder, but possibly not in t itself, and instead in the terms substituted for the variables $\vec{y}$; in other words, x is a *capturing* binder for substitution into $\vec{y}$. We define standard λ-abstraction as the special case $\lambda x.t \equiv x\langle x\rangle.t$, and generally, when we refer to $x\langle\vec{y}\rangle$ as a phantom-abstraction (rather than an abstraction) we assume $\vec{y} \neq x$. The **distributor** $u[\vec{x} \mid y\langle\vec{z}\rangle \, \overline{[\Gamma]}]$ binds the phantom-variables $\vec{x}$ in u, while its environment $\overline{[\Gamma]}$ will bind the variables in their covers; intuitively, it represents a set of explicit substitutions in which the variables $\vec{x}$ are expected to be captured.

The distributor is introduced when we wish to duplicate an abstraction, as depicted in Figure 4a. The sharing node (∘) duplicates the abstraction node, creating a distributor (depiced as the sharing and unsharing node (•), together with the bindings of the phantom-variables (depicted with a dashed line). The variables captured by the environment are the variables connected to sharing nodes linked with a dotted line. Notice one sharing node can be linked with multiple unsharing nodes, and vice versa. Duplication of applications also duplicates

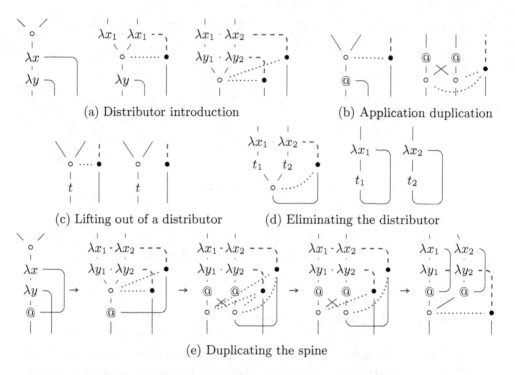

(a) Distributor introduction   (b) Application duplication

(c) Lifting out of a distributor   (d) Eliminating the distributor

(e) Duplicating the spine

Fig. 4: Graphical illustration of the distributor

the dotted line (Figure 4b), but these can be removed later if the term does not contain the variable bound to the unsharing (Figure 4c). These subterms are those which are not part of the spine. Eventually, we will reach a state where the only sharing node connected to the unsharing node is the one that shared the variable bound to the unsharing, allowing us to eliminate the distributor (Figure 4d). The purpose of the dotted line is similar to the brackets of optimal reduction graphs [21, 24], to supervise which sharing and unsharing match.

Terms are then pre-terms with sensible and correct bindings. To define terms, we first define *free* and *bound* variables and phantom variables; variables are bound by abstractions (not phantoms) and by sharings, while phantom-variables are bound by distributors.

Definition 4 (Free and Bound Variables). *The **free variables** $(-)_{fv}$ and **bound variables** $(-)_{bv}$ of a pre-term t are defined as follows*

$$(x)_{fv} = \{x\} \qquad\qquad (x)_{bv} = \{\}$$
$$(s\,t)_{fv} = (s)_{fv} \cup (t)_{fv} \qquad\qquad (s\,t)_{bv} = (s)_{bv} \cup (t)_{bv}$$
$$(x\langle x \rangle.t)_{fv} = (t)_{fv} - \{x\} \qquad\qquad (x\langle x \rangle.t)_{bv} = (t)_{bv} \cup \{x\}$$
$$(x\langle \vec{y} \rangle.t)_{fv} = (t)_{fv} \qquad\qquad (x\langle \vec{y} \rangle.t)_{bv} = (t)_{bv}$$
$$(u[\vec{x} \leftarrow t])_{fv} = (u)_{fv} \cup (t)_{fv} - \{\vec{x}\} \qquad\qquad (u[\vec{x} \leftarrow t])_{bv} = (u)_{bv} \cup (t)_{bv} \cup \{\vec{x}\}$$
$$(u[\vec{x}\,|\,y\langle y \rangle\,\overline{[\Gamma]}])_{fv} = (u\overline{[\Gamma]})_{fv} - \{y\} \qquad\qquad (u[\vec{x}\,|\,y\langle y \rangle\,\overline{[\Gamma]}])_{bv} = (u\overline{[\Gamma]})_{bv} \cup \{y\}$$

$$(u[\vec{x}\,|\,y\langle\,\vec{z}\,\rangle\,\overline{[\varGamma]}])_{fv} = (u\overline{[\varGamma]})_{fv} \cup \{y\} \qquad (u[\vec{x}\,|\,y\langle\,\vec{z}\,\rangle\,\overline{[\varGamma]}])_{bv} = (u\overline{[\varGamma]})_{bv}$$

Definition 5 (Free and Bound Phantom-Variables). *The **free phantom-variables** $(-)_{fp}$ and **bound phantom-variables** $(-)_{bp}$ of the pre-term t are defined as follows*

$$(x)_{fp} = \{\} \qquad\qquad\qquad (x)_{bp} = \{\}$$
$$(s\,t)_{fp} = (s)_{fp} \cup (t)_{fp} \qquad\qquad (s\,t)_{bp} = (s)_{bp} \cup (t)_{bp}$$
$$(x\langle\,x\,\rangle.t)_{fp} = (t)_{fp}$$
$$(c\langle\,\vec{x}\,\rangle.t)_{fp} = (t)_{fp} \cup \{c\} \qquad\qquad (c\langle\,\vec{x}\,\rangle.t)_{bp} = (t)_{bp}$$
$$(u[\vec{x} \leftarrow t])_{fp} = (u)_{fp} \cup (t)_{fp} \qquad\qquad (u[\vec{x} \leftarrow t])_{bp} = (u)_{bp} \cup (t)_{bp}$$
$$(u[\vec{x}\,|\,c\langle\,c\,\rangle\,\overline{[\varGamma]}])_{fp} = (u\overline{[\varGamma]})_{fp} - \{\vec{x}\}$$
$$(u[\vec{x}\,|\,c\langle\,\vec{y}\,\rangle\,\overline{[\varGamma]}])_{fp} = (u\overline{[\varGamma]})_{fp} \cup \{c\} - \{\vec{x}\} \qquad (u[\vec{x}\,|\,c\langle\,\vec{y}\,\rangle\,\overline{[\varGamma]}])_{bp} = (u\overline{[\varGamma]})_{bp} \cup \{\vec{x}\}$$

The **free covers** $(u)_{fc}$ and **bound covers** $(u)_{bc}$ are the covers associated with the free phantom-variables $(u)_{fp}$ respectively the bound phantom-variables $(u)_{bp}$ of u; that is, if x occurs as $x\langle\,\vec{a}\,\rangle$ in u and $x \in (u)_{fp}$ then $\langle\,\vec{a}\,\rangle \in (u)_{fc}$. When bound, x and the variables in $\vec{a}$ may be alpha-converted independently. When a distributor $u[\vec{x}\,|\,y\langle\,\vec{z}\,\rangle\,\overline{[\varGamma]}]$ binds the phantom-variables $\vec{x} = x_1,\ldots,x_n$ where each x_i occurs as $x_i\langle\,\vec{a}_i\,\rangle$ in u, then for technical convenience we may make the covers explicit in the distributor itself, and write

$$u[x_1\langle\,\vec{a}_1\,\rangle\ldots x_n\langle\,\vec{a}_n\,\rangle\,|\,y\langle\,\vec{z}\,\rangle\,\overline{[\varGamma]}]\ .$$

The environment $\overline{[\varGamma]}$ is expected to bind *exactly* the variables in the covers $\langle\,\vec{a}_i\,\rangle$. We apply this and other restrictions to define the terms of the calculus.

Definition 6. *Terms* $t \in \varLambda_a^S$ *are pre-terms with the following constraints*

1. *Each variable may occur at most once.*
2. *In a phantom-abstraction $x\langle\,\vec{y}\,\rangle.t$, $\{\vec{y}\} \subseteq (t)_{fv}$.*
3. *In a sharing $u[\vec{x} \leftarrow t]$, $\{\vec{x}\} \subseteq (u)_{fv}$.*
4. *In a distributor $u[x_1\langle\,\vec{a}_1\,\rangle\ldots x_n\langle\,\vec{a}_n\,\rangle\,|\,y\langle\,\vec{z}\,\rangle\,\overline{[\varGamma]}]$*
   (a) *$\{x_1,\ldots,x_n\} \subseteq (u)_{fp}$;*
   (b) *the variables in $\bigcup_{i \leq n}\{\vec{a}_i\}$ are free in u and bound by $\overline{[\varGamma]}$.*
   (c) *the variables in $\{\vec{z}\}$ occur freely in the environment $\overline{[\varGamma]}$.*

Example 1. Here we show some pre-terms that are not terms.

- $c\langle\,x\,\rangle.y$ (violates condition 2)
- $x\,y[x, z \leftarrow w]$ (violates condition 3)
- $e_2\langle\,w_2\,\rangle.w_2\,((e_1\langle\,w_1\,\rangle.w_1)\,z)[e_1\langle\,w_1\,\rangle, e_2\langle\,w_2\,\rangle\,|\,c\langle\,z\,\rangle\,[w_1, w_2 \leftarrow x\langle\,x\,\rangle.x\,y]]$
  (violates condition 4a)

We also work modulo permutation with respect to the variables in the cover of phantom-abstractions. Let $\vec{x}$ be a list of variables and let $\vec{x_P}$ be a permutation of that list, then the following terms are considered equal.

$$c\langle \vec{x} \rangle.t : \quad \cfrac{(A \to \Gamma) \wedge \Delta}{\cfrac{\Gamma^{\vec{x}} \wedge \Delta}{\Bigg\| t \atop C}}_{s}$$

$$u[\vec{x} \,|\, c\langle \vec{z} \rangle \overline{[\Gamma]}] : \quad \cfrac{C^c \to \cfrac{\cfrac{(C \to \Gamma) \wedge \Delta}{\cfrac{\Gamma^{\vec{z}} \wedge \Delta}{\Big\| [\Gamma] \atop \Sigma_1 \wedge \cdots \wedge \Sigma_n}}_{s} }{(C^{e_1} \to \Sigma_1^{x_1}) \wedge \cdots \wedge (C^{e_n} \to \Sigma_n^{x_n})} \wedge \Omega}_{d}$$
$$\overline{\quad (C \to \Sigma_1) \wedge \cdots \wedge (C \to \Sigma_n) \wedge \Omega \quad} \atop \Big\| u \atop E$$

Fig. 5: Typing derivations for phantom-abstractions and distributors

$$u[\vec{x} \leftarrow t] \sim u[\vec{x_P} \leftarrow t] \qquad\qquad y\langle \vec{x} \rangle.t \sim y\langle \vec{x_P} \rangle.t$$

Terms are typed with the typing system for Λ^S extended with the *distribution* inference rule. This rule is the result of computationally interpreting the medial rule as done in [16]. We obtain this variant of the medial rule due to the restriction for implications and to avoid introducing disjunction to the typing system. The terms of Λ_a^S are then typed as in both Figure 3 and Figure 5. Note environments are typed by the derivations of all its closures composed horizontally with the conjunction connective. Also note that in the case for phantom-abstraction is similar for that of an abstraction, where we replace one occurrence of the simple type A by the conjunction Γ.

3.1   Compilation and Readback.

We now define the translations between Λ_a^S and the original λ-calculus. First we define the interpretation $\Lambda \to \Lambda_a^S$ (*compilation*). Intuitively, it replaces each abstraction $\lambda x.-$ with the term $x\langle x \rangle.-[x_1, \ldots, x_n \leftarrow x]$ where $x_1, \ldots, x_n$ replace the occurrences of x. Actual substitutions are denoted as $\{t/x\}$. Let $|M|_x$ denote the number of occurrences of x in M, and if $|M|_x = n$ let $M\frac{n}{x}$ denote M with the occurrences of x replaced by fresh, distinct variables $x_1, \ldots, x_n$. First, the translation of a *closed* term M is $(\!|M|\!)'$, defined below

Definition 7 (Compilation). *The interpretation of λ terms, $(\!|\Lambda|\!)' : \Lambda \to \Lambda_a^S$, is defined as*

$$(\!|M\frac{n_1}{x_1} \ldots \frac{n_k}{x_k}|\!)'[x_1^1, \ldots, x_1^{n_1} \leftarrow x_1] \ldots [x_k^1, \ldots, x_k^{n_k} \leftarrow x_k]$$

where $x_1, \ldots, x_k$ are the free variables of M such that $|M|_{x_i} = n_i > 1$ and $(\!|-|\!)'$ is defined on terms as (where $n \neq 1$ in the abstraction case):

$$(\!|x|\!)' = x$$
$$(\!|M\,N|\!)' = (\!|M|\!)'\,(\!|N|\!)' \qquad (\!|\lambda x.M|\!)' = \begin{cases} x\langle x \rangle.(\!|M|\!)' & \text{if } |M|_x = 1 \\ x\langle x \rangle.(\!|M\frac{n}{x}|\!)'[x_1, \ldots, x_n \leftarrow x] & \text{if } |M|_x = n \end{cases}$$

The readback into the λ-calculus is slightly more complicated, specifically due to the bindings induced by the distributor. Interpreting a distributor construct as a λ-term requires (1) converting the phantom-abstractions it binds in

u into abstractions (2) collapsing the environment (3) maintaining the bindings between the converted abstractions and the intended variables located in the environment.

Definition 8. *Given a total function σ with domain D and codomain C, we* **overwrite** *the function with case $x \mapsto v$ where $x \in D$ and $v \in C$ such that*

$$\sigma[x \mapsto v](z) \quad := \quad \text{if } (x = z) \text{ then } v \text{ else } \sigma(z)$$

We use the map σ as part of the translation, the intuition is that for all bound variables x in the term we are translating, it should be that $\sigma(x) = x$. The purpose of the map γ is to keep track of the binding of phantom-variables.

Definition 9. *The interpretation $[\![- | - | -]\!] : \Lambda_a^S \times (V \to \Lambda) \times (V \to V) \to \Lambda$ is defined as*

$$[\![x | \sigma | \gamma]\!] = \sigma(x) \qquad [\![st | \sigma | \gamma]\!] = [\![s | \sigma | \gamma]\!] [\![t | \sigma | \gamma]\!]$$

$$[\![c\langle c \rangle.t | \sigma | \gamma]\!] = \lambda c.[\![t | \sigma[c \mapsto c] | \gamma]\!]$$

$$[\![c\langle x_1, \ldots, x_n \rangle.t | \sigma | \gamma]\!] = \lambda c.[\![t | \sigma[x_i \mapsto \sigma(x_i)\{c/\gamma(c)\}]_{i\in[n]} | \gamma]\!]$$

$$[\![u[x_1, \ldots, x_n \leftarrow t] | \sigma | \gamma]\!] = [\![u | \sigma[x_i \mapsto [\![t | \sigma | \gamma]\!]]_{i\in[n]} | \gamma]\!]$$

$$[\![u[e_1\langle \vec{w}_1 \rangle, \ldots, e_n\langle \vec{w}_n \rangle | c\langle c \rangle \overline{[\Gamma]}] | \sigma | \gamma]\!] = [\![u\overline{[\Gamma]} | \sigma | \gamma[e_i \mapsto c]_{i\in[n]}]\!]$$

$$[\![u[e_1\langle \vec{w}_1 \rangle, \ldots, e_n\langle \vec{w}_n \rangle | c\langle x_1, \ldots, x_m \rangle \overline{[\Gamma]}] | \sigma | \gamma]\!] = [\![u\overline{[\Gamma]} | \sigma' | \gamma[e_i \mapsto c]_{i\in[n]}]\!]$$

where $\sigma' = \sigma[x_i \mapsto \sigma(x_i)\{c/\gamma(c)\}]_{i\in[n]}$

The following Proposition justifies working modulo permutation equivalence.

Proposition 1. *For $s, t \in \Lambda_a^S$, if $s \sim t$ then $[\![s]\!] = [\![t]\!]$.*

3.2 Rewrite Rules.

Both the spinal atomic λ-calculus and the atomic λ-calculus of [16] follow atomic reduction steps, i.e. they apply on individual constructors. The biggest difference is that our calculus is capable of duplicating not only the skeleton but also the spine. The rewrite rules in our calculus make use of 3 operations, *substitution, book-keeping,* and *exorcism.* The operation **substitution** $t\{s/x\}$ propagates through the term t, and replaces the free occurences of the variable x with the term s. Moreover, if x occurs in the cover of a phantom-variable $e\langle \vec{y} \cdot x \rangle$, then substitution replaces the x in the cover with $(s)_{fv}$, resulting in $e\langle \vec{y} \cdot (s)_{fv} \rangle$. Although substitution performs some book-keeping on phantom-abstractions, we define an explicit notion of **book-keeping** $\{\vec{y}/e\}_b$ that updates the variables stored in a free cover i.e. for a term t, $e\langle \vec{x} \rangle \in (t)_{fc}$ then $e\langle \vec{y} \rangle \in (t\{\vec{y}/e\}_b)_{fc}$. The last operation we introduce is called **exorcism** $\{c\langle \vec{x} \rangle\}_e$. We perform exorcisms on phantom-abstractions to convert them to abstractions. Intuitively, this will be performed on phantom-abstractions with phantom-variables bound to a distributor when said distributor is eliminated. It converts phantom-abstractions to abstractions by introducing a sharing of the phantom-variable that captures the variables in the cover, i.e. $(c\langle \vec{x} \rangle.t)\{c\langle \vec{x} \rangle\}_e = c\langle c \rangle.t[\vec{x} \leftarrow c]$.

Proposition 2. *The translation $[\![\,u\,|\,\sigma\,|\,\gamma\,]\!]$ commutes with substitutions, book-keepings[1], and exorcisms[2] in the following way*

$$[\![\,u\{t/x\}\,|\,\sigma\,|\,\gamma\,]\!] = [\![\,u\,|\,\sigma[x \mapsto [\![\,t\,|\,\sigma\,|\,\gamma\,]\!]\,]\,|\,\gamma\,]\!]$$

$$[\![\,u\{\vec{x}/c\}_b\,|\,\sigma\,|\,\gamma\,]\!] = [\![\,u\,|\,\sigma\,|\,\gamma\,]\!]$$

$$[\![\,u\{c\langle x_1,\ldots,x_n\rangle\}_e\,|\,\sigma\,|\,\gamma\,]\!] = [\![\,u\,|\,\sigma[x_i \mapsto c]_{i\in[n]}\,|\,\gamma\,]\!]$$

(1) Given $c\langle\vec{y}\rangle \in (u)_{fc}$ where $\vec{x} \subseteq \vec{y}$ and for $z \in \vec{y}/\vec{x}$, $\gamma(c) \notin (\sigma(z))_{fv}$
(2) Given $c\langle\vec{x}\rangle \in (u)_{fc}$ or $\{\vec{x}\} \cap (u)_{fv} = \{\}$

Proof. See [25], proof of Proposition 18, 19, 20, 21.

Using these operations, we define the rewrite rules that allow for spinal duplication. Firstly we have beta reduction ($\leadsto_\beta$), which strictly requires an abstraction (not a phantom).

$$(x\langle x\rangle.t)\,s \leadsto_\beta t\{s/x\} \qquad\qquad \tag{β}$$

Here β-reduction is a linear operation, since the bound variable x occurs exactly once in the body t. Any duplication of the term t in the atomic λ-calculus proceeds via the sharing reductions.

The first set of sharing reduction rules move closures towards the outside of a term. Most of these rewrite rules only change the typing derivations in the way that subderivations are composed, with the exception of moving a closure out of scope of a distributor.

$$s[\Gamma]\,t \leadsto_L (s\,t)[\Gamma] \tag{l_1}$$

$$s\,t[\Gamma] \leadsto_L (s\,t)[\Gamma] \tag{l_2}$$

$$d\langle\vec{x}\rangle.t[\Gamma] \leadsto_L (d\langle\vec{x}\rangle.t)[\Gamma] \text{ if } \{\vec{x}\} \cap (t)_{fv} = \{\vec{x}\} \tag{l_3}$$

$$u[\vec{x} \leftarrow t[\Gamma]] \leadsto_L u[\vec{x} \leftarrow t][\Gamma] \tag{l_4}$$

For the case of lifting a closure outside a distributor, we use a notation $\|\,[\Gamma]\,\|$ to identify the variables captured by a closure, i.e. $\|\,[\vec{x} \leftarrow t]\,\| = \{\vec{x}\}$ and $\|\,[e_1\langle\vec{x_1}\rangle,\ldots,e_n\langle\vec{x_x}\rangle\,|\,c\langle c\rangle\overline{[\Gamma]}]\,\| = \{\vec{x_1},\ldots,\vec{x_n}\}$. Then let $\{\vec{z}\} = \|\,[\Gamma]\,\|$ in the following rewrite rule, where we remove $\vec{z}$ from the covers, that can only occur if $\{\vec{x}\} \cap ([\Gamma])_{fv} = \{\}$.

$$u[e_1\langle\vec{w}_1\rangle\ldots e_n\langle\vec{w}_n\rangle\,|\,c\langle\vec{x}\rangle\overline{[\Gamma]}[\Gamma]]$$
$$\leadsto_L u\{(\vec{w}_i \smallsetminus \vec{z})/e_i\}_{b_{i\in[n]}}[e_1\langle\vec{w}_1 \smallsetminus \vec{z}\rangle\ldots e_n\langle\vec{w}_n \smallsetminus \vec{z}\rangle\,|\,c\langle\vec{x}\rangle\overline{[\Gamma]}][\Gamma] \tag{l_5}$$

The graphical version of this rule is shown in Figure 4c, where we remove the edge only if there is no edge between t and the unsharing node. The proof rewrite rule corresponding with the rewrite rule l_5 can be broken down into two parts. The first part is readjusting how the derivations compose as shown below.

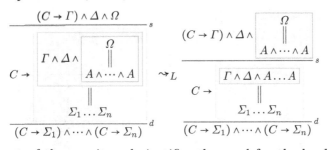

The second part of the rewrite rule justifies the need for the book-keeping operation. In the rewrite below, let A be the type of a variable z where $z \in \vec{z}$. After lifting, we want to remove the variable from the cover as to ensure correctness since the variables in the cover denote the variables captured by the environment. Book-keeping allows us to remove these variables simultaneously.

The lifting rules (l_i) are justified by the need to lift closures out of the distributor, as opposed to duplicating them. The second set of rewrite rules, consecutive sharings are compounded and unary sharings are applied as substitutions. For simplicity, in the equivalent proof rewrite step we only show the binary case.

$$u[\vec{w} \leftarrow y][y \cdot \vec{y} \leftarrow t] \rightsquigarrow_C u[\vec{w} \cdot \vec{y} \leftarrow t] \tag{c_1}$$

$$u[x \leftarrow t] \rightsquigarrow_C u\{t/x\} \tag{c_2}$$

$$\cfrac{\cfrac{A}{A \wedge \cfrac{A}{A \wedge A}\vartriangle}\vartriangle}{} \quad \rightsquigarrow_C \quad \cfrac{A}{A \wedge A \wedge A}\vartriangle \qquad \cfrac{A}{A}\vartriangle \ \rightsquigarrow_C \ A$$

The atomic steps for duplicating are given in the third and final set of rewrite rules. The first being the atomic duplication step of an application, which is the same rule used in [16]. The binary case proof rewrite steps for each rule are also provided. There are also shown graphically in (respectively) Figure 4b (where we maintain links between sharings and unsharings), Figure 4a, and Figure 4d (where the unsharing node is linked to exactly one connecting sharing node).

$$u[x_1 \ldots x_n \leftarrow s\,t] \rightsquigarrow_D u\{z_1\,y_1/x_1\} \ldots \{z_n\,y_n/x_n\}[z_1 \ldots z_n \leftarrow s][y_1 \ldots y_n \leftarrow t] \tag{d_1}$$

$$\frac{\dfrac{(A \to B) \wedge A}{B} @}{B \wedge B} \Delta \qquad \rightsquigarrow_D \qquad \frac{\dfrac{(A \to B)}{(A \to B) \wedge (A \to B)} \Delta \wedge \dfrac{B}{B \wedge B} \Delta}{\dfrac{(A \to B) \wedge A}{B} @ \wedge \dfrac{(A \to B) \wedge A}{B} @}$$

$$u[x_1, \ldots, x_n \leftarrow c\langle \vec{y} \rangle .t] \rightsquigarrow_D$$
$$u\{e_i\langle w_i \rangle .w_i / x_i\}_{i \in [n]}[e_1\langle w_1 \rangle \ldots e_n\langle w_n \rangle \,|\, c\langle \vec{y} \rangle \,[w_1, \ldots, w_n \leftarrow t]] \qquad (d_2)$$

$$\frac{\dfrac{(A \to B) \wedge \Gamma}{B \wedge \Gamma} s \quad A \to \; \Big\| \atop C}{(A \to C) \wedge (A \to C)} \Delta \qquad \rightsquigarrow_D \qquad \frac{\dfrac{(A \to B) \wedge \Gamma}{B \wedge \Gamma} s \quad A \to \; \Big\| \atop \dfrac{C}{C \wedge C}}{(A \to C) \wedge (A \to C)} d$$

$$u[e_1\langle \vec{w}_1 \rangle \ldots e_n\langle \vec{w}_n \rangle \,|\, c\langle c \rangle \,[\vec{w}_1, \ldots, \vec{w}_n \leftarrow c]] \rightsquigarrow_D u\{e_1\langle \vec{w}_1 \rangle\}_e \ldots \{e_n\langle \vec{w}_n \rangle\}_e \qquad (d_3)$$

$$\frac{A \to \dfrac{\overline{A} a}{A \wedge A} \Delta}{(A \to A) \wedge (A \to A)} d \qquad \rightsquigarrow_D \qquad \overline{A \to A} a \wedge \overline{A \to A} a$$

Example 2. The following example, illustrated in Figure 4e, is a reduction in the term calculus where we duplicate the spine of the term $[a_1, a_2 \leftarrow \lambda x.\lambda y.((\lambda z.z)y)x]$.

$$\rightsquigarrow_D \{\underline{x_1}\langle b_1 \rangle .b_1 / a_1\}\{\underline{x_2}\langle b_2 \rangle .b_2 / a_2\}[x_1\langle b_1 \rangle, x_2\langle b_2 \rangle \,|\, x\langle x \rangle [b_1, b_2 \leftarrow \underline{\lambda y}.((\lambda z.z)y)\underline{x}]]$$
$$\rightsquigarrow_D \{\underline{x_1}\langle c_1 \rangle .\underline{y_1}\langle c_1 \rangle c_1 / a_1\}\{\underline{x_2}\langle c_2 \rangle .\underline{y_2}\langle c_2 \rangle .c_2 / a_2\}$$
$$\quad [x_1\langle c_1 \rangle, x_2\langle c_2 \rangle \,|\, x\langle x \rangle [y_1\langle c_1 \rangle, y_2\langle c_2 \rangle \,|\, y\langle y \rangle [c_1, c_2 \leftarrow \underline{((\lambda z.z)y)\underline{x}}]]]$$
$$\rightsquigarrow_D \{\underline{x_1}\langle d_1, e_1 \rangle .\underline{y_1}\langle d_1, e_1 \rangle d_1 e_1 / a_1\}\{\underline{x_2}\langle d_2, e_2 \rangle .\underline{y_2}\langle d_2, e_2 \rangle .d_2 e_2 / a_2\}$$
$$\quad [x_1\langle d_1, e_1 \rangle, x_2\langle d_2, e_2 \rangle \,|\, x\langle x \rangle [y_1\langle d_1, e_1 \rangle, y_2\langle d_2, e_2 \rangle \,|\, y\langle y \rangle [d_1, d_2 \leftarrow (\lambda z.z)y][e_1, e_2 \leftarrow \underline{x}]]]$$
$$\rightsquigarrow_L \{\underline{x_1}\langle d_1, e_1 \rangle .\underline{y_1}\langle d_1 \rangle d_1 e_1 / a_1\}\{\underline{x_2}\langle d_2, e_2 \rangle .\underline{y_2}\langle d_2 \rangle .d_2 e_2 / a_2\}$$
$$\quad [x_1\langle d_1, e_1 \rangle, x_2\langle d_2, e_2 \rangle \,|\, x\langle x \rangle [y_1\langle d_1 \rangle, y_2\langle d_1 \rangle \,|\, y\langle y \rangle [d_1, d_2 \leftarrow (\lambda z.z)y]][e_1, e_2 \leftarrow \underline{x}]]$$
$$\rightsquigarrow_L \{\underline{x_1}\langle e_1 \rangle .\underline{y_1}\langle d_1 \rangle d_1 e_1 / a_1\}\{\underline{x_2}\langle e_2 \rangle .\underline{y_2}\langle d_2 \rangle .d_2 e_2 / a_2\}$$
$$\quad [x_1\langle e_1 \rangle, x_2\langle e_2 \rangle \,|\, x\langle x \rangle [e_1, e_2 \leftarrow \underline{x}]] \,[y_1\langle d_1 \rangle, y_2\langle d_2 \rangle \,|\, y\langle y \rangle [d_1, d_2(\lambda z.z)y]]$$
$$\rightsquigarrow_D \{\underline{\lambda x_1}.\underline{y_1}\langle d_1 \rangle d_1 \underline{x_1} / a_1\}\{\underline{\lambda x_2}.\underline{y_2}\langle d_2 \rangle .d_2 \underline{x_2} / a_2\} \,[y_1\langle d_1 \rangle, y_2\langle d_2 \rangle \,|\, y\langle y \rangle [d_1, d_2 \leftarrow (\lambda z.z)y]]$$

Reduction ($\rightsquigarrow_{(L,C,D,\beta)}$) preserves the conclusion of the derivation, and thus the following proposition is easy to observe.

Proposition 3. *If $s \rightsquigarrow_{(L,C,D,\beta)} t$ and $s : A$, then $t : A$.*

Definition 10. *For a term $t \in \Lambda_a^S$, if there does not exists a term $s \in \Lambda_a^S$ such that $t \rightsquigarrow_{(L,C,D)} s$ then it is said that t is in **sharing normal form**.*

The following Lemma not only proves we have good translations in Section 3.1, and shows duplication preserves denotation.

Lemma 1. *For a $t \in \Lambda_a^S$ in sharing normal form and a $N \in \Lambda$.*

$$\llbracket\, (\!|N|\!)\, \rrbracket = N \qquad\qquad (\!|\,\llbracket t \rrbracket\,|\!) = t \qquad\qquad \exists_{M \in \Lambda}.t = (\!|M|\!)$$

Otherwise if $s \leadsto_{(L,D,C)} t$ then $\llbracket\, s\,|\,\sigma\,|\,\gamma\, \rrbracket = \llbracket\, t\,|\,\sigma\,|\,\gamma\, \rrbracket$.

Proof. See [25, Lemma 24, Lemma 25].

Lemma 2. *Given a term $t \in \Lambda_a^S$, then $(\!|\,\llbracket t \rrbracket\,|\!)$ is t in sharing normal form.*

Proof. We can prove this by induction on the longest sharing reduction path from t. Our base case is already covered by Lemma 1. We are then interested in the inductive case, where t is not in sharing normal form. By Lemma 1, $\llbracket t \rrbracket = \llbracket t' \rrbracket$ where $t \leadsto_{(D,L,C)} t'$. By induction hypothesis, $(\!|\,\llbracket t' \rrbracket\,|\!)$ is in sharing normal form. Hence $(\!|\,\llbracket t \rrbracket\,|\!)$ is in sharing normal form. □

4   Strong Normalisation of Sharing Reductions

In order to show our calculus is strongly normalising, we first show that the sharing reduction rules are strongly normalising. We indite a measure on terms and show that this measure strictly decreases as sharing reduction progresses. Similar ideas and results can be found elsewhere: with *memory* in [20], the λ-I *calculus* in [6], the λ-*void calculus* [2], and the weakening $\lambda\mu$-calculus [17]. Our measure will consist of three components. First, the **height** of a term is a multiset of integers, that measures the number of constructors from each sharing node to the root of the term in its graphical notation. The height is defined on terms as $\mathcal{H}^i(-)$, where i is an integer. We say $\mathcal{H}(t)$ for $\mathcal{H}^1(t)$. We use $\uplus$ to denote the disjoint union of two multisets. We denote $\mathcal{H}^i([\Gamma_1]) \uplus \cdots \uplus \mathcal{H}^i([\Gamma_n])$ as $\mathcal{H}^i(\overline{[\Gamma]})$ for the environment $\overline{[\Gamma]} = [\Gamma_1], \ldots, [\Gamma_n]$.

Definition 11 (Sharing Height). *The sharing height $\mathcal{H}^i(t)$ of a term t is given below, where n is the number of closures in $\overline{[\Gamma]}$:*

$$\mathcal{H}^i(x) = \{\} \qquad\qquad \mathcal{H}^i(s\,t) = \mathcal{H}^{i+1}(s) \uplus \mathcal{H}^{i+1}(t)$$

$$\mathcal{H}^i(c\langle\, \vec{x}\,\rangle.t) = \mathcal{H}^{i+1}(t) \qquad\qquad \mathcal{H}^i(t[\Gamma]) = \mathcal{H}^i(t) \uplus \mathcal{H}^i([\Gamma]) \uplus \{i^1\}$$

$$\mathcal{H}^i([x_1, \ldots, x_n \leftarrow t]) = \mathcal{H}^{i+1}(t) \qquad \mathcal{H}^i([\vec{w}\,|\,c\langle\, \vec{x}\,\rangle\overline{[\Gamma]}]) = \mathcal{H}^{i+1}(\overline{[\Gamma]}) \uplus \{(i+1)^n\}$$

This measure then strictly decreases for the rewrite rules l_1, l_2, l_3, l_4 and l_5, i.e. if $t \leadsto_L u$ then $\mathcal{H}^i(t) > \mathcal{H}^i(u)$. The second measure we consider is the **weight** of a term. Intuitively this quantifies the remaining duplications, which are performed with $\leadsto_D$ reductions. If a term would be deleted, we assign it with a weight '1' to express that it is not duplicated. Calculating the weight requires an auxiliary function that assigns integer weights to the variables of a term. This function is defined on terms $\mathcal{V}^i(-)$, where i is an integer. To measure variables independently of binders is vital. It allows to measure distributors, which duplicate λ's but not the bound variable. Also, only bound variables for abstractions are measured since variables bound by sharings are substituted in the interpretation.

Definition 12 (Variable Weights). *The function $\mathcal{V}^i(t)$ returns a function that assigns integer weights to the free variables of t. It is defined by the below, where $f = \mathcal{V}^i(t)$ and $g = f(x_1) + \cdots + f(x_n)$ for each $x_i \in \vec{x}$.*

$$\mathcal{V}^i(x) = \{x \mapsto i\} \qquad\qquad \mathcal{V}^i(s\,t) = \mathcal{V}^i(s) \cup \mathcal{V}^i(t)$$

$$\mathcal{V}^i(c\langle c\rangle.t) = \mathcal{V}^i(t)/\{c\} \qquad\qquad \mathcal{V}^i(c\langle \vec{x}\rangle.t) = \mathcal{V}^i(t) \cup \{c \mapsto i\}$$

$$\mathcal{V}^i(t[\vec{x} \leftarrow s]) = \mathcal{V}^i(t)/\{\vec{x}\} \cup \mathcal{V}^g(s) \qquad \mathcal{V}^i(t[\leftarrow s]) = \mathcal{V}^i(t) \cup \mathcal{V}^1(s)$$

$$\mathcal{V}^i(t[e_1\langle \vec{w}_1\rangle \ldots e_n\langle \vec{w}_n\rangle \,|\, c\langle c\rangle \overline{[\Gamma]}]) = \mathcal{V}^i(t\overline{[\Gamma]})/\{c, e_1, \ldots, e_n\}$$

$$\mathcal{V}^i(t[e_1\langle \vec{w}_1\rangle \ldots e_n\langle \vec{w}_n\rangle \,|\, c\langle \vec{x}\rangle \overline{[\Gamma]}]) = \mathcal{V}^i(t\overline{[\Gamma]})/\{e_1, \ldots, e_n\} \cup \{c \mapsto i\}$$

The weight of a term can then be defined via the use of this auxiliary function. The auxiliary function is used when calculating the weight of a sharing, where the sharing weight of the variables bound by the sharing play a significant role in calculating the weight of the shared term. In the case of a weakening $[\leftarrow t]$, we assign an initial weight of 1. Again we say $\mathcal{W}(t) = \mathcal{W}^1(t)$.

Definition 13 (Sharing Weight). *The sharing weight $\mathcal{W}^i(t)$ of a term t is a multiset of integers computed by the function defined below, where $f = \mathcal{V}^i(t)$ and $g = f(x_1) + \cdots + f(x_n)$ for each $x_i \in \vec{x}$.*

$$\mathcal{W}^i(x) = \{\} \qquad\qquad \mathcal{W}^i(s\,t) = \mathcal{W}^i(s) \cup \mathcal{W}^i(t) \cup \{i\}$$

$$\mathcal{W}^i(c\langle c\rangle.t) = \mathcal{W}^i(t) \cup \{i\} \cup \{\mathcal{V}^i(t)(c)\} \quad \mathcal{W}^i(c\langle \vec{x}\rangle.t) = \mathcal{W}^i(t) \cup \{i\}$$

$$\mathcal{W}^i(t[\vec{x} \leftarrow s]) = \mathcal{W}^i(t) \cup \mathcal{W}^g(s) \qquad \mathcal{W}^i(t[\leftarrow s]) = \mathcal{W}^i(t) \cup \mathcal{W}^1(s)$$

$$\mathcal{W}^i(t[e_1\langle \vec{w}_1\rangle \ldots e_n\langle \vec{w}_n\rangle \,|\, c\langle c\rangle \overline{[\Gamma]}]) = \mathcal{W}^i(t\overline{[\Gamma]}) \cup \{\mathcal{V}^i(t\overline{[\Gamma]})(c)\}$$

$$\mathcal{W}^i(t[e_1\langle \vec{w}_1\rangle \ldots e_n\langle \vec{w}_n\rangle \,|\, c\langle \vec{x}\rangle \overline{[\Gamma]}]) = \mathcal{W}^i(t\overline{[\Gamma]})$$

This measure then strictly decreases on the rewrite rules d_1, d_2, d_3 and is unaffected by all the other sharing reduction rules, i.e. if $t \leadsto_D u$ then $\mathcal{W}^i(t) > \mathcal{W}^i(u)$. If $t \leadsto_{(L,C)} u$ then $\mathcal{W}^i(t) = \mathcal{W}^i(u)$. The third and last measure we consider is the **number of closures** in the term, where it can be easily observed that the rewrite rules c_1 and c_2 strictly decrease this measure, and that the $\leadsto_L$ rules do not alter the number of closures. We then use this along with height and weight to define a *sharing measure* on terms.

Definition 14. *The **sharing measure** of a Λ_a^S-term t is a triple $(\mathcal{W}(t), \mathcal{C}, \mathcal{H}(t))$, where $\mathcal{C}$ is the number of closures in the term t. We compare sharing measures by using the lexicographical preferences according to $\mathcal{W} > \mathcal{C} > \mathcal{H}$.*

Theorem 1. *Sharing reduction $\leadsto_{(D,L,C)}$ is strongly normalising.*

Now that we have proven the sharing reductions are strongly normalising, we can prove that they are confluent for closed terms.

Theorem 2. *The sharing reduction relation $\leadsto_{(D,L,C)}$ is confluent.*

Proof. Lemma 1 tells us that the preservation is preserved under reduction i.e. for $s \leadsto_{(D,L,C)} t$, $[\![s]\!] = [\![t]\!]$. Therefore given $t \leadsto^*_{(D,L,C)} s_1$ and $t \leadsto^*_{(D,L,C)} s_2$, $[\![t]\!] = [\![s_1]\!] = [\![s_2]\!]$. Since we know that sharing reductions are strongly normalising, we know there exists terms u_1 and u_2 in sharing normal form such that $s_1 \leadsto^*_{(D,L,C)} u_1$ and $s_2 \leadsto^*_{(D,L,C)} u_2$. Lemma 1 tells us that terms in sharing normal form are in correspondence with their denotations i.e. $(\!|[\![t]\!]|\!) = t$. Since by Lemma 1 we know $[\![u_1]\!] = [\![s_1]\!] = [\![s_2]\!] = [\![u_2]\!]$, and by Lemma 1 $(\!|[\![u_1]\!]|\!) = u_1$ and $(\!|[\![u_2]\!]|\!) = u_2$, we can conclude $u_1 = u_2$. Hence, we prove confluence.   □

5   Preservation of Strong Normalisation and Confluence

A β-step in our calculus may occur within a weakening, and therefore is simulated by zero β-steps in the λ-calculus. Therefore if there is an infinite reduction path located inside a weakening in Λ_a^S, then the reduction path is not preserved in the corresponding λ-term as there are no weakenings. To deal with this, just as done in [2, 16, 17], we make use of the **weakening calculus**. A β-step is non-deleting precisely because of the weakening construct. If a β-step would be deleting, then the weakening calculus would instead keep the deleted term around as 'garbage', which can continue to reduce unless explicitly 'garbage-collected' by extra (non-β) reduction steps. PSN has already be shown for the weakening calculus through the use of a perpetual strategy in [16]. A part of proving PSN is then using the weakening calculus to prove that if $t \in \Lambda_a^S$ has a infinite reduction path, then its translation into the weakening calculus also has an infinite reduction path.

Definition 15. *The w-terms of the weakening calculus (Λ_w) are*

$$T, U, V ::= x \mid \lambda x.T^* \mid UV \mid T[\leftarrow U] \mid \bullet \ (*) \ \text{where } x \in (T)_{fv}$$

The terms are variable, abstraction, application, weakening, and a bullet. In the weakening $T[\leftarrow U]$, the subterm U is *weakened*. The interpretation of atomic terms to weakening terms $[\![- \mid - \mid -]\!]_w$ can be seen as an extension of the translation into the λ-calculus (Definition 9).

Definition 16. *The interpretation $[\![- \mid - \mid -]\!]_w : \Lambda_a^S \times (V \to \Lambda_w) \times (V \to V) \to \Lambda_w$ with maps $\sigma : V \to \Lambda_w$ and $\gamma : V \to V$ is defined as an extension of the translation in (Definition 9) with the following additional special cases.*

$$[\![u[\leftarrow t] \mid \sigma \mid \gamma]\!]_w = [\![u \mid \sigma \mid \gamma]\!]_w[\leftarrow [\![t \mid \sigma \mid \gamma]\!]_w]$$

$$[\![u[\,\mid c\langle c\rangle \overline{[\Gamma]}] \mid \sigma \mid \gamma]\!]_w = [\![u \overline{[\Gamma]} \mid \sigma[c \mapsto \bullet] \mid \gamma]\!]_w$$

$$[\![u[\,\mid c\langle x_1, \ldots, x_n\rangle \overline{[\Gamma]}] \mid \sigma \mid \gamma]\!]_w = [\![u \overline{[\Gamma]} \mid \sigma' \mid \gamma]\!]_w$$

where $\sigma'(z) := $ if $z \in \{x_1, \ldots, x_n\}$ then $\sigma(z)\{\bullet/\gamma(c)\}$ else $\sigma(z)$

We say $[\![t]\!]^w = [\![t \mid I \mid I]\!]_w$ where I is the identity function. We also have translations of the weakening calculus to and from the λ-calculus. Both of these translations were provided in [16]. The interpretation $\lfloor - \rfloor$ from weakening terms to λ-terms discards all weakenings.

Definition 17. *The interpretation* $M \in \Lambda$, $(\!|-|\!)^{w} : \Lambda \to \Lambda_{w}$ *is defined below.*

$$(\!|x|\!)^{w} = x \quad (\!|M\,N|\!)^{w} = (\!|M|\!)^{w}\,(\!|N|\!)^{w} \quad (\!|\lambda x.N|\!)^{w} = \begin{cases} \lambda x.(\!|N|\!)^{w} & if\ x \in (N)_{fv} \\ \lambda x.(\!|N|\!)^{w}[\leftarrow x] & otherwise \end{cases}$$

The following equalities can be observed, where $\sigma^{\Lambda}(z) = \lfloor \sigma^{w}(z) \rfloor$.

Proposition 4. *For* $N \in \Lambda$ *and* $t \in \Lambda_{a}^{S}$ *the following properties hold*

$$\lfloor [\![t\,|\,\sigma^{w}\,|\,\gamma]\!]_{w} \rfloor = [\![t\,|\,\sigma^{\Lambda}\,|\,\gamma]\!] \qquad [\![(\!|N|\!)]\!]^{w} = (\!|N|\!)^{w} \qquad \lfloor (\!|N|\!)^{w} \rfloor = N$$

where for each $\{x \mapsto M\} \in \sigma^{w}$, $\{x \mapsto \lfloor M \rfloor\} \in \sigma^{\Lambda}$.

Definition 18. *In the weakening calculus,* β*-reduction is defined as follows, where* $\overline{[\Gamma]}$ *are weakening constructs.* $((\lambda x.T)\overline{[\Gamma]})\,U \to_{\beta} T\{U/x\}\overline{[\Gamma]}$

Proposition 5. *If* $N \in \Lambda$ *is strongly normalising, then so is* $(\!|N|\!)^{w}$.

When translating from Λ_{a}^{S} to Λ_{w}, weakenings are maintained whilst sharings are interpreted via substitution. Thus the reduction rules in the weakening calculus cover the spinal reductions for nullary distributors and weakenings.

Definition 19. *Weakening reduction* $(\to_{w})$ *proceeds as follows.*

$$U[\leftarrow T]V \to_{w} (U\,V)[\leftarrow T] \qquad\qquad U\,V[\leftarrow T] \to_{w} (U\,V)[\leftarrow T]$$

$$T[\leftarrow U[\leftarrow V]] \to_{w} T[\leftarrow U][\leftarrow V] \qquad T[\leftarrow \lambda x.U] \to_{w} T[\leftarrow U\{\bullet/x\}]$$

$$T[\leftarrow U\,V] \to_{w} T[\leftarrow U][\leftarrow V] \qquad\qquad T[\leftarrow \bullet] \to_{w} T$$

$$T[\leftarrow U] \to_{w} T^{(1)} \qquad\qquad \lambda x.T[\leftarrow U] \to_{w} (\lambda x.T)[\leftarrow U]^{(2)}$$

(1) if U *is a subterm of* T *and (2) if* $x \notin (U)_{fv}$

It is easy to see that these rules correspond to special cases of the sharing reduction rules for Λ_{a}^{S}. This resemblance is confirmed by the following Lemma, proven in [25, pp. 82-86]. We use this to show how Λ_{a}^{S} enjoys PSN.

Lemma 3. *If* $t \leadsto_{\beta} u$ *then* $[\![t]\!]^{w} \to_{\beta}^{+} [\![u]\!]^{w}$. *If* $t \leadsto_{(C,D,L)} u$ *and for any* $x \in (t)_{bv} \cup (t)_{fp}$ *such that for all* z, $x \notin (\sigma(z))_{fv}$.

$$[\![t\,|\,\sigma\,|\,\gamma]\!]_{w} \to_{w}^{*} [\![u\,|\,\sigma\,|\,\gamma]\!]_{w}$$

Lemma 4. *For* $t \in \Lambda_{a}^{S}$ *has an infinite reduction path, then* $[\![t]\!]^{w}$ *also has an infinite reduction path.*

Proof. Due to Theorem 2, we know that the infinite reduction path contains infinite β-steps. This means in the reduction sequence, between each β-step, there are finite many $\leadsto_{(D,L,C)}$ reduction steps. Lemma 3 says each $\leadsto_{(D,L,C)}$ step in Λ_{a}^{S} corresponds to zero or more weakening reductions $(\leadsto_{w}^{*})$. Lemma 3 says that each beta step in Λ_{a}^{S} corresponds to one or more β-steps in Λ_{w}. Therefore, it must be that $[\![t]\!]^{w}$ also has an infinite reduction path.   □

Theorem 3. *If $N \in \Lambda$ is strongly normalising, then so is $(\!| N |\!)$.*

Proof. For a given $N \in \Lambda$ that is strongly normalising, we know by Lemma 5 that $(\!| N |\!)^w$ is strongly normalising. Then $[\![(\!| N |\!)]\!]^w$ is strongly normalising, since Proposition 4 states that $(\!| N |\!)^w = [\![(\!| N |\!)]\!]^w$. Then by Lemma 4, which states that if $[\![t]\!]^w$ is strongly normalising, then t is strongly normalising, proves that $(\!| N |\!)$ is strongly normalising. □

We also prove confluence, which is already known for the λ-calculus [11]. We first observe that a β-step in the λ-calculus is simulated in Λ_a^S by one β-step followed by zero or more sharing reductions.

Lemma 5. *Given $N, M \in \Lambda$. If $N \leadsto_\beta M$, then $(\!| N |\!) \leadsto_\beta \leadsto^*_{(D,L,C)} (\!| M |\!)$.*

Proof. This is proven by Sherratt in [25, Lemma 67].

Theorem 4. *Given $t, s_1, s_2 \in \Lambda_a^S$. If $t \leadsto^*_{(\beta,D,L,C)} s_1$ and $t \leadsto^*_{(\beta,D,L,C)} s_2$, there exists a $u \in \Lambda_a^S$ such that $s_1 \leadsto^*_{(\beta,D,L,C)} u$ and $s_2 \leadsto^*_{(\beta,D,L,C)} u$.*

Proof. Suppose $t \leadsto^*_{(\beta,D,L,C)} s_1$ and $t \leadsto^*_{(\beta,D,L,C)} s_2$. Then we have $[\![t]\!] \leadsto^*_\beta [\![s_1]\!]$ and $[\![t]\!] \leadsto^*_\beta [\![s_2]\!]$. By the Church-Rosser theorem, there exists a $M \in \Lambda$ such that $[\![s_1]\!] \leadsto^*_\beta M$ and $[\![s_2]\!] \leadsto^*_\beta M$. Due to Lemma 2, $(\!| [\![s_1]\!] |\!) = s_1'$ and $(\!| [\![s_2]\!] |\!) = s_2'$ where $s_1', s_2' \in \Lambda_a^S$ in sharing normal form. Then thanks to Lemma 5 we know $s_1' \leadsto^*_{(\beta,D,L,C)} (\!| M |\!)$ and $s_2' \leadsto^*_{(\beta,D,L,C)} (\!| M |\!)$. Combined, we get confluence. □

6 Conclusion, related work, and future directions

We have studied the interaction between the switch and the medial rule, the two characteristic inference rules of deep inference. We built a Curry–Howard interpretation based on this interaction, whose resulting calculus not only has the ability to duplicate terms atomically but can also duplicate solely the spine of an abstraction such that beta reduction can proceed on the duplicates. We show that this calculus has natural properties with respect to the λ-calculus.

This work, which started as an investigation into the Curry-Howard correspondence of the switch rule [25], fits into a broader effort to give a computational interpretation to intuitionistic deep-inference proof theory. Brünnler and McKinley [9] give a natural reduction mechanism without medial (or switch), and observe that preservation of strong normalization fails. Guenot and Straßburger [14] investigate a different switch rule, corresponding to the implication-left rule of sequent calculus. He [17] extends the atomic λ-calculus to the $\lambda\mu$-calculus.

Our future goal is to develop the intuitionistic open deduction formalism towards optimal reduction [23, 21, 3], via the remaining medial and switch rules [26].

Acknowledgements We thank the anonymous reviewers for their comments.

References

1. Abadi, M., Cardelli, L., Curien, P.L., Lévy, J.J.: Explicit substitutions. Journal of Functional Programming **1**(4), 375–416 (1991)
2. Accattoli, B., Kesner, D.: Preservation of strong normalisation modulo permutations for the structural lambda-calculus. Logical Methods in Computer Science **8**(1) (2012)
3. Asperti, A., Guerrini, S.: The Optimal Implementation of Functional Programming Languages. Cambridge University Press (1998)
4. Balabonski, T.: A unified approach to fully lazy sharing. ACM SIGPLAN Notices **47**(1), 469–480 (2012)
5. Balabonski, T.: Weak Optimality, and the Meaning of Sharing. In: International Conference on Functional Programming (ICFP). pp. 263–274. Boston, United States (Sep 2013). https://doi.org/10.1145/2500365.2500606, https://hal.archives-ouvertes.fr/hal-00907056
6. Barendregt, H.P.: The Lambda Calculus – Its Syntax and Semantics, Studies in Logic and the Foundations of Mathematics, vol. 103. North-Holland (1984)
7. Berkling, K.J., Fehr, E.: A consistent extension of the lambda-calculus as a base for functional programming languages. Information and Control **55**, 89–101 (1982)
8. Blanc, T., Lévy, J.J., Maranget, L.: Sharing in the weak lambda-calculus. Processes, Terms and Cycles: Steps on the Road to Infinity: Essays Dedicated to Jan Willem Klop on the Occasion of His 60th Birthday **3838**, 70 (2005)
9. Brünnler, K., McKinley, R.: An algorithmic interpretation of a deep inference system. In: International Conference on Logic for Programming Artificial Intelligence and Reasoning (LPAR). pp. 482–496 (2008)
10. Brünnler, K., Tiu, A.: A local system for classical logic. In: 8th International Conference on Logic for Programming Artificial Intelligence and Reasoning (LPAR). LNCS, vol. 2250, pp. 347–361 (2001)
11. Church, A., Rosser, J.B.: Some properties of conversion. Transactions of the American Mathematical Society **39**(3), 472–482 (1936), http://www.jstor.org/stable/1989762
12. Cockett, R., Seely, R.: Weakly distributive categories. Journal of Pure and Applied Algebra **114**(2), 133–173 (1997)
13. Fernández, M., Mackie, I., Sinot, F.R.: Lambda-calculus with director strings. Applicable Algebra in Engineering, Communication and Computing **15**(6), 393–437 (2005)
14. Guenot, N., Straßburger, L.: Symmetric normalisation for intuitionistic logic. In: Joint Meeting of the Twenty-Third EACSL Annual Conference on Computer Science Logic (CSL) and the Twenty-Ninth Annual ACM/IEEE Symposium on Logic in Computer Science (LICS) (2014)
15. Guglielmi, A., Gundersen, T., Parigot, M.: A proof calculus which reduces syntactic bureaucracy. In: 21st International Conference on Rewriting Techniques and Applications (RTA). pp. 135–150 (2010)
16. Gundersen, T., Heijltjes, W., Parigot, M.: Atomic lambda-calculus: a typed lambda-calculus with explicit sharing. In: 28th Annual ACM/IEEE Symposium on Logic in Computer Science (LICS). pp. 311–320 (2013)
17. He, F.: The Atomic Lambda-Mu Calculus. Ph.D. thesis, University of Bath (2018)
18. Hendriks, D., van Oostrom, V.: Adbmal. In: 19th International Conference on Automated Deduction (CADE). LNCS, vol. 2741, pp. 136–150 (2003)

19. Kennaway, R., Sleep, R.: Director strings as combinators. ACM Transactions on Programming Languages and Systems (1988)
20. Klop, J.W.: Combinatory Reduction Systems. Ph.D. thesis, Utrecht University (1980)
21. Lamping, J.: An algorithm for optimal lambda calculus reduction. In: Proceedings of the 17th ACM SIGPLAN-SIGACT symposium on Principles of programming languages. pp. 16–30 (1990)
22. Launchbury, J.: A natural semantics for lazy evaluation. In: 20th ACM SIGPLAN-SIGACT symposium on Principles of programming languages (POPL). pp. 144–154 (1993)
23. Lévy, J.J.: Optimal reductions in the lambda-calculus. In: To H.B. Curry: Essays in Combinatory Logic, Lambda Calculus and Formalism. Academic Press (1980)
24. van Oostrom, V., van de Looij, K.J., Zwitserlood, M.: Lambdascope: another optimal implementation of the lambda-calculus. In: Workshop on Algebra and Logic on Programming Systems (ALPS) (2004)
25. Sherratt, D.R.: A lambda-calculus that achieves full laziness with spine duplication. Ph.D. thesis, University of Bath (2019)
26. Tiu, A.: A local system for intuitionistic logic. In: International Conference on Logic for Programming Artificial Intelligence and Reasoning (LPAR). pp. 242–256 (2006)
27. Wadsworth, C.P.: Semantics and Pragmatics of the Lambda-Calculus. Ph.D. thesis, University of Oxford (1971)

6

Local Local Reasoning:
A BI-Hyperdoctrine for Full Ground Store*

Miriam Polzer and Sergey Goncharov(✉)

FAU Erlangen-Nürnberg, Erlangen, Germany
{miriam.polzer,sergey.goncharov}@fau.de

Abstract. Modelling and reasoning about dynamic memory allocation is one of the well-established strands of theoretical computer science, which is particularly well-known as a source of notorious challenges in semantics, reasoning, and proof theory. We capitalize on recent progress on categorical semantics of *full ground store*, in terms of a *full ground store monad*, to build a corresponding semantics of a higher order logic over the corresponding programs. Our main result is a construction of an *(intuitionistic) BI-hyperdoctrine*, which is arguably the semantic core of higher order logic over local store. Although we have made an extensive use of the existing generic tools, certain principled changes had to be made to enable the desired construction: while the original monad works over total heaps (to disable dangling pointers), our version involves partial heaps (*heaplets*) to enable compositional reasoning using separating conjunction. Another remarkable feature of our construction is that, in contrast to the existing generic approaches, our BI-algebra does not directly stem from an internal categorical partial commutative monoid.

1 Introduction

Modelling and reasoning about dynamic memory allocation is a sophisticated subject in denotational semantics with a long history (e.g. [19,15,14,16]). Denotational models for dynamic references vary over a large spectrum, and in fact, in two dimensions: depending on the expressivity of the features being modelled (*ground store – full ground store – higher order store*) and depending on the amount of *intensional* information included in the model (*intensional – extensional*), using the terminology of Abramsky [1].

Recently, Kammar et al [9] constructed an extensional monad-based denotational model of the *full ground store*, i.e. permitting not only memory allocation for discrete values, but also storing mutually linked data. The key idea of the latter work is an explicit delineation between the target presheaf category [**W**, **Set**] on which the full ground store monad acts, and an auxiliary presheaf category [**E**, **Set**] of *initializations*, naturally hosting a *heap functor* H. The latter category also hosts a *hiding monad* P, which can be loosely understood as a semantic

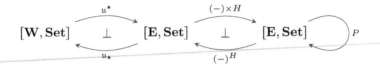

Fig. 1: Construction of the full ground store monad.

mechanism for idealized garbage collection. The full ground store monad is then assembled according to the scheme given in Fig. 1. As a slogan: the *local* store monad is a *global* store monad transform of the hiding monad sandwiched within a geometric morphism.

The fundamental reason, why extensional models of local store involve intricate constructions, such as presheaf categories is that the desirable program equalities include

$$\text{let } \ell := \text{new } v; \ell' := \text{new } w \text{ in } p \;\; = \;\; \text{let } \ell' := \text{new } w; \ell := \text{new } v \text{ in } p \qquad (\ell \not\equiv \ell')$$

$$\text{let } \ell := \text{new } v \text{ in ret } \star \;\; = \;\; \text{ret } \star$$

$$\text{let } \ell := \text{new } v \text{ in } (\text{if } \ell = \ell' \text{ then true else false}) \;\; = \;\; \text{false} \qquad (\ell \not\equiv \ell')$$

and these jointly do not have set-based models over countably infinite sets of locations [23, Proposition 6]. The first equation expresses irrelevance of the memory allocation order, the second expresses the fact that an unused cell is always garbage collected and the third guarantees that allocation of a fresh cell does indeed produce a cell different from any other. The aforementioned construction validates these equations and enjoys further pleasant properties, e.g. soundness and adequacy of a higher order language with user defined storable data structures.

The goal of our present work is to complement the semantics of programs over local store with a corresponding principled semantics of *higher order logic*. In order to be able to specify and reason modularly about local store, more specifically, we seek a model of higher order *separation logic* [21]. It has been convincingly argued in previous work on categorical models of separation logic [2,3] that a core abstraction device unifying such models is a notion of *BI-hyperdoctrine*, extending Lawvere's hyperdoctrines [10], which provide a corresponding abstraction for the first order logic. BI-hyperdoctrines are standardly built on *BI-algebras*, which are also standardly constructed from *partial commutative monoids (pcm)*, or more generally from *resource algebras* as in the IRIS state of the art advanced framework for higher order separation logic [8]. One subtlety our construction reveals is that it does not seem to be possible to obtain a *BI-algebra* following general recipes from a pcm (or a resource algebra), due to the inherent local nature of the storage model, which does not allow one to canonically map store contents into a global address space. Another subtlety is that the devised logic is necessarily non-classical, which is intuitively explained by the fact that the semantics of programs must be suitably irrelevant to garbage collection, and in our case this follows from entirely formal considerations (Yoneda lemma). It is also worth mentioning that for this reason the logical theory that we obtain is incompatible with the standard (classical or intuitionistic) predicate logic. E.g. the formula $\exists \ell. \, \ell \hookrightarrow 5$ is always valid in our setup, which expresses the fact that a heap *potentially* contains a cell equal to 5 (which need not be reachable) – this is in accord with the second equation above – and correspondingly, the formula $\forall \ell. \, \neg(\ell \hookrightarrow 5)$ is unsatisfiable. This and other similar phenomena are explained by the fact that our semantics essentially behaves as a Kripke semantics along two orthogonal axes: (proof relevant) *cell allocation* and (proof irrelevant) *cell accessibility*. While the latter captures a *programming* view of locality, the latter captures a *reasoning* view of locality, and as we argue (e.g. Example 26), they are generally mutually irreducible.

Related previous work   As we already pointed out, we take inspiration from the recent categorical approaches to modelling program semantics for dynamic references [9], as well as from higher order separation logic semantic frameworks [2]. Conceptually, the problem of combining separation logic with garbage collection mechanisms goes back to Reynolds [20], who indicated that standard semantics of separation logic in not compatible with garbage collection, which we also reinforce with our construction. Calcagno et al [4] addressed this issue by providing two models. The first model is based on total heaps, featuring the aforementioned effect of "potential" allocations. To cope with heap separation the authors introduced another model based on partial heaps, in which this effect again disappears, and has to be compensated by syntactic restrictions on the assertion language.

Plan of the paper   After preliminaries (Section 2), we give a modified presentation of a call-by-value language with full ground references and the full ground store monad (Sections 3 and 4) following the lines of [9]. In Section 5 we provide some general results for constructing semantics of higher order separation logics. The main development starts in Section 6 where we provide a construction of a BI-hyperdoctrine. We show some example illustrating our semantics in Section 7 and draw conclusions in Section 8.

2   Preliminaries

We assume basic familiarity with the elementary concepts of category theory [12,6], all the way up to monads, toposes, (co)ends and Kan extensions. We denote by $|\mathbf{C}|$ the class of objects of a category $\mathbf{C}$; we often suppress subscripts of natural transformation components if no confusion arises.

In this paper, we work with special kinds of *covariant presheaf toposes*, i.e. functor categories of the form $[\mathbf{C}, \mathbf{Set}]$, where $\mathbf{C}$ is small and satisfies the following *amalgamation condition*: for any $f \colon a \to b$ and $g \colon a \to c$ there exist $g' \colon b \to d$ and $f' \colon c \to d$ such that $f' \circ g = g' \circ f$. Such toposes are particularly well-behaved, and fall into the more general class of *De Morgan* toposes [7]. As presheaf toposes, De Morgan toposes are precisely characterized by the condition

$$(\text{put}) \quad \frac{\Gamma \vdash_{\mathsf{v}} \ell \colon \mathsf{Ref}_S \qquad \Gamma \vdash_{\mathsf{v}} v \colon \mathsf{CType}(S)}{\Gamma \vdash_{\mathsf{c}} \ell := v \colon 1} \qquad\qquad (\text{get}) \quad \frac{\Gamma \vdash_{\mathsf{v}} \ell \colon \mathsf{Ref}_S}{\Gamma \vdash_{\mathsf{c}} !\ell \colon \mathsf{CType}(S)}$$

$$\Gamma, \ell_1 \colon \mathsf{Ref}_{S_1}, \ldots, \ell_n \colon \mathsf{Ref}_{S_n} \vdash_{\mathsf{v}} v_1 \colon \mathsf{CType}(S_1)$$
$$\vdots$$
$$\Gamma, \ell_1 \colon \mathsf{Ref}_{S_1}, \ldots, \ell_n \colon \mathsf{Ref}_{S_n} \vdash_{\mathsf{v}} v_n \colon \mathsf{CType}(S_n)$$

$$(\text{new}) \quad \frac{\Gamma, \ell_1 \colon \mathsf{Ref}_{S_1}, \ldots, \ell_n \colon \mathsf{Ref}_{S_n} \vdash_{\mathsf{c}} p \colon A}{\Gamma \vdash_{\mathsf{c}} \mathsf{letref}\ \ell_1 := v_1, \ldots, \ell_n := v_n\ \mathsf{in}\ p \colon A}$$

Fig. 2: Term formation rules for memory management constructs.

that $2 = 1 + 1$ is a retract of the subobject classifier Ω. More specifically, our $\mathbf{C}$ support further useful structure, in particular, a strict monoidal tensor $\oplus$ with jointly epic injections in_1, in_2, forming an *independent coproduct* structure, as recently identified by Simpson [22]. Moreover, if the coslices $c \downarrow \mathbf{C}$ support independent products, we obtain *local independent coproducts* in $\mathbf{C}$, which are essentially cospans $c_1 \to c_1 \oplus_c c_2 \leftarrow c_2$ in $c \downarrow \mathbf{C}$. Given $\rho_1 \colon c \to c_1$ and $\rho_2 \colon c \to c_2$, we thus always have $\rho_1 \bullet \rho_2 \colon c_1 \to c_1 \oplus_c c_2$ and $\rho_2 \bullet \rho_1 \colon S_2 \to c_1 \oplus_c c_2$, such that $(\rho_1 \bullet \rho_2) \circ \rho_1 = (\rho_2 \bullet \rho_1) \circ \rho_2$, and as a consequence, $[\mathbf{C}, \mathbf{Set}]$ is a De Morgan topos. Intuitively, the category $\mathbf{C}$ represents worlds in the sense of *possible world semantics* [15,19]. A morphism $\rho \colon a \to b$ witnesses the fact that b is a *future world* w.r.t. a. Existence of local independent products intuitively ensures that diverse futures of a given world can eventually be unified in a canonical way.

Every functor $\mathfrak{f} \colon \mathbf{C} \to \mathbf{D}$ induces a functor $\mathfrak{f}^\star \colon [\mathbf{D}, \mathbf{Set}] \to [\mathbf{C}, \mathbf{Set}]$ by precomposition with $\mathfrak{f}$. By general considerations, there is a right adjoint $\mathfrak{f}_\star \colon [\mathbf{C}, \mathbf{Set}] \to [\mathbf{D}, \mathbf{Set}]$, computed as $\mathsf{Ran}_{\mathfrak{f}}$, the right Kan extension along $\mathfrak{f}$. This renders the adjunction $\mathfrak{f}^\star \dashv \mathfrak{f}_\star$, as a *geometric morphism*, in particular, $\mathfrak{f}^\star$ preserves all finite limits.

3   A Call-by-Value Language with Local References

To set the context, we consider the following higher order language of programs with local references by slightly adapting the language of Kammar et al [9] to match with the *fine-grain call-by-value* perspective [11]. This allows us to formally distinguish *pure* and *effectful* judgements. First, we postulate a collection of *cell sorts* $\mathcal{S}$ and then introduce further types with the grammar:

$$A, B \ldots ::= 0 \mid 1 \mid A \times B \mid A + B \mid A \to B \mid \mathsf{Ref}_S \qquad (S \in \mathcal{S}) \qquad (1)$$

A type is *first order* if it does not involve the function type constructors $A \to B$. We then fix a map CType, assigning a first order type to every given sort from $\mathcal{S}$. We show three term formation rules over these data in Fig. 2 specific to local store.

Here the v-indices at the turnstiles indicate *values* and the c-indices indicate *computations*. In **(put)** the cell referenced by ℓ is updated with a value v, **(get)** returns a value under the reference ℓ and **(new)** simultaneously allocates new cells filled with the values $v_1, \ldots, v_n$ and makes them accessible in p under the corresponding references $\ell_1, \ldots, \ell_n$. A fine-grain call-by-value language is interpreted standardly in a category with a monad, which in our case must additionally provide a semantics to the rules **(put)**, **(get)** and **(new)**. We present this monad in detail in the next section.

Example 1 (Doubly Linked Lists). Let $\mathcal{S} = \{DLList\}$ and let $\mathsf{CType}(DLList) = 2 \times (\mathsf{Ref}_{DLList} + 1) \times (\mathsf{Ref}_{DLList} + 1)$, which indicates that a list element is a Boolean (i.e. an element of $2 = 1 + 1$) and two pointers (forwards and backwards) to list elements, each of which may be missing. Note that we thus avoid empty lists and null-pointers: every list contains at least one element, and the elements added by $+1$ cannot be dereferenced. This example provides a suitable illustration for the letref construct. E.g. the program

$$\mathsf{letref}\ \ell_1 := (0, \mathsf{inr}\ \star, \mathsf{inl}\ \ell_2);\ \ell_2 := (1, \mathsf{inl}\ \ell_1, \mathsf{inr}\ \star)\ \mathsf{in}\ \mathsf{ret}\ \ell_1$$

simultaneously creates two list elements pointing to each other and returns a reference to the first one.

4 Full Ground Store in the Abstract

We proceed to present the full ground store monad by slightly tweaking the original construction [9] towards higher generality. The main distinction is that we do not recur to any specific program syntax and proceed in a completely axiomatic manner in terms of functors and natural transformations. This mainly serves the purpose of developing our logic in Section 6, which will require a coherent upgrade of the present model. Besides this, in this section we demonstrate flexibility of our formulation by showing that it also instantiates to the model previously developed by Plotkin and Power [16] (Theorem 8).

Our present formalization is parametric in three aspects: the set of *sorts* $\mathcal{S}$, the set of *locations* $\mathcal{L}$ and a map range, introduced below for interpreting $\mathcal{S}$. We assume that $\mathcal{L}$ is canonically isomorphic to the set of natural numbers $\mathbb{N}$ under $\#\colon \mathcal{L} \cong \mathbb{N}$. Using this isomorphism, we commonly use the "shift of $\ell \in \mathcal{L}$ by $n \in \mathbb{N}$", defined as follows: $\ell + n = \#^{-1}(\#\ell + n)$.

Heap layouts and abstract heap(let)s Let $\mathbf{W}$ be a category of *(heap) layouts* and injections defined as follows: an object $w \in |\mathbf{W}|$ is a finitely supported partial function $w\colon \mathcal{L} \rightharpoonup_{fin} \mathcal{S}$ and a morphism $\rho\colon w \to w'$ is a type preserving injection $\rho\colon \mathsf{dom}\ w \to \mathsf{dom}\ w'$, i.e. for all $l \in \mathsf{img}\ w$, $w(\ell) = w'(\rho(\ell))$. We will equivalently view w as a left-unique subset of $\mathcal{L} \times \mathcal{S}$ and hence use the notation $(\ell\colon S) \in w$ as an equivalent of $w(\ell) = S$. Injections $\rho\colon w \to w'$ with the property that $w(\ell\colon S) = \ell\colon S$ for all $(\ell\colon S) \in w$ we also call *inclusions* and write $w \subseteq w'$ instead of $\rho\colon w \to w'$, for obviously there is at most one inclusion from w to w'. If $w \subseteq w'$

then we call w a *sublayout* of w'. We next postulate

$$\text{range}\colon \mathcal{S} \to [\mathbf{W}, \mathbf{Set}].$$

The idea is, given a sort $S \in \mathcal{S}$ and a heap layout $w \in |\mathbf{W}|$, $\text{range}(S)(w)$ yields the set of possible values for cells of type S over w.

Example 2. Assuming the grammar (1) and a corresponding map CType, a generic type A is interpreted as a presheaf $\underline{A}\colon \mathbf{W} \to \mathbf{Set}$, by obvious structural induction, e.g. $\underline{A \times B} = \underline{A} \times \underline{B}$, except for the clause for Ref, for which $(\underline{\text{Ref}_S})w = w^{-1}(S)$. This yields the following definition for range: $\text{range}(S) = \text{CType}(S)$ [9].

Example 3 (Simple Store). By taking $\mathcal{S} = \{\star\}$, $\mathcal{L} = \mathbb{N}$ (natural numbers) and $\text{range}(\star)(w) = \mathcal{V}$ where $\mathcal{V}$ is a fixed set of *values*, we essentially obtain the model previously explored by Plotkin and Power [16]. We reserve the term *simple store* for this instance. Simple store is a ground store (since range is a constant functor), moreover this store is untyped (since $\mathcal{S} = \{\star\}$) and the locations $\mathcal{L}$ are precisely the natural numbers.

A *heap* over a layout w assigns to each $(\ell\colon S) \in w$ an element from $\text{range}(S)(w)$. More generally, a *heaplet* over w assigns an element from $\text{range}(S)(w)$ to *some*, possibly not all, $(\ell\colon S) \in w$. We thus define the following *heaplet bi-functor* $\mathcal{H}\colon \mathbf{W}^{\text{op}} \times \mathbf{W} \to \mathbf{Set}$:

$$\mathcal{H}(w^-, w^+) = \prod_{(\ell\colon S) \in w^-} \text{range}(S)(w^+)$$

and identify the elements of $\mathcal{H}(w^-, w^+)$ with heaplets and the elements of $\mathcal{H}(w, w)$ with heaps. Of course, we intend to use $\mathcal{H}(w^-, w^+)$ for such w^- and w^+ that the former is a sublayout of the latter. The contravariant action of H is given by projection and the covariant action is induced by functoriality of $\text{range}(S)$.

$$\text{pr}_{(\ell\colon S)}(\mathcal{H}(w^-, \rho_1\colon w_1^+ \to w_2^+)(\eta \in \mathcal{H}(w^-, w_1^+))) = \text{range}(S)(\rho_1)(\text{pr}_{(\ell\colon S)}\,\eta)$$

$$\text{pr}_{(\ell\colon S)}(\mathcal{H}(\rho_2\colon w_2^- \to w_1^-, w^+)(\eta \in \mathcal{H}(w_1^-, w^+))) = \text{pr}_{\rho_2(\ell\colon S)}\,\eta$$

The heaplet functor preserves independent coproduct, we overload the $\oplus$ operation with the isomorphism $\oplus\colon \mathcal{H}(w_1, w) \times \mathcal{H}(w_2, w) \cong \mathcal{H}(w_1 \oplus w_2, w)$.

Example 4. For illustration, consider the following simplistic example. Let $\mathcal{S} = \{Int, \text{Ref}_{Int}, \text{Ref}_{\text{Ref}_{Int}}, \dots\}$ where Int is meant to capture the ground type of integers and recursively, Ref_A is the type of pointers to A. Then, we put

$$\text{range}(Int)(w) = \mathbb{Z}, \quad \text{range}(\text{Ref}_S)(w) = w^{-1}(S) = \{\ell \in \text{dom } w \mid w(\ell) = S\}.$$

For a heaplet example, consider $w^- = \{\ell_1\colon Int, \ell_2\colon \text{Ref}_{Int}\}$ and $w^+ = \{\ell_1\colon Int, \ell_2\colon \text{Ref}_{Int}, \ell_3\colon Int\}$. Hence, w^- is a sublayout of w^+. By viewing the elements of $\mathcal{H}(w^-, w^+)$ as lists of assignments on w^-, we can define $s_1, s_2 \in \mathcal{H}(w^-, w^+)$ as follows: $s_1 = [\ell_1\colon Int \mapsto 5, \ell_2\colon \text{Ref}_{\text{int}} \mapsto \ell_1]$, $s_2 = [\ell_1\colon Int \mapsto 3, \ell_2\colon \text{Ref}_{\text{int}} \mapsto \ell_3]$. The heaplets s_1 and s_2 can be graphically presented as follows:

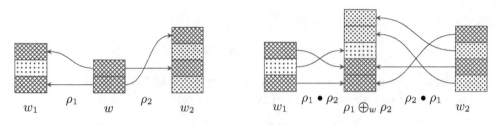

Fig. 3: Local independent coproduct

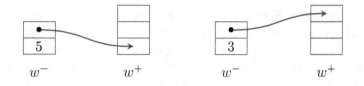

The category $\mathbf{W}$ supports (local) independent coproducts described in Section 2. These are constructed as follows. For $w, w' \in |\mathbf{C}|$, $w \oplus w' = w \cup \{\ell + n + 1 : S \mid (\ell, c) \in w'\}$ with n being the largest index for which w is defined on $\#^{-1}(n)$. This yields a strict monoidal structure $\oplus : \mathbf{W} \times \mathbf{W} \to \mathbf{W}$. Intuitively, $w_1 \oplus w_2$ is a canonical disjoint sum of w_1 and w_2, but note that $\oplus$ is not a coproduct in $\mathbf{W}$ (e.g. there is no $\nabla : 1 \oplus 1 \to 1$, for $\mathbf{W}$ only contains injections). For every $\rho : w_1 \to w_2$, there is a canonical complement $\rho^{\mathsf{c}} : w_2 \ominus \rho \to w_2$ whose domain $w_2 \ominus \rho = w_2 \smallsetminus \operatorname{img} \rho$ consists of all such cells $(\ell : S) \in w_2$ that ρ misses. Given two morphisms $\rho_1 : w \to w_1$ and $\rho_2 : w \to w_2$, we define the local independent coproduct $w_1 \oplus_w w_2$ as the layout consisting of the locations from w, and the ones from w_1 and w_2 which are neither in the image of ρ_1 nor in the image of ρ_2:

$$\rho_1 \oplus_w \rho_2 = w \oplus (w_1 \ominus \rho_1) \oplus (w_2 \ominus \rho_2).$$

There are morphisms $w_1 \xrightarrow{\ \rho_1 \bullet \rho_2\ } \rho_1 \oplus_w \rho_2$ and $w_2 \xrightarrow{\ \rho_2 \bullet \rho_1\ } \rho_1 \oplus_w \rho_2$ such that

$$
\begin{array}{ccc}
w & \xrightarrow{\ \rho_2\ } & w_2 \\
{\scriptstyle \rho_1} \downarrow & & \downarrow {\scriptstyle \rho_2 \bullet \rho_1} \\
w_1 & \xrightarrow{\ \rho_1 \bullet \rho_2\ } & \rho_1 \oplus_w \rho_2
\end{array}
$$

Fig. 3 illustrates this definition with a concrete example.

Initialization and hiding Note that in the simple store model (Definition 3), $\mathcal{H}$ is equivalently a contravariant functor $H : \mathbf{W}^{\mathrm{op}} \to \mathbf{Set}$ with $Hw = \mathcal{V}^w$, hence $\mathcal{H}$ can be placed e.g. in $[\mathbf{W}^{\mathrm{op}}, \mathbf{Set}]$. In general, $\mathcal{H}$ is mix-variant, which calls for a more ingenious category where H could be placed. Designing such category is indeed the key insight of [9]. Closely following this work, we introduce a category $\mathbf{E}$, whose objects are the same as those of $\mathbf{W}$, and the morphisms $\epsilon \in \mathbf{E}(w, w')$, called *initializations*, consist of an injection $\rho : w \to w'$ and a heaplet $\eta \in \mathcal{H}(w' \ominus \rho, w')$:

$$\mathbf{E}(w, w') = \sum\nolimits_{\rho\,:\,w \to w'} \mathcal{H}(w' \ominus \rho, w').$$

Recall that the morphism $\rho\colon w \to w'$ represents a move from a world with w allocated memory cells a world with w' allocated memory cells. A morphism of $\mathbf{E}$ is a morphism of $\mathbf{W}$ augmented with a heaplet part η, which provides the information how the newly allocated cells in $w' \ominus \rho$ are filled. The heap functor now can be viewed as a representable presheaf $H\colon \mathbf{E} \to \mathbf{Set}$ essentially because by definition, $Hw = \mathcal{H}(w, w) \cong \mathbf{E}(\emptyset, w)$. Let us agree to use the notation $\epsilon\colon w \rightsquigarrow w'$ for morphisms in $\mathbf{E}$ to avoid confusion with the morphisms in $\mathbf{W}$.

Like $\mathbf{W}$, $\mathbf{E}$ supports local independent coproducts, but remarkably $\mathbf{E}$ does not have vanilla independent coproducts, due to the fact that $\mathbf{E}$ does not have an initial object. That is, in turn, because defining an inital morphism would amount to defining canonical fresh values for newly allocated cells, but those need not exist. The local independent coproducts of $\mathbf{W}$ and $\mathbf{E}$ agree in the sense that we can *promote* an initialization $(\rho_2, \eta)\colon w \rightsquigarrow w_2$ along an injection $\rho_1\colon w \to w_1$ to obtain an initialization $\rho_1 \bullet (\rho_2, \eta)\colon w_1 \rightsquigarrow \rho_1 \oplus_{w_1} \rho_2$. This is accomplished by mapping the heaplet structure η forward along $\rho_2 \bullet \rho_1\colon w_2 \to \rho_1 \oplus_w \rho_2$.

Hiding monad   Recall that the local store is supposed to be insensitive to garbage collection. This is captured by identifying the stores that agree on their observable parts using the *hiding monad* P defined on $[\mathbf{E}, \mathbf{Set}]$ as follows:

$$(PX)w = \int^{\rho\,:\,w \to w' \in w \downarrow \mathfrak{u}} Xw'. \tag{2}$$

Here, $\mathfrak{u}\colon \mathbf{E} \to \mathbf{W}$ is the obvious heaplet discarding functor $\mathfrak{u}(\rho, \eta) = \rho$. Intuitively, in (2), we view the locations of w as public and the ones of $w' \ominus \rho$ as private. The integral sign denotes a *coend*, which in this case is just an ordinary colimit on $\mathbf{Set}$ and is computed as a quotient of $\sum_{\rho\,:\,w \to w' \in w \downarrow \mathfrak{u}} Xw'$ under the equivalence relation $\sim$ obtained as a symmetric-transitive closure of the relation

$$(\rho\colon w \to w_1, x \in Xw_1) \preceq (\mathfrak{u}\epsilon \circ \rho\colon w \to w_2, (X\epsilon)(x) \in Xw_2) \qquad (\epsilon\colon w_1 \rightsquigarrow w_2)$$

Note that $\preceq$ is a preorder. Moreover, it enjoys the following *diamond property*.

Proposition 5. *If* $(\rho, x) \preceq (\rho_1, x_1)$ *and* $(\rho, x) \preceq (\rho_2, x_2)$ *then* $(\rho_1, x_1) \preceq (\rho', x')$ *and* $(\rho_2, x_2) \preceq (\rho', x')$ *for a suitable* (ρ', x').
    Hence $(\rho_1, x_1) \sim (\rho_2, x_2)$ *iff* $(\rho_1, x_1) \preceq (\rho, x)$, $(\rho_2, x_2) \preceq (\rho, x)$ *for some* (ρ, x).

Example 6. To illustrate the equivalence relation $\sim$ behind P, we revisit the setting of Example 4. Consider the following situations:

Here, the solid lines indicate public locations and the dotted lines indicate private locations. The left equivalence holds because the private locations are not reachable from the public ones by references (depicted as arrows). On the right, although the public parts are equal, the reachable cells of the private parts reveal the distinction, preventing the equivalence under $\sim$. Intuitively, hiding identifies those heaps that agree both on their public and reachable private part.

The covariant action of PX (on $\mathbf{E}$) is defined via promotion of initializations:

$$(PX)(\epsilon\colon w_1 \rightsquigarrow w_2)(\rho\colon w_1 \to w_1', x \in Xw_1')_\sim$$
$$= (\mathfrak{u}\epsilon \bullet \rho\colon w_2 \to \rho \oplus_{w_1} \mathfrak{u}\epsilon, X(\rho \bullet \epsilon)(x))_\sim.$$

Furthermore, there is a contravariant hiding operation (on $\mathbf{W}$) given by the canonical action of the coend: for $\rho\colon w \to w'$, we define $\mathsf{hide}_\rho\colon PXw' \to PXw$:

$$\mathsf{hide}_\rho(\rho'\colon w' \to w'', x \in Xw'')_\sim \; = (\rho' \circ \rho, x)_\sim \tag{3}$$

This allows us to regard P both as a functor $[\mathbf{E}, \mathbf{Set}] \to [\mathbf{E}, \mathbf{Set}]$ and as a functor $[\mathbf{E}, \mathbf{Set}] \to [\mathbf{W}^{\mathrm{op}}, \mathbf{Set}]$.

Full ground store monad　We now have all the necessary ingredients to obtain the full ground store monad T on $[\mathbf{W}, \mathbf{Set}]$. This monad is assembled by composing the functors in Fig. 1 in the following way. First, observe that $(P(- \times H))^H$ is a standard (global) store monad transform of P on $[\mathbf{E}, \mathbf{Set}]$. This monad is sandwiched between the adjunction $\mathfrak{u}_\star \vdash \mathfrak{u}^\star$ induced by $\mathfrak{u}$ (see Section 2). Since any monad itself resolves into an adjunction, sandwiching in it between an adjunction again yields a monad. In summary,

$$T = \left([\mathbf{W}, \mathbf{Set}] \xrightarrow{\mathfrak{u}^\star} [\mathbf{E}, \mathbf{Set}] \xrightarrow{P(- \times H)^H} [\mathbf{E}, \mathbf{Set}] \xrightarrow{\mathfrak{u}_\star} [\mathbf{W}, \mathbf{Set}]\right). \tag{4}$$

Theorem 7. *The monad T, defined by (4) is strong.*

Proof. The proof is a straightforward generalization of the proof in [9].　　□

We can recover the monad previously developed by Plotkin and Power [16] by resorting to the simple store (Example 3).

Theorem 8. *Under the simple store model T is isomorphic to the local store monad from [16]:*

$$(TX)w \cong \left(\int^{\rho\colon w\to w' \in w \downarrow \mathbf{W}} Xw' \times \mathcal{V}^{w'}\right)^{\mathcal{V}^w}.$$

Using (4), one obtains the requisite semantics to the language in Fig. 2 using the standard clauses of fine-grain call-by-value [11], except for the special clauses for **(put)**, **(get)** and **(new)**, which require special operations of the monad:

$$\mathsf{get}\colon \mathfrak{u}^\star\underline{\mathsf{Ref}}_S \times H \to \mathfrak{u}^\star\underline{\mathsf{CType}}(S) \times H$$
$$\mathsf{put}\colon (\mathfrak{u}^\star\underline{\mathsf{Ref}}_S \times \mathfrak{u}^\star\underline{\mathsf{CType}}(S)) \times H \to 1 \times H$$
$$\mathsf{new}\colon \mathfrak{u}^\star(\underline{\mathsf{CType}}(S)^{\underline{\mathsf{Ref}}_S}) \times H \to P(\mathfrak{u}^\star\underline{\mathsf{Ref}}_S \times H)$$

5 Intermezzo: BI-Hyperdoctrines and BI-Algebras

To be able to give a categorical notion of higher order logic over local store, following Biering et al [2], we aim to construct a *BI-hyperdoctrine*.

Note that algebraic structures, such as monoids and Heyting algebras can be straightforwardly internalized in any category with finite products, which gives rise to *internal monoids*, *internal Heyting algebras*, etc. The situation changes when considering non-algebraic properties. In particular, recall that a Heyting algebra A is *complete* iff it has arbitrary joins, which are preserved by binary meets. The corresponding categorical notion is essentially obtained from spelling out generic definitions from internal category theory [6, B2] and is as follows.

Definition 9 (Internally Complete Heyting Algebras). An internal Heyting (Boolean) algebra A in a finitely complete category $\mathbf{C}$ is *internally complete* if for every $f \in \mathbf{C}(I, J)$, there exist *indexed joins* $\bigvee_f \colon \mathbf{C}(I, A) \to \mathbf{C}(J, A)$, left order-adjoint to $(-) \circ f \colon \mathbf{C}(J, A) \to \mathbf{C}(I, A)$ such that for any pullback square on the left, the corresponding diagram on the right commutes (*Beck-Chevalley condition*):

$$
\begin{array}{ccc}
I & \xrightarrow{\ f\ } & J \\
{\scriptstyle g}\downarrow & \lrcorner & \downarrow{\scriptstyle h} \\
I' & \xrightarrow[\ f'\ ]{} & J'
\end{array}
\qquad\qquad
\begin{array}{ccc}
\mathbf{C}(J, A) & \xrightarrow{(-)\circ f} & \mathbf{C}(I, A) \\
{\scriptstyle \bigvee_h}\downarrow & & \downarrow{\scriptstyle \bigvee_g} \\
\mathbf{C}(J', A) & \xrightarrow[(-)\circ f']{} & \mathbf{C}(I', A)
\end{array}
$$

It follows generally that existence of indexed joins $\bigvee$ implies existence of indexed meets $\bigwedge$, which then satisfy dual conditions ([6, Corollary 2.4.8]).

Remark 10 (Binary Joins/Meets). The adjointness condition for indexed joins means precisely that $\bigvee_f \phi \leqslant \psi$ iff $\phi \leqslant \psi \circ f$ for every $\phi \colon I \to A$ and every $\psi \colon J \to A$. If $\mathbf{C}$ has binary coproducts, by taking $f = \nabla \colon X + X \to X$ we obtain that $\bigvee_\nabla \phi \leqslant \psi$ iff $\phi \leqslant [\psi, \psi]$ iff $\phi \circ \mathsf{inl} \leqslant \psi$ and $\phi \circ \mathsf{inr} \leqslant \psi$. This characterizes $\bigvee_\nabla [\phi_1, \phi_2] \colon X \to A$ as the binary join of $\phi_1, \phi_2 \colon X \to A$. Binary meets are characterized analogously.

Definition 11 ((First Order) (BI-)Hyperdoctrine). Let $\mathbf{C}$ be a category with finite products. A *first order hyperdoctrine over* $\mathbf{C}$ is a functor $S \colon \mathbf{C}^{\mathsf{op}} \to \mathbf{Poset}$ with the following properties:

1. given $X \in |\mathbf{C}|$, SX is a Heyting algebra;
2. given $f \in \mathbf{C}(X, Y)$, $Sf \colon SY \to SX$ is a Heyting algebra morphism;
3. for any product projection $\mathsf{fst} \colon X \times Y \to X$, there are $(\exists Y)_X \colon S(X \times Y) \to SX$ and $(\forall Y)_X \colon S(X \times Y) \to SX$, which are respective left and right order-adjoints of $S\,\mathsf{fst} \colon S(X \times Y) \to SX$, naturally in X;
4. for every $X \in |\mathbf{C}|$, there is $=_X \in S(X \times X)$ such that for all $\phi \in S(X \times X)$, $\top \leqslant (S\langle \mathsf{id}_X, \mathsf{id}_X \rangle)(\phi)$ iff $=_X \leqslant \phi$.

If additionally

$$\frac{\Gamma \vdash_\mathsf{v} v \colon A \quad \Gamma \vdash \phi \colon \mathsf{P}A}{\Gamma \vdash \phi(v) \colon \mathrm{prop}} \qquad \frac{\Gamma, x \colon A \vdash \phi \colon \mathrm{prop}}{\Gamma \vdash x.\,\phi \colon \mathsf{P}A} \qquad \frac{\Gamma \vdash_\mathsf{v} \ell \colon \mathsf{Ref}_S \quad \Gamma \vdash_\mathsf{v} v \colon \mathsf{CType}(S)}{\Gamma \vdash \ell \hookrightarrow v \colon \mathrm{prop}}$$

$$\frac{\Gamma \vdash \phi \colon \mathsf{P}A}{\Gamma \vdash Q\,\phi \colon \mathrm{prop}} \quad (Q \in \{\forall, \exists\}) \qquad \frac{\Gamma \vdash_\mathsf{v} v \colon A \quad \Gamma \vdash_\mathsf{v} w \colon A}{\Gamma \vdash v = w \colon \mathrm{prop}}$$

$$\frac{}{\Gamma \vdash c \colon \mathrm{prop}} \quad (c \in \{\top, \bot\}) \qquad \frac{\Gamma \vdash \phi \colon \mathrm{prop} \quad \Gamma \vdash \psi \colon \mathrm{prop}}{\Gamma \vdash \phi \,\$\, \psi \colon \mathrm{prop}} \quad (\$ \in \{\wedge, \vee, \Rightarrow, \star, \twoheadrightarrow\})$$

Fig. 4: Term formation rules for the higher order separation logic.

5. given $X \in |\mathbf{C}|$, SX is a *BI-algebra*, i.e. a commutative monoid equipped with a right order-adjoint to multiplication;
6. given $f \in \mathbf{C}(X, Y)$, $Sf \colon SY \to SX$ is a BI-algebra morphism,

then S is called a *first order BI-hyperdoctrine*.

In a *(higher order) hyperdoctrine*, $\mathbf{C}$ is additionally required to be Cartesian closed and every SX is required to be poset-isomorphic to $\mathbf{C}(X, A)$ for a suitable internal Heyting algebra $A \in |\mathbf{C}|$ naturally in X. Such a hyperdoctrine is a *BI-hyperdoctrine* if moreover A is an internal BI-algebra.

Proposition 12. *Every internally complete Heyting algebra A in a Cartesian closed category $\mathbf{C}$ with finite limits gives rise to a canonical hyperdoctrine $\mathbf{C}(-, A)$: for every X, $\mathbf{C}(X, A)$ is a poset under $f \leqslant g$ iff $f \wedge g = f$.*

Proof. Clearly, every $\mathbf{C}(X, A)$ is a Heyting algebra and every $\mathbf{C}(f, A)$ is a Heyting algebra morphism. The quantifies are defined mutually dually as follows:

$$(\exists Y)_X (\phi \colon X \times Y \to A) = \bigvee\nolimits_{\mathsf{fst} \colon X \times Y \to X} \phi,$$

$$(\forall Y)_X (\phi \colon X \times Y \to A) = \bigwedge\nolimits_{\mathsf{fst} \colon X \times Y \to X} \phi.$$

Naturality in X follows from the corresponding Beck-Chevalley conditions.

Finally, internal equality $=_X \colon X \times X \to A$ is defined as $\bigvee_{\langle \mathsf{id}_X, \mathsf{id}_X \rangle} \top$.   □

A standard way to obtain an (internally) complete BI-algebra is to resort to ordered partial commutative monoids [18].

Definition 13 (Ordered PCM [18]). An *ordered partial commutative monoid (pcm)* is a tuple $(\mathcal{M}, \mathcal{E}, \cdot, \leqslant)$ where $\mathcal{M}$ is a set, $\mathcal{E} \subseteq \mathcal{M}$ is a set of *units*, *multiplication* $\cdot$ is a partial binary operation on $\mathcal{M}$, and $\leqslant$ is a preorder on $\mathcal{M}$, satisfying an number of axioms (see [18] for details).

We note that using general recipes [3], for every internal ordered pcm M in a topos $\mathbf{C}$ with subobject classifier Ω, $\mathbf{C}(- \times M, \Omega)$ forms a BI-hyperdoctrine, on particular, if $\mathbf{C} = \mathbf{Set}$ then $\mathbf{Set}(- \times M, 2)$ is a BI-hyperdoctrine.

6 A Higher Order Logic for Full Ground Store

We proceed to develop a local version of separation logic using semantic principles explored in the previous sections. That is, we seek an interpretation for the language in Fig. 4 in the category $[\mathbf{W}, \mathbf{Set}]$ over the type system (1), extended with *predicate types* $\mathsf{P}A$. The judgements $\Gamma \vdash \phi$: prop type formulas depending on a variable context Γ. Additionally, we have judgements of the form $\Gamma \vdash \phi$: $\mathsf{P}A$ for *predicates in context*. Both kinds of judgements are mutually convertible using the standard application-abstraction routine. Note that expressions for quantifiers $\exists x. \phi$ are thus obtained in two steps: by forming a predicate $x. \phi$, and subsequently applying $\exists$. Apart from the standard logical connectives, we postulate *separating conjunction* $\star$ and *separating implication* $-\!\!\star$.

Our goal is to build a BI-hyperdoctrine, using the recipes, summarized in the previous section. That is, we construct a certain internal BI-algebra Θ in $[\mathbf{W}, \mathbf{Set}]$, and subsequently conclude that $[-, \Theta]$ is a BI-hyperdoctrine in question. In what follows, most of the effort is invested into constructing an internally complete Boolean algebra $\check{\mathcal{P}} \circ (\hat{P}\hat{H})$ (hence $[-, \check{\mathcal{P}} \circ (\hat{P}\hat{H})]$ is a hyperdoctrine), from which Θ is carved out as a subfunctor, identified by an upward closure condition. Here, $\check{\mathcal{P}}$ is a contravariant powerset functor, and $\hat{P}$ and $\hat{H}$ are certain modifications of the hiding and the heap functors from Section 4. As we shall see, the move from $\check{\mathcal{P}} \circ (\hat{P}\hat{H})$ to Θ remedies the problem of the former that the natural separation conjunction operator $\star$ on it does not have unit (Remark 19).

In order to model resource separation, we must identify a domain of logical assertions over partial heaps, i.e. heaplets, instead of total heaps. We thus need to derive a unary (covariant) heaplet functor from the binary, mix-variant one $\mathcal{H}$ used before. We must still cope not only with heaplets, but with partially hidden heaplets, to model information hiding. A seemingly natural candidate functor for hidden heaplets is the composition

$$P\left(\mathbf{E} \xrightarrow{\sum_{w \subseteq -} \mathcal{H}(w, -)} \mathbf{Set}\right) : \mathbf{W}^{\mathrm{op}} \to \mathbf{Set}.$$

One problem of this definition is that the equivalence relation $\sim$ underlying the construction of P (2) is too fine. Consider, for example, $e_w = (\emptyset \subseteq w, \star) \in \sum_{w' \subseteq w} \mathcal{H}(w', w)$. Then $(\mathsf{id}: w \to w, e_w) \not\prec (\mathsf{inl}: w \to w \oplus \{\star: 1\}, e_{w \oplus \{\star: 1\}})$, i.e. two hidden heaplets would not be equivalent if one extends the other by an inaccessible hidden cell. In order to arrive at a more reasonable model of logical assertions, we modify the previous model by replacing the category of initializations $\mathbf{E}$ is a category $\hat{\mathbf{E}}$ of *partial initializations*. This will induce a hiding monad $\hat{P}$ over $[\hat{\mathbf{E}}, \mathbf{Set}]$ using exactly the same formula (2) as for P.

A partial initialization is a pair (ρ, η) with $\rho \in \mathbf{W}(w_1^-, w_2^+)$ and $\eta \in \sum_{w^- \subseteq w_2^+ \ominus \rho} \mathcal{H}(w^-, w_2^+)$. Let $\hat{\mathbf{E}}$ be the category of heap layouts and partial initializations. Analogously to $\mathfrak{u}$, there is an obvious partial-heap-forgetting functor $\hat{\mathfrak{u}}: \hat{\mathbf{E}} \to \mathbf{W}$. Let $\hat{H}: \hat{\mathbf{E}} \to \mathbf{Set}$ be the following *heaplet functor*:

$$\hat{H}w = \sum_{w' \subseteq w} \mathcal{H}(w', w).$$

Given a partial initialization $\epsilon = (\rho\colon w \to w', (w'' \subseteq w' \ominus \rho, \eta \in \mathcal{H}(w'', w')))\colon w \rightsquigarrow w'$, $\hat{H}\epsilon\colon \hat{H}w \to \hat{H}w'$ extends a given heaplet over w to a heaplet over w' via η:

$$(\hat{H}\epsilon)(w_1 \subseteq w, \eta' \in \mathcal{H}(w_1, w)) = (\rho[w_1] \cup w'' \subseteq w', \eta'')$$

where $\eta'' \in \mathcal{H}(\rho[w_1] \cup w'' \subseteq w', w')$ is as follows

$$\mathsf{pr}_{\rho(\ell\colon S)}\,\eta'' = \mathsf{range}(S)(\rho)(\mathsf{pr}_{(\ell\colon S)}\,\eta') \qquad\qquad ((\ell\colon S) \in w_1)$$

$$\mathsf{pr}_{(\ell\colon S)}\,\eta'' = \mathsf{pr}_{(\ell\colon S)}\,\eta \qquad\qquad ((\ell\colon S) \in w'')$$

With $\hat{\mathbf{E}}$ and $\hat{H}$ as above instead of $\mathbf{E}$ and H, the framework described in Section 4 transforms coherently.

Remark 14. Let us fix a fresh symbol $\boxtimes$, and note that

$$\hat{H}w = \sum\nolimits_{w' \subseteq w} \prod\nolimits_{(\ell\colon S) \in w'} \mathsf{range}(S)(w) \cong \prod\nolimits_{(\ell\colon S) \in w} (\mathsf{range}(S)(w) \uplus \{\boxtimes\}),$$

meaning that the passage from $\mathbf{E}$, H and P to $\hat{\mathbf{E}}$, $\hat{H}$ and $\hat{P}$ is equivalent to extending the **range** function with designated values $\boxtimes$ for *inaccessible locations*. We prefer to think of $\boxtimes$ this way and not as a content of *dangling pointers*, to emphasize that we deal with a *reasoning phenomenon* and not with a *programming phenomenon*, for our programs neither create nor process dangling pointers.

For the next proposition we need the following concrete description of the set $\hat{\mathfrak{u}}_\star(2^X)w$ as the end $\int_{\rho\colon w \to w' \in w \downarrow \hat{\mathfrak{u}}} \mathbf{Set}(Xw', 2)$: this set is a space of dependent functions ϕ sending every injection $\rho\colon w \to w'$ to a corresponding subset of Xw', and satisfying the constraint: $x \in \phi(\rho)$ iff $(X\,\epsilon)(x) \in \phi(\hat{\mathfrak{u}}\,\epsilon \circ \rho)$ for every $\epsilon\colon w' \rightsquigarrow w''$.

Proposition 15. *The following diagram commutes up to isomorphism:*

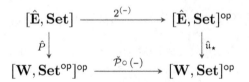

(using the fact that $[\mathbf{W}, \mathbf{Set}^{\mathrm{op}}]^{\mathrm{op}} \cong [\mathbf{W}^{\mathrm{op}}, \mathbf{Set}]$*) where* $\check{\mathcal{P}}$ *is the contravariant powerset functor* $\check{\mathcal{P}}\colon \mathbf{Set}^{\mathrm{op}} \to \mathbf{Set}$ *and for every* $X\colon \hat{\mathbf{E}} \to \mathbf{Set}$ *the relevant isomorphism* $\Phi_w\colon \hat{\mathfrak{u}}_\star(2^X)w \cong \check{\mathcal{P}}(\hat{P}Xw)$ *is as follows:*

$$(\rho\colon w \to w', x \in Xw')_\sim \in \Phi_w(\phi \in \hat{\mathfrak{u}}_\star(2^X)w) \iff x \in \phi(\rho). \qquad (5)$$

Let us clarify the significance of Proposition 15. The exponential $2^{\hat{H}}$ in $[\hat{\mathbf{E}}, \mathbf{Set}]$ can be thought of as a carrier of Boolean predicates over $\hat{H}$, and as we see next those form an internally complete Boolean algebra, which is carried from $[\hat{\mathbf{E}}, \mathbf{Set}]$ to $[\mathbf{W}, \mathbf{Set}]$ by $\hat{\mathfrak{u}}_\star$. The alternative route via $\hat{P}$ and $\check{\mathcal{P}}$ induces a Boolean algebra of predicates over hidden heaplets $\hat{P}\hat{H}$ directly in $[\mathbf{W}, \mathbf{Set}]$. The equivalence established in Proposition 15 witnesses agreement of these two structures.

Theorem 16. *For every* $X\colon \hat{\mathbf{E}} \to \mathbf{Set}$, $\check{\mathcal{P}} \circ (\hat{P}X)$ *is an internally complete Boolean algebra in* $[\mathbf{W}, \mathbf{Set}]$ *under*

$$\left(\bigvee_f \phi\colon I \to \check{\mathcal{P}} \circ (\hat{P}X)\right)_w (j \in Jw)$$
$$= \{(\rho\colon w \to w', x \in Xw')_\sim \mid \exists \epsilon\colon w' \rightsquigarrow w'', \exists i \in Iw''.$$
$$f_{w''}(i) = J(\hat{\mathbf{u}}\,\epsilon \circ \rho)(j) \wedge (\mathrm{id}_{w''}, (X\,\epsilon)(x))_\sim \in \phi_{w''}(i)\},$$

$$\left(\bigwedge_f \phi\colon I \to \check{\mathcal{P}} \circ (\hat{P}X)\right)_w (j \in Jw)$$
$$= \{(\rho\colon w \to w', x \in Xw')_\sim \mid \forall \epsilon\colon w' \rightsquigarrow w'', \forall i \in Iw''.$$
$$f_{w''}(i) = J(\hat{\mathbf{u}}\,\epsilon \circ \rho)(j) \Rightarrow (\mathrm{id}_{w''}, (X\,\epsilon)(x))_\sim \in \phi_{w''}(i)\}.$$

for every $f\colon I \to J$, *and the corresponding Boolean algebra operations are computed as set-theoretic unions, intersections and complements.*

By Theorem 16, we obtain a hyperdoctrine $[-, \check{\mathcal{P}} \circ (\hat{P}\hat{H})]$, which provides us with a model of (classical) higher order logic in $[\mathbf{W}, \mathbf{Set}]$. In particular, this allows us to interpret the language from Fig. 4 over $[\mathbf{W}, \mathbf{Set}]$ excluding the separation logic constructs, in such a way that

$$[\![\Gamma \vdash \phi\colon \mathrm{prop}]\!]\colon \underline{\Gamma} \to \check{\mathcal{P}} \circ (\hat{P}\hat{H}), \qquad [\![\Gamma \vdash \phi\colon \mathrm{P}A]\!]\colon \underline{\Gamma} \times \underline{A} \to \check{\mathcal{P}} \circ (\hat{P}\hat{H})$$

where $\underline{\Gamma} = \underline{A_1} \times \ldots \times \underline{A_n}$ for $\Gamma = (x_1\colon A_1, \ldots, x_n\colon A_n)$ where, additionally to the standard clauses, $\underline{\mathrm{P}A} = \check{\mathcal{P}} \circ \hat{P}(\mathbf{u}^\star \underline{A} \times \hat{H})$. The latter interpretation of predicate types $\mathrm{P}A$ is justified by the natural isomorphism:

$$(\check{\mathcal{P}} \circ (\hat{P}\hat{H}))^X \cong (\hat{\mathbf{u}}_\star(2^{\hat{H}}))^X \cong \hat{\mathbf{u}}_\star((2^{\hat{H}})^{\hat{\mathbf{u}}^\star X}) \cong \check{\mathcal{P}} \circ (\hat{P}(\hat{\mathbf{u}}^\star X \times \hat{H})).$$

Here, the first and the last transitions are by Φ from Proposition 15 and the middle one is due to the fact that clearly both $(\hat{\mathbf{u}}_\star(-))^X \vdash \hat{\mathbf{u}}^\star(X \times (-))$ and $\hat{\mathbf{u}}_\star((-)^{\hat{\mathbf{u}}^\star X}) \vdash \hat{\mathbf{u}}^\star(X \times (-))$.

Since every set $\hat{H}w$ models a heaplet in the standard sense [18], we can equip $\hat{H}w$ with a standard pointer model structure.

Proposition 17. *For every* $w \in |\mathbf{W}|$, $(\hat{H}w, \{(\emptyset \subseteq w, \star)\}, \cdot, \leqslant)$ *is an ordered pcm where for every* $w \in |\mathbf{W}|$, $\hat{H}w$ *is partially ordered as follows:*

$$(w_1 \subseteq w, \mathcal{H}(w_1 \subseteq w_2, w)\eta \in \mathcal{H}(w_1, w)) \leqslant (w_2 \subseteq w, \eta \in \mathcal{H}(w_2, w)) \quad (w_1 \subseteq w_2)$$

and for $w_1 \subseteq w$, $w_2 \subseteq w$ *and* $\eta_1 \in \mathcal{H}(w_1, w)$, $\eta_2 \in \mathcal{H}(w_2, w)$, $(w_1 \subseteq w, \eta_1) \cdot (w_2 \subseteq w, \eta_2)$ *equals* $(w_1 \cup w_2, \eta_1 \cup \eta_2)$ *if* $w_1 \cap w_2 = \emptyset$, *and otherwise undefined.*

As indicated in Section 5, we automatically obtain a BI-algebra structure over the set of all subsets of $\hat{H}w$. The same strategy does not apply to $\hat{P}\hat{H}w$, roughly because we cannot predict mutual arrangement of hidden partitions of two heaplets wrt to each other, for we do not have a global reference space for pointers as contrasted to the standard separation logic setting. We thus define a separating conjunction operator directly on every $\check{\mathcal{P}}(\hat{P}\hat{H}w)$ as follows:

$$\phi \star_w \psi = \{(\rho\colon w \to w', (w_1 \uplus w_2 \subseteq w', \eta \in \mathcal{H}(w_1 \uplus w_2, w')))_\sim \mid$$
$$(\rho, (w_1 \subseteq w', \mathcal{H}(w_1 \subseteq w_1 \uplus w_2, w')\eta))_\sim \in \phi,$$
$$(\rho, (w_2 \subseteq w', \mathcal{H}(w_2 \subseteq w_1 \uplus w_2, w')\eta))_\sim \in \psi\}.$$

Lemma 18. *The operator $\star_w$ on $\check{\mathcal{P}}(\hat{P}\hat{H}w)$ satisfies the following properties.*

1. *$\star_w$ is natural in w.*
2. *$\star_w$ is associative and commutative.*
3. *$(\rho\colon w \to w', (w'' \subseteq w', \eta \in \mathcal{H}(w'', w')))_\sim \in \phi \star_w \psi$ if and only if there exist w_1, w_2 such that $w_1 \uplus w_2 = w''$, $(\rho, (w_1 \subseteq w', \mathcal{H}(w_1 \subseteq w'', w')\eta))_\sim \in \phi$ and $(\rho, (w_2 \subseteq w', \mathcal{H}(w_2 \subseteq w'', w')\eta))_\sim \in \psi$.*

Property (3) specifically tells us that any representative of an equivalence class contained in a separating conjunction can be split in such a way that the respective pieces belong to the arguments of the separating conjunction.

Remark 19. The only candidate for the unit of the separating conjunction $\star_w$ would be the emptiness predicate $\mathsf{empty}_w\colon 1 \to \check{\mathcal{P}}(\hat{P}\hat{H}w)$, identifying precisely the empty heaplets. However, empty_w is not natural in w. In fact, it follows by Yoneda lemma that there are exactly two natural transformations $1 \to \check{\mathcal{P}} \circ (\hat{P}\hat{H})$, which are the total truth and the total false, none of which is a unit for $\star_w$.

Remark 19 provides a formal argument why we cannot interpret classical separation logic over $\check{\mathcal{P}} \circ (\hat{P}\hat{H})$. We thus proceed to identify for every w a subset of $\check{\mathcal{P}}(\hat{P}\hat{H}w)$, for which the total truth predicate becomes the unit of the separating conjunction. Concretely, let Θ be the subfunctor of $\check{\mathcal{P}} \circ (\hat{P}\hat{H})$ identified by the following *upward closure condition*: $\phi \in \Theta w$ if

$$(\rho, \eta)_\sim \in \phi,\ \eta \leqslant \eta' \qquad \text{imply} \qquad (\rho, \eta')_\sim \in \phi.$$

Lemma 20. *Θ is an internal complete sublattice of $\check{\mathcal{P}} \circ (\hat{P}\hat{H})$, i.e. the inclusion $\iota\colon \Theta \hookrightarrow \check{\mathcal{P}} \circ (\hat{P}\hat{H})$ preserves all meets and all joins. This canonically equips Θ with an internally complete Heyting algebra structure.*

Proof (Sketch). The key idea is to establish a retraction (ι, cl) with $\mathsf{cl} \circ \iota = \mathsf{id}$. The requisite structure is then transferred from $\check{\mathcal{P}} \circ (\hat{P}\hat{H})$ to Θ along it. The Heyting implication for Θ is obtained using the standard formula $(\phi \Rightarrow \psi) = \bigvee\{\xi \mid \phi \wedge \xi \leqslant \psi\}$ interpreted in the internal language. □

Lemma 21. *Separating conjunction preserves upward closure: for $\phi, \psi \in \Theta w$, $\phi \star_w \psi = \mathsf{cl}_w(\phi \star_w \psi)$.*

Lemma 22. *Θ is a BI-algebra: $\star_w$ is obtained by restriction from $\check{\mathcal{P}}(\hat{P}\hat{H}w)$ by Lemma 21, $\hat{P}\hat{H}w$ is the unit for it and*

$$\phi \twoheadrightarrow_w \psi = \{(\rho, \eta)_\sim \in \Theta w \mid \forall \rho'\colon w \to w', \eta_1, \eta_2 \in \hat{H}w', \eta_1 \cdot \eta_2 \text{ defined } \wedge$$
$$(\rho, \eta) \sim (\rho', \eta_1) \wedge (\rho', \eta_2)_\sim \in \phi \Rightarrow (\rho', \eta_1 \cdot \eta_2)_\sim \in \psi\}.$$

- $s, \rho, \eta \models \top$
- $s, \rho, \eta \models \phi \wedge \psi$ if $s, \rho, \eta \models \phi$ and $s, \rho, \eta \models \psi$
- $s, \rho, \eta \models \phi \vee \psi$ if $s, \rho, \eta \models \phi$ or $s, \rho, \eta \models \psi$
- $s, \rho, \eta \models \phi \Rightarrow \psi$ if for all $(\rho, \eta) \sim (\rho', \eta')$ and $\eta' \leqslant \eta''$,
  $s, \rho', \eta'' \models \phi$ implies $s, \rho', \eta'' \models \psi$
- $s, \rho, \eta \models \phi(v)$ if $s, \rho, (([\![\Gamma \vdash_{\mathsf{v}} v \colon A]\!]_{w'} \circ \underline{\Gamma}\rho)s, \eta) \models \phi$
- $s, \rho, (a, \eta) \models x.\phi$ if $a = (X\rho)b$ and $(s, b), \rho, \eta \models \phi$
- $s, \rho, \eta \models \ell \hookrightarrow v$ if $\eta = (w'' \subseteq w', \delta \in \mathcal{H}(w'', w'))$ and
  $\delta(r \colon S) = ([\![\Gamma \vdash_{\mathsf{v}} v \colon \mathsf{CType}(S)]\!]_{w'} \circ \underline{\Gamma}\rho)s$
  where $([\![\Gamma \vdash_{\mathsf{v}} \ell \colon \mathsf{Ref}_S]\!]_{w'} \circ \underline{\Gamma}\rho)s = (r \colon S) \in w''$
- $s, \rho, \eta \models v = u$ if $([\![\Gamma \vdash_{\mathsf{v}} v \colon A]\!]_{w''} \circ \underline{\Gamma}\rho' \circ \underline{\Gamma}\rho)(s) = ([\![\Gamma \vdash_{\mathsf{v}} u \colon A]\!]_{w''} \circ \underline{\Gamma}\rho' \circ \underline{\Gamma}\rho)(s)$
  for some $\rho' \colon w' \to w''$
- $s, \rho, \eta \models \phi \star \psi$ if for suitable w_1, w_2, $\eta \in \mathcal{H}(w_1 \uplus w_2, w')$,
  $s, \rho, (w_1 \subseteq w', \mathcal{H}(w_1 \subseteq w_1 \uplus w_2, w')\eta) \models \phi$ and
  $s, \rho, (w_2 \subseteq w', \mathcal{H}(w_2 \subseteq w_1 \uplus w_2, w')\eta) \models \psi$
- $s, \rho, \eta \models \phi \mathbin{-\!\star} \psi$ if for all $(\rho', \eta_1) \sim (\rho, \eta)$ and for all η_2 such that $\eta_1 \cdot \eta_2$ is defined,
  $s, \rho', \eta_2 \models \phi$ implies $s, \rho', \eta_1 \cdot \eta_2 \models \psi$
- $s, \rho, \eta \models \exists\phi$ if $\underline{\Gamma}(\hat{\mathsf{u}}\epsilon \circ \rho)s, \mathrm{id}_{w''}, (a, \hat{H}\epsilon \circ \eta) \models \phi$ for some $\epsilon \colon w' \rightsquigarrow w''$, $a \in \underline{A}w''$
- $s, \rho, \eta \models \forall\phi$ if $\underline{\Gamma}(\hat{\mathsf{u}}\epsilon \circ \rho)s, \mathrm{id}_{w''}, (a, \hat{H}\epsilon \circ \eta) \models \phi$ for all $\epsilon \colon w' \rightsquigarrow w''$, $a \in \underline{A}w''$

Fig. 5: Semantics of the logic.

Proof. In view of Lemma 20, we are left to show that the given operations are natural and that Θ is an internal BI-algebra w.r.t. them. Since BI-algebras form a variety [5], it suffices to show that each Θw is a BI-algebra. By Lemma 18 (ii), it suffices to show that every $(-) \star_w \phi$ preserves arbitrary joins, for then we can use the standard formula to calculate $\phi \mathbin{-\!\star}_w \psi$, which happens to be natural in w:

$$\phi \mathbin{-\!\star}_w \psi = \bigcup \{\xi \mid \phi \star_w \xi \leqslant \psi\}.$$

By unfolding the right-hand side, we obtain the expression for $\mathbin{-\!\star}_w$ figuring in the statement of the lemma. $\qquad\square$

Theorem 23. *Θ is an internally complete Heyting BI-algebra, hence $[-, \Theta]$ is a BI-hyperdoctrine.*

Proof. Follows from Lemmas 20 and 22. $\qquad\square$

This now provides us with a complete semantics of the language in Fig. 4 with $[\![\Gamma \vdash \phi \colon \mathsf{prop}]\!] \colon \underline{\Gamma} \to \Theta$ and $[\![\Gamma \vdash \phi \colon \mathsf{P}A]\!] \colon \underline{\Gamma} \to \underline{P}A$ where $\underline{P}A$ is the upward closed subfunctor of $\check{\mathcal{P}} \circ (\hat{P}(\hat{\mathsf{u}}\underline{A} \times \hat{H}))$, with upward closure only on the $\hat{H}$-part, which is isomorphic to $\Theta^{\underline{A}}$. The resulting semantics is defined in Fig. 5 where we write $s, \rho, \eta \models \phi$ for $(\rho, \eta)_\sim \in [\![\Gamma \vdash \phi \colon \mathsf{prop}]\!](s)$ and $s, \rho, (a, \eta) \models \phi$ for $(\rho, (a, \eta))_\sim \in [\![\Gamma \vdash \phi \colon \mathsf{P}A]\!](s)$. The following properties [4] are then automatic.

Proposition 24. – (Monotonicity) *If* $s, \rho, \eta \models \phi$ *and* $\eta \leqslant \eta'$ *then* $s, \rho, \eta' \models \phi$.
  – (Shrinkage) *If* $s, \rho, \eta \models \phi$, $\eta' \leqslant \eta$ *and* η' *contains all cells reachable from* s *and* w *then* $s, \rho, \eta' \models \phi$.

7 Examples

Let us illustrate subtle features of our semantics by some examples.

Example 25. Consider the formula $\exists \ell \colon \mathsf{Ref}_{\mathsf{Int}} . \ell \hookrightarrow 5$ from the introduction in the empty context $-$. Then $-, \rho, \eta \models \exists \ell. \ell \hookrightarrow 5$ iff for some $\epsilon \colon w' \rightsquigarrow w''$, and some $x \in \underline{\mathsf{Ref}_{\mathsf{Int}}}w''$, $x, \mathsf{id}_{w''}, (\hat{H}\epsilon)\eta \models \ell' \hookrightarrow 5$. The latter is true iff $\mathsf{pr}_x((\hat{H}\epsilon)\eta) = 5$. Note that w' may not contain ℓ and it is always possible to choose ϵ so that w'' contains ℓ and $\mathsf{pr}_x((\hat{H}\epsilon)\eta) = 5$. Hence, the original formula is always valid.

Example 26. The clauses in Fig. 5 are very similar to the standard Kripke semantics of intuitionistic logic. Note however, that the clause for implication strikingly differs from the expected one

$\quad - s, \rho, \eta \models \phi \Rightarrow \psi \quad$ if $\quad$ for all $\eta \leqslant \eta'$, $s, \rho, \eta' \models \phi$ implies $s, \rho, \eta' \models \psi$,

though. The latter is indeed not validated by our semantics, as witnessed by the following example. Consider the following formulas ϕ and ψ respectively:

$$\ell \colon \mathsf{Ref}_{\mathsf{Ref}_{Int}} \vdash \exists \ell'. \exists x. \ell \hookrightarrow \ell' \wedge \ell' \hookrightarrow x \colon \mathsf{prop} \tag{6}$$

$$\ell \colon \mathsf{Ref}_{\mathsf{Ref}_{Int}} \vdash \exists \ell'. \ell \hookrightarrow \ell' \wedge \ell' \hookrightarrow 6 \colon \mathsf{prop} \tag{7}$$

The first formula is valid over heaplets, in which ℓ refers to a reference to some integer, while the second one is only valid over heaplets, in which ℓ refers to a reference to 6. Any $\eta' \geqslant \eta = (\mathsf{id}_w, (\{\ell''\} \subseteq \{\ell, \ell''\}, [\ell'' \mapsto 6]))$ satisfies both (6) and (7) or none of them. However, the implication $\phi \Rightarrow \psi$ still is not valid over η in our semantics, for

$$\eta \sim (w \hookrightarrow w \oplus (\ell' \colon Int), (\{\ell', \ell''\} \subseteq \{\ell, \ell', \ell''\}, [\ell' \mapsto 5, \ell'' \mapsto 6]))$$
$$\leqslant (w \hookrightarrow w \oplus (\ell' \colon Int), (\{\ell, \ell', \ell''\} \subseteq \{\ell, \ell', \ell''\}, [\ell \mapsto \ell', \ell' \mapsto 5, \ell'' \mapsto 6]))$$

and the latter heaplet validates ϕ but not ψ.

Example 27. Least μ and greatest ν fixpoints can be encoded in higher order logic [2]. As an example, consider

$$isList = \mu\gamma. \ell. \ \ell \hookrightarrow null \vee \exists \ell', x. \ell \hookrightarrow (x, \ell') \star \gamma(\ell'),$$

which specifies the fact that ℓ is a pointer to a head of a list (eliding coproduct injections in $\mathsf{inl}\ null$ and $\mathsf{inr}(x, \ell')$). By definition, *isList* satisfies the following recursive equation:

$$isList(\ell) = \ell \hookrightarrow null \vee \exists \ell', x. \ell \hookrightarrow (x, \ell') \star isList(\ell')$$

Let us expand the semantics of the right hand side. We have

$[\![\ell \colon \mathsf{Ref}_{\mathsf{list}}, \mathit{isList} \colon \mathsf{P}(\mathsf{Ref}_{\mathsf{list}}) \vdash l \hookrightarrow \mathit{null} \vee \exists \ell', x. \ell \hookrightarrow (x, \ell') \star \mathit{isList}(\ell')]\!]_w (\mathit{isList})$

$= \{ (\rho \colon w \to w', (\mathsf{Ref}_{\mathsf{list}} \rho)(\ell), \delta \in \hat{H} w')_{\sim} \mid \mathsf{pr}_{\rho(\ell)}(\delta) = \mathit{null} \} \cup$

$\quad\quad [\![\ell \colon \mathsf{Ref}_{\mathsf{list}}, \mathit{isList} \colon \mathsf{P}(\mathsf{Ref}_{\mathsf{list}}) \vdash \exists \ell', x. \ell \hookrightarrow (x, \ell') \star \mathit{isList}(\ell')]\!]_w (\mathit{isList})$

$= \{ (\rho \colon w \to w', (\mathsf{Ref}_{\mathsf{list}} \rho)(\ell), \delta \in \hat{H} w')_{\sim} \mid$

$\quad\quad \mathsf{pr}_{\rho(\ell)}(\delta) = \mathit{null} \vee \exists \ell', x. \, \mathsf{pr}_{\rho(\ell)} \delta = (x, \ell') \wedge (\rho, \ell', \delta \smallsetminus \rho(\ell))_{\sim} \in \mathit{isList} \}$

where $\delta \smallsetminus \rho(\ell)$ denotes the δ with the cell $\rho(\ell)$ removed. In summary, $(\rho \colon w \to w', (\mathsf{Ref}_{\mathsf{list}} \rho)(\ell), \delta \in \hat{H} w')_{\sim}$ is in $[\![\ell \colon \mathsf{Ref}_{\mathsf{list}}, \mathit{isList} \colon \mathsf{P}(\mathsf{Ref}_{\mathsf{list}}) \vdash \mathit{isList}(\ell)]\!]_w (\mathit{isList})$ if and only if either $\mathsf{pr}_{\rho(\ell)} \delta = \mathit{null}$ or there exists an $l' \in w'$ such that $\mathsf{pr}_{\rho(\ell)} \delta = (x, \ell')$ and $(\rho, \ell', \delta \smallsetminus \rho(\ell))_{\sim} \in \mathit{isList}$.

8 Conclusions and Further Work

Compositionality is an uncontroversial desirable property in semantics and reasoning, which admits strikingly different, but equally valid interpretations, as becomes particularly instructive when modelling dynamic memory allocation. From the programming perspective it is desirable to provide compositional means for keeping track of integrity of the underlying data, in particular, for preventing *dangling pointers*. Reasoning however inherently requires introduction of partially defined data, such as *heaplets*, which due to the compositionality principle must be regarded as first class semantic units.

Here we have made a step towards reconciling recent extensional monad-based denotational semantic for full-ground store [9] with higher order categorical reasoning frameworks [2] by constructing a suitable intuitionistic BI-hyperdoctrine. Much remains to be done. A highly desirable ingredient, which is currently missing in our logic in Fig. 4 is a construct relating programs and logical assertions, such as the following dynamic logic style modality

$$\frac{\Gamma \vdash_{\mathsf{c}} p \colon A \quad\quad \Gamma \vdash \phi \colon \mathsf{P} A}{\Gamma \vdash [p]\phi \colon \mathrm{prop}}$$

which would allow us e.g. in a standard way to encode *Hoare triples* $\{\phi\}p\{\psi\}$ as implications $\phi \Rightarrow [p]\psi$. This is difficult due to the outlined discrepancy in the semantics for construction and reasoning. The categories of initializations for p and ϕ and the corresponding hiding monads are technically incompatible. In future work we aim to deeply analyse this phenomenon and develop a semantics for such modalities in a principled fashion.

Orthogonally to these plans we are interested in further study of the full ground store monad and its variants. One interesting research direction is developing algebraic presentations of these monads in terms of operations and equations [17]. Certain generic methods [13] were proposed for the simple store case (Example 3), and it remains to be seen if these can be generalized to the full ground store case.

References

1. Samson Abramsky. Intensionality, definability and computation. In Alexandru Baltag and Sonja Smets, editors, *Johan van Benthem on Logic and Information Dynamics*, pages 121–142. Springer, 2014.

2. Bodil Biering, Lars Birkedal, and Noah Torp-Smith. BI-hyperdoctrines, higher-order separation logic, and abstraction. *ACM Trans. Program. Lang. Syst.*, 29(5), 2007.

3. Ales Bizjak and Lars Birkedal. On models of higher-order separation logic. *Electr. Notes Theor. Comput. Sci.*, 336:57–78, 2018.

4. Cristiano Calcagno, Peter O'Hearn, and Richard Bornat. Program logic and equivalence in the presence of garbage collection. *Theoretical Computer Science*, 298(3):557 – 581, 2003. Foundations of Software Science and Computation Structures.

5. Nikolaos Galatos, Peter Jipsen, Tomasz Kowalski, and Hiroakira Ono. *Residuated Lattices: An Algebraic Glimpse at Substructural Logics, Volume 151*. Elsevier Science, San Diego, CA, USA, 1st edition, 2007.

6. Peter Johnstone. *Sketches of an elephant: A topos theory compendium*. Oxford logic guides. Oxford Univ. Press, New York, 2002.

7. Peter T Johnstone. Conditions related to De Morgan's law. In *Applications of sheaves*, pages 479–491. Springer, 1979.

8. Ralf Jung, Robbert Krebbers, Jacques-Henri Jourdan, Aleš Bizjak, Lars Birkedal, and Derek Dreyer. Iris from the ground up: A modular foundation for higher-order concurrent separation logic. *Journal of Functional Programming*, 28:e20, 2018.

9. Ohad Kammar, Paul Blain Levy, Sean K. Moss, and Sam Staton. A monad for full ground reference cells. In *32nd Annual ACM/IEEE Symposium on Logic in Computer Science, LICS 2017*, pages 1–12, 2017.

10. William Lawvere. Adjointness in foundations. *Dialectica*, 23(3-4):281–296, 1969.

11. Paul Blain Levy, John Power, and Hayo Thielecke. Modelling environments in call-by-value programming languages. *Inf. & Comp*, 185:2003, 2002.

12. Saunders Mac Lane. *Categories for the Working Mathematician*. Springer, 1971.

13. Kenji Maillard and Paul-André Melliès. A fibrational account of local states. In *30th Annual ACM/IEEE Symposium on Logic in Computer Science, LICS 2015*, pages 402–413. IEEE Computer Society, 2015.

14. Peter O'Hearn and Robert D. Tennent. Semantics of local variables. *Applications of categories in computer science*, 177:217–238, 1992.

15. Frank Joseph Oles. *A Category-theoretic Approach to the Semantics of Programming Languages*. PhD thesis, Syracuse University, Syracuse, NY, USA, 1982.

16. Gordon Plotkin and John Power. Notions of computation determine monads. In *FoSSaCS'02*, volume 2303 of *LNCS*, pages 342–356. Springer, 2002.

17. Gordon Plotkin and John Power. Algebraic operations and generic effects. *Appl. Cat. Struct.*, 11(1):69–94, 2003.

18. David J. Pym, Peter W. O'Hearn, and Hongseok Yang. Possible worlds and resources: the semantics of BI. *Theor. Comput. Sci.*, 315:257–305, May 2004.

19. John Reynolds. The essence of ALGOL. In Peter W. O'Hearn and Robert D. Tennent, editors, *ALGOL-like Languages, Volume 1*, pages 67–88. Birkhauser Boston Inc., Cambridge, MA, USA, 1997.

20. John Reynolds. Intuitionistic reasoning about shared mutable data structure. In *Millennial Perspectives in Computer Science*, pages 303–321. Palgrave, 2000.

21. John Reynolds. Separation logic: A logic for shared mutable data structures. In *17th Annual IEEE Symposium on Logic in Computer Science, LICS 2002*, pages 55–74. IEEE Computer Society, 2002.

22. Alex Simpson. Category-theoretic structure for independence and conditional independence. *Electr. Notes Theor. Comput. Sci.*, 336:281–297, 2018.
23. Sam Staton. Instances of computational effects: An algebraic perspective. In *Proc. 28th Annual ACM/IEEE Symposium on Logic in Computer Science (LICS 2013)*, pages 519–519, June 2013.

7

The Inconsistent Labelling Problem of Stutter-Preserving Partial-Order Reduction

Thomas Neele[1](✉), Antti Valmari[2], and Tim A.C. Willemse[1]

[1] Eindhoven University of Technology, Eindhoven, The Netherlands
{t.s.neele, t.a.c.willemse}@tue.nl
[2] University of Jyväskylä, Jyväskylä, Finland
antti.valmari@jyu.fi

Abstract. In model checking, partial-order reduction (POR) is an effective technique to reduce the size of the state space. Stubborn sets are an established variant of POR and have seen many applications over the past 31 years. One of the early works on stubborn sets shows that a combination of several conditions on the reduction is sufficient to preserve stutter-trace equivalence, making stubborn sets suitable for model checking of linear-time properties. In this paper, we identify a flaw in the reasoning and show with a counter-example that stutter-trace equivalence is not necessarily preserved. We propose a solution together with an updated correctness proof. Furthermore, we analyse in which formalisms this problem may occur. The impact on practical implementations is limited, since they all compute a correct approximation of the theory.

1 Introduction

In formal methods, model checking is a technique to automatically decide the correctness of a system's design. The many interleavings of concurrent processes can cause the state space to grow exponentially with the number of components, known as the *state-space explosion* problem. *Partial-order reduction* (POR) is one technique that can alleviate this problem. Several variants of POR exist, such as *ample sets* [11], *persistent set* [7] and *stubborn sets* [16,21]. For each of those variants, sufficient conditions for preservation of stutter-trace equivalence have been identified. Since LTL without the next operator (LTL_{-X}) is invariant under finite stuttering, this allows one to check most LTL properties under POR.

However, the correctness proofs for these methods are intricate and not reproduced often. For stubborn sets, LTL_{-X}-preserving conditions and an accompanying correctness result were first presented in [15], and discussed in more detail in [17]. While trying to reproduce the proof for [17, Theorem 2] (see also Theorem 1 in the current work), we ran into an issue while trying to prove a certain property of the construction used in the original proof [17, Construction 1]. This led us to discover that stutter-trace equivalence is not necessarily preserved. We will refer to this as the *inconsistent labelling problem*. The essence of the problem is that POR in general, and the proofs in [17] in particular, reason mostly about actions, which label the transitions. The only relevance of the state labelling is that it determines which actions are *visible*. On the other hand, stutter-trace equivalence and the LTL semantics are purely based on state labels. The correctness proof in [17] does not deal properly with this disparity. Further investigation shows that the same problem also occurs in two works of Beneš *et al.* [2,3], who apply ample sets to state/event LTL model checking.

Consequently, any application of stubborn sets in LTL_{-X} model checking is possibly unsound, both for safety and liveness properties. In literature, the correctness of several theories [9,10,18] relies on the incorrect theorem.

Our contributions are as follows:

- We prove the existence of the inconsistent labelling problem with a counter-example. This counter-example is valid for weak stubborn sets and, with a small modification, in a non-deterministic setting for strong stubborn sets.
- We propose to strengthen one of the stubborn set conditions and show that this modification resolves the issue (Theorem 2).
- We analyse in which circumstances the inconsistent labelling problem occurs and, based on the conclusions, discuss its impact on existing literature. This includes a thorough analysis of Petri nets and several different notions of invisible transitions and atomic propositions.

Our investigation shows that probably all practical implementations of stubborn sets compute an approximation which resolves the inconsistent labelling problem. Furthermore, POR methods based on the standard independence relation, such as ample sets and persistent sets, are not affected.

The rest of the paper is structured as follows. In Section 2, we introduce the basic concepts of stubborn sets and stutter-trace equivalence, which is not preserved in the counter-example of Section 3. A solution to the inconsistent labelling problem is discussed in Section 4, together with an updated correctness proof. Sections 5 and 6 discuss several settings in which correctness is not affected. Finally, Section 7 presents related work and Section 8 presents a conclusion.

2   Preliminaries

Since LTL relies on state labels and POR relies on edge labels, we assume the existence of some fixed set of atomic propositions AP to label the states and a fixed set of edge labels Act, which we will call *actions*. Actions are typically denoted with the letter a.

Definition 1. *A labelled state transition system, short LSTS, is a directed graph $TS = (S, \rightarrow, \hat{s}, L)$, where:*

- *S is the state space;*
- *$\rightarrow \subseteq S \times Act \times S$ is the transition relation;*
- *$\hat{s} \in S$ is the initial state; and*
- *$L : S \rightarrow 2^{AP}$ is a function that labels states with atomic propositions.*

We write $s \xrightarrow{a} t$ whenever $(s, a, t) \in \rightarrow$. A *path* is a (finite or infinite) alternating sequence of states and actions: $s_0 \xrightarrow{a_1} s_1 \xrightarrow{a_2} s_2 \ldots$. We sometimes omit the intermediate and/or final states if they are clear from the context or not relevant, and write $s \xrightarrow{a_1 \ldots a_n} t$ or $s \xrightarrow{a_1 \ldots a_n}$ for finite paths and $s \xrightarrow{a_1 a_2 \ldots}$ for infinite paths. Paths that start in the initial state $\hat{s}$ are called *initial paths*. Given a path $\pi = s_0 \xrightarrow{a_1} s_1 \xrightarrow{a_2} s_2 \ldots$, the *trace* of π is the sequence of state labels observed along π, *viz.* $L(s_0)L(s_1)L(s_2)\ldots$. An action a is *enabled* in a state s, notation $s \xrightarrow{a}$, if and only if there is a transition $s \xrightarrow{a} t$ for some t. In a given LSTS TS, $enabled_{TS}(s)$ is the set of all enabled actions in a state s. A set $\mathcal{I}$ of *invisible* actions is chosen such that if (but not necessarily only if) $a \in \mathcal{I}$, then for all states s and t, $s \xrightarrow{a} t$ implies $L(s) = L(t)$. Note that this definition allows the set $\mathcal{I}$ to be under-approximated. An action that is not invisible is called *visible*. We say TS is *deterministic* if and only if $s \xrightarrow{a} t$ and $s \xrightarrow{a} t'$ imply $t = t'$, for all states s, t and t' and actions a. To indicate that TS is not necessarily deterministic, we say TS is *non-deterministic*.

2.1   Stubborn sets

In POR, *reduction functions* play a central role. A reduction function $r : S \rightarrow 2^{Act}$ indicates which transitions to explore in each state. When starting at the initial state $\hat{s}$, a reduction function induces a *reduced LSTS* as follows.

Definition 2. *Let $TS = (S, \rightarrow, \hat{s}, L)$ be an LSTS and $r : S \rightarrow 2^{Act}$ a reduction function. Then the reduced LSTS induced by r is defined as $TS_r = (S_r, \rightarrow_r, \hat{s}, L_r)$, where L_r is the restriction of L on S_r, and S_r and $\rightarrow_r$ are the smallest sets such that the following holds:*

- *$\hat{s} \in S_r$; and*
- *If $s \in S_r$, $s \xrightarrow{a} t$ and $a \in r(s)$, then $t \in S_r$ and $s \xrightarrow{a}_r t$.*

Note that we have $\rightarrow_r \subseteq \rightarrow$. In the remainder of this paper, we will assume the reduced LSTS is finite. This is essential for the correctness of the approach detailed below. In general, a reduction function is not guaranteed to preserve almost any property of an LSTS. Below, we list a number of conditions that have been proposed in literature; they aim to preserve LTL_{-X}. Here, we call an action a a *key action* in s iff for all paths $s \xrightarrow{a_1 \ldots a_n} s'$ such that $a_1 \notin r(s), \ldots, a_n \notin r(s)$, it holds that $s' \xrightarrow{a}$. We typically denote key actions by a_{key}.

D0   If $enabled(s) \neq \emptyset$, then $r(s) \cap enabled(s) \neq \emptyset$.

D1   For all $a \in r(s)$ and $a_1 \notin r(s), \ldots, a_n \notin r(s)$, if $s \xrightarrow{a_1} \cdots \xrightarrow{a_n} s_n \xrightarrow{a} s'_n$, then there are states $s', s'_1, \ldots, s'_{n-1}$ such that $s \xrightarrow{a} s' \xrightarrow{a_1} s'_1 \xrightarrow{a_2} \cdots \xrightarrow{a_n} s'_n$.

D2   Every enabled action in $r(s)$ is a key action in s.

D2w   If $enabled(s) \neq \emptyset$, then $r(s)$ contains a key action in s.

V   If $r(s)$ contains an enabled visible action, then it contains all visible actions.

I   If an invisible action is enabled, then $r(s)$ contains an invisible key action.

L   For every visible action a, every cycle in the reduced LSTS contains a state s such that $a \in r(s)$.

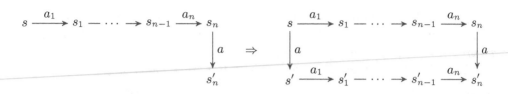

Fig. 1: Visual representation of condition **D1**.

These conditions are used to define *strong* and *weak* stubborn sets in the following way.

Definition 3. *A reduction function* $r : S \to 2^{Act}$ *is a* strong stubborn set *iff for all states* $s \in S$, *the conditions* **D0, D1, D2, V, I, L** *all hold.*

Definition 4. *A reduction function* $r : S \to 2^{Act}$ *is a* weak stubborn set *iff for all states* $s \in S$, *the conditions* **D1, D2w, V, I, L** *all hold.*

Below, we also use 'weak/strong stubborn set' to refer to the set of actions $r(s)$ in some state s. First, note that key actions are always enabled, by setting $n = 0$. Furthermore, a stubborn set can never introduce new deadlocks, either by **D0** or **D2w**. Condition **D1** enforces that a key action $a_{\text{key}} \in r(s)$ does not disable other paths that are not selected for the stubborn set. A visual representation of condition **D1** can be found in Figure 1. When combined, **D1** and **D2w** are sufficient conditions for preservation of deadlocks. Condition **V** enforces that the paths $s \xrightarrow{a_1 \ldots a_n a} s'_n$ and $s \xrightarrow{a a_1 \ldots a_n} s'_n$ in **D1** contain the same sequence of visible actions. The purpose of condition **I** is to preserve the possibility to perform an invisible action, if one is enabled. Finally, we have condition **L** to deal with the *action-ignoring problem*, which occurs when an action is never selected for the stubborn set and always ignored. Since we assume that the reduced LSTS is finite, it suffices to reason in **L** about every cycle instead of every infinite path. The combination of **I** and **L** helps to preserve divergences (infinite paths containing only invisible actions).

Conditions **D0** and **D2** together imply **D2w**, and thus every strong stubborn set is also a weak stubborn set. Since the reverse does not necessarily hold, weak stubborn sets might offer more reduction.

2.2 Weak and Stutter Equivalence

To reason about the similarity of an LSTS *TS* and its reduced LSTS TS_r, we introduce the notions of *weak equivalence*, which operates on actions, and *stutter equivalence*, which operates on states. The definitions are generic, so that they can also be used in Section 6.

Definition 5. *Two paths* π *and* π' *are* weakly equivalent with respect to a set of actions A, *notation* $\pi \sim_A \pi'$, *if and only if they are both finite or both infinite and their respective projections on* $Act \setminus A$ *are equal.*

Definition 6. *The* no-stutter trace *under labelling L of a path $s_0 \xrightarrow{a_1} s_1 \xrightarrow{a_2} \ldots$ is the sequence of those $L(s_i)$ such that $i = 0$ or $L(s_i) \neq L(s_{i-1})$. Paths π and π' are* stutter equivalent *under L, notation $\pi \triangleq_L \pi'$, iff they are both finite or both infinite, and they yield the same no-stutter trace under L.*

We typically consider weak equivalence with respect to the set of invisible actions $\mathcal{I}$. In that case, we write $\pi \sim \pi'$. We also omit the subscript for stutter equivalence when reasoning about the standard labelling function and write $\pi \triangleq \pi'$. Remark that stutter equivalence is invariant under finite repetitions of state labels, hence its name. We lift both equivalences to LSTSs, and say that TS and TS' are *weak-trace equivalent* iff for every initial path π in TS, there is a weakly equivalent initial path π' in TS' and vice versa. Likewise, TS and TS' are *stutter-trace equivalent* iff for every initial path π in TS, there is a stutter equivalent initial path π' in TS' and vice versa.

In general, weak equivalence and stutter equivalence are incomparable, even for initial paths. However, for some LSTSs, these notions can be related in a certain way. We formalise this in the following definition.

Definition 7. *Let TS be an LSTS and π and π' two paths in TS that both start in some state s. Then, TS is* labelled consistently *iff $\pi \sim \pi'$ implies $\pi \triangleq \pi'$.*

Note that if an LSTS is labelled consistently, then in particular all weakly equivalent initial paths are also stutter equivalent. Hence, if an LSTS TS is labelled consistently and weak-trace equivalent to a subgraph TS', then TS and TS' are also stutter-trace equivalent.

Stubborn sets as defined in the previous section aim to preserve stutter-trace equivalence between the original and the reduced LSTS. The motivation behind this is that two stutter-trace equivalent LSTSs satisfy exactly the same formulae [1] in LTL_{-X}. The following theorem, which is frequently cited in literature [9,10,18], aims to show that stubborn sets indeed preserve stutter-trace equivalence. Its original formulation reasons about the validity of an arbitrary LTL_{-X} formula. Here, we give the alternative formulation based on stutter-trace equivalence.

Theorem 1. *[17, Theorem 2] Given an LSTS TS and a weak/strong stubborn set r, then the reduced LSTS TS_r is stutter-trace equivalent to TS.*

The original proof correctly concludes that the stubborn set method preserves the order of visible actions in the reduced LSTS, *i.e.*, $TS \sim TS_r$. However, this only implies preservation of stutter-trace equivalence ($TS \triangleq TS_r$) if the full LSTS is labelled consistently, so Theorem 1 is invalid in the general case. In the next section, we will see a counter-example which exploits this fact.

3　Counter-Example

Consider the LSTS in Figure 2, which we will refer to as TS^C. There is only one atomic proposition q, which holds in the grey states and is false in the other states. The initial state $\hat{s}$ is marked with an incoming arrow. First, note that this LSTS is deterministic. The actions a_1, a_2 and a_3 are visible and a and a_{key} are invisible. By setting $r(\hat{s}) = \{a, a_{\mathsf{key}}\}$, which is a weak stubborn set, we obtain a reduced LSTS TS_r^C that does not contain the dashed states and transitions. The original LSTS contains the trace $\emptyset\{q\}\emptyset\emptyset\{q\}^\omega$, obtained by following the path with actions $a_1 a_2 a a_3^\omega$. However, the reduced LSTS does not contain a stutter equivalent trace. This is also witnessed by the LTL$_{-X}$ formula $\Box(q \Rightarrow \Box(q \lor \Box\neg q))$, which holds for TS_r^C, but not for TS^C.

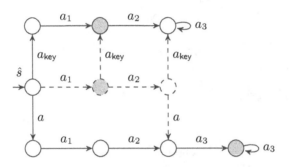

Fig. 2: Counter-example showing that stubborn sets do not preserve stutter-trace equivalence. Grey states are labelled with $\{q\}$. The dashed transitions and states are not present in the reduced LSTS.

A very similar example can be used to show that strong stubborn sets suffer from the same problem. Consider again the LSTS in Figure 2, but assume that $a = a_{\mathsf{key}}$, making the LSTS non-deterministic. Now, $r(\hat{s}) = \{a\}$ is a strong stubborn set and again the trace $\emptyset\{q\}\emptyset\emptyset\{q\}^\omega$ is not preserved in the reduced LSTS. In Section 4.3, we will see why the inconsistent labelling problem does not occur for deterministic systems under strong stubborn sets.

The core of the problem lies in the fact that condition **D1**, even when combined with **V**, does not enforce that the two paths it considers are stutter equivalent. Consider the paths $s \xrightarrow{a}$ and $s \xrightarrow{a_1 a_2 a}$ and assume that $a \in r(s)$ and $a_1 \notin r(s), a_2 \notin r(s)$. Condition **V** ensures that at least one of the following two holds: (i) a is invisible, or (ii) a_1 and a_2 are invisible. Half of the possible scenarios are depicted in Figure 3; the other half are symmetric. Again, the grey states (and only those states) are labelled with $\{q\}$.

The two cases delimited with a solid line are problematic. In both LSTSs, the paths $s \xrightarrow{a_1 a_2 a} s'$ and $s \xrightarrow{a a_1 a_2} s'$ are weakly equivalent, since a is invisible. However, they are not stutter equivalent, and therefore these LSTSs are not labelled consistently. The topmost of these two LSTSs forms the core of the counter-example TS^C, with the rest of TS^C serving to satisfy condition **D2/D2w**.

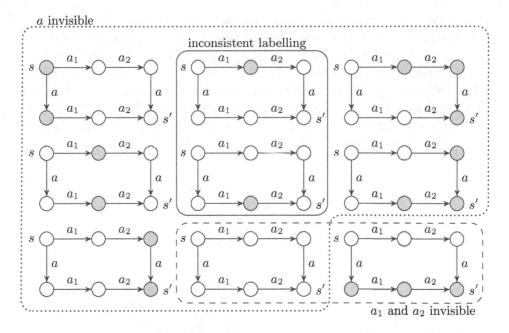

Fig. 3: Nine possible scenarios when $a \in r(s)$ and $a_1 \notin r(s), a_2 \notin r(s)$, according to conditions **D1** and **V**. The dotted and dashed lines indicate when a or a_1, a_2 are invisible, respectively.

4   Strengthening Condition D1

To fix the issue with inconsistent labelling, we propose to strengthen condition **D1** as follows.

D1' For all $a \in r(s)$ and $a_1 \notin r(s), \ldots, a_n \notin r(s)$, if $s \xrightarrow{a_1} s_1 \xrightarrow{a_2} \cdots \xrightarrow{a_n} s_n \xrightarrow{a}$ s'_n, then there are states $s', s'_1, \ldots, s'_{n-1}$ such that $s \xrightarrow{a} s' \xrightarrow{a_1} s'_1 \xrightarrow{a_2} \cdots \xrightarrow{a_n}$ s'_n. Furthermore, if a is invisible, then $s_i \xrightarrow{a} s'_i$ for every $1 \leq i < n$.

This new condition **D1'** provides a form of *local* consistent labelling when one of $a_1, \ldots, a_n$ is visible. In this case, **V** implies that a is invisible and, consequently, the presence of transitions $s_i \xrightarrow{a} s'_i$ implies $L(s_i) = L(s'_i)$. Hence, the problematic cases of Figure 3 are resolved; a correctness proof is given below.

Condition **D1'** is very similar to condition **C1** [5], which is common in the context of ample sets. However, **C1** requires that action a is *globally* independent of each of the actions $a_1, \ldots, a_n$, while **D1'** merely requires a kind of *local* independence. Persistent sets [7] also rely on a condition similar to **D1'**, and require local independence.

4.1   Implementation

In practice, most, if not all, implementations of stubborn sets approximate **D1** based on a binary relation $\leadsto_s$ on actions. This relation may (partly) depend on the current state s and it is defined such that **D1** can be satisfied by ensuring that if $a \in r(s)$ and $a \leadsto_s a'$, then also $a' \in r(s)$. A set satisfying **D0**, **D1**, **D2**, **D2w**, **V** and/or **I** can be found by searching for a suitable *strongly connected component* in the graph $(Act, \leadsto_s)$. Condition **L** is dealt with by other techniques.

Practical implementations construct $\leadsto_s$ by analysing how any two actions a and a' interact. If a is enabled, the simplest (but not necessarily the best possible) strategy is to make $a \leadsto_s a'$ if and only if a and a' access at least one variable in common. This can be relaxed, for instance, by not considering commutative accesses, such as writing to and reading from a FIFO buffer. As a result, $\leadsto_s$ can only detect reduction opportunities in (sub)graphs of the shape

$$
\begin{array}{ccccccc}
s & \xrightarrow{a_1} & s_1 & - \cdots \to & s_{n-1} & \xrightarrow{a_n} & s_n \\
\downarrow a & & \downarrow a & & \downarrow a & & \downarrow a \\
s' & \xrightarrow{a_1} & s'_1 & - \cdots \to & s'_{n-1} & \xrightarrow{a_n} & s'_n
\end{array}
$$

where $a \in r(s)$ and $a_1 \notin r(s), \ldots, a_n \notin r(s)$. The presence of the vertical a transitions in $s_1, \ldots, s_{n-1}$ implies that **D1'** is also satisfied by such implementations.

4.2 Correctness

To show that **D1'** indeed resolves the inconsistent labelling problem, we reproduce the construction in the original proof [17, Construction 1] in two lemmata and show that it preserves stutter equivalence. Below, recall that $\to_r$ indicates which transitions occur in the reduced state space.

Lemma 1. *Let r be a weak stubborn set, where condition **D1** is replaced by **D1'**, and $\pi = s_0 \xrightarrow{a_1} \cdots \xrightarrow{a_n} s_n \xrightarrow{a} s'_n$ a path such that $a_1 \notin r(s_0), \ldots, a_n \notin r(s_0)$ and $a \in r(s_0)$. Then, there is a path $\pi' = s_0 \xrightarrow{a}_r s'_0 \xrightarrow{a_1} \cdots \xrightarrow{a_n} s'_n$ such that $\pi \triangleq \pi'$.*

Proof. The existence of π' follows directly from condition **D1'**. Due to condition **V** and our assumption that $a_1 \notin r(s_0), \ldots, a_n \notin r(s_0)$, it cannot be the case that a is visible and at least one of $a_1, \ldots, a_n$ is visible. If a is invisible, then the traces of $s_0 \xrightarrow{a_1} \cdots \xrightarrow{a_n} s_n$ and $s'_0 \xrightarrow{a_1} \cdots \xrightarrow{a_n} s'_n$ are equivalent, since **D1'** implies that $s_i \xrightarrow{a} s'_i$ for every $0 \leq i \leq n$, so $L(s'_i) = L(s_i)$. Otherwise, if all of $a_1, \ldots, a_n$ are invisible, then the sequences of labels observed along π and π' have the shape $L(s_0)^{n+1} L(s'_0)$ and $L(s_0)L(s'_0)^{n+1}$, respectively. We conclude that $\pi \triangleq \pi'$. $\square$

Lemma 2. *Let r be a weak stubborn set, where condition **D1** is replaced by **D1'**, and $\pi = s_0 \xrightarrow{a_1} s_1 \xrightarrow{a_2} \ldots$ a path such that $a_i \notin r(s_0)$ for any a_i that occurs in π. Then, the following holds:*

- *If π is of finite length $n > 0$, there exist an action a_{key}, a state s'_n such that $s_n \xrightarrow{a_{key}} s'_n$ and a path $\pi' = s_0 \xrightarrow{a_{key}}_r s'_0 \xrightarrow{a_1} \cdots \xrightarrow{a_n} s'_n$.*
- *If π is infinite, there exists a path $\pi' = s_0 \xrightarrow{a_{key}}_r s'_0 \xrightarrow{a_1} s'_1 \xrightarrow{a_2} \ldots$ for some action a_{key}.*

In either case, $\pi \triangleq \pi'$.

Proof. Let K be the set of key actions in s. If a_1 is invisible, K contains at least one invisible action, due to **I**. Otherwise, if a_1 is visible, we reason that K is not empty (condition **D2w**) and all actions in $r(s_0)$, and thus also all actions in K, are invisible, due to **V**. In the remainder, let a_{key} be an invisible key action.

In case π has finite length n, the existence of $s_n \xrightarrow{a_{\mathsf{key}}} s'_n$ and $s_0 \xrightarrow{a_{\mathsf{key}}}_r s'_0 \xrightarrow{a_1} \cdots \xrightarrow{a_n} s'_n$ follows from the definition of key actions and **D1'**, respectively.

If π is infinite, we can apply the definition of key actions and **D1'** successively to obtain a path $\pi_i = s_0 \xrightarrow{a_{\mathsf{key}}} s'_0 \xrightarrow{a_1} \cdots \xrightarrow{a_i} s'_i$ for every $i \geq 0$, with $s_j \xrightarrow{a_{\mathsf{key}}} s'_j$ for every $1 \leq j < i$. Since the reduced state space is finite, infinitely many of these paths must use the same state as s'_0. At most one of them ends at s'_0 (the one with $i = 0$), so infinitely many continue from s'_0. Of them, infinitely many must use the same s'_1, again because the reduced state space is finite. Again, at most one of them is lost because of ending at s'_1. This reasoning can continue without limit, proving the existence of $\pi' = s_0 \xrightarrow{a_{\mathsf{key}}}_r s'_0 \xrightarrow{a_1} s'_1 \xrightarrow{a_2} \dots$, with $s_j \xrightarrow{a_{\mathsf{key}}} s'_j$ for every $j \geq 0$.

Since a_{key} is invisible, we have $L(s_j) = L(s'_j)$ for every $j \geq 0$. This implies $\pi \triangleq \pi'$. $\qquad\qquad\qquad\qquad\qquad\qquad\qquad\qquad\qquad\qquad\qquad\qquad\qquad$ □

Lemmata 1 and 2 coincide with branches 1 and 2 of [17, Construction 1], respectively, but contain the stronger result that $\pi \triangleq \pi'$. Thus, when applied in the proof of [17, Theorem 2] (see also Theorem 1), this yields the result that stubborn sets with condition **D1'** preserve stutter-trace equivalence.

Theorem 2. *Given an LSTS TS and weak/strong stubborn set r, where condition **D1** is replaced by **D1'**, then the reduced LSTS TS_r is stutter-trace equivalent to TS.*

We do not reproduce the complete proof, but provide insight into the application of the lemmata with the following example.

Example 1. Consider the path obtained by following $a_1 a_2 a_3$ in Figure 4. Lemmata 1 and 2 show that $a_1 a_2 a_3$ can always be mimicked in the reduced LSTS, while preserving stutter equivalence. In this case, the path is mimicked by the path corresponding to $a_{\mathsf{key}} a_2 a_1 a'_{\mathsf{key}} a_3$, drawn with dashes. The new path reorders the actions a_1, a_2 and a_3 according to the construction of Lemma 1 and introduces the key actions a_{key} and a'_{key} according to Lemma 2. $\qquad\qquad$ □

We remark that Lemma 2 also holds if the reduced LSTS is infinite, but finitely branching.

4.3 Deterministic LSTSs

As already noted in Section 3, strong stubborn sets for deterministic systems do not suffer from the inconsistent labelling problem. The following lemma, which also appeared as [20, Lemma 4.2], shows why.

Lemma 3. *For deterministic LSTSs, conditions **D1** and **D2** together imply **D1'**.*

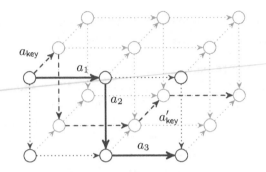

Fig. 4: Example of how the trace a_1, a_2, a_3 can be mimicked by introducing additional actions and moving a_2 to the front (dashed trace). Transitions that are drawn in parallel have the same label.

5 Safe Logics

In this section, we will identify two logics, *viz.* reachability and CTL_{-X}, which are not affected by the inconsistent labelling problem. This is either due to their limited expressivity or the extra POR conditions that are required.

5.1 Reachability properties

Although the counter-example of Section 3 shows that stutter-trace equivalence is in general not preserved by stubborn sets, some fragments of LTL_{-X} are preserved. One such class of properties is reachability properties, which are of the shape $\Box f$ or $\Diamond f$, where f is a formula not containing temporal operators.

Theorem 3. *Let TS be an LSTS, r a reduction function that satisfies either* **D0**, **D1**, **D2**, **V** *and* **L** *or* **D1**, **D2w**, **V** *and* **L** *and* TS_r *the reduced LSTS. For all possible labellings* $l \subseteq AP$, *TS contains a path to a state s such that* $L(s) = l$ *iff* TS_r *contains a path to a state* s' *such that* $L(s') = l$.

Proof. The 'if' case is trivial, since TS_r is a subgraph of TS. For the 'only if' case, we reason as follows. Let $TS = (S, \rightarrow, \hat{s}, L)$ be an LSTS and $\pi = s_0 \xrightarrow{a_1} \cdots \xrightarrow{a_n} s_n$ a path such that $s_0 = \hat{s}$. We mimic this path by repeatedly taking some enabled action a that is in the stubborn set, according to the following schema. Below, we assume the path to be mimicked contains at least one visible action. Otherwise, its first state would have the same labelling as s_n.

1. If there is an i such that $a_i \in r(s_0)$, we consider the smallest such i, i.e., $a_1 \notin r(s_0), \ldots, a_{i-1} \notin r(s_0)$. Then, we can shift a_i forward by **D1**, move towards s_n along $s_0 \xrightarrow{a_i} s_0'$ and continue by mimicking $s_0' \xrightarrow{a_1} \cdots \xrightarrow{a_{i-1}} s_i \xrightarrow{a_{i+1}} \cdots \xrightarrow{a_n} s_n$.
2. If all of $a_1 \notin r(s_0), \ldots, a_n \notin r(s_0)$, then, by **D0** and **D2** or by **D2w**, there is a key action a_{key} in s_0. By the definition of key actions and **D1**, a_{key} leads to a state s_0' from which we can continue mimicking the path $s_0' \xrightarrow{a_1} s_1' \xrightarrow{a_2} \cdots \xrightarrow{a_n} s_n'$. Note that $L(s_n) = L(s_n')$, since a_{key} is invisible by condition **V**.

The second case cannot be repeated infinitely often, due to condition **L**. Hence, after a finite number of steps, we reach a state s'_n with $L(s'_n) = L(s_n)$.   □

We remark that more efficient mechanisms for reachability checking under POR have been proposed, such as condition **S** [21], which can replace **L**, or conditions based on *up-sets* [13]. Another observation is that model checking of LTL_{-X} properties can be reduced to reachability checking by computing the cross-product of a Büchi automaton and an LSTS [1], in the process resolving the inconsistent labelling problem. Peled [12] shows how this approach can be combined with POR, but please see [14].

5.2 Deterministic LSTSs and CTL_{-X} Model Checking

In this section, we will consider the inconsistent labelling problem in the setting of CTL_{-X} model checking. When applying stubborn sets in that context, stronger conditions are required to preserve the branching structure that CTL_{-X} reasons about. Namely, the original LSTS must be deterministic and one more condition needs to be added [5]:

C4 Either $r(s) = Act$ or $r(s) \cap enabled(s) = \{a\}$ for some $a \in Act$.

We slightly changed its original formulation to match the setting of stubborn sets. A weaker condition, called **Ä8**, which does not require determinism of the whole LSTS is proposed in [19]. With **C4**, strong and weak stubborn sets collapse, as shown by the following lemma.

Lemma 4. *Conditions **D2w** and **C4** together imply **D0** and **D2**.*

Proof. Let *TS* be an LSTS, s a state and r a reduction function that satisfies **D2w** and **C4**. Condition **D0** is trivially implied by **C4**. Using **C4**, we distinguish two cases: either $r(s)$ contains precisely one enabled action a, or $r(s) = Act$. In the former case, this single action a must be a key action, according to **D2w**. Hence, **D2**, which requires that all enabled actions in $r(s)$ are key actions, is satisfied. Otherwise, if $r(s) = Act$, we consider an arbitrary action a that satisfies **D2**'s precondition that $s \xrightarrow{a}$. Given a path $s \xrightarrow{a_1...a_n}$, the condition that $a_1 \notin r(s), \ldots, a_n \notin r(s)$ only holds if $n = 0$. We conclude that **D2**'s condition $s \xrightarrow{a_1...a_n a}$ is satisfied by the assumption $s \xrightarrow{a}$.   □

It follows from Lemmata 3 and 4 and Theorem 2 that CTL_{-X} model checking of deterministic systems with stubborn sets does not suffer from the inconsistent labelling problem. The same holds for condition **Ä8**, as already shown in [19].

6 Petri Nets

Petri nets are a widely-known formalism for modelling concurrent processes and have seen frequent use in the application of stubborn-set theory [4,10,21,22]. A Petri net contains a set of *places* P and a set of *structural transitions* T.

Arcs between places and structural transitions are weighted according to a total function $W : (P \times T) \cup (T \times P) \to \mathbb{N}$. The state space of the underlying LSTS is the set $\mathcal{M}$ of all *markings*; a marking m is a function $P \to \mathbb{N}$, which assigns a number of *tokens* to each place. The LSTS contains a transition $m \xrightarrow{t} m'$ iff $m(p) \geq W(p,t)$ and $m'(p) = m(p) - W(p,t) + W(t,p)$ for all places $p \in P$. As before, we assume the LSTS contains some labelling function $L : \mathcal{M} \to 2^{AP}$. More details on the labels are given below. Note that markings and structural transitions take over the role of states and actions respectively. The set of markings reachable under $\to$ from some *initial marking* $\hat{m}$ is denoted $\mathcal{M}_{reach}$.

Example 2. Consider the Petri net with initial marking $\hat{m}$ below on the left. Here, all arcs are weighted 1, except for the arc from p_5 to t_2, which is weighted 2. Its LSTS is infinite, but the reachable substructure is depicted on the right. The number of tokens in each of the places $p_1, \ldots, p_6$ is inscribed in the nodes, the state labels (if any) are written beside the nodes.

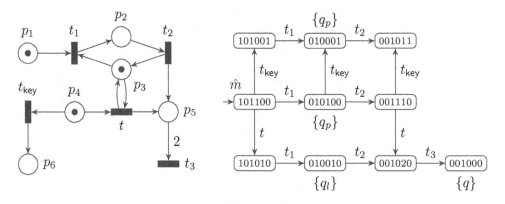

The LSTS practically coincides with the counter-example of Section 3. Only the self-loops are missing and the state labelling, with atomic propositions q, q_p and q_l, differs slightly; the latter will be explained later. For now, note that t and t_{key} are invisible and that the trace $\emptyset\{q_p\}\emptyset\emptyset\{q\}$, which occurs when firing transitions $t_1t_2tt_3$ from $\hat{m}$, can be lost when reducing with weak stubborn sets. □

In the remainder of this section, we fix a Petri net $(P, T, W, \hat{m})$ and its LSTS $(\mathcal{M}, \to, \hat{m}, L)$. Below, we consider three different types of atomic propositions. Firstly, polynomial propositions [4] are of the shape $f(p_1, \ldots, p_n) \bowtie k$ where f is a polynomial over $p_1, \ldots, p_n$, $\bowtie \in \{<, \leq, >, \geq, =, \neq\}$ and $k \in \mathbb{Z}$. Such a proposition holds in a marking m iff $f(m(p_1), \ldots, m(p_n)) \bowtie k$. A linear proposition [10] is similar, but the function f over places must be linear and $f(0, \ldots, 0) = 0$, *i.e.*, linear propositions are of the shape $k_1p_1 + \cdots + k_np_n \bowtie k$, where $k_1, \ldots, k_n, k \in \mathbb{Z}$. Finally, we have arbitrary propositions [22], whose shape is not restricted and which can hold in any given set of markings.

Several other types of atomic propositions can be encoded as polynomial propositions. For example, *fireable*(t) [4,10], which holds in a marking m iff t is enabled in m, can be encoded as $\prod_{p \in P} \prod_{i=0}^{W(p,t)-1}(p - i) \geq 1$. The proposition *deadlock*, which holds in markings where no structural transition is enabled, does not require special treatment in the context of POR, since it is already preserved by **D1** and **D2w**. The sets containing all linear and polynomial propositions are henceforward called AP_l and AP_p, respectively. The corresponding labelling functions are defined as $L_l(m) = L(m) \cap AP_l$ and $L_p(m) = L(m) \cap AP_p$ for all markings m. Below, the two stutter equivalences $\triangleq_{L_l}$ and $\triangleq_{L_p}$ that follow from the new labelling functions are abbreviated $\triangleq_l$ and $\triangleq_p$, respectively. Note that $AP \supseteq AP_p \supseteq AP_l$ and $\triangleq \subseteq \triangleq_p \subseteq \triangleq_l$.

For the purpose of introducing several variants of invisibility, we reformulate and generalise the definition of invisibility from Section 2. Given an atomic proposition $q \in AP$, a relation $\mathcal{R} \subseteq \mathcal{M} \times \mathcal{M}$ is *q-invisible* if and only if $(m, m') \in \mathcal{R}$ implies $q \in L(m) \Leftrightarrow q \in L(m')$. We consider a structural transition t *q-invisible* iff its corresponding relation $\{(m, m') \mid m \xrightarrow{t} m'\}$ is *q-invisible*. Invisibility is also lifted to sets of atomic propositions: given a set $AP' \subseteq AP$, relation $\mathcal{R}$ is AP'-*invisible* iff it is *q-invisible* for all $q \in AP'$. If $\mathcal{R}$ is AP-invisible, we plainly say that $\mathcal{R}$ is *invisible*. AP'-invisibility and invisibility carry over to structural transitions. We sometimes refer to invisibility as *ordinary invisibility* for emphasis. Note that the set of invisible structural transitions $\mathcal{I}$ is no longer an under-approximation, but contains exactly those structural transitions t for which $m \xrightarrow{t} m'$ implies $L(m) = L(m')$ (cf. Section 2).

We are now ready to introduce three orthogonal variations on invisibility. Firstly, relation $\mathcal{R} \subseteq \mathcal{M} \times \mathcal{M}$ is *reach q-invisible* [21] iff $\mathcal{R} \cap (\mathcal{M}_{reach} \times \mathcal{M}_{reach})$ is *q-invisible*, *i.e.*, all the pairs of reachable markings $(m, m') \in \mathcal{R}$ agree on the labelling of q. Secondly, $\mathcal{R}$ is *value q-invisible* if (i) q is polynomial and for all $(m, m') \in \mathcal{R}$, $f(m(p_1), \ldots, m(p_n)) = f(m'(p_1), \ldots, m'(p_n))$; or if (ii) q is not polynomial and $\mathcal{R}$ is *q-invisible*. Intuitively, this means that the value of polynomial f never changes between two markings $(m, m') \in \mathcal{R}$. Reach and value invisibility are lifted to structural transitions and sets of atomic propositions as before, *i.e.*, by taking $\mathcal{R} = \{(m, m') \mid m \xrightarrow{t} m'\}$ when considering invisibility of t. Finally, we introduce another way to lift invisibility to structural transitions: t is *strongly q-invisible* iff the set $\{(m, m') \mid \forall p \in P : m'(p) = m(p) + W(t, p) - W(p, t)\}$ is *q-invisible*. Strong invisibility does not take the presence of a transition $m \xrightarrow{t} m'$ into account, and purely reasons about the effects of t. Value invisibility and strong in-

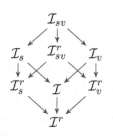

Fig. 5: Lattice of sets of invisible actions. Arrows represent a subset relation.

visibility are new in the current work, although strong invisibility was inspired by the notion of invisibility that is proposed by Varpaaniemi in [22].

We indicate the sets of all value, reach and strongly invisible structural transitions with $\mathcal{I}_v$, $\mathcal{I}^r$ and $\mathcal{I}_s$ respectively. Since $\mathcal{I}_v \subseteq \mathcal{I}$, $\mathcal{I}_s \subseteq \mathcal{I}$ and $\mathcal{I} \subseteq \mathcal{I}^r$, the set of all their possible combinations forms the lattice shown in Figure 5. In the remainder, the weak equivalence relations that follow from each of the eight invisibility notions are abbreviated, *e.g.*, $\sim_{\mathcal{I}^r_{sv}}$ becomes $\sim^r_{sv}$.

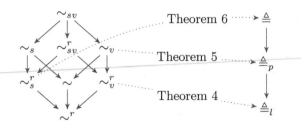

Fig. 6: Two lattices containing variations of weak equivalence and stutter equivalence, respectively. Solid arrows indicate a subset relation inside the lattice; dotted arrows follow from the indicated theorems and show when the LSTS of a Petri net is labelled consistently.

Example 3. Consider again the Petri net and LSTS from Example 2. We can define q_l and q_p as linear and polynomial propositions, respectively:

- $q_l := p_3 + p_4 + p_6 = 0$ is a linear proposition, which holds when neither p_3, p_4 nor p_6 contains a token. Structural transition t is q_l-invisible, because $m \xrightarrow{t} m'$ implies that $m(p_3) = m'(p_3) \geq 1$, and thus neither m nor m is labelled with q_l. On the other hand, t is not value q_l-invisible (by the transition $101100 \xrightarrow{t} 101010$) or strongly reach q_l-invisible (by 010100 and 010010). However, t_{key} is strongly value q_l-invisible: it moves a token from p_4 to p_6 and hence never changes the value of $p_3 + p_4 + p_6$.
- $q_p := (1 - p_3)(1 - p_5) = 1$ is a polynomial proposition, which holds in all reachable markings m where $m(p_3) = 0$ and $m(p_5) = 0$. Structural transition t is reach value q_p-invisible, but not q_p-invisible (by $002120 \xrightarrow{t} 002030$) or strongly reach q_p invisible. Strong value q_p-invisibility of t_{key} follows immediately from the fact that the adjacent places of t_{key}, *viz.* p_4 and p_6, do not occur in the definition of q_p.

This yields the state labelling which is shown in Example 2.   □

Given a weak equivalence relation $R_\sim$ and a stutter equivalence relation $R_{\triangleq}$, we write $R_\sim \preceq R_{\triangleq}$ to indicate that $R_\sim$ and $R_{\triangleq}$ yield consistent labelling. We spend the rest of this section investigating under which notions of invisibility and propositions from the literature, the LSTS of a Petri net is labelled consistently. More formally, we check for each weak equivalence relation $R_\sim$ and each stutter equivalence relation $R_{\triangleq}$ whether $R_\sim \preceq R_{\triangleq}$. This tells us when existing stubborn set theory can be applied without problems. The two lattices containing all weak and stuttering equivalence relations are depicted in Figure 6; each dotted arrow represents a consistent labelling result. Before we continue, we first introduce an auxiliary lemma.

Lemma 5. *Let I be a set of invisible structural transitions and L some labelling function. If for all $t \in I$ and paths $\pi = m_0 \xrightarrow{t_1} m_1 \xrightarrow{t_2} \ldots$ and $\pi' = m_0 \xrightarrow{t} m'_0 \xrightarrow{t_1} m'_1 \xrightarrow{t_2} \ldots$, it holds that $\pi \triangleq_L \pi'$, then $\sim_I \preceq \triangleq_L$.*

Proof. We assume that the following holds for all paths and $t \in I$:

$$m_0 \xrightarrow{t_1} m_1 \xrightarrow{t_2} \cdots \triangleq_L m_0 \xrightarrow{t} m_0' \xrightarrow{t_1} m_1' \xrightarrow{t_2} \cdots \qquad (\dagger)$$

We consider two initial paths π and π' such that $\pi \sim_I \pi'$ and prove that $\pi \triangleq_L \pi'$. The proof proceeds by induction on the combined number of invisible structural transitions (taken from I) in π and π'. In the base case, π and π' contain only visible structural transitions, and $\pi \sim_I \pi'$ implies $\pi = \pi'$ since Petri nets are deterministic. Hence, $\pi \triangleq_L \pi'$.

For the induction step, we take as hypothesis that, for all initial paths π and π' that together contain at most k invisible structural transitions, $\pi \sim_I \pi'$ implies $\pi \triangleq_L \pi'$. Let π and π' be two arbitrary initial paths such that $\pi \sim_I \pi'$ and the total number of invisible structural transitions contained in π and π' is k. We consider the case where an invisible structural transition is introduced in π', the other case is symmetric. Let $\pi' = \sigma_1 \sigma_2$ for some σ_1 and σ_2. Let $t \in I$ be some invisible structural transition and $\pi'' = \sigma_1 t \sigma_2'$ such that σ_2 and σ_2' contain the same sequence of structural transitions. Clearly, we have $\pi' \sim_I \pi''$. Here, we can apply our original assumption $(\dagger)$, to conclude that $\sigma_2 \triangleq t \sigma_2'$, i.e., the extra stuttering step t thus does not affect the labelling of the remainder of π''. Hence, we have $\pi' \triangleq_L \pi''$ and, with the induction hypothesis, $\pi \triangleq_L \pi''$. Note that π and π'' together contain $k + 1$ invisible structural transitions.

In case π and π' together contain an infinite number of invisible structural transitions, $\pi \sim_I \pi'$ implies $\pi \triangleq_L \pi'$ follows from the fact that the same holds for all finite prefixes of π and π' that are related by $\sim_I$. $\qquad \square$

The following theorems each focus on a class of atomic propositions and show which notion of invisibility is required for the LSTS of a Petri net to be labelled consistently. In the proofs, we use a function d_t, defined as $d_t(p) = W(t, p) - W(p, t)$ for all places p, which indicates how structural transition t changes the state. Furthermore, we also consider functions of type $P \to \mathbb{N}$ as vectors of type $\mathbb{N}^{|P|}$. This allows us to compute the pairwise addition of a marking m with d_t $(m + d_t)$ and to indicate that t does not change the marking $(d_t = 0)$.

Theorem 4. *Under reach value invisibility, the LSTS underlying a Petri net is labelled consistently for linear propositions, i.e., $\sim_v^r \preceq \triangleq_l$.*

Proof. Let $t \in \mathcal{I}_v^r$ be a reach value invisible structural transition such that there exist reachable markings m and m' with $m \xrightarrow{t} m'$. If such a t does not exist, then $\sim_v^r$ is the reflexive relation and $\sim_v^r \preceq \triangleq_l$ is trivially satisfied. Otherwise, let $q := f(p_1, \ldots, p_n) \bowtie k$ be a linear proposition. Since t is reach value invisible and f is linear, we have $f(m) = f(m') = f(m + d_t) = f(m) + f(d_t)$ and thus $f(d_t) = 0$. It follows that, given two paths $\pi = m_0 \xrightarrow{t_1} m_1 \xrightarrow{t_2} \ldots$ and $\pi' = m_0 \xrightarrow{t} m_0' \xrightarrow{t_1} m_1' \xrightarrow{t_2} \ldots$, the addition of t does not influence f, since $f(m_i) = f(m_i) + f(d_t) = f(m_i + d_t) = f(m_i')$ for all i. As a consequence, t also does not influence q. With Lemma 5, we deduce that $\sim_v^r \preceq \triangleq_l$. $\qquad \square$

Whereas in the linear case one can easily conclude that π and π' are stutter equivalent under f, in the polynomial case, we need to show that f is constant under all value invisible structural transitions t, even in markings where t is not enabled. This follows from the following proposition.

Proposition 1. *Let $f : \mathbb{N}^n \to \mathbb{Z}$ be a polynomial function, $a, b \in \mathbb{N}^n$ two constant vectors and $c = a - b$ the difference between a and b. Assume that for all $x \in \mathbb{N}^n$ such that $x \geq b$, where $\geq$ denotes pointwise comparison, it holds that $f(x) = f(x + c)$. Then, f is constant in the vector c, i.e., $f(x) = f(x + c)$ for all $x \in \mathbb{N}^n$.*

Proof. Let f, a, b and c be as above and let $\mathbf{1} \in \mathbb{N}^n$ be the vector containing only ones. Given some arbitrary $x \in \mathbb{N}^n$, consider the function $g_x(t) = f(x + t \cdot \mathbf{1} + c) - f(x + t \cdot \mathbf{1})$. For sufficiently large t, it holds that $x + t \cdot \mathbf{1} \geq b$, and it follows that $g_x(t) = 0$ for all sufficiently large t. This can only be the case if g_x is the zero polynomial, *i.e.*, $g_x(t) = 0$ for all t. As a special case, we conclude that $g_x(0) = f(x + c) - f(x) = 0$. □

The intuition behind this is that $f(x + c) - f(x)$ behaves like the directional derivative of f with respect to c. If the derivative is equal to zero in infinitely many x, f must be constant in the direction of c. We will apply this result in the following theorem.

Theorem 5. *Under value invisibility, the LSTS underlying a Petri net is labelled consistently for polynomial propositions, i.e., $\sim_v \preceq \triangleq_p$.*

Proof. Let $t \in \mathcal{I}_v$ be a value invisible structural transition, m and m' two markings with $m \xrightarrow{t} m'$, and $q := f(p_1, \ldots, p_n) \bowtie k$ a polynomial proposition. Note that infinitely many such (not necessarily reachable) markings exist in $\mathcal{M}$, so we can apply Proposition 1 to obtain $f(m) = f(m + d_t)$ for all markings m. It follows that, given two paths $\pi = m_0 \xrightarrow{t_1} m_1 \xrightarrow{t_2} \ldots$ and $\pi' = m_0 \xrightarrow{t} m_0' \xrightarrow{t_1} m_1' \xrightarrow{t_2} \ldots$, the addition of t does not alter the value of f, since $f(m_i) = f(m_i + d_t) = f(m_i')$ for all i. As a consequence, t also does not change the labelling of q. Application of Lemma 5 yields $\sim_v \preceq \triangleq_p$. □

Varpaaniemi shows that the LSTS of a Petri net is labelled consistently for arbitrary propositions under his notion of invisibility [22, Lemma 9]. Our notion of strong visibility, and especially strong reach invisibility, is weaker than Varpaaniemi's invisibility, so we generalise the result to $\sim_s^r \preceq \triangleq$.

Theorem 6. *Under strong reach visibility, the LSTS underlying a Petri net is labelled consistently for arbitrary propositions, i.e., $\sim_s^r \preceq \triangleq$.*

Proof. Let $t \in \mathcal{I}_s^r$ be a strongly reach invisible structural transition and $\pi = m_0 \xrightarrow{t_1} m_1 \xrightarrow{t_2} \ldots$ and $\pi' = m_0 \xrightarrow{t} m_0' \xrightarrow{t_1} m_1' \xrightarrow{t_2} \ldots$ two paths. Since, $m_i' = m_i + d_t$ for all i, it holds that either (i) $d_t = 0$ and $m_i = m_i'$ for all i; or (ii) each pair (m_i, m_i') is contained in $\{(m, m') \mid \forall p \in P : m'(p) = m(p) + W(t, p) - W(p, t)\}$, which is the set that underlies strong reach invisibility of t. In both cases, $L(m_i) = L(m_i')$ for all i. It follows from Lemma 5 that $\sim_s^r \preceq \triangleq$. □

To show that the results of the above theorems cannot be strengthened, we provide two negative results.

Theorem 7. *Under ordinary invisibility, the LSTS underlying a Petri net is not necessarily labelled consistently for arbitrary propositions, i.e., $\sim\; \not\trianglelefteq \triangleq$.*

Proof. Consider the Petri net from Example 2 with the arbitrary proposition q_l. Disregard q_p for the moment. Structural transition t is q_l-invisible, hence the paths corresponding to $t_1 t_2 t t_3$ and $t t_1 t_2 t_3$ are weakly equivalent under ordinary invisibility. However, they are not stutter equivalent.   □

Theorem 8. *Under reach value invisibility, the LSTS underlying a Petri net is not necessarily labelled consistently for polynomial propositions, i.e., $\sim_v^r \not\trianglelefteq \triangleq_p$.*

Proof. Consider the Petri net from Example 2 with the polynomial proposition $q_p := (1 - p_3)(1 - p_5) = 1$ from Example 3. Disregard q_l in this reasoning. Structural transition t is reach value q_p-invisible, hence the paths corresponding to $t_1 t_2 t t_3$ and $t t_1 t_2 t_3$ are weakly equivalent under reach value invisibility. However, they are not stutter equivalent for polynomial propositions.   □

It follows from Theorems 7 and 8 and transitivity of $\subseteq$ that Theorems 4, 5 and 6 cannot be strengthened further. In terms of Figure 6, this means that the dotted arrows cannot be moved downward in the lattice of weak equivalences and cannot be moved upward in the lattice of stutter equivalences. The implications of these findings on related work will be discussed in the next section.

7   Related Work

There are many works in literature that apply stubborn sets. We will consider several works that aim to preserve LTL$_{-X}$ and discuss whether they are correct when it comes to the problem presented in the current work.

Liebke and Wolf [10] present an approach for efficient CTL model checking on Petri nets. For some formulas, they can reduce CTL model checking to LTL model checking, which allows greater reductions under POR. They rely on the incorrect LTL preservation theorem, and since they apply the techniques on Petri nets with ordinary invisibility, their theory is incorrect (Theorem 7). Similarly, the overview of stubborn set theory presented by Valmari and Hansen in [21] applies reach invisibility and does not necessarily preserve LTL$_{-X}$. Varpaaniemi [22] also applies stubborn sets to Petri nets, but relies on a visibility notion that is stronger than strong invisibility. The correctness of these results is thus not affected (Theorem 6). The approach of Bønneland *et al.* [4] operates on two-player Petri nets, but only aims to preserve reachability and consequently does not suffer from the inconsistent labelling problem.

A generic implementation of weak stubborn sets is proposed by Laarman *et al.* [9]. They use abstract concepts such as guards and transition groups to implement POR in a way that is agnostic of the input language. The theory they present includes condition **D1**, which is too weak, but the accompanying implementation follows the framework of Section 4.1, and thus it is correct by Theorem 2 The implementations proposed in [21,23] are similar, albeit specific for Petri nets.

Others [6,8] perform action-based model checking and thus strive to preserve weak trace equivalence or inclusion. As such, they do not suffer from the problems discussed here, which applies only to state labels.

Although Beneš *et al.* [2,3] rely on ample sets, and not on stubborn sets, they also discuss weak trace equivalence and stutter-trace equivalence. In fact, they present an equivalence relation for traces that is a combination of weak and stutter equivalence. The paper includes a theorem that weak equivalence implies their new state/event equivalence [2, Theorem 6.5]. However, the counter-example on the right shows that this consistent la-belling theorem does not hold. Here, the action τ is in-visible, and the two paths in this transition system are thus weakly equivalent. However, they are not stutter equivalent, which is a special case of state/event equiv-alence. Although the main POR correctness result [2,

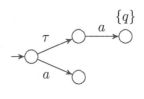

Corollary 6.6] builds on the incorrect consistent labelling theorem, its correctness does not appear to be affected. An alternative proof can be constructed based on Lemmas 1 and 2.

The current work is not the first to point out mistakes in POR theory. In [14], Siegel presents a flaw in an algorithm that combines POR and on-the-fly model checking [12]. In that setting, POR is applied on the product of an LSTS and a Büchi automaton. Let q be a state of the LSTS and s a state of the Büchi au-tomaton. While investigating a transition $(q, s) \xrightarrow{a} (q', s')$, condition **C3**, which—like condition **L**—aims to solve the action ignoring problem, incorrectly sets $r(q, s') = enabled(q)$ instead of $r(q, s) = enabled(q)$.

8   Conclusion

We discussed the inconsistent labelling problem for preservation of stutter-trace equivalence with stubborn sets. The issue is relatively easy to repair by strength-ening condition **D1**. For Petri nets, altering the definition of invisibility can also resolve inconsistent labelling depending on the type of atomic propositions. The impact on applications presented in related works seems to be limited: the prob-lem is typically mitigated in the implementation, since it is very hard to compute **D1** exactly. This is also a possible explanation for why the inconsistent labelling problem has not been noticed for so many years.

Since this is not the first error found in POR theory [14], a more rigorous approach to proving its correctness, *e.g.* using proof assistants, would provide more confidence.

References

1. Baier, C., Katoen, J.P.: Principles of model checking. MIT Press (2008)

2. Beneš, N., Brim, L., Buhnova, B., Ern, I., Sochor, J., Vařeková, P.: Partial order reduction for state/event LTL with application to component-interaction automata. Science of Computer Programming **76**(10), 877–890 (2011). https://doi.org/10.1016/j.scico.2010.02.008

3. Beneš, N., Brim, L., Černá, I., Sochor, J., Vařeková, P., Zimmerova, B.: Partial Order Reduction for State/Event LTL. In: IFM 2009. LNCS, vol. 5423, pp. 307–321 (2009). https://doi.org/10.1007/978-3-642-00255-7_21

4. Bønneland, F.M., Jensen, P.G., Larsen, K.G., Muñiz, M.: Partial Order Reduction for Reachability Games. In: CONCUR 2019. vol. 140, pp. 23:1–23:15 (2019). https://doi.org/10.4230/LIPIcs.CONCUR.2019.23

5. Gerth, R., Kuiper, R., Peled, D., Penczek, W.: A Partial Order Approach to Branching Time Logic Model Checking. Information and Computation **150**(2), 132–152 (1999). https://doi.org/10.1006/inco.1998.2778

6. Gibson-Robinson, T., Hansen, H., Roscoe, A.W., Wang, X.: Practical Partial Order Reduction for CSP. In: NFM 2015. LNCS, vol. 9058, pp. 188–203 (2015). https://doi.org/10.1007/978-3-319-17524-9_14

7. Godefroid, P.: Partial-Order Methods for the Verification of Concurrent Systems, LNCS, vol. 1032. Springer (1996). https://doi.org/10.1007/3-540-60761-7

8. Hansen, H., Lin, S., Liu, Y., Nguyen, T.K., Sun, J.: Diamonds Are a Girl's Best Friend: Partial Order Reduction for Timed Automata with Abstractions. In: CAV 2014. LNCS, vol. 8559, pp. 391–406 (2014). https://doi.org/10.1007/978-3-319-08867-9_26

9. Laarman, A., Pater, E., van de Pol, J., Hansen, H.: Guard-based partial-order reduction. STTT **18**(4), 427–448 (2016). https://doi.org/10.1007/s10009-014-0363-9

10. Liebke, T., Wolf, K.: Taking Some Burden Off an Explicit CTL Model Checker. In: Petri Nets 2019. LNCS, vol. 11522, pp. 321–341 (2019). https://doi.org/10.1007/978-3-030-21571-2_18

11. Peled, D.: All from One, One for All: on Model Checking Using Representatives. In: CAV 1993. LNCS, vol. 697, pp. 409–423 (1993). https://doi.org/10.1007/3-540-56922-7_34

12. Peled, D.: Combining partial order reductions with on-the-fly model-checking. FMSD **8**(1), 39–64 (1996). https://doi.org/10.1007/BF00121262

13. Schmidt, K.: Stubborn sets for model checking the EF/AG fragment of CTL. Fundamenta Informaticae **43**(1-4), 331–341 (2000)

14. Siegel, S.F.: What's Wrong with On-the-Fly Partial Order Reduction. In: CAV 2019. LNCS, vol. 11562, pp. 478–495 (2019). https://doi.org/10.1007/978-3-030-25543-5_27

15. Valmari, A.: A Stubborn Attack on State Explosion. In: CAV 1990. LNCS, vol. 531, pp. 156–165 (1991). https://doi.org/10.1007/BFb0023729

16. Valmari, A.: Stubborn sets for reduced state space generation. In: Advances in Petri Nets. vol. 483, pp. 491–515 (1991). https://doi.org/10.1007/3-540-53863-1_36

17. Valmari, A.: A Stubborn Attack on State Explosion. Formal Methods in System Design **1**(4), 297–322 (1992). https://doi.org/10.1007/BF00709154

18. Valmari, A.: The state explosion problem. In: ACPN 1996. LNCS, vol. 1491, pp. 429–528 (1996). https://doi.org/10.1007/3-540-65306-6_21

19. Valmari, A.: Stubborn Set Methods for Process Algebras. In: POMIV 1996. DIMACS, vol. 29, pp. 213–231 (1997). https://doi.org/10.1090/dimacs/029/12

20. Valmari, A.: Stop It, and Be Stubborn! TECS **16**(2), 46:1–46:26 (2017). https://doi.org/10.1145/3012279

21. Valmari, A., Hansen, H.: Stubborn Set Intuition Explained. In: ToPNoC XII. LNCS, vol. 10470, pp. 140–165 (2017). https://doi.org/10.1007/978-3-662-55862-1_7
22. Varpaaniemi, K.: On Stubborn Sets in the Verification of Linear Time Temporal Properties. FMSD **26**(1), 45–67 (2005). https://doi.org/10.1007/s10703-005-4594-y
23. Wolf, K.: Petri Net Model Checking with LoLA 2. In: Petri Nets 2018. LNCS, vol. 10877, pp. 351–362 (2018). https://doi.org/10.1007/978-3-319-91268-4_18

Neural Flocking: MPC-based Supervised Learning of Flocking Controllers

(✉)Usama Mehmood[1], Shouvik Roy[1], Radu Grosu[2], Scott A. Smolka[1], Scott D. Stoller[1], and Ashish Tiwari[3]

[1] Stony Brook University, Stony Brook NY, USA
umehmood@cs.stonybrook.edu
[2] Technische Universitat Wien, Wien, Austria
[3] Microsoft Research, San Francisco CA, USA

Abstract. We show how a symmetric and fully distributed flocking controller can be synthesized using Deep Learning from a centralized flocking controller. Our approach is based on *Supervised Learning*, with the centralized controller providing the training data, in the form of trajectories of state-action pairs. We use Model Predictive Control (MPC) for the centralized controller, an approach that we have successfully demonstrated on flocking problems. MPC-based flocking controllers are high-performing but also computationally expensive. By learning a symmetric and distributed neural flocking controller from a centralized MPC-based one, we achieve the best of both worlds: the neural controllers have high performance (on par with the MPC controllers) and high efficiency. Our experimental results demonstrate the sophisticated nature of the distributed controllers we learn. In particular, the neural controllers are capable of achieving myriad flocking-oriented control objectives, including flocking formation, collision avoidance, obstacle avoidance, predator avoidance, and target seeking. Moreover, they generalize the behavior seen in the training data to achieve these objectives in a significantly broader range of scenarios. In terms of verification of our neural flocking controller, we use a form of statistical model checking to compute confidence intervals for its convergence rate and time to convergence.

Keywords: Flocking · Model Predictive Control · Distributed Neural Controller · Deep Neural Network · Supervised Learning

1 Introduction

With the introduction of Reynolds rule-based model [16, 17], it is now possible to understand the flocking problem as one of distributed control. Specifically, in this model, at each time-step, each agent executes a control law given in terms of the weighted sum of three competing forces to determine its next acceleration. Each of these forces has its own rule: *separation* (keep a safe distance away from your neighbors), *cohesion* (move towards the centroid of your neighbors), and *alignment* (steer toward the average heading of your neighbors). Reynolds

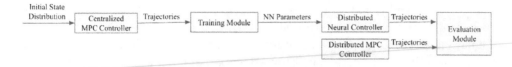

Fig. 1: Neural Flocking Architecture

controller is *distributed*; i.e., it is executed separately by each agent, using information about only itself and nearby agents, and without communication. Furthermore, it is *symmetric*; i.e., every agent runs the same controller (same code).

We subsequently showed that a simpler, more declarative approach to the flocking problem is possible [11]. In this setting, flocking is achieved when the agents combine to minimize a system-wide *cost function*. We presented centralized and distributed solutions for achieving this form of "declarative flocking" (DF), both of which were formulated in terms of Model-Predictive Control (MPC) [2].

Another advantage of DF over the ruled-based approach exemplified by Reynolds model is that it allows one to consider additional control objectives (e.g., obstacle and predator avoidance) simply by extending the cost function with additional terms for these objectives. Moreover, these additional terms are typically quite straightforward in nature. In contrast, deriving behavioral rules that achieve the new control objectives can be a much more challenging task.

An issue with MPC is that computing the next control action can be computationally expensive, as MPC searches for an action sequence that minimizes the cost function over a given prediction horizon. This renders MPC unsuitable for real-time applications with short control periods, for which flocking is a prime example. Another potential problem with MPC-based approaches to flocking is its performance (in terms of achieving the desired flight formation), which may suffer in a fully distributed setting.

In this paper, we present *Neural Flocking* (NF), a new approach to the flocking problem that uses Supervised Learning to learn a symmetric and fully distributed flocking controller from a centralized MPC-based controller. By doing so, we achieve the best of both worlds: high performance (on par with the MPC controllers) in terms of meeting flocking flight-formation objectives, and high efficiency leading to real-time flight controllers. Moreover, our NF controllers can easily be parallelized on hardware accelerators such as GPUs and TPUs.

Figure 1 gives an overview of the NF approach. A high-performing centralized MPC controller provides the labeled training data to the learning agent: a symmetric and distributed neural controller in the form of a deep neural network (DNN). The training data consists of trajectories of state-action pairs, where a state contains the information known to an agent at a time step (e.g., its own position and velocity, and the position and velocity of its neighbors), and the action (the label) is the acceleration assigned to that agent at that time step by the centralized MPC controller.

We formulate and evaluate NF in a number of essential flocking scenarios: basic flocking with inter-agent collision avoidance, as in [11], and more advanced scenarios with additional objectives, including obstacle avoidance, predator avoidance, and target seeking by the flock. We conduct an extensive performance evaluation of NF. Our experimental results demonstrate the sophisticated nature of NF controllers. In particular, they are capable of achieving all of the stated control objectives. Moreover, they generalize the behavior seen in the training data in order to achieve these objectives in a significantly broader range of scenarios. In terms of verification of our neural controller, we use a form of statistical model checking [5, 10] to compute confidence intervals for its rate of convergence to a flock and for its time to convergence.

2   Background

We consider a set of n dynamic agents $\mathcal{A} = \{1, \ldots, n\}$ that move according to the following discrete-time equations of motion:

$$
\begin{aligned}
p_i(k + 1) &= p_i(k) + dt \cdot v_i(k), \quad |v_i(k)| < \bar{v} \\
v_i(k + 1) &= v_i(k) + dt \cdot a_i(k), \quad |a_i(k)| < \bar{a}
\end{aligned}
\tag{1}
$$

where $p_i(k) \in \mathbb{R}^2$, $v_i(k) \in \mathbb{R}^2$, $a_i(k) \in \mathbb{R}^2$ are the position, velocity and acceleration of agent $i \in \mathcal{A}$ respectively at time step k, and $dt \in \mathbb{R}^+$ is the time step. The magnitudes of velocities and accelerations are bounded by $\bar{v}$ and $\bar{a}$, respectively. Acceleration $a_i(k)$ is the control input for agent i at time step k. The acceleration is updated after every η time steps i.e., $\eta \cdot dt$ is the control period. The flock *configuration* at time step k is thus given by the following vectors (in boldface):

$$
\mathbf{p}(k) = [p_1^T(k) \cdots p_n^T(k)]^T
\tag{2}
$$

$$
\mathbf{v}(k) = [v_1^T(k) \cdots v_n^T(k)]^T
\tag{3}
$$

$$
\mathbf{a}(k) = [a_1^T(k) \cdots a_n^T(k)]^T
\tag{4}
$$

The configuration vectors are referred to without the time indexing as $\mathbf{p}$, $\mathbf{v}$, and $\mathbf{a}$. The *neighborhood* of agent i at time step k, denoted by $\mathcal{N}_i(k) \subseteq \mathcal{A}$, contains its $\mathcal{N}$-nearest neighbors, i.e., the $\mathcal{N}$ other agents closest to it. We use this definition (in Section 2.2 to define a distributed-flocking cost function) for simplicity, and expect that a radius-based definition of neighborhood would lead to similar results for our distributed flocking controllers.

2.1   Model-Predictive Control

Model-Predictive control (MPC) [2] is a well-known control technique that has recently been applied to the flocking problem [11, 19, 20]. At each control step, an optimization problem is solved to find the optimal sequence of control actions (agent accelerations in our case) that minimizes a given cost function with respect to a predictive model of the system. The first control action of the optimal control sequence is then applied to the system; the rest is discarded. In the computation of the cost function, the predictive model is evaluated for a finite prediction horizon of T control steps.

MPC-based flocking models can be categorized as *centralized* or *distributed*. A *centralized* model assumes that complete information about the flock is available to a single "global" controller, which uses the states of all agents to compute their next optimal accelerations. The following optimization problem is solved by a centralized MPC controller at each control step k:

$$\min_{\mathbf{a}(k|k),\ldots,\mathbf{a}(k+T-1|k) < \bar{a}} \quad J(k) + \lambda \cdot \sum_{t=0}^{T-1} \|\mathbf{a}(k+t \mid k)\|^2 \tag{5}$$

The first term $J(k)$ is the centralized model-specific cost, evaluated for T control steps (this embodies the predictive aspect of MPC), starting at time step k. It encodes the control objective of minimizing the cost function $J(k)$. The second term, scaled by a weight $\lambda > 0$, penalizes large control inputs: $\mathbf{a}(k+t \mid k)$ are the predictions made at time step k for the accelerations at time step $k+t$.

In *distributed MPC*, each agent computes its acceleration based only on its own state and its local knowledge, e.g., information about its neighbors:

$$\min_{a_i(k|k),\ldots,a_i(k+T-1|k) < \bar{a}} \quad J_i(k) + \lambda \cdot \sum_{t=0}^{T-1} \|a_i(k+t \mid k)\|^2 \tag{6}$$

$J_i(k)$ is the distributed, model-specific cost function for agent i, analogous to $J(k)$. In a distributed setting where an agent's knowledge of its neighbors' behavior is limited, an agent cannot calculate the exact future behavior of its neighbors. Hence, the predictive aspect of $J_i(k)$ must rely on some assumption about that behavior during the prediction horizon. Our distributed cost functions are based on the assumption that the neighbors have zero accelerations during the prediction horizon. While this simple design is clearly not completely accurate, our experiments show that it still achieves good results.

2.2 Declarative Flocking

Declarative flocking (DF) is a high-level approach to designing flocking algorithms based on defining a suitable cost function for MPC [11]. This is in contrast to the operational approach, where a set of rules are used to capture flocking behavior, as in Reynolds model. For basic flocking, the DF cost function contains two terms: (1) a *cohesion* term based on the squared distance between each pair of agents in the flock; and (2) a *separation* term based on the inverse of the squared distance between each pair of agents. The flock evolves toward a configuration in which these two opposing forces are balanced. The cost function J^C for centralized DF, i.e., centralized MPC (CMPC), is as follows:

$$J^C(\mathbf{p}) = \frac{2}{|\mathcal{A}| \cdot (|\mathcal{A}| - 1)} \cdot \sum_{i \in \mathcal{A}} \sum_{j \in \mathcal{A}, i < j} \|p_{ij}\|^2 + \omega_s \cdot \frac{1}{\|p_{ij}\|^2} \tag{7}$$

where ω_s is the weight of the separation term and controls the density of the flock. The cost function is normalized by the number of pairs of agents, $\frac{|\mathcal{A}|\cdot(|\mathcal{A}-1|)}{2}$; as such, the cost does not depend on the size of the flock. The control law for CMPC is given by Eq. (5), with $J(k) = \sum_{t=1}^{T} J^{C}\left(\mathbf{p}(k+t \mid k)\right)$.

The basic flocking cost function for distributed DF is similar to that for CMPC, except that the cost function J_i^D for agent i is computed over its set of neighbors $\mathcal{N}_i(k)$ at time k:

$$J_i^{\mathrm{D}}\left(\mathbf{p}(k)\right) = \frac{1}{|\mathcal{N}_i(k)|} \cdot \sum_{j \in \mathcal{N}_i(k)} \|p_{ij}\|^2 + \omega_s \cdot \sum_{j \in \mathcal{N}_i(k)} \frac{1}{\|p_{ij}\|^2} \qquad (8)$$

The control law for agent i is given by Eq. (6), with $J_i(k) = \sum_{t=1}^{T} J_i^{\mathrm{D}}\left(\mathbf{p}(k+t \mid k)\right)$.

3   Additional Control Objectives

The cost functions for basic flocking given in Eqs. (7) and (8) are designed to ensure that in the steady state, the agents are well-separated. Additional goals such as obstacle avoidance, predator avoidance, and target seeking are added to the MPC formulation as weighted cost-function terms. Different objectives can be combined by including the corresponding terms in the cost function as a weighted sum.

Cost-Function Term for Obstacle Avoidance. We consider multiple rectangular obstacles which are distributed randomly in the field. For a set of m rectangular obstacles $\mathcal{O} = \{\mathcal{O}_1, \mathcal{O}_2, ..., \mathcal{O}_m\}$, we define the cost function term for obstacle avoidance as:

$$J_{OA}(\mathbf{p}, \mathbf{o}) = \frac{1}{|\mathcal{A}||\mathcal{O}|} \sum_{i \in \mathcal{A}} \sum_{j \in \mathcal{O}} \frac{1}{\left\|p_i - o_j^{(i)}\right\|^2} \qquad (9)$$

where $\mathbf{o}$ is the set of points on the obstacle boundaries and $o_j^{(i)}$ is the point on the obstacle boundary of the jth obstacle $\mathcal{O}_j$ that is closest to the ith agent.

Cost-Function Term for Target Seeking. This term is the average of the squared distance between the agents and the target. Let g denote the position of the fixed target. Then the target-seeking term is as defined as

$$J_{TS}(\mathbf{p}) = \frac{1}{|\mathcal{A}|} \sum_{i \in \mathcal{A}} \|p_i - g\|^2 \qquad (10)$$

Cost-Function Term for Predator Avoidance. We introduce a single predator, which is more agile than the flocking agents: its maximum speed and acceleration are a factor of f_p greater than $\bar{v}$ and $\bar{a}$, respectively, with $f_p > 1$. Apart from being more agile, the predator has the same dynamics as the agents, given by

Eq. (1). The control law for the predator consists of a single term that causes it to move toward the centroid of the flock with maximum acceleration.

For a flock of n agents and one predator, the cost-function term for predator avoidance is the average of the inverse of the cube of the distances between the predator and the agents. It is given by:

$$J_{PA}\left(\mathbf{p}, p_{pred}\right) = \frac{1}{|\mathcal{A}|} \sum_{i \in \mathcal{A}} \frac{1}{\|p_i - p_{pred}\|^3} \qquad (11)$$

where p_{pred} is the position of the predator. In contrast to the separation term in Eqs. (5)-(6), which we designed to ensure inter-agent collision avoidance, the predator-avoidance term has a cube instead of a square in the denominator. This is to reduce the influence of the predator on the flock when the predator is far away from the flock.

NF Cost-Function Terms. The MPC cost functions used in our examination of Neural Flocking are weighted sums of the cost function terms introduced above. We refer to the first term of our centralized DF cost function $J^C(\mathbf{p})$ (see Eq. (7)) as $J_{cohes}(\mathbf{p})$ and the second as $J_{sep}(\mathbf{p})$. We use the following cost functions J_1, J_2, and J_3 for basic flocking with collision avoidance, obstacle avoidance with target seeking, and predator avoidance, respectively.

$$J_1(\mathbf{p}) = J_{cohes}(\mathbf{p}) + \omega_s \cdot J_{sep}(\mathbf{p}) \qquad (12a)$$

$$J_2(\mathbf{p}, \mathbf{o}) = J_{cohes}(\mathbf{p}) + \omega_s \cdot J_{sep}(\mathbf{p}) + \omega_o \cdot J_{OA}(\mathbf{p}, \mathbf{o}) + \omega_t \cdot J_{TS}(\mathbf{p}) \qquad (12b)$$

$$J_3(\mathbf{p}, p_{pred}) = J_{cohes}(\mathbf{p}) + \omega_s \cdot J_{sep}(\mathbf{p}) + \omega_p \cdot J_{PA}(\mathbf{p}, p_{pred}) \qquad (12c)$$

where ω_s is the weight of the separation term, ω_o is the weight of the obstacle avoidance term, ω_t is the weight of the target-seeking term, and ω_p is the weight of the predator-avoidance term. Note that J_1 is equivalent to J^C (Eq. (7)). The weight ω_s of the separation term is experimentally chosen to ensure that the distance between agents, throughout the simulation, is at least d_{min}, the minimum inter-agent distance representing collision avoidance. Similar considerations were given to the choice of values for ω_o and ω_p. The specific values we used for the weights are: $\omega_s = 2000$, $\omega_o = 1500$, $\omega_t = 10$, and $\omega_p = 500$.

We experimented with an alternative strategy for introducing inter-agent collision avoidance, obstacle avoidance, and predator avoidance into the MPC problem, namely, as *constraints* of the form $d_{min} - p_{ij} < 0$, $d_{min} - \|p_i - o_j^{(i)}\| < 0$, and $d_{min} - \|p_i - p_{pred}\| < 0$, respectively. Using the theory of exact penalty functions [12], we recast the constrained MPC problem as an equivalent unconstrained MPC problem by converting the constraints into a weighted *penalty term*, which is then added to the MPC cost function. This approach rendered the optimization problem difficult to solve due to the non-smoothness of the penalty term. As a result, constraint violations in the form of collisions were observed during simulation.

4 Neural Flocking

We learn a *distributed neural controller* (DNC) for the flocking problem using training data in the form of trajectories of state-action pairs produced by a CMPC controller. In addition to basic flocking with inter-agent collision avoidance, the DNC exhibits a number of other flocking-related behaviors, including obstacle avoidance, target seeking, and predator avoidance. We also show how the learned behavior exhibited by the DNC generalizes over a larger number of agents than what was used during training to achieve successful collision-free flocking in significantly larger flocks.

We use *Supervised Learning* to train the DNC. Supervised Learning learns a function that maps an input to an output based on example sequences of input-output pairs. In our case, the trajectory data obtained from CMPC contains both the training inputs and corresponding labels (outputs): the state of an agent in the flock (and that of its nearest neighbors) at a particular time step is the input, and that agent's acceleration at the same time step is the label.

4.1 Training Distributed Flocking Controllers

We use Deep Learning to synthesize a distributed and symmetric neural controller from the training data provided by the CMPC controller. Our objective is to learn basic flocking, obstacle avoidance with target seeking, and predator avoidance. Their respective CMPC-based cost functions are given in Sections 2.2 and 3. All of these control objectives implicitly also include inter-agent collision avoidance by virtue of the separation term in Eq. 7.

For each of these control objectives, DNC training data is obtained from CMPC trajectory data generated for $n = 15$ agents, starting from initial configurations in which agent positions and velocities are uniformly sampled from $[-15, 15]^2$ and $[0, 1]^2$, respectively. All training trajectories are 1,000 time steps in duration.

We further ensure that the initial configurations are *recoverable*; i.e., no two agents are so close to each other that they cannot avoid a collision by resorting to maximal accelerations. We learn a single DNC from the state-action pairs of all n agents. This yields a symmetric distributed controller, which we use for each agent in the flock during evaluation.

Basic Flocking. Trajectory data for basic flocking is generated using the cost function given in Eq. (7). We generate 200 trajectories, each of which (as noted above) is 1,000 time steps long. The input to the NN is the position and velocity of each agent along with the positions and velocities of its $\mathcal{N}$-nearest neighbors. This yields $200 \cdot 1,000 \cdot 15 = 3M$ total training samples.

Let us refer to the agent (the DNC) being learned as $\mathcal{A}_0$. Since we use neighborhood size $\mathcal{N} = 14$, the input to the NN is of the form $[p_0^x \; p_0^y \; v_0^x \; v_0^y \; p_1^x \; p_1^y \; v_1^x \; v_1^y \; \ldots \; p_{14}^x \; p_{14}^y \; v_{14}^x \; v_{14}^y]$, where p_0^x, p_0^y are the position coordinates and v_0^x, v_0^y velocity coordinates for agent $\mathcal{A}_0$, and $p_{1\ldots14}^x$, $p_{1\ldots14}^y$ and $v_{1\ldots14}^x$, $v_{1\ldots14}^y$ are the position and velocity vectors of its neighbors. Since this input vector has 60 components, the input to the NN consists of 60 features.

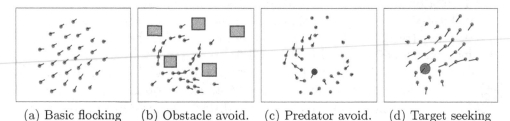

(a) Basic flocking   (b) Obstacle avoid.   (c) Predator avoid.   (d) Target seeking

Fig. 2: Snapshots of DNC flocking behaviors for 30 agents

Obstacle Avoidance with Target Seeking. For obstacle avoidance with target seeking, we use CMPC with the cost function given in Eq. (12b). The target is located beyond the obstacles, forcing the agents to move through the obstacle field. For the training data, we generate 100 trajectories over 4 different obstacle fields (25 trajectories per obstacle field). The input to the NN consists of the 92 features $[p_0^x \; p_0^y \; v_0^x \; v_0^y \; o_0^x \; o_0^y \cdots p_{14}^x \; p_{14}^y \; v_{14}^x \; v_{14}^y \; o_{14}^x \; o_{14}^y \; g^x \; g^y]$, where o_0^x, o_0^y is the closest point on any obstacle to agent $\mathcal{A}_0$; $o_{1\ldots14}^x$, $o_{1\ldots14}^y$ give the closest point on any obstacle for the 14 neighboring agents, and g^x, g^y is the target location.

Predator Avoidance. The CMPC cost function for predator avoidance is given in Eq. (12c). The position, velocity, and the acceleration of the predator are denoted by p_{pred}, v_{pred}, a_{pred}, respectively. We take $f_p = 1.40$; hence $\bar{v}_{pred} = 1.40\,\bar{v}$ and $\bar{a}_{pred} = 1.40\,\bar{a}$. The input features to the NN are the positions and velocities of agent $\mathcal{A}_0$ and its $\mathcal{N}$-nearest neighbors, and the position and velocity of the predator. The input with 64 features thus has the form $[p_0^x \; p_0^y \; v_0^x \; v_0^y \cdots p_{14}^x \; p_{14}^y \; v_{14}^x \; v_{14}^y \; p_{pred}^x \; p_{pred}^y \; v_{pred}^x \; v_{pred}^y]$.

5 Experimental Evaluation

This section contains the results of our extensive performance analysis of the distributed neural flocking controller (DNC), taking into account various control objectives: basic flocking with collision avoidance, obstacle avoidance with target seeking, and predator avoidance. As illustrated in Fig. 1, this involves running CMPC to generate the training data for the DNCs, whose performance we then compare to that of the DMPC and CMPC controllers. We also show that the DNC flocking controllers generalize the behavior seen in the training data to achieve successful collision-free flocking in flocks significantly larger in size than those used during training. Finally, we use Statistical Model Checking to obtain confidence intervals for DNC's correctness/performance.

5.1 Preliminaries

The CMPC and DMPC control problems defined in Section 2.1 are solved using MATLAB fmincon optimizer. In the training phase, the size of the flock is

$n = 15$. For obstacle-avoidance with target-seeking, we use 5 obstacles with the target located at [60,50]. The simulation time is 100, $dt = 0.1$ time units, and $\eta = 3$, where (recall) $\eta \cdot dt$ is the control period. Further, the agent velocity and acceleration bounds are $\bar{v} = 2.0$ and $\bar{a} = 1.5$.

We use $d_{min} = 1.5$ as the minimum inter-agent distance for collision avoidance, $d_{min}^{obs} = 1$ as the minimum agent-obstacle distance for obstacle avoidance, and $d_{min}^{pred} = 1.5$ as the minimum agent-predator distance for predator avoidance. For initial configurations, recall that agent positions and velocities are uniformly sampled from $[-15, 15]^2$ and $[0, 1]^2$, respectively, and we ensure that they are *recoverable*; i.e., no two agents are so close to each other that they cannot avoid a collision when resorting to maximal accelerations. The predator starts at rest from a fixed location at a distance of 40 from the flock center.

For training, we considered 15 agents and 200 trajectories per agent, each trajectory 1,000 time steps in length. This yielded a total of 3,000,000 training samples. Our neural controller is a fully connected feed-forward Deep Neural Network (DNN), with 5 hidden layers, 84 neurons per hidden layer, and with a ReLU activation function. We use an iterative approach for choosing the DNN hyperparameters and architecture where we continuously improve our NN, until we observe satisfactory performance by the DNC.

For training the DNNs, we use Keras [3], which is a high-level neural network API written in Python and capable of running on top of TensorFlow. To generate the NN model, Keras uses the Adam optimizer [8] with the following settings: $lr = 10^{-2}$, $\beta_1 = 0.9$, $\beta_2 = 0.999$, $\epsilon = 10^{-8}$. The batch size (number of samples processed before the model is updated) is 2,000, and the number of epochs (number of complete passes through the training dataset) used for training is 1,000. For measuring training loss, we use the mean-squared error metric.

For basic flocking, DNN input vectors have 60 features and the number of trainable DNN parameters is 33,854. For flocking with obstacle-avoidance and target-seeking, input vectors have 92 features and the number of trainable parameters is 36,542. Finally, for flocking with predator-avoidance, input vectors have 64 features and the resulting number of trainable DNN parameters is 34,190.

To test the trained DNC, we generated 100 simulations (runs) for each of the desired control objectives: basic flocking with collision avoidance, flocking with obstacle avoidance and target seeking, and flocking with predator avoidance. The results presented in Tables 1, were obtained using the same number of agents and obstacles and the same predator as in the training phase. We also ran tests that show DNC controllers can achieve collision-free flocking with obstacle avoidance where the numbers of agents and obstacles are greater than those used during training.

5.2   Results for Basic Flocking

We use flock diameter, inter-agent collision count and velocity convergence [20] as performance metrics for flocking behavior. At any time step, the *flock diameter* $D(\mathbf{p}) = \max_{(i,j) \in \mathcal{A}} \|p_{ij}\|$ is the largest distance between any two agents in the flock. We calculate the average converged diameter by averaging the flock diameter

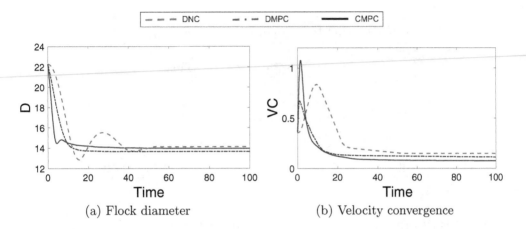

(a) Flock diameter   (b) Velocity convergence

Fig. 3: Performance comparison for basic flocking with collision avoidance, averaged over 100 test runs.

in the final time step of the simulation over the 100 runs. An inter-agent collision (IC) occurs when the distance between two agents at any point in time is less than d_{min}. The IC rate (ICR) is the average number of ICs per test-trajectory timestep. The velocity convergence $VC(\mathbf{v}) = (1/n) \left(\sum_{i \in \mathcal{A}} \|v_i - (\sum_{j=1}^{n} v_j)/n\|^2 \right)$ is the average of the squared magnitude of the discrepancy between the velocities of agents and the flock's average velocity. For all the metrics, lower values are better, indicating a denser and more coherent flock with fewer collisions. A successful flocking controller should also ensure that values of $D(\mathbf{p})$ and $VC(\mathbf{v})$ eventually stabilize.

Fig. 3 and Table 1 compare the performance of the DNC on the basic-flocking problem for 15 agents to that of the MPC controllers. Although the DMPC and CMPC outperform the DNC, the difference is marginal. An important advantage of the DNC over DMPC is that they are much faster. Executing a DNC controller requires a modest number of arithmetic operations, whereas executing an MPC controller requires simulation of a model and controller over the prediction horizon. In our experiments, on average, the CMPC takes 1209 msec of CPU time for the entire flock and DMPC takes 58 msec of CPU time per agent, whereas the DNC takes only 1.6 msec.

Table 1: Performance comparison for BF with 15 agents on 100 test runs

	Avg. Conv. Diameter	ICR	Velocity Convergence
DNC	14.13	0	0.15
DMPC	13.67	0	0.11
CMPC	13.84	0	0.10

Table 2: DNC Performance Generalization for BF

Agents	Avg. Conv. Diameter	Conv. Rate (%)	Avg. Conv. Time	ICR
15	14.13	100	52.15	0
20	16.45	97	58.76	0
25	19.81	94	64.11	0
30	23.24	92	72.08	0
35	30.57	86	83.84	0.008
40	38.66	81	95.32	0.019

5.3 Results for Obstacle and Predator Avoidance

For obstacle and predator avoidance, collision rates are used as a performance metric. An obstacle-agent collision (OC) occurs when the distance between an agent and the closest point on any obstacle is less than d_{min}^{obs}. A predator-agent collision (PC) occurs when the distance between an agent and the predator is less than d_{min}^{pred}. The OC rate (OCR) is the average number of OCs per test-trajectory time-step, and the PC rate (PCR) is defined similarly. Our test results show that the DNC, along with the DMPC and CMPC, is collision-free (i.e., each of ICR, OCR, and PCR is zero) for 15 agents, with the exception of DMPC for predator avoidance where PCR = 0.013. We also observed that the flock successfully reaches the target location in all 100 test runs.

5.4 DNC Generalization Results

Tables 2–3 present DNC generalization results for basic flocking (BF), obstacle avoidance (OA), and predator avoidance (PA), with the number of agents ranging from 15 (the flock size during training) to 40. In all of these experiments, we use a neighborhood size of $\mathcal{N} = 14$, the same as during training. Each controller was evaluated with 100 test runs. The performance metrics in Table 2 are the average converged diameter, convergence rate, average convergence time, and ICR.

The convergence rate is the fraction of successful flocks over 100 runs. The collection of agents is said to have converged to a flock (with collision avoidance) if the value of the global cost function is less than the convergence threshold. We use a convergence threshold of $J_1(\mathbf{p}) \leq 150$, which was chosen based on its proximity to the value achieved by CMPC. We use the cost function from Eq. 12a to calculate our success rate because we are showing convergence rate for basic flocking. The average convergence time is the time when the global cost function first drops below the success threshold and remains below it for the rest of the run, averaged over all 100 runs. Even with a local neighborhood of size 14, the results demonstrate that the DNC can successfully generalize to a large number of agents for all of our control objectives.

Table 3: DNC Generalization Performance for OA and PA

Agents	OA		PA	
	ICR	OCR	ICR	PCR
15	0	0	0	0
20	0	0	0	0
25	0	0	0	0
30	0	0	0	0
35	0.011	0.009	0.013	0.010
40	0.021	0.018	0.029	0.023

5.5 Statistical Model Checking Results

We use Monte Carlo (MC) approximation as a form of Statistical Model Checking [5,10] to compute confidence intervals for the DNC's convergence rate to a flock with collision avoidance and for the (normalized) convergence time. The convergence rate is the fraction of successful flocks over N runs. The collection of agent is said to have converged to a successful flock with collision avoidance if the global cost function $J_1(\mathbf{p}) \leq 150$, where $J_1(\mathbf{p})$ is cost function for basic flocking defined in Eq. 12a.

The main idea of MC is to use N random variables, $Z_1, \ldots, Z_N$, also called samples, IID distributed according to a random variable Z with mean μ_Z, and to take the sum $\tilde{\mu}_Z = (Z_1 + \ldots + Z_N)/N$ as the value approximating the mean μ_Z. Since an exact computation of μ_Z is almost always intractable, an MC approach is used to compute an (ϵ, δ)-approximation of this quantity.

Additive Approximation [6] is an (ϵ, δ)-approximation scheme where the mean μ_Z of an RV Z is approximated with absolute error ϵ and probability $1 - \delta$:

$$Pr[\mu_Z - \epsilon \leq \tilde{\mu}_Z \leq \mu_Z + \epsilon] \geq 1 - \delta \tag{13}$$

where $\tilde{\mu}_Z$ is an approximation of μ_Z. An important issue is to determine the number of samples N needed to ensure that $\tilde{\mu}_Z$ is an (ϵ, δ)-approximation of μ_Z. If Z is a Bernoulli variable expected to be large, one can use the Chernoff-Hoeffding instantiation of the Bernstein inequality and take N to be $N = 4\ln(2/\delta)/\epsilon^2$, as in [6]. This results in the *additive approximation algorithm* [5], defined in Algorithm 1.

We use this algorithm to obtain a joint (ϵ, δ)-approximation of the mean convergence rate and mean normalized convergence time for the DNC. Each sample Z_i is based on the result of an execution obtained by simulating the system starting from a random initial state, and we take $Z = (B, R)$, where B is a Boolean variable indicating whether the agents converged to a flock during the execution, and R is a real value denoting the normalized convergence time. The normalized convergence time is the time when the global cost function first drops below the convergence threshold and remains below it for the rest of the run, measured as a fraction of the total duration of the run. The assumptions

---

Algorithm 1: Additive Approximation Algorithm

Input: (ϵ, δ) with $0 < \epsilon < 1$ and $0 < \delta < 1$
Input: Random variables Z_i, IID
Output: $\tilde{\mu}_Z$ approximation of μ_Z
$N = 4\ln(2/\delta)/\epsilon^2$;
for $(i=0; i \leq N; i++)$ **do**
$\quad \lfloor \ S = S + Z_i$;
$\tilde{\mu}_Z = S/N$; **return** $\tilde{\mu}_Z$;

Table 4: SMC results for DNC convergence rate and normalized convergence time; $\epsilon = 0.01$, $\delta = 0.0001$

Agents	$\tilde{\mu}_{CR}$	$\tilde{\mu}_{CT}$
15	0.99	0.53
20	0.97	0.58
25	0.94	0.65
30	0.91	0.71
35	0.86	0.84
40	0.80	0.95

about Z required for validity of the additive approximation hold, because RV B is a Bernoulli variable, the convergence rate is expected to be large (i.e., closer to 1 than to 0), and the proportionality constraint of the Bernstein inequality is also satisfied for RV R.

In these experiments, the initial configurations are sampled from the same distributions as in Section 5.1, and we set $\epsilon = 0.01$ and $\delta = 0.0001$, to obtain $N = 396{,}140$. We perform the required set of N simulations for 15, 20, 25, 30, 35 and 40 agents. Table 4 presents the results, specifically, the (ϵ, δ)-approximations $\tilde{\mu}_{CR}$ and $\tilde{\mu}_{CT}$ of the mean convergence rate and the mean normalized convergence time, respectively. While the results for the convergence rate are (as expected) numerically similar to the results in Table 2, the results in Table 4 are much stronger, because they come with the guarantee that they are (ϵ, δ)-approximations of the actual mean values.

6   Related Work

In [18], a flocking controller is synthesized using multi-agent reinforcement learning (MARL) and natural evolution strategies (NES). The target model from which the system learns is Reynolds flocking model [16]. For training purposes, a list of metrics called *entropy* are chosen, which provide a measure of the collective behavior displayed by the target model. As the authors of [18] observe, this technique does not quite work: although it consistently leads to agents forming recognizable patterns during simulation, agents self-organized into a cluster instead of flowing like a flock.

In [9], reinforcement learning and flocking control are combined for the purpose of predator avoidance, where the learning module determines safe spaces in which the flock can navigate to avoid predators. Their approach to predator avoidance, however, isn't distributed as it requires a majority consensus by the flock to determine its action to avoid predators. They also impose an α-lattice structure [13] on the flock. In contrast, our approach is geometry-agnostic and achieves predator avoidance in a distributed manner.

In [7], an uncertainty-aware reinforcement learning algorithm is developed to estimate the probability of a mobile robot colliding with an obstacle in an unknown environment. Their approach is based on bootstrap neural networks using dropouts, allowing it to process raw sensory inputs. Similarly, a learning-based approach to robot navigation and obstacle avoidance is presented in [14]. They train a model that maps sensor inputs and the target position to motion commands generated by the ROS [15] navigation package. Our work in contrast considers obstacle avoidance (and other control objectives) in a multi-agent flocking scenario under the simplifying assumption of full state observation.

In [4], an approach based on Bayesian inference is proposed that allows an agent in a heterogeneous multi-agent environment to estimate the navigation model and goal of each of its neighbors. It then uses this information to compute a plan that minimizes inter-agent collisions while allowing the agent to reach its goal. Flocking formation is not considered.

7   Conclusions

With the introduction of Neural Flocking (NF), we have shown how machine learning in the form of Supervised Learning can bring many benefits to the flocking problem. As our experimental evaluation confirms, the symmetric and fully distributed neural controllers we derive in this manner are capable of achieving a multitude of flocking-oriented objectives, including flocking formation, inter-agent collision avoidance, obstacle avoidance, predator avoidance, and target seeking. Moreover, NF controllers exhibit real-time performance and generalize the behavior seen in the training data to achieve these objectives in a significantly broader range of scenarios.

Ongoing work aims to determine whether a DNC can perform as well as the centralized MPC controller for agent models that are significantly more realistic than our current point-based model. For this purpose, we are using transfer learning to train a DNC that can achieve acceptable performance on realistic quadrotor dynamics [1], starting from our current point-model-based DNC. This effort also involves extending our current DNC from 2-dimensional to 3-dimensional spatial coordinates. If successful, and preliminary results are encouraging, this line of research will demonstrate that DNCs are capable of achieving flocking with complex realistic dynamics.

For future work, we plan to investigate a distance-based notion of agent neighborhood as opposed to our current nearest-neighbors formulation. Furthermore, motivated by the quadrotor study of [21], we will seek to combine MPC with reinforcement learning in the framework of guided policy search as an alternative solution technique for the NF problem.

References

1. Bouabdallah, S.: Design and control of quadrotors with application to autonomous flying (2007)
2. Camacho, E.F., Bordons Alba, C.: Model Predictive Control. Springer (2007)
3. Chollet, F., et al.: Keras (2015), https://github.com/keras-team/keras.git
4. Godoy, J., Karamouzas, I., Guy, S.J., Gini, M.: Moving in a crowd: Safe and efficient navigation among heterogeneous agents. In: Proceedings of the Twenty-Fifth International Joint Conference on Artificial Intelligence. pp. 294–300. IJCAI'16, AAAI Press (2016)
5. Grosu, R., Peled, D., Ramakrishnan, C.R., Smolka, S.A., Stoller, S.D., Yang, J.: Using statistical model checking for measuring systems. In: 6th International Symposium, ISoLA 2014. Corfu, Greece (Oct 2014)
6. Hérault, T., Lassaigne, R., Magniette, F., Peyronnet, S.: Approximate probabilistic model checking. In: Steffen, B., Levi, G. (eds.) Verification, Model Checking, and Abstract Interpretation. pp. 73–84. Springer Berlin Heidelberg, Berlin, Heidelberg (2004)
7. Kahn, G., Villaflor, A., Pong, V., Abbeel, P., Levine, S.: Uncertainty-aware reinforcement learning for collision avoidance. arXiv preprint arXiv:1702.01182. pp. 1–12 (2017)
8. Kingma, D.P., Ba, J.: Adam: A method for stochastic optimization. In: 3rd International Conference on Learning Representations, ICLR 2015, San Diego, CA, USA, May 7-9, 2015, Conference Track Proceedings (2015)
9. La, H.M., Lim, R., Sheng, W.: Multirobot cooperative learning for predator avoidance. IEEE Transactions on Control Systems Technology $23(1)$, 52–63 (2015)
10. Larsen, K.G., Legay, A.: Statistical model checking: Past, present, and future. In: 6th International Symposium, ISoLA 2014. Corfu, Greece (Oct 2014)
11. Mehmood, U., Paoletti, N., Phan, D., Grosu, R., Lin, S., Stoller, S.D., Tiwari, A., Yang, J., Smolka, S.A.: Declarative vs rule-based control for flocking dynamics. In: Proceedings of SAC 2018, 33rd Annual ACM Symposium on Applied Computing. pp. 816–823 (2018)
12. Nocedal, J., Wright, S.J.: Numerical Optimization. Springer, New York, NY, USA, second edn. (2006)
13. Olfati-Saber, R.: Flocking for multi-agent dynamic systems: Algorithms and theory. IEEE Transactions on automatic control $51(3)$, 401–420 (2006)
14. Pfeiffer, M., Schaeuble, M., Nieto, J.I., Siegwart, R., Cadena, C.: From perception to decision: A data-driven approach to end-to-end motion planning for autonomous ground robots. In: 2017 IEEE International Conference on Robotics and Automation, ICRA 2017, Singapore, Singapore, May 29 - June 3, 2017. pp. 1527–1533 (2017)
15. Quigley, M., Conley, K., Gerkey, B.P., Faust, J., Foote, T., Leibs, J., Wheeler, R., Ng, A.Y.: ROS: an open-source robot operating system. In: ICRA Workshop on Open Source Software (2009)
16. Reynolds, C.W.: Flocks, herds and schools: A distributed behavioral model. SIGGRAPH Comput. Graph. $21(4)$ (Aug 1987)
17. Reynolds, C.W.: Steering behaviors for autonomous characters. In: Proceedings of Game Developers Conference 1999. pp. 763–782 (1999)

18. Shimada, K., Bentley, P.: Learning how to flock: Deriving individual behaviour from collective behaviour with multi-agent reinforcement learning and natural evolution strategies. In: Proceedings of the Genetic and Evolutionary Computation Conference Companion. pp. 169–170. ACM (2018)

19. Zhan, J., Li, X.: Flocking of multi-agent systems via model predictive control based on position-only measurements. IEEE Transactions on Industrial Informatics **9**(1), 377–385 (2013)

20. Zhang, H.T., Cheng, Z., Chen, G., Li, C.: Model predictive flocking control for second-order multi-agent systems with input constraints. IEEE Transactions on Circuits and Systems I: Regular Papers **62**(6), 1599–1606 (2015)

21. Zhang, T., Kahn, G., Levine, S., Abbeel, P.: Learning deep control policies for autonomous aerial vehicles with MPC-guided policy search. In: 2016 IEEE International Conference on Robotics and Automation, ICRA 2016, Stockholm, Sweden, May 16-21, 2016. pp. 528–535 (2016)

Quantum Programming with Inductive Datatypes: Causality and Affine Type Theory

Romain Péchoux[1], Simon Perdrix[1], Mathys Rennela[2], and Vladimir Zamdzhiev[1 (✉)]

[1] Université de Lorraine, CNRS, Inria, LORIA, F 54000 Nancy, France
{romain.pechoux|simon.perdrix|vladimir.zamdzhiev}@loria.fr
[2] Leiden University, Leiden, The Netherlands
m.p.a.rennela@liacs.leidenuniv.nl

Abstract. Inductive datatypes in programming languages allow users to define useful data structures such as natural numbers, lists, trees, and others. In this paper we show how inductive datatypes may be added to the quantum programming language QPL. We construct a sound categorical model for the language and by doing so we provide the first detailed semantic treatment of user-defined inductive datatypes in quantum programming. We also show our denotational interpretation is invariant with respect to big-step reduction, thereby establishing another novel result for quantum programming. Compared to classical programming, this property is considerably more difficult to prove and we demonstrate its usefulness by showing how it immediately implies computational adequacy at all types. To further cement our results, our semantics is entirely based on a physically natural model of von Neumann algebras, which are mathematical structures used by physicists to study quantum mechanics.

Keywords: Quantum programming · Inductive types · Adequacy

1 Introduction

Quantum computing is a computational paradigm which takes advantage of quantum mechanical phenomena to perform computation. A quantum computer can solve problems which are out of reach for classical computers (e.g. factorisation of large numbers [24], solving large linear systems [8]). The recent developments of quantum technologies points out the necessity of filling the gap between theoretical quantum algorithms and the actual (prototypes of) quantum computers. As a consequence, quantum software and in particular quantum programming languages play a key role in the future development of quantum computing. The present paper makes several theoretical contributions towards the design and denotational semantics of quantum programming languages.

Our development is based around the quantum programming language QPL [23] which we extend with inductive datatypes. Our paper is the first to construct a denotational semantics for user-defined inductive datatypes in quantum programming. In the spirit of the original QPL, our type system is *affine* (discarding of arbitrary variables is allowed, but copying is restricted). We also extend QPL with a copy operation for *classical data*, because this is an admissible operation in quantum mechanics which improves programming convenience. The addition of inductive datatypes requires a departure from the original denotational semantics of QPL, which are based on finite-dimensional quantum structures, and we consider instead (possibly infinite-dimensional) quantum structures based on *W*-algebras* (also known as *von Neumann algebras*), which have been used by physicists in the study of quantum foundations [25]. As such, our semantic treatment is physically natural and our model is more accessible to physicists and experts in quantum computing compared to most other denotational models.

QPL is a first-order programming language which has *procedures*, but it does not have lambda abstractions. Thus, there is no use for a !-modality and we show how to model the copy operation by describing the canonical comonoid structure of all classical types (including the inductive ones).

An important notion in quantum mechanics is the idea of *causality* which has been formulated in a variety of different ways. In this paper, we consider a simple operational interpretation of causality: if the output of a physical process is discarded, then it does not matter which process occurred [10]. In a symmetric monoidal category $\mathbf{C}$ with tensor unit I, this can be understood as requiring that for any morphism (process) $f : A_1 \to A_2$, it must be the case that $\diamond_{A_2} \circ f = \diamond_{A_1}$, where $\diamond_{A_i} : A_i \to I$ is the discarding map (process) at the given objects. This notion ties in very nicely with our affine language, because we have to show that the interpretation of values is causal, i.e., values are always discardable.

A major contribution of this paper is that we prove the denotational semantics is invariant with respect to both small-step reduction and big-step reduction. The latter is more difficult in quantum programming and our paper is the first to demonstrate such a result. As a corollary, we obtain computational adequacy.

2   Syntax of QPL

The syntax of QPL (including our extensions) is summarised in Figure 1. A well-formed type context, denoted $\vdash \Theta$, is simply a list of distinct type variables. A type A is well-formed in type context Θ, denoted $\Theta \vdash A$, if the judgement can be derived according to the following rules (see [1,6] for a more detailed exposition):

$$\frac{\vdash \Theta}{\Theta \vdash \Theta_i} \qquad \frac{\vdash \Theta}{\Theta \vdash I} \qquad \frac{\vdash \Theta}{\Theta \vdash \mathbf{qbit}} \qquad \frac{\Theta \vdash A \qquad \Theta \vdash B}{\Theta \vdash A \star B} \star \in \{+, \otimes\} \qquad \frac{\Theta, X \vdash A}{\Theta \vdash \mu X.A}$$

A type A is *closed* if $\cdot \vdash A$. Note that nested type induction is allowed. Henceforth, we implicitly assume that all types we are dealing with are well-formed.

Example 1. The type of natural numbers is defined as $\mathbf{Nat} \equiv \mu X.I + X$. Lists of a closed type $\cdot \vdash A$ are defined as $\mathbf{List}(A) \equiv \mu Y.I + A \otimes Y$.

Notice that our type system is not equipped with a !-modality. Indeed, in the absence of function types, there is no reason to introduce it. Instead, we specify

Types	A, B	$::= X \mid I \mid \mathbf{qbit} \mid A + B \mid A \otimes B \mid \mu X.A$
Classical Types	P, R	$::= X \mid I \mid P + R \mid P \otimes R \mid \mu X.P$
Terms	M, N	$::= \mathbf{new\ unit}\ u \mid \mathbf{discard}\ x \mid y = \mathbf{copy}\ x \mid \mathbf{new\ qbit}\ q \mid$

$b = \mathbf{measure}\ q \mid q_1, \ldots, q_n\ \mathbin{*\!=} S \mid M; N \mid \mathbf{skip} \mid$
$\mathbf{while}\ b\ \mathbf{do}\ M \mid x = \mathbf{left}_{A,B} M \mid x = \mathbf{right}_{A,B} M \mid$
$\mathbf{case}\ y\ \mathbf{of}\ \{\mathbf{left}\ x_1 \rightarrow M \mid \mathbf{right}\ x_2 \rightarrow N\} \mid$
$x = (x_1, x_2) \mid (x_1, x_2) = x \mid y = \mathbf{fold}\ x \mid y = \mathbf{unfold}\ x \mid$
$\mathbf{proc}\ f :: x : A \rightarrow y : B\ \{M\} \mid y = f(x)$

Variable contexts	Γ, Σ	$::= x_1 : A_1, \ldots, x_n : A_n$
Procedure contexts Π		$::= f_1 : A_1 \rightarrow B_1, \ldots, f_n : A_n \rightarrow B_n$

$$\overline{\Pi \vdash \langle \Gamma \rangle\ \mathbf{new\ unit}\ u\ \langle \Gamma, u : I \rangle} \qquad \overline{\Pi \vdash \langle \Gamma, x : A \rangle\ \mathbf{discard}\ x\ \langle \Gamma \rangle}$$

$$\frac{P \text{ is a classical type}}{\Pi \vdash \langle \Gamma, x : P \rangle\ y = \mathbf{copy}\ x\ \langle \Gamma, x : P, y : P \rangle} \qquad \overline{\Pi \vdash \langle \Gamma \rangle\ \mathbf{skip}\ \langle \Gamma \rangle}$$

$$\frac{\Pi \vdash \langle \Gamma \rangle\ M\ \langle \Gamma' \rangle \qquad \Pi \vdash \langle \Gamma' \rangle\ N\ \langle \Sigma \rangle}{\Pi \vdash \langle \Gamma \rangle\ M; N\ \langle \Sigma \rangle}$$

$$\frac{\Pi \vdash \langle \Gamma, b : \mathbf{bit} \rangle\ M\ \langle \Gamma, b : \mathbf{bit} \rangle}{\Pi \vdash \langle \Gamma, b : \mathbf{bit} \rangle\ \mathbf{while}\ b\ \mathbf{do}\ M\ \langle \Gamma, b : \mathbf{bit} \rangle}$$

$$\overline{\Pi \vdash \langle \Gamma \rangle\ \mathbf{new\ qbit}\ q\ \langle \Gamma, q : \mathbf{qbit} \rangle} \qquad \overline{\Pi \vdash \langle \Gamma, q : \mathbf{qbit} \rangle\ b = \mathbf{measure}\ q\ \langle \Gamma, b : \mathbf{bit} \rangle}$$

$$\frac{S \text{ is a unitary of arity } n}{\Pi \vdash \langle \Gamma, q_1 : \mathbf{qbit}, \ldots, q_n : \mathbf{qbit} \rangle\ q_1, \ldots, q_n\ \mathbin{*\!=} S\ \langle \Gamma, q_1 : \mathbf{qbit}, \ldots, q_n : \mathbf{qbit} \rangle}$$

$$\overline{\Pi \vdash \langle \Gamma, x : A \rangle\ y = \mathbf{left}_{A,B}\ x\ \langle \Gamma, y : A + B \rangle}$$

$$\overline{\Pi \vdash \langle \Gamma, x : B \rangle\ y = \mathbf{right}_{A,B}\ x\ \langle \Gamma, y : A + B \rangle}$$

$$\frac{\Pi \vdash \langle \Gamma, x_1 : A \rangle\ M_1\ \langle \Sigma \rangle \qquad \Pi \vdash \langle \Gamma, x_2 : B \rangle\ M_2\ \langle \Sigma \rangle}{\Pi \vdash \langle \Gamma, y : A + B \rangle\ \mathbf{case}\ y\ \mathbf{of}\ \{\mathbf{left}_{A,B}\ x_1 \rightarrow M_1 \mid \mathbf{right}_{A,B}\ x_2 \rightarrow M_2\ \}\ \langle \Sigma \rangle}$$

$$\overline{\Pi \vdash \langle \Gamma, x_1 : A, x_2 : B \rangle\ x = (x_1, x_2)\ \langle \Gamma, x : A \otimes B \rangle}$$

$$\overline{\Pi \vdash \langle \Gamma, x : A \otimes B \rangle\ (x_1, x_2) = x\ \langle \Gamma, x_1 : A, x_2 : B \rangle}$$

$$\overline{\Pi \vdash \langle \Gamma, x : A[\mu X.A/X] \rangle\ y = \mathbf{fold}_{\mu X.A}\ x\ \langle \Gamma, y : \mu X.A \rangle}$$

$$\overline{\Pi \vdash \langle \Gamma, x : \mu X.A \rangle\ y = \mathbf{unfold}\ x\ \langle \Gamma, y : A[\mu X.A/X] \rangle}$$

$$\frac{\Pi, f : A \rightarrow B \vdash \langle x : A \rangle\ M\ \langle y : B \rangle}{\Pi \vdash \langle \Gamma \rangle\ \mathbf{proc}\ f :: x : A \rightarrow y : B\ \{M\}\ \langle \Gamma \rangle}$$

$$\overline{\Pi, f : A \rightarrow B \vdash \langle \Gamma, x : A \rangle\ y = f(x)\ \langle \Gamma, y : B \rangle}$$

Fig. 1: Syntax and formation rules for QPL terms.

the subset of types where copying is an admissible operation. The *classical types* are a subset of our types defined in Figure 1. They are characterised by the property that variables of classical types may be copied, whereas variables of non-classical types may not be copied (see the rule for copying in Figure 1).

We use small Latin letters (e.g. x, y, u, q, b) to range over *term variables*. More specifically, q ranges over variables of type **qbit**, u over variables of unit type I, b over variables of type **bit** $:= I + I$ and x, y range over variables of arbitrary type. We use Γ and Σ to range over *variable contexts*. A variable context is a function from term variables to *closed types*, which we write as $\Gamma = x_1 : A_1, \ldots, x_n : A_n$.

We use f, g to range over *procedure names*. Every procedure name f has an *input type* A and an *output type* B, denoted $f : A \to B$, where A and B are closed types. We use Π to range over *procedure contexts*. A procedure context is a function from procedure names to pairs of procedure input-output types, denoted $\Pi = f_1 : A_1 \to B_1, \ldots, f_n : A_n \to B_n$.

Remark 2. Unlike lambda abstractions, procedures cannot be passed to other procedures as input arguments, nor can they be returned as output.

A *term judgement* has the form $\Pi \vdash \langle \Gamma \rangle \ M \ \langle \Sigma \rangle$ (see Figure 1) and indicates that term M is well-formed in procedure context Π with input variable context Γ and output variable context Σ. All types occurring within it are closed.

The intended interpretation of the quantum rules are as follows. The term **new qbit** q prepares a new qubit q in state $|0\rangle\langle 0|$. The term $q_1, \ldots, q_n \ *= S$ applies a unitary operator S to a sequence of qubits in the standard way. The term $b = \textbf{measure}\ q$ performs a quantum measurement on qubit q and stores the measurement outcome in bit b. The measured qubit is destroyed in the process.

The no-cloning theorem of quantum mechanics [28] shows that arbitrary qubits cannot be copied. Because of this, copying is restricted only to classical types, as indicated in Figure 1, and this allows us to avoid runtime errors. Like the original QPL [23], our type system is also *affine* and so any variable can be discarded (see the formation rule for the term **discard** x in Figure 1).

3 Operational Semantics of QPL

In this section we describe the operational semantics of QPL. The central notion is that of a *program configuration* which provides a complete description of the current state of program execution. It consists of four components that must satisfy some coherence properties: (1) the term which remains to be executed; (2) a *value assignment*, which is a function that assigns formal expressions to variables as a result of execution; (3) a *procedure store* which keeps track of what procedures have been defined so far and (4) the *quantum state* computed so far.

Value Assignments. A *value* is an expression defined by the following grammar:

$$v, w ::= * \mid n \mid \textbf{left}_{A,B} v \mid \textbf{right}_{A,B} v \mid (v, w) \mid \textbf{fold}_{\mu X.A} v$$

where n ranges over the natural numbers. Think of $*$ as representing the unique value of unit type I and of n as representing a pointer to the n-th qubit of a quantum state ρ. Specific values of interest are $\mathtt{ff} := \mathbf{left}_{I,I}*$ and $\mathtt{tt} := \mathbf{right}_{I,I}*$ which correspond to **false** and **true** respectively.

A *qubit pointer context* is a set Q of natural numbers. A value v of type A is well-formed in qubit pointer context Q, denoted $Q \vdash v : A$, if the judgement is derivable from the following rules:

$$\frac{}{\cdot \vdash * : I} \qquad \frac{}{\{n\} \vdash n : \mathbf{qbit}} \qquad \frac{Q \vdash v : A}{Q \vdash \mathbf{left}_{A,B}v : A + B} \qquad \frac{Q \vdash v : B}{Q \vdash \mathbf{right}_{A,B}v : A + B}$$

$$\frac{Q_1 \vdash v : A \qquad Q_2 \vdash w : B \qquad Q_1 \cap Q_2 = \varnothing}{Q_1, Q_2 \vdash (v,w) : A \otimes B} \qquad \frac{Q \vdash v : A[\mu X.A/X]}{Q \vdash \mathbf{fold}_{\mu X.A}v : \mu X.A}$$

If v is well-formed, then its type and qubit pointer context are uniquely determined. If $Q \vdash v : P$ with P classical, then we say v is a *classical value*.

Lemma 3. *If $Q \vdash v : P$ is a well-formed classical value, then $Q = \cdot$.*

A *value assignment* is a function from term variables to values, which we write as $V = \{x_1 = v_1, \ldots, x_n = v_n\}$, where x_i are variables and v_i are values. A value assignment is *well-formed* in qubit pointer context Q and variable context Γ, denoted $Q; \Gamma \vdash V$, if V has exactly the same variables as Γ, so that $\Gamma = \{x_1 : A_1, \ldots, x_n : A_n\}$, and $Q = Q_1, \ldots, Q_n$, s.t. $Q_i \vdash v_i : A_i$. Such a splitting of Q is necessarily unique, if it exists, and some of the Q_i may be empty.

Procedure Stores. A *procedure store* is a set of procedure definitions, written as:

$$\Omega = \{f_1 :: x_1 : A_1 \to y_1 : B_1 \{M_1\}, \ldots, f_n :: x_n : A_n \to y_n : B_n \{M_n\}\}.$$

A procedure store is *well-formed* in procedure context Π, written $\Pi \vdash \Omega$, if the judgement is derivable via the following rules:

$$\frac{}{\cdot \vdash \cdot} \qquad \frac{\Pi \vdash \Omega \qquad \Pi, f : A \to B \vdash \langle x : A \rangle M \langle y : B \rangle}{\Pi, f : A \to B \vdash \Omega, f :: x : A \to y : B \{M\}}$$

Program Configurations. A *program configuration* is a quadruple $(M \mid V \mid \Omega \mid \rho)$, where M is a term, V is a value assignment, Ω is a procedure store and $\rho \in \mathbb{C}^{2^n \times 2^n}$ is a finite-dimensional density matrix with $0 \leq \mathrm{tr}(\rho) \leq 1$. The density matrix ρ represents a (mixed) quantum state and its trace may be smaller than one because we also use it to encode probability information (see Remark 4). We write $dim(\rho) = n$ to indicate that the dimension of ρ is n.

A *well-formed* program configuration is a configuration $(M \mid V \mid \Omega \mid \rho)$, where there exist (necessarily unique) Π, Γ, Σ, Q, such that: (1) $\Pi \vdash \langle \Gamma \rangle M \langle \Sigma \rangle$ is a well-formed term; (2) $Q; \Gamma \vdash V$ is a well-formed value assignment; (3) $\Pi \vdash \Omega$ is a well-formed procedure store; and (4) $Q = \{1, 2, \ldots, dim(\rho)\}$. We write $\Pi; \Gamma; \Sigma; Q \vdash (M \mid V \mid \Omega \mid \rho)$ to indicate this situation. The formation rules enforce that the qubits of ρ and the qubit pointers from V are in a 1-1 correspondence.

$$(\textbf{new unit } u \mid V \mid \Omega \mid \rho) \rightsquigarrow (\textbf{skip} \mid V, u = * \mid \Omega \mid \rho)$$

$$(\textbf{discard } x \mid V, x = v \mid \Omega \mid \rho) \rightsquigarrow (\textbf{skip} \mid r_v(V) \mid \Omega \mid tr_v(\rho))$$

$$(y = \textbf{copy } x \mid V, x = v \mid \Omega \mid \rho) \rightsquigarrow (\textbf{skip} \mid V, x = v, y = v \mid \Omega \mid \rho)$$

$$(\textbf{new qbit } q \mid V \mid \Omega \mid \rho) \rightsquigarrow (\textbf{skip} \mid V, q = dim(\rho) + 1 \mid \Omega \mid \rho \otimes |0\rangle\langle0|)$$

$$(\vec{q} \mathrel{*}= S \mid V, \vec{q} = \vec{m} \mid \Omega \mid \rho) \rightsquigarrow (\textbf{skip} \mid V, \vec{q} = \vec{m} \mid \Omega \mid S_{\vec{m}}(\rho))$$

$$(b = \textbf{measure } q \mid V, q = m \mid \Omega \mid \rho) \rightsquigarrow (\textbf{skip} \mid r_m(V), b = \texttt{ff} \mid \Omega \mid {}_m\langle0|\rho|0\rangle_m)$$

$$(b = \textbf{measure } q \mid V, q = m \mid \Omega \mid \rho) \rightsquigarrow (\textbf{skip} \mid r_m(V), b = \texttt{tt} \mid \Omega \mid {}_m\langle1|\rho|1\rangle_m)$$

$$\frac{}{(\textbf{skip}; P \mid V \mid \Omega \mid \rho) \rightsquigarrow (P \mid V \mid \Omega \mid \rho)} \qquad \frac{(P \mid V \mid \Omega \mid \rho) \rightsquigarrow (P' \mid V' \mid \Omega' \mid \rho')}{(P; Q \mid V \mid \Omega \mid \rho) \rightsquigarrow (P'; Q \mid V' \mid \Omega' \mid \rho')}$$

$$(\textbf{while } b \textbf{ do } M \mid V, b = \texttt{ff} \mid \Omega \mid \rho) \rightsquigarrow (\textbf{skip} \mid V, b = \texttt{ff} \mid \Omega \mid \rho)$$

$$(\textbf{while } b \textbf{ do } M \mid V, b = \texttt{tt} \mid \Omega \mid \rho) \rightsquigarrow (M; \textbf{while } b \textbf{ do } M \mid V, b = \texttt{tt} \mid \Omega \mid \rho)$$

$$(y = \textbf{left } x \mid V, x = v \mid \Omega \mid \rho) \rightsquigarrow (\textbf{skip} \mid V, y = \textbf{left } v \mid \Omega \mid \rho)$$

$$(y = \textbf{right } x \mid V, x = v \mid \Omega \mid \rho) \rightsquigarrow (\textbf{skip} \mid V, y = \textbf{right } v \mid \Omega \mid \rho)$$

$$(\textbf{case } y \textbf{ of } \{\textbf{left } x_1 \to M_1 \mid \textbf{right } x_2 \to M_2 \} \mid V, y = \textbf{left } v \mid \Omega \mid \rho) \rightsquigarrow (M_1 \mid V, x_1 = v \mid \Omega \mid \rho)$$

$$(\textbf{case } y \textbf{ of } \{\textbf{left } x_1 \to M_1 \mid \textbf{right } x_2 \to M_2 \} \mid V, y = \textbf{right } v \mid \Omega \mid \rho) \rightsquigarrow (M_2 \mid V, x_2 = v \mid \Omega \mid \rho)$$

$$(x = (x_1, x_2) \mid V, x_1 = v_1, x_2 = v_2 \mid \Omega \mid \rho) \rightsquigarrow (\textbf{skip} \mid V, x = (v_1, v_2) \mid \Omega \mid \rho)$$

$$((x_1, x_2) = x \mid V, x = (v_1, v_2) \mid \Omega \mid \rho) \rightsquigarrow (\textbf{skip} \mid V, x_1 = v_1, x_2 = v_2 \mid \Omega \mid \rho)$$

$$(y = \textbf{fold } x \mid V, x = v \mid \Omega \mid \rho) \rightsquigarrow (\textbf{skip} \mid V, y = \textbf{fold } v \mid \Omega \mid \rho)$$

$$(y = \textbf{unfold } x \mid V, x = \textbf{fold } v \mid \Omega \mid \rho) \rightsquigarrow (\textbf{skip} \mid V, y = v \mid \Omega \mid \rho)$$

$$(\textbf{proc } f :: x : A \to y : B \{M\} \mid V \mid \Omega \mid \rho) \rightsquigarrow (\textbf{skip} \mid V \mid \Omega, f :: x : A \to y : B \{M\} \mid \rho)$$

$$(y_1 = f(x_1) \mid V, x_1 = v \mid \Omega, f :: x_2 : A \to y_2 : B \{M\} \mid \rho) \rightsquigarrow$$
$$(M_\alpha \mid V, x_1 = v \mid \Omega, f :: x_2 : A \to y_2 : B \{M\} \mid \rho)$$

Fig. 2: Small Step Operational semantics of QPL.

The small step semantics is defined for configurations $(M \mid V \mid \Omega \mid \rho)$ by induction on M in Figure 2 and we now explain the notations used therein.

In the rule for discarding, we use two functions that depend on a value v. They are tr_v, which modifies the quantum state ρ by tracing out all of its qubits which are used in v, and r_v which simply reindexes the value assignment, so that the pointers within $r_v(V)$ correctly point to the corresponding qubits of $tr_v(\rho)$, which is potentially of smaller dimension than ρ. Formally, for a well-formed value v, let Q and A be the unique qubit pointer context and type, such that $Q \vdash v : A$. Then $tr_v(\rho)$ is the quantum state obtained from ρ by tracing out all qubits specified by Q. Given a value assignment $V = \{x_1 = v_1, \ldots x_n = v_n\}$, then $r_v(V) = \{x_1 = r'_v(v_1), \ldots, x_n = r'_v(v_n)\}$, where:

$$
r'_v(w) = \begin{cases}
*, & \text{if } w = * \\
k - |\{i \in Q \mid i < k\}|, & \text{if } w = k \in \mathbb{N} \\
\textbf{left } r'_v(w'), & \text{if } w = \textbf{left } w' \\
\textbf{right } r'_v(w'), & \text{if } w = \textbf{right } w' \\
(r'_v(w_1), r'_v(w_2)), & \text{if } w = (w_1, w_2) \\
\textbf{fold } r'_v(w'), & \text{if } w = \textbf{fold } w'
\end{cases}
$$

In the rule for unitaries, the superoperator $S_{\vec{m}}$ applies the unitary S to the vector of qubits specified by $\vec{m}$. In the rules for measurement, the m-th qubit of ρ is measured in the computational basis, the measured qubit is destroyed in the process and the measurement outcome is stored in the bit b. More specifically, $|i\rangle_m = I_{2^{m-1}} \otimes |i\rangle \otimes I_{2^{n-m}}$ and $_m\langle i|$ is its adjoint, for $i \in \{0, 1\}$, and where I_n is the identity matrix in $\mathbb{C}^{n \times n}$.

Remark 4. Because of the way we decided to handle measurements, reduction $(- \rightsquigarrow -)$ is a *nondeterministic* operation, where we encode the probabilities of reduction within the trace of our density matrices in a similar way to [9]. Equivalently, we may see the reduction relation as *probabilistic* provided that we normalise all density matrices and decorate the reductions with the appropriate probability information as specified by the Born rule of quantum mechanics. The nondeterministic view leads to a more concise and clear presentation and because of this we have chosen it over the probabilistic view.

The introduction rule for procedures simply defines a procedure which is added to the procedure store. In the rule for calling procedures, the term M_α is α-equivalent to M and is obtained from it by renaming the input x_2 to x_1, renaming the output y_2 to y_1 and renaming all other variables within M to some fresh names, so as to avoid conflicts with the input, output and the rest of the variables within V.

Theorem 5 (Subject reduction). *If $\Pi; \Gamma; \Sigma; Q \vdash (M \mid V \mid \Omega \mid \rho)$ and $(M \mid V \mid \Omega \mid \rho) \rightsquigarrow (M' \mid V' \mid \Omega' \mid \rho')$, then $\Pi'; \Gamma'; \Sigma; Q' \vdash (M' \mid V' \mid \Omega' \mid \rho')$, for some (necessarily unique) contexts Π', Γ', Q' and where Σ is invariant.*

Assumption 6. *From now on we assume all configurations are well-formed.*

```
while b do {
  new qbit q;
  q *= H;
  discard b;
  b = measure q
}
```

(a) A term M

$$(M \mid \mathtt{b} = \mathtt{tt} \mid \cdot \mid 1)$$

$$(M \mid \mathtt{b} = \mathtt{tt} \mid \cdot \mid 0.5) \quad (\mathbf{skip} \mid \mathtt{b} = \mathtt{ff} \mid \cdot \mid 0.5)$$

$$(M \mid \mathtt{b} = \mathtt{tt} \mid \cdot \mid 0.25) \quad (\mathbf{skip} \mid \mathtt{b} = \mathtt{ff} \mid \cdot \mid 0.25)$$

$$(\mathbf{skip} \mid \mathtt{b} = \mathtt{ff} \mid \cdot \mid 0.125)$$

(b) A reduction graph involving M

Fig. 3: Example of a term and of a reduction graph.

A configuration $(M \mid V \mid \Omega \mid \rho)$ is said to be *terminal* if $M = \mathbf{skip}$. Program execution finishes at terminal configurations, which are characterised by the property that they do not reduce any further. We will use calligraphic letters $(\mathcal{C}, \mathcal{D}, \ldots)$ to range over configurations and we will use $\mathcal{T}$ to range over terminal configurations. For a configuration $\mathcal{C} = (M \mid V \mid \Omega \mid \rho)$, we write for brevity $\mathrm{tr}(\mathcal{C}) := \mathrm{tr}(\rho)$ and we shall say $\mathcal{C}$ is *normalised* whenever $\mathrm{tr}(\mathcal{C}) = 1$. We say that a configuration $\mathcal{C}$ is *impossible* if $\mathrm{tr}(\mathcal{C}) = 0$ and we say it is *possible* otherwise.

Theorem 7 (Progress). *If $\mathcal{C}$ is a configuration, then either $\mathcal{C}$ is terminal or there exists a configuration $\mathcal{D}$, such that $\mathcal{C} \rightsquigarrow \mathcal{D}$. Moreover, if $\mathcal{C}$ is not terminal, then $\mathrm{tr}(\mathcal{C}) = \sum_{\mathcal{C} \rightsquigarrow \mathcal{D}} \mathrm{tr}(\mathcal{D})$ and there are at most two such configurations $\mathcal{D}$.*

In the situation of the above theorem, the probability of reduction is given by $\Pr(\mathcal{C} \rightsquigarrow \mathcal{D}) := \mathrm{tr}(\mathcal{D})/\mathrm{tr}(\mathcal{C})$, for any possible $\mathcal{C}$ (see Remark 4) and Theorem 7 shows the total probability of all single-step reductions is 1. If $\mathcal{C}$ is impossible, then $\mathcal{C}$ occurs with probability 0 and subsequent reductions are also impossible.

Probability of Termination. Given configurations $\mathcal{C}$ and $\mathcal{D}$ let $\mathrm{Seq}_n(\mathcal{C}, \mathcal{D}) := \{\mathcal{C}_0 \rightsquigarrow \cdots \rightsquigarrow \mathcal{C}_n \mid \mathcal{C}_0 = \mathcal{C} \text{ and } \mathcal{C}_n = \mathcal{D}\}$, and let $\mathrm{Seq}_{\leq n}(\mathcal{C}, \mathcal{D}) = \bigcup_{i=0}^{n} \mathrm{Seq}_n(\mathcal{C}, \mathcal{D})$. Finally, let $\mathrm{TerSeq}_{\leq n}(\mathcal{C}) := \bigcup_{\mathcal{T} \text{ terminal}} \mathrm{Seq}_{\leq n}(\mathcal{C}, \mathcal{T})$. In other words, $\mathrm{TerSeq}_{\leq n}(\mathcal{C})$ is the set of all reduction sequences from $\mathcal{C}$ which terminate in at most n steps (including 0 if $\mathcal{C}$ is terminal). For every terminating reduction sequence $r = (\mathcal{C} \rightsquigarrow \cdots \rightsquigarrow \mathcal{T})$, let $\mathrm{End}(r) := \mathcal{T}$, i.e. $\mathrm{End}(r)$ is simply the (terminal) end-point of the sequence.

For any configuration $\mathcal{C}$, the sequence $\left(\sum_{r \in \mathrm{TerSeq}_{\leq n}(\mathcal{C})} \mathrm{tr}(\mathrm{End}(r)) \right)_{n \in \mathbb{N}}$ is increasing with upper bound $\mathrm{tr}(\mathcal{C})$ (follows from Theorem 7). For any possible $\mathcal{C}$, we define:

$$\mathrm{Halt}(\mathcal{C}) := \bigvee_{n=0}^{\infty} \sum_{r \in \mathrm{TerSeq}_{\leq n}(\mathcal{C})} \mathrm{tr}(\mathrm{End}(r))/\mathrm{tr}(\mathcal{C})$$

which is exactly the *probability of termination* of $\mathcal{C}$. This is justified, because $\mathrm{Halt}(\mathcal{T}) = 1$, for any terminal (and possible) configuration $\mathcal{T}$ and $\mathrm{Halt}(\mathcal{C}) = \sum_{\substack{\mathcal{C} \rightsquigarrow \mathcal{D} \\ \mathcal{D} \text{ possible}}} \Pr(\mathcal{C} \rightsquigarrow \mathcal{D})\mathrm{Halt}(\mathcal{D})$. We write $\rightsquigarrow_*$ for the transitive closure of $\rightsquigarrow$.

```
proc GHZnext :: l : ListQ -> l : ListQ {
  new qbit q;
  case l of
      nil -> q*=H;
          l = q :: nil
   | q' :: l' -> q',q *= CNOT;
              l = q :: q' :: l'
}

proc GHZ :: n : Nat -> l : ListQ {
  case n of
      zero -> l = nil
   | s(n') -> l = GHZnext(GHZ(n'))
}
```

(a) Procedures for generating GHZ$_n$.

$$(1 = \text{GHZ(n)} \mid n = s(s(s(\text{zero}))) \mid \Omega \mid 1)$$
$$\downarrow^*$$
$$(1 = \text{GHZnext(l)} \mid 1 = 2 :: 1 :: \text{nil} \mid \Omega \mid \gamma_2)$$
$$\downarrow$$
$$(\text{new qbit q}; \cdots \mid 1 = 2 :: 1 :: \text{nil} \mid \Omega \mid \gamma_2)$$
$$\downarrow$$
$$(\text{case l of } \cdots \mid 1 = 2 :: 1 :: \text{nil}, q = 3 \mid \Omega \mid \gamma_2 \otimes |0\rangle\langle 0|)$$
$$\downarrow^*$$
$$(\text{q',q *=CNOT}; \cdots \mid 1' = 1 :: \text{nil}, q = 3, q' = 2 \mid \Omega \mid \gamma_2 \otimes |0\rangle\langle 0|)$$
$$\downarrow$$
$$(1 = q :: q' :: 1' \mid 1' = 1 :: \text{nil}, q = 3, q' = 2 \mid \Omega \mid \gamma_3)$$
$$\downarrow^*$$
$$(\textbf{skip} \mid 1 = 3 :: 2 :: 1 :: \text{nil} \mid \Omega \mid \gamma_3)$$

(b) A reduction sequence producing GHZ$_3$.

Fig. 4: Example with lists of qubits and a recursive procedure.

Example 8. Consider the term M in Figure 3. The body of the **while** loop (3a) has the effect of performing a fair coin toss (realised through quantum measurement in the standard way) and storing the outcome in variable b. Therefore, starting from configuration $\mathcal{C} = (M \mid \text{b} = \text{tt} \mid \cdot \mid 1)$, as in Subfigure 3b, the program has the effect of tossing a fair coin until ff shows up. The set of terminal configurations reachable from $\mathcal{C}$ is $\{(\textbf{skip} \mid \text{b} = \text{ff} \mid \cdot \mid 2^{-i}) \mid i \in \mathbb{N}_{\geq 1}\}$ and the last component of each configuration is a 1×1 density matrix which is exactly the probability of reducing to the configuration. Therefore $\text{Halt}(\mathcal{C}) = \sum_{i=1}^{\infty} 2^{-i} = 1$.

Example 9. The GHZ$_n$ state is defined as $\gamma_n := (|0\rangle^{\otimes n} + |1\rangle^{\otimes n})(\langle 0|^{\otimes n} + \langle 1|^{\otimes n})/2$. In Figure 4, we define a procedure GHZ, which given a natural number n, generates the state γ_n, which is represented as a list of qubits of length n. The procedure (4a) uses an auxiliary procedure GHZnext, which given a list of qubits representing the state γ_n, returns the state γ_{n+1} again represented as a list of qubits. The two procedures make use of some (hopefully obvious) syntactic sugar. In 4b, we also present the last few steps of a reduction sequence which produces γ_3 starting from configuration $(1 = \text{GHZ(n)} \mid n = s(s(s(\text{zero}))) \mid \Omega \mid 1)$, where Ω contains the above mentioned procedures. In the reduction sequence we only show the term in evaluating position and we omit some intermediate steps. The type ListQ is a shorthand for **List(qbit)** from Example 1.

4   W*-algebras

In this section we describe our denotational model. It is based on W*-algebras, which are algebras of observables (i.e. physical entities), with interesting domain-theoretic properties. We recall some background on W*-algebras and their categorical structure. We refer the reader to [25] for an encyclopaedic account on W*-algebras.

Domain-theoretic Preliminaries. Recall that a directed subset of a poset P is a non-empty subset $X \subseteq P$ in which every pair of elements of X has an upper bound in X. A poset P is a *directed-complete partial order* (*dcpo*) if each directed subset has a supremum. A poset P is *pointed* if it has a least element, usually denoted by $\perp$. A monotone map $f : P \to Q$ between posets is *Scott-continuous* if it preserves suprema of directed subsets. If P and Q are pointed and f preserves the least element, then we say f is *strict*. We write **DCPO** (**DCPO**$_{\perp !}$) for the category of (pointed) dcpo's and (strict) Scott-continuous maps between them.

Definition of W-algebras.* A *complex algebra* is a complex vector space V equipped with a bilinear multiplication $(- \cdot -) : V \times V \to V$, which we write as juxtaposition. A *Banach algebra* A is a complex algebra A equipped with a submultiplicative norm $\| - \| : A \to \mathbb{R}_{\geq 0}$, i.e. $\forall x, y \in A : \|xy\| \leq \|x\|\|y\|$. A *-*algebra* A is a complex algebra A with an involution $(-)^* : A \to A$ such that $(x^*)^* = x$, $(x + y)^* = (x^* + y^*)$, $(xy)^* = y^* x^*$ and $(\lambda x)^* = \bar{\lambda} x^*$, for $x, y \in A$ and $\lambda \in \mathbb{C}$. A *C*-algebra* is a Banach *-algebra A which satisfies the C*-identity, i.e. $\|x^* x\| = \|x\|^2$ for all $x \in A$. A C*-algebra A is *unital* if it has an element $1 \in A$, such that for every $x \in A : x1 = 1x = x$. All C*-algebras in this paper are unital and for brevity we regard unitality as part of their definition.

Example 10. The algebra $M_n(\mathbb{C})$ of $n \times n$ complex matrices is a C*-algebra. In particular, the set of complex numbers $\mathbb{C}$ has a C*-algebra structure since $M_1(\mathbb{C}) \cong \mathbb{C}$. More generally, the $n \times n$ matrices valued in a C*-algebra A also form a C*-algebra $M_n(A)$. The C*-algebra of qubits is **qbit** $:= M_2(\mathbb{C})$.

An element $x \in A$ of a C*-algebra A is called *positive* if $\exists y \in A : x = y^* y$. The *poset of positive elements* of A is denoted A^+ and its order is given by $x \leq y$ iff $(y - x) \in A^+$. The *unit interval* of A is the subposet $[0, 1]_A \subseteq A^+$ of all positive elements x such that $0 \leq x \leq 1$.

Let $f : A \to B$ be a linear map between C*-algebras A and B. We say that f is *positive* if it preserves positive elements. We say that f is *completely positive* if it is n-positive for every $n \in \mathbb{N}$, i.e. the map $M_n(f) : M_n(A) \to M_n(B)$ defined for every matrix $[x_{i,j}]_{1 \leq i,j \leq n} \in M_n(A)$ by $M_n(f)([x_{i,j}]_{1 \leq i,j \leq n}) = [f(x_{i,j})]_{1 \leq i,j \leq n}$ is positive. The map f is called *multiplicative, involutive, unital* if it preserves multiplication, involution, and the unit, respectively. The map f is called *subunital* whenever the inequalities $0 \leq f(1) \leq 1$ hold. A *state* on a C*-algebra A is a completely positive unital map $s : A \to \mathbb{C}$.

Although W*-algebras are commonly defined in topological terms (as C*-algebras closed under several operator topologies) or equivalently in algebraic terms (as C*-algebras which are their own bicommutant), one can also equivalently define them in domain-theoretic terms [19], as we do next.

A completely positive map between C*-algebras is *normal* if its restriction to the unit interval is Scott-continuous [19, Proposition A.3]. A *W*-algebra* is a

C*-algebra A such that the unit interval $[0,1]_A$ is a dcpo, and A has a separating set of normal states: for every $x \in A^+$, if $x \neq 0$, then there is a normal state $s : A \to \mathbb{C}$ such that $s(x) \neq 0$ [25, Theorem III.3.16].

A linear map $f : A \to B$ between W*-algebras A and B is called an *NCPSU-map* if f is normal, completely positive and subunital. The map f is called an *NMIU-map* if f is normal, multiplicative, involutive and unital. We note that every NMIU-map is necessarily an NCPSU-map and that W*-algebras are closed under formation of matrix algebras as in Example 10.

Categorical Structure. Let $\mathbf{W}^*_{\mathrm{NCPSU}}$ be the category of W*-algebras and NCPSU-maps and let $\mathbf{W}^*_{\mathrm{NMIU}}$ be its full-on-objects subcategory of NMIU-maps. Throughout the rest of the paper let $\mathbf{C} := (\mathbf{W}^*_{\mathrm{NCPSU}})^{\mathrm{op}}$ and let $\mathbf{V} := (\mathbf{W}^*_{\mathrm{NMIU}})^{\mathrm{op}}$. QPL types are interpreted as functors $[\![\Theta \vdash A]\!] : \mathbf{V}^{|\Theta|} \to \mathbf{V}$ and closed QPL types as objects $[\![A]\!] \in \mathrm{Ob}(\mathbf{V}) = \mathrm{Ob}(\mathbf{C})$. One should think of $\mathbf{V}$ as the category of *values*, because the interpretation of our values from §3 are indeed $\mathbf{V}$-morphisms. General QPL terms are interpreted as morphisms of $\mathbf{C}$, so one should think of $\mathbf{C}$ as the category of *computations*. We now describe the categorical structure of $\mathbf{V}$ and $\mathbf{C}$ and later we justify our choice for working in the opposite categories.

Both $\mathbf{C}$ and $\mathbf{V}$ have a symmetric monoidal structure when equipped with the spatial tensor product, denoted here by $(- \otimes -)$, and tensor unit $I := \mathbb{C}$ [11, Section 10]. Moreover, $\mathbf{V}$ is symmetric monoidal closed and also complete and cocomplete [11]. $\mathbf{C}$ and $\mathbf{V}$ have finite coproducts, given by direct sums of W*-algebras [2, Proposition 4.7.3]. The coproduct of objects A and B is denoted by $A + B$ and the coproduct injections are denoted $\mathrm{left}_{A,B} : A \to A + B$ and $\mathrm{right}_{A,B} : B \to A + B$. Given morphisms $f : A \to C$ and $g : B \to C$, we write $[f,g] : A + B \to C$ for the unique cocone morphism induced by the coproduct. Moreover, coproducts distribute over tensor products [2, §4.6]. More specifically, there exists a natural isomorphism $d_{A,B,C} : A \otimes (B + C) \to (A \otimes B) + (A \otimes C)$ which satisfies the usual coherence conditions. The initial object in $\mathbf{C}$ is moreover a zero object and is denoted 0. The W*-algebra of bits is $\mathbf{bit} := I + I = \mathbb{C} \oplus \mathbb{C}$.

The categories $\mathbf{V}, \mathbf{C}$ and $\mathbf{Set}$ are related by symmetric monoidal adjunctions:

$$\mathbf{Set} \underset{G}{\overset{F}{\rightleftarrows}} \mathbf{V} \underset{R}{\overset{J}{\rightleftarrows}} \mathbf{C} \qquad\qquad \text{[26, pp. 11]}$$

and the subcategory inclusion J preserves coproducts and tensors up to equality.

Interpreting QPL within $\mathbf{C}$ and $\mathbf{V}$ is not an ad hoc trick. In physical terms, this corresponds to adopting the *Heisenberg picture* of quantum mechanics and this is usually done when working with infinite-dimensional W*-algebras (like we do). Semantically, this is necessary, because (1) our type system has conditional branching and we need to interpret QPL terms within a category with finite coproducts; (2) we have to be able to compute parameterised initial algebras to interpret inductive datatypes. The category $\mathbf{W}^*_{\mathrm{NCPSU}}$ has finite products, but it does *not* have coproducts, so by interpreting QPL terms within $\mathbf{C} = (\mathbf{W}^*_{\mathrm{NCPSU}})^{\mathrm{op}}$ we solve problem (1). For (2), the monoidal closure of $\mathbf{V} = (\mathbf{W}^*_{\mathrm{NMIU}})^{\mathrm{op}}$ is crucial, because it implies the tensor product preserves ω-colimits.

$\mathrm{tr} : M_n(\mathbb{C}) \to \mathbb{C}$	$\mathrm{new}_\rho : \mathbb{C} \to M_{2^n}(\mathbb{C})$	$\mathrm{meas} : M_2(\mathbb{C}) \to \mathbb{C} \oplus \mathbb{C}$	$\mathrm{unitary}_S : M_{2^n}(\mathbb{C}) \to M_{2^n}(\mathbb{C})$
$\mathrm{tr} :: A \mapsto \sum_i A_{i,i}$	$\mathrm{new}_\rho :: a \mapsto a\rho$	$\mathrm{meas} :: \begin{pmatrix} a & b \\ c & d \end{pmatrix} \mapsto \begin{pmatrix} a & d \end{pmatrix}$	$\mathrm{unitary}_S :: A \mapsto SAS^\dagger$
$\mathrm{tr}^\dagger : \mathbb{C} \to M_n(\mathbb{C})$	$\mathrm{new}_\rho^\dagger : M_{2^n}(\mathbb{C}) \to \mathbb{C}$	$\mathrm{meas}^\dagger : \mathbb{C} \oplus \mathbb{C} \to M_2(\mathbb{C})$	$\mathrm{unitary}_S^\dagger : M_{2^n}(\mathbb{C}) \to M_{2^n}(\mathbb{C})$
$\mathrm{tr}^\dagger :: a \mapsto aI_n$	$\mathrm{new}_\rho^\dagger :: A \mapsto \mathrm{tr}(A\rho)$	$\mathrm{meas}^\dagger :: \begin{pmatrix} a & d \end{pmatrix} \mapsto \begin{pmatrix} a & 0 \\ 0 & d \end{pmatrix}$	$\mathrm{unitary}_S^\dagger :: A \mapsto S^\dagger AS$

Fig. 5: A selection of maps in the Schrödinger picture ($f : A \to B$) and their Hermitian adjoints ($f^\dagger : B \to A$) used in the Heisenberg picture.

Convex Sums. In both $\mathbf{C}$ and $\mathbf{W}^*_{\mathrm{NCPSU}}$, morphisms are closed under *convex sums*, which are defined pointwise, as usual. More specifically, given NCPSU-maps $f_1, \ldots, f_n : A \to B$ and real numbers $p_i \in [0,1]$ with $\sum_i p_i \leq 1$, then the map $\sum_i p_i f_i : A \to B$ is also an NCPSU-map.

Order-enrichment. For W*-algebras A and B, we define a partial order on $\mathbf{C}(A, B)$ by : $f \leq g$ iff $g - f$ is a completely positive map. Equipped with this order, our category $\mathbf{C}$ is $\mathbf{DCPO}_{\perp!}$-enriched [3, Theorem 4.3]. The least element in $\mathbf{C}(A, B)$ is also a zero morphism and is given by the map $\mathbf{0} : A \to B$, defined by $\mathbf{0}(x) = 0$. Also, the coproduct structure and the symmetric monoidal structure are both $\mathbf{DCPO}_{\perp!}$-enriched [2, Corollary 4.9.15] [3, Theorem 4.5].

Quantum Operations. For convenience, our operational semantics adopts the *Schrödinger picture* of quantum mechanics, which is the picture most experts in quantum computing are familiar with. However, as we have just explained, our denotational semantics has to adopt the Heisenberg picture. The two pictures are equivalent in finite dimensions and we will now show how to translate from one to the other. By doing so, we provide an explicit description (in both pictures) of the required quantum maps that we need to interpret QPL.

Consider the maps in Figure 5. The map *tr* is used to trace out (or discard) parts of quantum states. Density matrices ρ are in 1-1 correspondence with the maps *new*$_\rho$, which we use in our semantics to describe (mixed) quantum states. The *meas* map simply measures a qubit in the computational basis and returns a bit as measurement outcome. The *unitary*$_S$ map is used for application of a unitary S. These maps work as described in the Schrödinger picture of quantum mechanics, i.e., the category $\mathbf{W}^*_{\mathrm{NCPSU}}$. For every map $f : A \to B$ among those mentioned, $f^\dagger : B \to A$ indicates its Hermitian adjoint [3]. In the Heisenberg picture, composition of maps is done in the opposite way, so we simply write $f^\ddagger := (f^\dagger)^{\mathrm{op}} \in \mathbf{C}(A, B)$ for the Hermitian adjoint of f when seen as a morphism in $(\mathbf{W}^*_{\mathrm{NCPSU}})^{\mathrm{op}} = \mathbf{C}$. Thus, the mapping $(-)^\ddagger$ translates the above operations from the Schrödinger picture (the category $\mathbf{W}^*_{\mathrm{NCPSU}}$) to the Heisenberg picture (the category $\mathbf{C}$) of quantum mechanics.

---

[3] This adjoint exists, because A and B are *finite-dimensional* W*-algebras which therefore have the structure of a Hilbert space when equipped with the Hilbert-Schmidt inner product [27, pp. 145].

Parameterised Initial Algebras. In order to interpret inductive datatypes, we need to be able to compute parameterised initial algebras for the functors induced by our type expressions. $\mathbf{V}$ is ideal for this, because it is cocomplete and monoidal closed and so all type expressions induce functors on $\mathbf{V}$ which preserve ω-colimits.

Definition 11 (cf. [6, §6.1]). *Given a category $\mathbf{A}$ and a functor $T : \mathbf{A}^n \to \mathbf{A}$, with $n \geq 1$, a parameterised initial algebra for T is a pair $(T^\sharp, \phi^T)$, such that:*

- *$T^\sharp : \mathbf{A}^{n-1} \to \mathbf{A}$ is a functor;*
- *$\phi^T : T \circ \langle Id, T^\sharp \rangle \Rightarrow T^\sharp : \mathbf{A}^{n-1} \to \mathbf{A}$ is a natural isomorphism;*
- *For every $A \in \mathrm{Ob}(\mathbf{A}^{n-1})$, the pair $(T^\sharp A, \phi^T_A)$ is an initial $T(A, -)$-algebra.*

Proposition 12. *Every ω-cocontinuous functor $T : \mathbf{V}^n \to \mathbf{V}$ has a parameterised initial algebra $(T^\sharp, \phi^T)$ with $T^\sharp : \mathbf{V}^{n-1} \to \mathbf{V}$ being ω-cocontinuous.*

Proof. $\mathbf{V}$ is cocomplete, so this follows from [13, §4.3]. $\qquad\square$

5   Denotational Semantics of QPL

In this section we describe the denotational semantics of QPL.

5.1   Interpretation of Types

The interpretation of a type $\Theta \vdash A$ is a functor $[\![\Theta \vdash A]\!] : \mathbf{V}^{|\Theta|} \to \mathbf{V}$, defined by induction on the derivation of $\Theta \vdash A$ in Figure 6. As usual, one has to prove this assignment is well-defined by showing the required initial algebras exist.

Proposition 13. *The assignment in Figure 6 is well-defined.*

Proof. By induction, every $[\![\Theta \vdash A]\!]$ is an ω-cocontinuous functor and thus it has a parameterised initial algebra by Proposition 12. $\qquad\square$

Lemma 14 (Type Substitution). *Given types $\Theta, X \vdash A$ and $\Theta \vdash B$, then:*

$$[\![\Theta \vdash A[B/X]]\!] = [\![\Theta, X \vdash A]\!] \circ \langle Id, [\![\Theta \vdash B]\!] \rangle.$$

Proof. Straightforward induction. $\qquad\square$

For simplicity, the interpretation of terms is only defined on closed types and so we introduce more concise notation for them. For any closed type $\cdot \vdash A$ we write for convenience $[\![A]\!] := [\![\cdot \vdash A]\!](\ast) \in \mathrm{Ob}(\mathbf{V})$, where $\ast$ is the unique object of the terminal category $\mathbf{1}$. Notice also that $[\![A]\!] \in \mathrm{Ob}(\mathbf{C}) = \mathrm{Ob}(\mathbf{V})$.

Definition 15. *Given a closed type $\cdot \vdash \mu X.A$, we define an isomorphism (in $\mathbf{V}$):*

$$\mathrm{fold}_{\mu X.A} : [\![A[\mu X.A/X]]\!] = [\![X \vdash A]\!][\![\mu X.A]\!] \cong [\![\mu X.A]\!] : \mathrm{unfold}_{\mu X.A}$$

where the equality is Lemma 14 and the iso is the initial algebra structure.

Example 16. The interpretation of the types from Example 1 are $[\![\mathbf{Nat}]\!] = \bigoplus_{i=0}^{\omega} \mathbb{C}$ and $[\![\mathbf{List}(A)]\!] = \bigoplus_{i=0}^{\omega} [\![A]\!]^{\otimes i}$. Specifically, $[\![\mathbf{List}(\mathbf{qbit})]\!] = \bigoplus_{i=0}^{\omega} \mathbb{C}^{2^i \times 2^i}$.

$$[\![\Theta \vdash A]\!] : \mathbf{V}^{|\Theta|} \to \mathbf{V}$$
$$[\![\Theta \vdash \Theta_i]\!] = \Pi_i$$
$$[\![\Theta \vdash I]\!] = K_I$$
$$[\![\Theta \vdash \mathbf{qbit}]\!] = K_{\mathbf{qbit}}$$
$$[\![\Theta \vdash A + B]\!] = + \circ \langle [\![\Theta \vdash A]\!], [\![\Theta \vdash B]\!] \rangle$$
$$[\![\Theta \vdash A \otimes B]\!] = \otimes \circ \langle [\![\Theta \vdash A]\!], [\![\Theta \vdash B]\!] \rangle$$
$$[\![\Theta \vdash \mu X.A]\!] = [\![\Theta, X \vdash A]\!]^{\sharp}$$

Fig. 6: Interpretations of types. K_A is the constant-A-functor.

$$[\![\cdot \vdash * : I]\!] := \mathrm{id}_I$$
$$[\![\{n\} \vdash n : \mathbf{qbit}]\!] := \mathrm{id}_{\mathbf{qbit}}$$
$$[\![Q \vdash \mathbf{left}_{A,B}v : A + B]\!] := \mathrm{left} \circ [\![v]\!]$$
$$[\![Q \vdash \mathbf{right}_{A,B}v : A + B]\!] := \mathrm{right} \circ [\![v]\!]$$
$$[\![Q_1, Q_2 \vdash (v, w) : A \otimes B]\!] := [\![v]\!] \otimes [\![w]\!]$$
$$[\![Q \vdash \mathbf{fold}_{\mu X.A}v : \mu X.A]\!] := \mathrm{fold} \circ [\![v]\!]$$

Fig. 7: Interpretation of values.

$[\![\Pi \vdash \langle \Gamma \rangle \ \mathbf{new\ unit}\ u\ \langle \Gamma, u : I \rangle]\!] := \pi \mapsto r^{-1}$
$[\![\Pi \vdash \langle \Gamma, x : A \rangle \ \mathbf{discard}\ x\ \langle \Gamma \rangle]\!] := \pi \mapsto (r \circ (\mathrm{id} \otimes \diamond))$
$[\![\Pi \vdash \langle \Gamma, x : P \rangle \ y = \mathbf{copy}\ x\ \langle \Gamma, x : P, y : P \rangle]\!] := \pi \mapsto (\mathrm{id} \otimes \triangle)$
$[\![\Pi \vdash \langle \Gamma \rangle \ \mathbf{new\ qbit}\ q\ \langle \Gamma, q : \mathbf{qbit} \rangle]\!] := \pi \mapsto \left((\mathrm{id} \otimes \mathrm{new}^{\ddagger}_{|0\rangle\langle 0|}) \circ r^{-1} \right)$
$[\![\Pi \vdash \langle \Gamma, q : \mathbf{qbit} \rangle \ b = \mathbf{measure}\ q\ \langle \Gamma, b : \mathbf{bit} \rangle]\!] := \pi \mapsto (\mathrm{id} \otimes \mathrm{meas}^{\ddagger})$
$[\![\Pi \vdash \langle \Gamma, \vec{q} : \overrightarrow{\mathbf{qbit}} \rangle \ \vec{q} \mathrel{*}= S\ \langle \Gamma, \vec{q} : \overrightarrow{\mathbf{qbit}} \rangle]\!] := \pi \mapsto \left(\mathrm{id} \otimes \mathrm{unitary}^{\ddagger}_S \right)$
$[\![\Pi \vdash \langle \Gamma \rangle \ M; N\ \langle \Sigma \rangle]\!] := \pi \mapsto ([\![N]\!](\pi) \circ [\![M]\!](\pi))$
$[\![\Pi \vdash \langle \Gamma \rangle \ \mathbf{skip}\ \langle \Gamma \rangle]\!] := \pi \mapsto \mathrm{id}$
$[\![\Pi \vdash \langle \Gamma, b : \mathbf{bit} \rangle \ \mathbf{while}\ b\ \mathbf{do}\ M\ \langle \Gamma, b : \mathbf{bit} \rangle]\!] := \pi \mapsto \mathrm{lfp}(W_{[\![M]\!](\pi)})$
$[\![\Pi \vdash \langle \Gamma, x : A \rangle \ y = \mathbf{left}_{A,B}\ x\ \langle \Gamma, y : A + B \rangle]\!] := \pi \mapsto (\mathrm{id} \otimes \mathrm{left}_{A,B})$
$[\![\Pi \vdash \langle \Gamma, x : B \rangle \ y = \mathbf{right}_{A,B}\ x\ \langle \Gamma, y : A + B \rangle]\!] := \pi \mapsto \left(\mathrm{id} \otimes \mathrm{right}_{A,B} \right)$
$[\![\Pi \vdash \langle \Gamma, y : A + B \rangle \ \mathbf{case}\ y\ \mathbf{of}\ \{\mathbf{left}\ x_1 \to M_1 \mid \mathbf{right}\ x_2 \to M_2\}\ \langle \Sigma \rangle]\!] :=$
$\qquad \pi \mapsto ([\![M_1]\!](\pi), [\![M_2]\!](\pi)] \circ d)$
$[\![\Pi \vdash \langle \Gamma, x_1 : A, x_2 : B \rangle \ x = (x_1, x_2)\ \langle \Gamma, x : A \otimes B \rangle]\!] := \pi \mapsto \mathrm{id}$
$[\![\Pi \vdash \langle \Gamma, x : A \otimes B \rangle \ (x_1, x_2) = x\ \langle \Gamma, x_1 : A, x_2 : B \rangle]\!] := \pi \mapsto \mathrm{id}$
$[\![\Pi \vdash \langle \Gamma, x : A[\mu X.A/X] \rangle \ y = \mathbf{fold}\ x\ \langle \Gamma, y : \mu X.A \rangle]\!] := \pi \mapsto (\mathrm{id} \otimes \mathrm{fold})$
$[\![\Pi \vdash \langle \Gamma, x : \mu X.A \rangle \ y = \mathbf{unfold}\ x\ \langle \Gamma, y : A[\mu X.A/X] \rangle]\!] := \pi \mapsto (\mathrm{id} \otimes \mathrm{unfold})$
$[\![\Pi \vdash \langle \Gamma \rangle \ \mathbf{proc}\ f :: x : A \to y : B\ \{M\}\ \langle \Gamma \rangle]\!] := \pi \mapsto \mathrm{id}$
$[\![\Pi, f : A \to B \vdash \langle \Gamma, x : A \rangle \ y = f(x)\ \langle \Gamma, y : B \rangle]\!] := (\pi, f) \mapsto (\mathrm{id} \otimes f),$
where r is the right monoidal unit. For simplicity, we omit the monoidal associator.

Fig. 8: Interpretation of QPL terms.

5.2   Copying and Discarding

Our type system is affine, so we have to construct discarding maps at all types. The tensor unit I is a terminal object in $\mathbf{V}$ (but not in $\mathbf{C}$) which leads us to the next definition.

Definition 17 (Discarding map). *For any W*-algebra A, let $\diamond_A : A \to I$ be the unique morphism of $\mathbf{V}$ with the indicated domain and codomain.*

We will see that all values admit an interpretation as $\mathbf{V}$-morphisms and are therefore discardable. In physical terms, this means values are causal (in the sense mentioned in the introduction). Of course, this is not true for the interpretation of general terms (which correspond to $\mathbf{C}$-morphisms).

Our language is equipped with a copy operation on classical data, so we have to explain how to copy classical values. We do this by constructing a copy map defined at all *classical* types using results from [13,14].

Proposition 18. *Using the categorical data of* $\mathbf{Set} \begin{array}{c} \xrightarrow{F} \\ \perp \\ \xleftarrow{G} \end{array} \mathbf{V}$ *, one can define a copy map $\triangle_{[\![P]\!]} : [\![P]\!] \to [\![P]\!] \otimes [\![P]\!]$ for every classical type $\cdot \vdash P$, such that the triple $([\![P]\!], \triangle_{[\![P]\!]}, \diamond_{[\![P]\!]})$ forms a cocommutative comonoid in $\mathbf{V}$.*

We shall later see that the interpretations of our *classical* values are comonoid homomorphisms (w.r.t. Proposition 18) and therefore they may be copied.

5.3   Interpretation of Terms

Given a variable context $\Gamma = x_1 : A_1, \ldots, x_n : A_n$, we interpet it as the object $[\![\Gamma]\!] := [\![A_1]\!] \otimes \cdots \otimes [\![A_n]\!] \in \mathrm{Ob}(\mathbf{C})$. The interpretation of a procedure context $\Pi = f_1 : A_1 \to B_1, \ldots, f_n : A_n \to B_n$ is defined to be the pointed dcpo $[\![\Pi]\!] := \mathbf{C}(A_1, B_1) \times \cdots \times \mathbf{C}(A_n, B_n)$. A term $\Pi \vdash \langle \Gamma \rangle \, M \, \langle \Sigma \rangle$ is interpreted as a Scott-continuous function $[\![\Pi \vdash \langle \Gamma \rangle \, M \, \langle \Sigma \rangle]\!] : [\![\Pi]\!] \to \mathbf{C}([\![\Gamma]\!], [\![\Sigma]\!])$ defined by induction on the derivation of $\Pi \vdash \langle \Gamma \rangle \, M \, \langle \Sigma \rangle$ in Figure 8. For brevity, we often write $[\![M]\!] := [\![\Pi \vdash \langle \Gamma \rangle \, M \, \langle \Sigma \rangle]\!]$, when the contexts are clear or unimportant.

We now explain some of the notation used in Figure 8. The rules for manipulating qubits use the morphisms $\mathrm{new}^{\ddagger}_{|0\rangle\langle 0|}, \mathrm{meas}^{\ddagger}$ and $\mathrm{unitary}^{\ddagger}_S$ which are defined in §4. For the interpretation of **while** loops, given an arbitrary morphism $f : A \otimes \mathbf{bit} \to A \otimes \mathbf{bit}$ of $\mathbf{C}$, we define a Scott-continuous endofunction

$$W_f : \mathbf{C}\,(A \otimes \mathbf{bit}, A \otimes \mathbf{bit}) \to \mathbf{C}(A \otimes \mathbf{bit}, A \otimes \mathbf{bit})$$

$$W_f(g) = \big[\mathrm{id} \otimes \mathrm{left}_{I,I}, \; g \circ f \circ (\mathrm{id} \otimes \mathrm{right}_{I,I})\big] \circ d_{A,I,I},$$

where the isomorphism $d_{A,I,I} : A \otimes (I + I) \to (A \otimes I) + (A \otimes I)$ is explained in §4. For any pointed dcpo D and Scott-continuous function $h : D \to D$, its *least fixpoint* is $\mathrm{lfp}(h) := \bigvee_{i=0}^{\infty} h^i(\perp)$, where $\perp$ is the least element of D.

Remark 19. The term semantics for defining and calling procedures does not involve any fixpoint computations. The required fixpoint computations are done when interpreting procedure stores, as we shall see next.

5.4   Interpretation of Configurations

Before we may interpret program configurations, we first have to describe how to interpret values and procedure stores.

Interpretation of Values. A qubit pointer context Q is interpreted as the object $[\![Q]\!] = \mathbf{qbit}^{\otimes |Q|}$. A value $Q \vdash v : A$ is interpreted as a morphism in $\mathbf{V}$ $[\![Q \vdash v : A]\!] : [\![Q]\!] \to [\![A]\!]$, which we abbreviate as $[\![v]\!]$ if Q and A are clear from context. It is defined by induction on the derivation of $Q \vdash v : A$ in Figure 7.

For the next theorem, recall that if $Q \vdash v : A$ is a classical value, then $Q = \cdot$.

Theorem 20. *Let $Q \vdash v : A$ be a value. Then:*

1. *$[\![v]\!]$ is discardable (i.e. causal). More specifically, $\diamond_{[\![A]\!]} \circ [\![v]\!] = \diamond_{[\![Q]\!]} = \mathrm{tr}^{\ddagger}$.*
2. *If A is classical, then $[\![v]\!]$ is copyable, i.e., $\triangle_{[\![A]\!]} \circ [\![v]\!] = ([\![v]\!] \otimes [\![v]\!]) \circ \triangle_I$.*

We see that, as promised, interpretations of values may always be discarded and interpretations of classical values may also be copied. Next, we explain how to interpret value contexts. For a value context $Q; \Gamma \vdash V$, its interpretation is the morphism:

$$[\![Q; \Gamma \vdash V]\!] = \left([\![Q]\!] \xrightarrow{\cong} [\![Q_1]\!] \otimes \cdots \otimes [\![Q_n]\!] \xrightarrow{[\![v_1]\!] \otimes \cdots \otimes [\![v_n]\!]} [\![\Gamma]\!] \right),$$

where $Q_i \vdash v_i : A_i$ is the splitting of Q (see §3) and $[\![\Gamma]\!] = [\![A_1]\!] \otimes \cdots \otimes [\![A_n]\!]$. Some of the Q_i can be empty and this is the reason why the definition depends on a coherent natural isomorphism. We write $[\![V]\!]$ as a shorthand for $[\![Q; \Gamma \vdash V]\!]$. Obviously, $[\![V]\!]$ is also causal thanks to Theorem 20.

Interpretation of Procedure Stores. The interpretation of a well-formed procedure store $\Pi \vdash \Omega$ is an element of $[\![\Pi]\!]$, i.e. a $|\Pi|$-tuple of morphisms from $\mathbf{C}$. It is defined by induction on $\Pi \vdash \Omega$:

$$[\![\cdot \vdash \cdot]\!] = ()$$
$$[\![\Pi, f : A \to B \vdash \Omega, f :: x : A \to y : B \{M\}]\!] = ([\![\Omega]\!], \mathrm{lfp}([\![M]\!]([\![\Omega]\!], -))).$$

Interpretation of Configurations. Density matrices $\rho \in M_{2^n}(\mathbb{C})$ are in 1-1 correspondence with $\mathbf{W}^*_{\mathrm{NCPSU}}$-morphisms $\mathrm{new}_\rho : \mathbb{C} \to M_{2^n}(\mathbb{C})$ which are in turn in 1-1 correspondence with $\mathbf{C}$-morphisms $\mathrm{new}_\rho^{\ddagger} : I \to \mathbf{qbit}^{\otimes n}$. Using this observation, we can now define the interpretation of a configuration $\mathcal{C} = (M \mid V \mid \Omega \mid \rho)$ with $\Pi; \Gamma; \Sigma; Q \vdash (M \mid V \mid \Omega \mid \rho)$ to be the morphism

$$[\![\Pi; \Gamma; \Sigma; Q \vdash (M \mid V \mid \Omega \mid \rho)]\!] :=$$

$$\left(I \xrightarrow{\mathrm{new}_\rho^{\ddagger}} \mathbf{qbit}^{\otimes \dim(\rho)} \xrightarrow{[\![Q; \Gamma \vdash V]\!]} [\![\Gamma]\!] \xrightarrow{[\![\Pi \vdash \langle \Gamma \rangle \; M \; \langle \Sigma \rangle]\!]([\![\Pi \vdash \Omega]\!])} [\![\Sigma]\!] \right).$$

For brevity, we simply write $[\![(M \mid V \mid \Omega \mid \rho)]\!]$ or even just $[\![\mathcal{C}]\!]$ to refer to the above morphism.

5.5　Soundness, Adequacy and Big-step Invariance

Since our operational semantics allows for branching, *soundness* is showing that the interpretation of configurations is equal to the sum of small-step reducts.

Theorem 21 (Soundness). *For any non-terminal configuration $\mathcal{C}$:*

$$\llbracket \mathcal{C} \rrbracket = \sum_{\mathcal{C} \leadsto \mathcal{D}} \llbracket \mathcal{D} \rrbracket.$$

Proof. By induction on the shape of the term component of $\mathcal{C}$. □

Remark 22. The above sum and all sums that follow are well-defined convex sums of NCPSU-maps where the probability weights p_i have been encoded in the density matrices.

A natural question to ask is whether $\llbracket \mathcal{C} \rrbracket$ is also equal to the (potentially infinite) sum of all terminal configurations that $\mathcal{C}$ reduces to. In other words, is the interpretation of configurations also invariant with respect to big-step reduction. This is indeed the case and proving this requires considerable effort.

Theorem 23 (Big-step Invariance). *For any configuration $\mathcal{C}$, we have:*

$$\llbracket \mathcal{C} \rrbracket = \bigvee_{n=0}^{\infty} \sum_{r \in \mathrm{TerSeq}_{\leq n}(\mathcal{C})} \llbracket \mathrm{End}(r) \rrbracket$$

The above theorem is the main result of our paper. This is a powerful result, because with big-step invariance in place, computational adequacy[4] at all types is now a simple consequence of the causal properties of our interpretation. Observe that for any configuration $\mathcal{C}$, we have a subunital map $\diamond \circ \llbracket \mathcal{C} \rrbracket : \mathbb{C} \to \mathbb{C}$ and evaluating it at 1 yields a real number $(\diamond \circ \llbracket \mathcal{C} \rrbracket)(1) \in [0,1]$.

Theorem 24 (Adequacy). *For any normalised $\mathcal{C}$: $(\diamond \circ \llbracket \mathcal{C} \rrbracket)(1) = \mathrm{Halt}(\mathcal{C})$.*

If $\mathcal{C}$ is not normalised, then adequacy can be recovered simply by normalising: $(\diamond \circ \llbracket \mathcal{C} \rrbracket)(1) = \mathrm{tr}(\mathcal{C})\mathrm{Halt}(\mathcal{C})$, for any possible configuration $\mathcal{C}$. The adequacy formulation of [17] and [5] is now a special case of our more general formulation.

Corollary 25. *Let M be a closed program of unit type, i.e. $\cdot \vdash \langle \cdot \rangle\, M\, \langle \cdot \rangle$. Then:*

$$\llbracket (M \mid \cdot \mid \cdot \mid 1) \rrbracket (1) = \mathrm{Halt}(M \mid \cdot \mid \cdot \mid 1).$$

Proof. By Theorem 24 and because $\diamond_I = \mathrm{id}$. □

---

[4] Recall that a computational adequacy result has to establish an equivalent *purely denotational* characterisation of the operational notion of non-termination.

6　Conclusion and Related Work

There are many quantum programming languages described in the literature. For a survey see [7] and [16, pp. 129]. Some circuit programming languages (e.g. Proto-Quipper [21,22,15]), generate quantum circuits, but do not necessarily support executing quantum measurements. Here we focus on quantum languages which support measurement and which have either inductive datatypes or some computational adequacy result.

Our work is the first to present a detailed semantic treatment of user-defined inductive datatypes for quantum programming. In [17] and [5], the authors show how to interpret a quantum lambda calculus extended with a datatype for lists, but their syntax does not support any other inductive datatypes. These languages are equipped with lambda abstractions, whereas our language has only support for procedures. Lambda abstractions are modelled using constructions from quantitative semantics of linear logic in [17] and techniques from game semantics in [5]. We believe our model is simpler and certainly more physically natural, because we work only with mathematical structures used by physicists in their study of quantum mechanics. Both [17] and [5] prove an adequacy result for programs of unit type. In [20], the authors discuss potential categorical models for inductive datatypes in quantum programming, but there is no detailed semantic treatment provided and there is no adequacy result, because the language lacks recursion.

Other quantum programming languages without inductive datatypes, but which prove computational adequacy results include [9,12]. A model based on W*-algebras for a quantum lambda calculus without recursion or inductive datatypes was described in a recent manuscript [4]. In that model, it appears that currying is *not* a Scott-continuous operation, and if so, the addition of recursion renders the model neither sound, nor adequate. For this reason, we use procedures and not lambda abstractions in our language.

To conclude, we presented two novel results in quantum programming: (1) we provided a denotational semantics for a quantum programming language with inductive datatypes; (2) we proved that our denotational semantics is invariant with respect to big-step reduction. We also showed that the latter result is quite powerful by demonstrating how it immediately implies computational adequacy.

Our denotational model is based on W*-algebras, which are used by physicists to study quantum foundations. We hope this would make it useful for developing static analysis methods (based on abstract interpretation) that can be used for entanglement detection [18] and we plan on investigating this in future work.

Acknowledgements. We thank Andre Kornell, Bert Lindenhovius and Michael Mislove for discussions regarding this paper. We also thank the anonymous referees for their feedback. MR acknowledges financial support from the Quantum Software Consortium, under the Gravitation programme of the Dutch Research Council NWO. The remaining authors were supported by the French projects ANR-17-CE25-0009 SoftQPro, ANR-17-CE24-0035 VanQuTe and PIA-GDN/Quantex.

References

1. Abadi, M., Fiore, M.P.: Syntactic Considerations on Recursive Types. In: Proceedings, 11th Annual IEEE Symposium on Logic in Computer Science, New Brunswick, New Jersey, USA, July 27-30, 1996. pp. 242–252. IEEE Computer Society (1996). https://doi.org/10.1109/LICS.1996.561324

2. Cho, K.: Semantics for a Quantum Programming Language by Operator Algebras (2014), Master Thesis, University of Tokyo.

3. Cho, K.: Semantics for a Quantum Programming Language by Operator Algebras. New Generation Comput. **34**(1-2), 25–68 (2016). https://doi.org/10.1007/s00354-016-0204-3

4. Cho, K., Westerbaan, A.: Von Neumann Algebras form a Model for the Quantum Lambda Calculus (2016), `http://arxiv.org/abs/1603.02133`, manuscript.

5. Clairambault, P., de Visme, M., Winskel, G.: Game semantics for quantum programming. PACMPL **3**(POPL), 32:1–32:29 (2019). https://doi.org/10.1145/3290345

6. Fiore, M.P.: Axiomatic Domain Theory in Categories of Partial Maps. Ph.D. thesis, University of Edinburgh, UK (1994)

7. Gay, S.J.: Quantum programming languages: survey and bibliography. Mathematical Structures in Computer Science **16**(4), 581–600 (2006). https://doi.org/10.1017/S0960129506005378

8. Harrow, A.W., Hassidim, A., Lloyd, S.: Quantum Algorithm for Linear Systems of Equations. Phys. Rev. Lett. **103**, 150502 (Oct 2009). https://doi.org/10.1103/PhysRevLett.103.150502

9. Hasuo, I., Hoshino, N.: Semantics of higher-order quantum computation via geometry of interaction. Ann. Pure Appl. Logic **168**(2), 404–469 (2017). https://doi.org/10.1016/j.apal.2016.10.010

10. Kissinger, A., Uijlen, S.: A categorical semantics for causal structure. In: 32nd Annual ACM/IEEE Symposium on Logic in Computer Science, LICS 2017, Reykjavik, Iceland, June 20-23, 2017. pp. 1–12. IEEE Computer Society (2017). https://doi.org/10.1109/LICS.2017.8005095

11. Kornell, A.: Quantum collections. International Journal of Mathematics **28**(12), 1750085 (2017). https://doi.org/10.1142/S0129167X17500859

12. Lago, U.D., Faggian, C., Valiron, B., Yoshimizu, A.: The geometry of parallelism: classical, probabilistic, and quantum effects. In: Castagna, G., Gordon, A.D. (eds.) Proceedings of the 44th ACM SIGPLAN Symposium on Principles of Programming Languages, POPL 2017, Paris, France, January 18-20, 2017. pp. 833–845. ACM (2017), `http://dl.acm.org/citation.cfm?id=3009859`

13. Lindenhovius, B., Mislove, M., Zamdzhiev, V.: LNL-FPC: The Linear/Non-linear Fixpoint Calculus `https://arxiv.org/abs/1906.09503`, submitted.

14. Lindenhovius, B., Mislove, M., Zamdzhiev, V.: Mixed linear and non-linear recursive types. Proc. ACM Program. Lang. **3**(ICFP), 111:1–111:29 (Jul 2019). https://doi.org/10.1145/3341715

15. Lindenhovius, B., Mislove, M.W., Zamdzhiev, V.: Enriching a Linear/Non-linear Lambda Calculus: A Programming Language for String Diagrams. In: Dawar, A., Grädel, E. (eds.) Proceedings of the 33rd Annual ACM/IEEE Symposium on Logic in Computer Science, LICS 2018, Oxford, UK, July 09-12, 2018. pp. 659–668. ACM (2018). https://doi.org/10.1145/3209108.3209196

16. Mosca, M., Roetteler, M., Selinger, P.: Quantum Programming Languages (Dagstuhl Seminar 18381). Dagstuhl Reports **8**(9), 112–132 (2019). https://doi.org/10.4230/DagRep.8.9.112

17. Pagani, M., Selinger, P., Valiron, B.: Applying quantitative semantics to higher-order quantum computing. In: Jagannathan, S., Sewell, P. (eds.) The 41st Annual ACM SIGPLAN-SIGACT Symposium on Principles of Programming Languages, POPL '14, San Diego, CA, USA, January 20-21, 2014. pp. 647–658. ACM (2014). https://doi.org/10.1145/2535838.2535879

18. Perdrix, S.: Quantum Entanglement Analysis Based on Abstract Interpretation. In: Alpuente, M., Vidal, G. (eds.) Static Analysis, 15th International Symposium, SAS 2008, Valencia, Spain, July 16-18, 2008. Proceedings. Lecture Notes in Computer Science, vol. 5079, pp. 270–282. Springer (2008). https://doi.org/10.1007/978-3-540-69166-2_18

19. Rennela, M.: Operator Algebras in Quantum Computation (2013), Master Thesis, Université Paris 7 Denis Diderot.

20. Rennela, M., Staton, S.: Classical Control and Quantum Circuits in Enriched Category Theory. Electr. Notes Theor. Comput. Sci. **336**, 257–279 (2018). https://doi.org/10.1016/j.entcs.2018.03.027

21. Rios, F., Selinger, P.: A Categorical Model for a Quantum Circuit Description Language. In: QPL (2017). https://doi.org/10.4204/EPTCS.266.11

22. Ross, N.J.: Algebraic and Logical Methods in Quantum Computation (2015), Ph.D. thesis, Dalhousie University.

23. Selinger, P.: Towards a quantum programming language. Mathematical Structures in Computer Science **14**(4), 527–586 (2004). https://doi.org/10.1017/S0960129504004256

24. Shor, P.W.: Polynomial-Time Algorithms for Prime Factorization and Discrete Logarithms on a Quantum Computer. SIAM Review **41**(2), 303–332 (1999). https://doi.org/10.1137/S0036144598347011

25. Takesaki, M.: Theory of Operator Algebras. Vol. I, II and III. Springer-Verlag, Berlin (2002)

26. Westerbaan, A.: Quantum Programs as Kleisli Maps. In: Duncan, R., Heunen, C. (eds.) Proceedings 13th International Conference on Quantum Physics and Logic, QPL 2016, Glasgow, Scotland, 6-10 June 2016. EPTCS, vol. 236, pp. 215–228 (2016). https://doi.org/10.4204/EPTCS.236.14

27. Westerbaan, B.: Dagger and Dilation in the Category of Von Neumann algebras. Ph.D. thesis, Radboud University (2018), http://arxiv.org/abs/1803.01911

28. Wootters, W.K., Zurek, W.H.: A single quantum cannot be cloned. Nature **299**(5886), 802–803 (1982)

Timed Negotiations*

S. Akshay[1]($\boxtimes$), Blaise Genest[2], Loïc Hélouët[3], and Sharvik Mital[1]

[1] IIT Bombay, Mumbai, India {akshayss,sharky}@cse.iitb.ac.in
[2] Univ Rennes, CNRS, IRISA, Rennes, France blaise.genest@irisa.fr
[3] Univ Rennes, Inria, Rennes, France loic.helouet@inria.fr

Abstract. Negotiations were introduced in [6] as a model for concurrent systems with multiparty decisions. What is very appealing with negotiations is that it is one of the very few non-trivial concurrent models where several interesting problems, such as soundness, i.e. absence of deadlocks, can be solved in PTIME [3]. In this paper, we introduce the model of timed negotiations and consider the problem of computing the minimum and the maximum execution times of a negotiation. The latter can be solved using the algorithm of [10] computing costs in negotiations, but surprisingly minimum execution time cannot.
This paper proposes new algorithms to compute both minimum and maximum execution time, that work in much more general classes of negotiations than [10], that only considered sound and deterministic negotiations. Further, we uncover the precise complexities of these questions, ranging from PTIME to Δ_2^P-complete. In particular, we show that computing the minimum execution time is more complex than computing the maximum execution time in most classes of negotiations we consider.

1 Introduction

Distributed systems are notoriously difficult to analyze, mainly due to the explosion of the number of configurations that have to be considered to answer even simple questions. A challenging task is then to propose models on which analysis can be performed with tractable complexities, preferably within polynomial time. Free choice Petri nets are a classical model of distributed systems that allow for efficient verification, in particular when the nets are 1-safe [4,5].

Recently, [6] introduced a new model called *negotiations* for workflows and business processes. A negotiation describes how processes interact in a distributed system: a subset of processes in a node of the system take a synchronous decisions among several *outcomes*. The effect of this outcome sends contributing processes to a new set of nodes. The execution of a negotiation ends when processes reach a *final configuration*. Negotiations can be deterministic (once an outcome is fixed, each process knows its unique successor node) or not.

Negotiations are an interesting model since several properties can be decided with a reasonable complexity. The question of *soundness*, i.e., deadlock-freedom:

whether from every reachable configuration one can reach a final configuration, is PSPACE-complete. However, for deterministic negotiations, it can be decided in PTIME [7]. The decision procedure uses reduction rules. Reduction techniques were originally proposed for Petri nets [2, 8, 11, 16]. The main idea is to define transformations rules that produce a model of smaller size w.r.t. the original model, while preserving the property under analysis. In the context of negotiations, [7, 3] proposed a sound and complete set of soundness-preserving reduction rules and algorithms to apply these rules efficiently. The question of soundness for deterministic negotiations was revisited in [9] and showed NLOGSPACE-complete using anti patterns instead of reduction rules. Further, they show that the PTIME result holds even when relaxing determinism [9]. Negotiation games have also been considered to decide whether one particular process can force termination of a negotiation. While this question is EXPTIME-complete in general, for sound and deterministic negotiations, it becomes PTIME [12].

While it is natural to consider cost or time in negotiations (e.g. think of the Brexit negotiation where time is of the essence, and which we model as running example in this paper), the original model of negotiations proposed by [6] is only qualitative. Recently, [10] has proposed a framework to associate costs to the executions of negotiations, and adapt a static analysis technique based on reduction rules to compute end-to-end cost functions that are not sensitive to scheduling of concurrent nodes. For sound *and* deterministic negotiations, the end-to-end cost can be computed in $O(n.(C + n))$, where n is the size of the negotiation and C the time needed to compute the cost of an execution. Requiring soundness or determinism seems perfectly reasonable, but asking sound *and* deterministic negotiations is too restrictive: it prevents a process from waiting for decisions of other processes to know how to proceed.

In this paper, we revisit time in negotiations. We attach time intervals to outcomes of nodes. We want to compute maximal and minimal executions times, for negotiations that are not necessarily sound and deterministic. Since we are interested in minimal and maximal execution time, cycles in negotiations can be either bypassed or lead to infinite maximal time. Hence, we restrict this study to acyclic negotiations. Notice that time can be modeled as a cost, following [10], and the maximal execution time of a sound and deterministic negotiation can be computed in PTIME using the algorithm from [10]. Surprisingly however, we give an example (Example 3) for which the minimal execution time cannot be computed in PTIME by this algorithm.

The first contribution of the paper shows that reachability (whether at least one run of a negotiation terminates) is NP-complete, already for (untimed) deterministic acyclic negotiations. This implies that computing minimal or maximal execution time for deterministic (but unsound) acyclic negotiations cannot be done in PTIME (unless NP=PTIME). We characterize precisely the complexities of different decision variants (threshold, equality, etc.), with complexities ranging from (co-)NP-complete to Δ_2^P.

We thus turn to negotiations that are sound but not necessarily deterministic. Our second contribution is a new algorithm, not based on reduction rules, to compute the maximal execution time in PTIME for sound negotiations. It is based on computing the maximal execution time of critical paths in the negotiations. However, we show that *minimal* execution time cannot be computed in PTIME for sound negotiations (unless NP=PTIME): deciding whether the minimal execution time is lower than T is NP-complete, even for T given in unary, using a reduction from a Bin packing problem. This shows that minimal execution time is harder to compute than maximal execution time.

Our third contribution consists in defining a class in which the minimal execution time can be computed in (pseudo) PTIME. To do so, we define the class of k-layered negotiations, for k fixed, that is negotiations where nodes can be organized into layers of at most k nodes at the same depth. These negotiations can be executed without remembering more than k nodes at a time. In this case, we show that computing the maximal execution time is PTIME, even if the negotiation is neither deterministic nor sound. The algorithm, not based on reduction rules, uses the k-layer restriction in order to navigate in the negotiation while considering only a polynomial number of configurations. For minimal execution time, we provide a pseudo PTIME algorithm, that is PTIME if constants are given in unary. Finally, we show that the size of constants do matter: deciding whether the minimal execution time of a k-layered negotiation is less than T is NP-complete, when T is given in binary. We show this by reducing from a Knapsack problem, yet again emphasizing that the minimal execution time of a negotiation is harder to compute than its maximal execution time.

This paper is organized as follows. Section 2 introduces the key ingredients of negotiations, determinism and soundness, known results in the untimed setting, and provides our running example modeling the Brexit negotiation. Section 3 introduces time in negotiations, gives a semantics to this new model, and formalizes several decision problems on maximal and minimal durations of runs in timed negotiations. We recall the main results of the paper in Section 4. Then, Section 5 considers timed execution problems for deterministic negotiations, Section 6 for sound negotiations, and section 7 for layered negotiations. Proof details for the last three sections are given in an extended version of this paper [1].

2 Negotiations: Definitions and Brexit example

In this section, we recall the definition of negotiations, of some subclasses (acyclic and deterministic), as well as important problems (soundness and reachability).

Definition 1 (Negotiation [6, 10]). *A negotiation over a finite set of processes P is a tuple $\mathcal{N} = (N, n_0, n_f, \mathcal{X})$, where:*

- *N is a finite set of nodes. Each node is a pair $n = (P_n, R_n)$ where $P_n \subseteq P$ is a non empty set of processes participating in node n, and R_n is a finite set of outcomes of node n (also called results), with $R_{n_f} = \{r_f\}$. We denote by R the union of all outcomes of nodes in N.*
- *n_0 is the first node of the negotiation and n_f is the final node. Every process in P participates in both n_0 and n_f.*

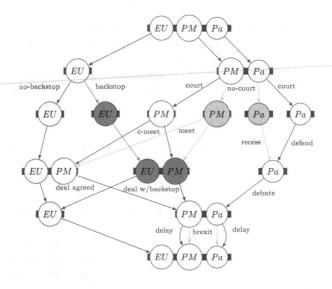

Fig. 1. A (sound but non-deterministic) negotiation modeling Brexit.

- For all $n \in N$, $\mathcal{X}_n : P_n \times R_n \to 2^N$ is a map defining the transition relation from node n, with $\mathcal{X}_n(p,r) = \emptyset$ iff $n = n_f, r = r_f$. We denote $\mathcal{X} : N \times P \times R \to 2^N$ the partial map defined on $\bigcup_{n \in N}(\{n\} \times P_n \times R_n)$, with $\mathcal{X}(n,p,a) = \mathcal{X}_n(p,a)$ for all p,a.

Intuitively, at a node $n = (P_n, R_n)$ in a negotiation, all processes of P_n have to agree on a common outcome r chosen from R_n. Once this outcome r is chosen, every process $p \in P_n$ is ready to move to any node prescribed by $\mathcal{X}(n,p,r)$. A new node m can only start when all processes of P_m are ready to move to m.

Example 1. We illustrate negotiations by considering a simplified model of the Brexit negotiation, see Figure 1. There are 3 processes, $P = \{EU, PM, Pa\}$. At first EU decides whether or not to enforce a backstop in any deal (outcome backstop) or not (outcome no-backstop). In the meantime, PM decides to proroge Pa, and Pa can choose or not to appeal to court (outcome court/no court). If it goes to court, then PM and Pa will take some time in court (c-meet, defend), before PM can meet EU to agree on a deal. Otherwise, Pa goes to recess, and PM can meet EU directly. Once EU and PM agreed on a deal, PM tries to convince Pa to vote the deal. The final outcome is whether the deal is voted, or whether Brexit is delayed.

Definition 2 (Deterministic negotiations). *A process $p \in P$ is deterministic iff, for every $n \in N$ and every outcome r of n, $\mathcal{X}(n,p,r)$ is a singleton. A negotiation is deterministic iff all its processes are deterministic. It is weakly non-deterministic [9] (called weakly deterministic in [3]) iff, for every node n, one of the processes in P_n is deterministic. Last, it is very weakly non-deterministic [9] (called weakly deterministic in [6]) iff, for every n, every $p \in P_n$ and every outcome r of n, there exists a deterministic process q such that $q \in P_{n'}$ for every $n' \in \mathcal{X}(n,p,r)$.*

In deterministic negotiations, once an outcome is chosen, each process knows the next node it will be involved in. In (very-)weakly non-deterministic negotiations, the next node might depend upon the outcome chosen in other nodes by other processes. However, once the outcomes have been chosen for all current nodes, there is only one next node possible for each process. Observe that the class of deterministic negotiations is isomorphic to the class of free choice workflow nets [10]. In Example 1, the Brexit negotiation is non-deterministic, because process PM is non-deterministic. Indeed, consider outcomes c-$meet$: it allows two nodes, according to whether the backstop is enforced or not, which is a decision taken by process EU.

Semantics: A *configuration* [3] of a negotiation is a mapping $M : P \to 2^N$. Intuitively, it tells for each process p the set $M(p)$ of nodes p is ready to engage in. The semantics of a negotiation is defined in terms of moves from a configuration to the next one. The *initial* M_0 and *final* M_f configurations, are given by $M_0(p) = \{n_0\}$ and $M_f(p) = \emptyset$ respectively for every process $p \in P$. A configuration M *enables* node n if $n \in M(p)$ for every $p \in P_n$. When n is enabled, a decision at node n can occur, and the participants at this node choose an outcome $r \in R_n$. The occurrence of (n, r) produces the configuration M' given by $M'(p) = \mathcal{X}(n, p, r)$ for every $p \in P_n$ and $M'(p) = M(p)$ for remaining processes in $P \setminus P_n$. Moving from M to M' after choosing (n, r) is called a *step*, denoted $M \xrightarrow{n,r} M'$. A *run* of $\mathcal{N}$ is a sequence $(n_1, r_1), (n_2, r_2)...(n_k, r_k)$ such that there is a sequence of configurations $M_0, M_1, \ldots, M_k$ and every (n_i, r_i) is a step between M_{i-1} and M_i. A run starting from the initial configuration and ending in the final configuration is called a *final run*. By definition, its last step is (n_f, r_f).

An important class of negotiations in the context of timed negotiations is acyclic negotiations, where infinite sequence of steps is impossible:

Definition 3 (Acyclic negotiations). *The* graph *of a negotiation $\mathcal{N}$ is the labeled graph $G_\mathcal{N} = (V, E)$ where $V = N$, and $E = \{((n, (p, r), n') \mid n' \in \mathcal{X}(n, p, r)\}$, with pairs of the form (p, r) being the labels. A negotiation is acyclic iff its graph is acyclic. We denote by $Paths(G_\mathcal{N})$ the set of paths in the graph of a negotiation. These paths are of form $\pi = (n_0, (p_0, r_0), n_1) \ldots (n_{k-1}, (p_k, r_k), n_k)$.*

The Brexit negotiation of Fig.1 is an example of acyclic negotiation. Despite their apparent simplicity, negotiations may express involved behaviors as shown with the Brexit example. Indeed two important questions in this setting are whether there is some way to reach a final node in the negotiation from (i) the initial node and (ii) any reachable node in the negotiation.

Definition 4 (Soundness and Reachability).

1. *A negotiation is* sound *iff every run from the initial configuration can be extended to a final run. The problem of soundness is to check if a given negotiation is sound.*
2. *The problem of reachability asks if a given negotiation has a final run.*

Notice that the Brexit negotiation of Fig.1 is sound (but not deterministic). It seems hard to preserve the important features of this negotiation while being both sound *and* deterministic. The problem of soundness has received considerable attention. We summarize the results about soudness in the next theorem:

Theorem 1. *Determining whether a negotiation is sound is PSPACE-Complete. For (very-)weakly non-deterministic negotiations, it is co-NP-complete [9]. For acyclic negotiations, it is in DP and co-NP-Hard [6]. Determining whether an acyclic weakly non-deterministic negotiation is sound is in PTIME [3, 9]. Finally, deciding soundness for deterministic negotiations is NLOGSPACE-complete [9].*

Checking reachability is NP-complete, even for deterministic acyclic negotiations (surprisingly, we did not find this result stated before in the literature):

Proposition 1. *Reachability is NP-complete for acyclic negotiations, even if the negotiation is deterministic.*

Proof (sketch). One can guess a run of size $\leq |\mathcal{N}|$ in polynomial time, and verify if it reaches n_f, which gives the inclusion in NP. The hardness part comes from a reduction from 3-CNF-SAT that can be found in the proof of Theorem 3. □

k-Layered Acyclic Negotiations

We introduce a new class of negotiations which has good algorithmic properties, namely k-layered acyclic negotiations, for k fixed. Roughly speaking, nodes of a k-layered acyclic negotiations can be arranged in layers, and these layers contain at most k nodes. Before giving a formal definition, we need to define the depth of nodes in $\mathcal{N}$.

First, a *path* in a negotiation is a sequence of nodes $n_0 \dots n_\ell$ such that for all $i \in \{1, \dots, \ell - 1\}$, there exists p_i, r_i with $n_{i+1} \in \mathcal{X}(n_i, p_i, r_i)$. The *length* of a path $n_0, \dots, n_\ell$ is ℓ. The *depth* depth(n) of a node n is the maximal length of a path from n_0 to n (recall that $\mathcal{N}$ is acyclic, so this number is always finite).

Definition 5. *An acyclic negotiation is* layered *if for all node n, every path reaching n has length depth(n). An acyclic negotiation is k-layered if it is layered, and for all $\ell \in \mathbb{N}$, there are at most k nodes at depth ℓ.*

The Brexit example of Fig. 1 is 6-layered. Notice that a layered negotiation is necessarily k-layered for some $k \leq |\mathcal{N}| - 2$. Note also that we can always transform an acyclic negotiation $\mathcal{N}$ into a layered acyclic negotiation $\mathcal{N}'$, by adding dummy nodes: for every node $m \in \mathcal{X}(n, p, r)$ with depth$(m) >$ depth$(n) + 1$, we can add several nodes $n_1, \dots n_\ell$ with $\ell =$ depth$(m) - ($depth$(n) + 1)$, and processes $P_{n_i} = \{p\}$. We compute a new relation $\mathcal{X}'$ such that $\mathcal{X}'(n, p, r) = \{n_1\}$, $\mathcal{X}(n_\ell, p, r) = \{m\}$ and for every $i \in 1..\ell - 1$, $\mathcal{X}(n_i, p, r) = n_{i+1}$. This transformation is polynomial: the resulting negotiation is of size up to $|\mathcal{N}| \times |\mathcal{X}| \times |P|$. The proof of the following Theorem can be found in [1].

Theorem 2. *Let $k \in \mathbb{N}^+$. Checking reachability or soundness for a k-layered acyclic negotiation $\mathcal{N}$ can be done in PTIME.*

3   Timed Negotiations

In many negotiations, time is an important feature to take into account. For instance, in the Brexit example, with an initial node starting at the begining of September 2019, there are 9 weeks to pass a deal till the 31st October deadline.

   We extend negotiations by introducing timing constraints on outcomes of nodes, inspired by timed Petri nets [14] and by the notion of negotiations with costs [10]. We use time intervals to specify lower and upper bounds for the duration of negotiations. More precisely, we attach time intervals to pairs (n, r) where n is a node and r an outcome. In the rest of the paper, we denote by $\mathcal{I}$ the set of intervals with endpoints that are non-negative integers or ∞. For convenience we only use closed intervals in this paper (except for ∞), but the results we show can also be extended to open intervals with some notational overhead. Intuitively, outcome r can be taken at a node n with associated time interval $[a, b]$ only after a time units have elapsed from the time all processes contributing to n are ready to engage in n, and at most b time units later.

Definition 6. *A* timed negotiation *is a pair $(\mathcal{N}, \gamma)$ where $\mathcal{N}$ is a negotiation, and $\gamma : N \times R \to \mathcal{I}$ associates an interval to each pair (n, r) of node and outcome such that $r \in R_n$. For a given node n and outcome r, we denote by $\gamma^-(n, r)$ (resp. $\gamma^+(n, r)$) the lower bound (resp. the upper bound) of $\gamma(n, r)$.*

Example 2. In the Brexit example, we define the following timed constraints γ. We only specify the outcome names, as the timing only depends upon them. Backstop and no-backstop both take between 1 and 2 weeks: $\gamma(\text{backstop}) = \gamma(\text{no-backstop}) = [1, 2]$. In case of no-court, recess takes 5 weeks $\gamma(\text{recess}) = [5, 5]$, and PM can meet EU immediatly $\gamma(\text{meet}) = [0, 0]$. In case of court action, PM needs to spend 2 weeks in court $\gamma(\text{c-meet}) = [2, 2]$, and depending on the court delay and decision, Pa needs between 3 (court overules recess) to 5 (court confirms recess) weeks, $\gamma(\text{defend}) = [3, 5]$. Agreeing on a deal can take anywhere from 2 weeks to 2 years (104 weeks): $\gamma(\text{deal agreed}) = [2, 104]$—some would say infinite time is even possible! It needs more time with the backstop, $\gamma(\text{deal w/backstop}) = [5, 104]$. All other outcomes are assumed to be immediate, i.e., associated with $[0, 0]$.

Semantics: A *timed valuation* is a map $\mu : P \to \mathbb{R}^{\geq 0}$ that associates a non-negative real value to every process. A *timed configuration* is a pair (M, μ) where M is a configuration and μ a timed valuation. There is a *timed step* from (M, μ) to (M', μ'), denoted $(M, \mu) \xrightarrow{(n,r)} (M', \mu')$, if (i) $M \xrightarrow{(n,r)} M'$, (ii) $p \notin P_n$ implies $\mu'(p) = \mu(p)$ (iii) $\exists d \in \gamma(n, r)$ such that $\forall p \in P_n$, we have $\mu'(p) = \max_{p' \in P_n} \mu(p') + d$ (d is the duration of node n).

   Intuitively a timed step $(M, \mu) \xrightarrow{(n,r)} (M', \mu')$ depicts a decision taken at node n, and how long each process of P_n waited in that node before taking decision (n, r). The last process engaged in n must wait for a duration contained in $\gamma(n, r)$. However, other processes may spend a time greater than $\gamma^+(n, r)$.

A *timed run* is a sequence of steps $\rho = (M_0, \mu_0) \xrightarrow{e_1} (M_1, \mu_1) \ldots (M_k, \mu_k)$ where M_0 is the initial configuration, $\mu_0(p) = 0$ for every $p \in P$, and each $(M_i, \mu_i) \xrightarrow{e_i} (M_{i+1}, \mu_{i+1})$ is a timed step. It is *final* if $M_k = M_f$. Its *execution time* $\delta(\rho)$ is defined as $\delta(\rho) = \max_{p \in P} \mu_k(p)$.

Notice that we only attached timing to processes, not to individual steps. With our definition of runs, timing on steps may not be monotonous (i.e., non-decreasing) along the run, while timing on processes is. Viewed by the lens of concurrent systems, the timing is monotonous on the partial orders of the system rather than the linearization. It is not hard to restrict paths, if necessary, to have a monotonous timing on steps as well. In this paper, we are only interested in execution time, which does not depend on the linearization considered.

Given a timed negotiation $\mathcal{N}$, we can now define the minimum and maximum execution time, which correspond to optimistic or pessimistic views:

Definition 7. *Let $\mathcal{N}$ be a timed negotiation. Its* minimum execution time, *denoted* $mintime(\mathcal{N})$ *is the minimal $\delta(\rho)$ over all final timed run ρ of $\mathcal{N}$. We define the* maximal execution time $maxtime(\mathcal{N})$ *of $\mathcal{N}$ similarly.*

Given $T \in \mathbb{N}$, the main problems we consider in this paper are the following:

- The mintime problem, i.e., do we have $mintime(\mathcal{N}) \leq T$?.
  In other words, does there exist a final timed run ρ with $\delta(\rho) \leq T$?
- The maxtime problem, i.e., do we have $maxtime(\mathcal{N}) \leq T$?.
  In other words, does $\delta(\rho) \leq T$ for every final timed run ρ?

These questions have a practical interest : in the Brexit example, the question "is there a way to have a vote on a deal within 9 weeks ?" is indeed a minimum execution time problem. We also address the equality variant of these decision problems, i.e., $mintime(\mathcal{N}) = T$: is there a final run of $\mathcal{N}$ that terminates in exactly T time units and no other final run takes less than T time units? Similarly for $maxtime(\mathcal{N}) = T$.

Example 3. We use Fig. 1 to show that it is not easy to compute the minimal execution time, and in particular one cannot use the algorithm from [10] to compute it. Consider the node n with $P_n = \{PM, Pa\}$ and $R_n = \{\text{court}, \text{no\_court}\}$. If the outcome is court, then PM needs 2 weeks before (s)he can talk to EU and Pa needs at least 3 weeks before he can debate. However, if the outcome is no_court, then PM need not wait before (s)he can talk to EU, but Pa wastes 5 weeks in recess. This means that one needs to remember different alternatives which could be faster in the end, depending on the future. On the other hand, the algorithm from [10] attaches one minimal time to process Pa, and one minimal time to process PM. No matter the choices (0 or 2 for PM and 3 or 5 for Pa), there will be futures in which the chosen number will over or underapproximate the real minimal execution time (this choice is not explicit in [10])[4].

---

[4] the authors of [10] acknowledged the issue with their algorithm for mintime.

For maximum execution time, it is not an issue to attach to each node a unique maximal execution time. The reason for the asymmetry between minimal and maximal execution times of a negotiation is that the execution time of a path is $\max_{p \in P} \mu_k(p)$, for μ_k the last timed valuation, which breaks the symmetry between min and max.

4 High level view of the main results

In this section, we give a high-level description of our main results. Formal statements can be found in the sections where they are proved. We gather in Fig. 2 the precise complexities for the minimal and the maximal execution time problems for 3 classes of negotiations that we describe in the following. Since we are interested in minimum and maximum execution time, cycles in negotiations can be either bypassed or lead to infinite maximal time. Hence, while we define timed negotiations in general, we always restrict to acyclic negotiations (such as Brexit) while stating and proving results.

In [10], a PTIME algorithm is given to compute different costs for negotiations that are both sound *and* deterministic. One limitation of this result is that it cannot compute the minimum execution time, as explained in Example 3. A second limitation is that the class of sound and deterministic negotiations is quite restrictive: it cannot model situations where the next node a process participates in depends on the outcome from another process, as in the Brexit example. We thus consider classes where one of these restrictions is dropped.

We first consider (Section 5) negotiations that are deterministic, but without the soundness restriction. We show that for this class, no timed problem we consider can be solved in PTIME (unless NP=PTIME). Further, we show that the equality problems $(maxtime/mintime(\mathcal{N}) = T)$, are complete for the complexity class DP, i.e., at the second level of the Boolean Hierarchy [15].

We then consider (Section 6) the class of negotiations that are sound, but not necessarily deterministic. We show that maximum execution time can be solved in PTIME, and propose a new algorithm. However, the minimum execution time cannot be computed in PTIME (unless NP=PTIME). Again for the mintime equality problem we have a matching DP-completeness result.

	Deterministic	Sound	k-layered
Max $\leq T$	co-NP-complete (Thm. 3)	PTIME (Prop. 3)	PTIME (Thm. 6)
Max $= T$	DP-complete (Prop. 2)		
Min $\leq T$	NP-complete (Thm. 3)	NP-complete* (Thm. 5)	pseudo-PTIME (Thm. 8) / NP-complete** (Thm. 7)
Min $= T$	DP-complete (Prop. 2)	DP-complete* (Prop. 4)	pseudo-PTIME (Thm. 8)

Fig. 2. Results for acyclic timed negotiations. *DP* refers to the complexity class, Difference Polynomial time [15], the second level of the Boolean Hierarchy.
* hardness holds even for very weakly non-deterministic negotiations, and T in unary.
** hardness holds even for sound and very weakly non-deterministic negotiations.

Finally, in order to obtain a polytime algorithm to compute the minimum execution time, we consider the class of k-layered negotiations (see Section 7): Given $k \in \mathbb{N}$, we can show that $maxtime(\mathcal{N})$ can be computed in PTIME for k-layered negotiations. We also show that while the $mintime(\mathcal{N}) \leq T$? problem is weakly NP-complete for k-layered negotiations, we can compute $mintime(\mathcal{N})$ in pseudo-PTIME, i.e. in PTIME if constants are given in unary.

5 Deterministic Negotiations

We start by considering the class of deterministic acyclic negotiations. We show that both maximal and minimal execution times cannot be computed in PTIME (unless NP=PTIME), as the threshold problems are (co-)NP-complete.

Theorem 3. *The* $mintime(\mathcal{N}) \leq T$ *decision problem is NP complete, and the* $maxtime(\mathcal{N}) \leq T$ *decision problem is co-NP-complete for acyclic deterministic timed negotiations.*

Proof. For $mintime(\mathcal{N}) \leq T$, containment in NP is easy: we just need to guess a run ρ (of polynomial size as $\mathcal{N}$ is acyclic), consider the associated timed run ρ^- where all decisions are taken at their earliest possible dates, and check whether $\delta(\rho^-) \leq T$, which can be done in time $O(|\mathcal{N}| + \log T)$.

For the hardness, we give the proof in two steps. First, we start with a proof of Proposition 1 that reachability problem is NP-hard using reduction of 3-CNF SAT, i.e., given a formula ϕ, we build a deterministic negotiation $\mathcal{N}_\phi$ s.t. ϕ is satisfiable iff $\mathcal{N}_\phi$ has a final run. In a second step, we introduce timings on this negotiation and show that $mintime(\mathcal{N}_\phi) \leq T$ iff ϕ is satisfiable.

Step 1: Reducing 3-CNF-SAT to Reachability problem.

Given a Boolean formula ϕ with variables $v_i, 1 \leq i \leq n$ and clauses $c_j, 1 \leq j \leq m$, for each variable v_i we define the sets of clauses $S_{i,\mathbf{t}} = \{c_j \mid v_i$ is present in $c_j\}$ and $S_{i,\mathbf{f}} = \{c_j \mid \neg v_i$ is present in $c_j\}$. Clauses in $S_{i,\mathbf{t}}$ and $S_{i,\mathbf{f}}$ are naturally ordered: $c_i < c_j$ iff $i < j$. We denote these elements $S_{i,\mathbf{t}}(1) < S_{i,\mathbf{t}}(2) < \ldots$. Similarly for set $S_{i,\mathbf{f}}$.

Now, we construct a negotiation $\mathcal{N}_\phi$ (as depicted in Figure 3) with a process V_i for each variable v_i and a process C_j for each clause c_j:

- Initial node n_0 has a single outcome r taking each process C_j to node $Lone_{c_j}$, and each process V_i to node $Lone_{v_i}$.
- $Lone_{c_j}$ has three outcomes: if literal $v_i \in c_j$, then t_i is an outcome, taking C_j to $Pair_{c_j,v_i}$, and if literal $\neg v_i \in c_j$, then f_i is an outcome, taking C_j to $Pair_{c_j,\neg v_i}$.
- The outcomes of $Lone_{v_i}$ are $\mathtt{true}$ and $\mathtt{false}$. Outcome $\mathtt{true}$ brings V_i to node $Tlone_{v_i,1}$ and outcome $\mathtt{false}$ brings V_i to node $Flone_{v_i,1}$.
- We have a node $Tlone_{v_i,j}$ for each $j \leq |S_{i,\mathbf{t}}|$ and $Flone_{v_i,j}$ for each $j \leq |S_{i,\mathbf{f}}|$, with V_i as only process. Let $c_r = S_{i,\mathbf{t}}(j)$. Node $Tlone_{v_i,j}$ has two outcomes $vton$ bringing V_i to $Tlone_{v_i,j+1}$ (or n_f if $j = |S_{i,\mathbf{t}}|$), and $vtoc_{i,r}$ bringing V_i to $Pair_{c_r,v_i}$. The two outcomes from $Flone_{v_i,j}$ are similar.

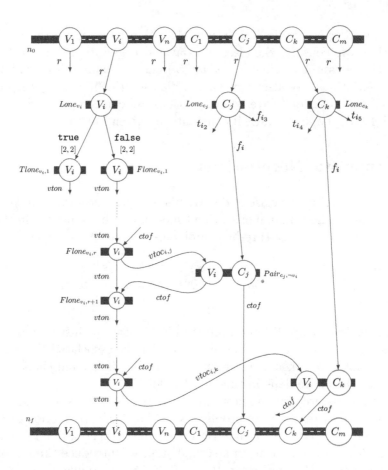

Fig. 3. A part of $\mathcal{N}_\phi$ where clause c_j is $(i_2 \vee \neg i \vee \neg i_3)$ and clause c_k is $(i_4 \vee \neg i \vee i_5)$. Timing is $[0,0]$ whereever not mentioned

– Node $Pair_{c_r,v_i}$ has V_i and C_r as its processes and one outcome $ctof$ which takes process C_r to final node n_f and process V_i to $Tlone_{v_i,j+1}$ (with $c_r = S_{i,\mathbf{t}}(j)$), or to n_f if $j = |S_{i,\mathbf{t}}|$. Node $Pair_{c_r,\neg v_i}$ is defined in the same way from $Flone_{v_i,j}$.

With this we claim that $\mathcal{N}_\phi$ has a final run iff ϕ is satisfiable which completes the first step of the proof. We give a formal proof of this claim in Appendix A of [1]. Observe that the negotiation $\mathcal{N}_\phi$ constructed is deterministic and acyclic (but it is not sound).

Step 2: Before we introduce timing on $\mathcal{N}_\phi$, we introduce a new outcome r' at n_0 which takes all processes to n_f. Now, the timing function γ associated with $\mathcal{N}_\phi$ is: $\gamma(n_0, r) = [2,2]$ and $\gamma(n_0, r') = [3,3]$ and $\gamma(n, r) = [0,0]$, for all node $n \neq n_0$ and all $r \in R_n$. Then, $mintime(\mathcal{N}_\phi) \leq 2$ iff ϕ has a satisfiable assignment: if $mintime(\mathcal{N}_\phi) \leq 2$, there is a run with decision r taken at n_0 which is final. But existence of any such final run implies satisfiability of ϕ. For reverse implication, if ϕ is satisfiable, then the corresponding run for satisfying assignment takes 2 time units, which means that $mintime(\mathcal{N}_\phi) \leq 2$.

Similarly, we can prove that the MaxTime problem is co-NP complete by changing $\gamma(n_0, r') = [1,1]$ and asking if $maxtime(\mathcal{N}_\phi) > 1$ for the new $\mathcal{N}_\phi$. The answer will be yes iff ϕ is satisfiable. $\square$

We now consider the related problem of checking if $mintime(\mathcal{N}) = T$ (or if $maxtime(\mathcal{N}) = T$). These problems are harder than their threshold variant under usual complexity assumptions: they are DP-complete (Difference Polynomial time class, i.e., second level of the Boolean Hierarchy, defined as intersection of a problem in NP and one in co-NP [15]).

Proposition 2. *The $mintime(\mathcal{N}) = T$ and $maxtime(\mathcal{N}) = T$ decision problems are DP-complete for acyclic deterministic negotiations.*

Proof. We only give the proof for *mintime* (the proof for *maxtime* is given in Appendix A of [1]). Indeed, it is easy to see that this problem is in DP, as it can be written as $mintime(\mathcal{N}) \leq T$ which is in NP and $\neg(mintime(\mathcal{N}) \leq T - 1))$, which is in co-NP. To show hardness, we use the negotiation constructed in the above proof as a gadget, and show a reduction from the SAT-UNSAT problem (a standard DP-complete problem).

The SAT-UNSAT Problem asks given two Boolean expressions ϕ and ϕ', both in CNF forms with three literals per clause, is it true that ϕ is satisfiable and ϕ' is unsatisfiable? SAT-UNSAT is known to be DP-complete [15]. We reduce this problem to $mintime(\mathcal{N}) = T$.

Given ϕ, ϕ', we first make the corresponding negotiations $\mathcal{N}_\phi$ and $\mathcal{N}_{\phi'}$ as in the previous proof. Let n_0 and n_f be the initial and final nodes of $\mathcal{N}_\phi$ and n_0' and n_f' be the initial and final nodes of $\mathcal{N}_{\phi'}$. (Similarly, for other nodes we write $'$ above the nodes to signify they belong to $\mathcal{N}_{\phi'}$.)

In the negotiation $\mathcal{N}_{\phi'}$, we introduce a new node n_{all}, in which all the processes participate (see Figure 4). The node n_{all} has a single outcome r'_{all} which sends all the processes to n_f. Also, for node n_0', apart from the outcome r which sends all processes to different nodes, there is another outcome r_{all} which sends all the processes to n_{all}. Now we merge the nodes n_f and n_0' and call the merged node n_{sep}. Also nodes n_0 and n_f' now have all the processes of $\mathcal{N}_\phi$ and $\mathcal{N}_{\phi'}$ participating in them. This merged process gives us a new negotiation $\mathcal{N}_{\phi,\phi'}$ in which the structure above n_{sep} is same as $\mathcal{N}_\phi$ while below it is same as $\mathcal{N}_{\phi'}$. Node n_{sep} now has all the processes of $\mathcal{N}_\phi$ and $\mathcal{N}_{\phi'}$ participating in it. The outcomes of n_{sep} will be same as that of n_0' (r_{all}, r). For both the outcomes of n_{sep} the processes corresponding to $\mathcal{N}_\phi$ directly go to n_f of the $\mathcal{N}_{\phi,\phi'}$. Similarly n_0 of $\mathcal{N}_{\phi,\phi'}$ which is same n_0 of $\mathcal{N}_\phi$, sends processes corresponding to $\mathcal{N}_{\phi'}$ directly to n_{sep} for all its outcomes. We now define timing function γ for $\mathcal{N}_{\phi,\phi'}$ which is as follows: $\gamma(Lone'_{v_i}, r) = [1,1]$ for all $v_i \in \phi'$ and $r \in \{\texttt{true}, \texttt{false}\}$, $\gamma(n_{all}, r'_{all}) = [2,2]$ and $\gamma(n, r) = [0,0]$ for all other outcomes of nodes. With this construction, one can conclude that $mintime(\mathcal{N}_{\phi,\phi'}) = 2$ iff ϕ is satisfiable and ϕ' is unsatisfiable (see [1] for details). This completes the reduction and hence proves DP-hardness. $\square$

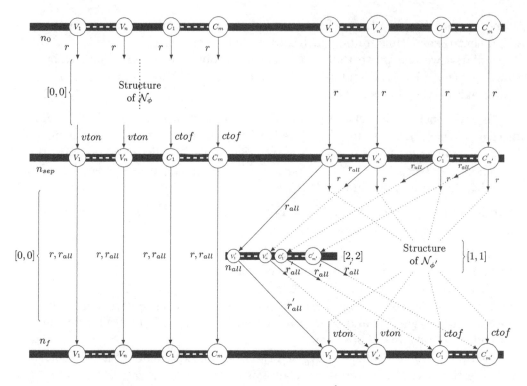

Fig. 4. Structure of $\mathcal{N}_{\phi,\phi'}$

Finally, we consider a related problem of computing the min and max time. To consider the decision variant, we rephrase this problem as checking whether an arbitrary bit of the minimum execution time is 1. Perhaps surprisingly, we obtain that this problem goes even beyond DP, the second level of the Boolean Hierarchy and is in fact hard for Δ_2^P (second level of the *polynomial* hierarchy), which contains the entire Boolean Hierarchy. Formally,

Theorem 4. *Given an acyclic deterministic timed negotiation and a positive integer k, computing the kth bit of the maximum/minimum execution time is Δ_2^P-complete.*

Finally, we remark that if we were interested in the optimization variant and not the decision variant of the problem, the above proof can be adapted to show that these variants are OptP-complete (as defined in [13]). But as optimization is not the focus of this paper, we avoid formal details of this proof.

6   Sound Negotiations

Sound negotiations are negotiations in which every run can be extended to a final run, as in Fig. 1. In this section, we show that $maxtime(\mathcal{N})$ can be computed in PTIME for sound negotiations, hence giving PTIME complexities for the $maxtime(\mathcal{N}) \leq T$? and $maxtime(\mathcal{N}) = T$? questions. However, we show that $mintime(\mathcal{N}) \leq T$ is NP-complete for sound negotiations, and that $mintime(\mathcal{N}) = T$ is DP-complete, even if T is given in unary.

Consider the graph $G_\mathcal{N}$ of a negotiation $\mathcal{N}$. Let $\pi = (n_0, (p_0, r_0), n_1) \cdots$ $(n_k, (p_k, r_k), n_{k+1})$ be a path of $G_\mathcal{N}$. We define the *maximal execution time* of a path π as the value $\delta^+(\pi) = \sum_{i \in 0..k} \gamma^+(n_i, r_i)$. We say that a path $\pi = (n_0, (p_0, r_0), n_1) \cdots (n_\ell, (p_\ell, r_\ell), n_{\ell+1})$ is a path of some run $\rho = (M_1, \mu_1) \xrightarrow{(n_1, r_1')} \cdots (M_k, \mu_k)$ if $r_0, \ldots, r_\ell$ is a subword of $r_1', \ldots, r_k'$.

Lemma 1. *Let $\mathcal{N}$ be an acyclic and sound timed negotiation. Then $maxtime(\mathcal{N})$ $= \max_{\pi \in Paths(G_\mathcal{N})} \delta^+(\pi) + \gamma^+(n_f, r_f)$.*

Proof. Let us first prove that $maxtime(\mathcal{N}) \geq \max_{\pi \in Paths(G_\mathcal{N})} \delta^+(\pi) + \gamma^+(n_f, r_f)$. Consider any path π of $G_\mathcal{N}$, ending in some node n. First, as $\mathcal{N}$ is sound, we can compute a run ρ_π such that π is a path of ρ_π, and ρ_π ends in a configuration in which n is enabled. We associate with ρ_π the timed run ρ_π^+ which associates to every node the latest possible execution date. We have easily $\delta(\rho_\pi^+) \geq \delta^+(\pi)$, and then we obtain $\max_{\pi \in Paths(G_\mathcal{N})} \delta(\rho_\pi^+) \geq \max_{\pi \in Paths(G_\mathcal{N})} \delta^+(\pi)$. As $maxtime(\mathcal{N})$ is the maximal duration over all runs, it is hence necessarily greater than $\max_{\pi \in Paths(G_\mathcal{N})} \delta(\rho_\pi^+) + \gamma^+(n_f, r_f)$.

We now prove that $maxtime(\mathcal{N}) \leq \max_{\pi \in Paths(G_\mathcal{N})} \delta^+(\pi) + \gamma^+(n_f, r_f)$. Take any timed run $\rho = (M_1, \mu_1) \xrightarrow{(n_1, r_1)} \cdots (M_k, \mu_k)$ of $\mathcal{N}$ with a unique maximal node n_k. We show that there exists a path π of ρ such that $\delta(\rho) \leq \delta^+(\pi)$ by induction on the length k of ρ. The initialization is trivial for $k = 1$. Let $k \in \mathbb{N}$. Because n_k is the unique maximal node of ρ, we have $\delta^+(\rho) = \max_{p \in P_{n_k}} \mu_{k-1}(p) + \gamma^+(n_k, r_k)$. We choose one p_{k-1} maximizing $\mu_{k-1}(p)$. Let $\ell < k$ be the maximal index of a decision involving process p_{k-1} (i.e. $p_{k-1} \in P_{n_\ell}$). Now, consider the timed run ρ' subword of ρ, but with n_ℓ as unique maximal node (that is, it is ρ where nodes $n_i, i > \ell$ has been removed, but also where some nodes $n_i, i < \ell$ have been removed if they are not causally before n_ℓ (in particular, $P_{n_i} \cap P_{n_\ell} = \emptyset$).)

By definition, we have that $\delta^+(\rho) = \delta^+(\rho') + \gamma^+(n_\ell, r_\ell) + \gamma^+(n_k, r_k)$. We apply the induction hypothesis on ρ', and obtain a path π' of ρ' ending in n_ℓ such that $\delta^+(\rho') + \gamma^+(n_\ell, r_\ell) \leq \delta^+(\pi')$. It suffices to consider path $\pi = \pi'.(n_\ell, (p_{k-1}, r_\ell), n_k)$ to prove the inductive step $\delta^+(\rho) \leq \delta^+(\pi) + \gamma^+(n_k, r_k)$.

Thus $maxtime(\mathcal{N}) = \max \delta^+(\rho) \leq \max_{\pi \in Paths(G_\mathcal{N})} \delta^+(\pi) + \gamma^+(n_f, r_f)$. $\square$

Lemma 1 gives a way to evaluate the maximal execution time. This amounts to finding a path of maximal weight in an acyclic graph, which is a standard PTIME problem that can be solved using standard max-cost calculation.

Proposition 3. *Computing the maximal execution time for an acyclic sound negotiation $\mathcal{N} = (N, n_0, n_f, \mathcal{X})$ can be done in time $O(|N| + |\mathcal{X}|)$.*

A direct consequence is that $maxtime(\mathcal{N}) \leq T$ and $maxtime(\mathcal{N}) = T$ problems can be solved in polynomial time when $\mathcal{N}$ is sound. Notice that if $\mathcal{N}$ is deterministic but not sound, then Lemma 1 does not hold: we only have an inequality.

We now turn to $mintime(\mathcal{N})$. We show that it is strictly harder to compute for sound negotiations than $maxtime(\mathcal{N})$.

Theorem 5. $mintime(\mathcal{N}) \leq T$ *is NP-complete in the strong sense for sound acyclic negotiations, even if $\mathcal{N}$ is very weakly non-deterministic.*

Proof (sketch). First, we can decide $mintime(\mathcal{N}) \leq T$ in NP. Indeed, one can guess a final (untimed) run ρ of size $\leq |N|$, consider ρ^- the timed run corresponding to ρ where all outcomes are taken at the earliest possible dates, and compute in linear time $\delta(\rho^-)$, and check that $\delta(\rho^-) \leq T$.

The hardness part is obtained by reduction from the **Bin Packing** problem. The reduction is similar to Knapsack, that we will present in Thm. 7. The difference is that we use ℓ bins in parallel, rather than 2 processes, one for the weight and one for the value. The hardness is thus strong, but the negotiation is not k-layered for a bounded k (it is $2\ell + 1$ bounded, with ℓ depending on the input). A detailed proof is given in Appendix B of [1]. □

We show that $mintime(\mathcal{N}) = T$ is harder to decide than $mintime(\mathcal{N}) \leq T$, with a proof similar to Prop. 2.

Proposition 4. *The $mintime(\mathcal{N}) = T$? decision problem is DP-complete for sound acyclic negotiations, even if it is very weakly non-deterministic.*

An open question is whether the minimal execution time can be computed in PTIME if the negotiation is both sound and deterministic. The reduction from Bin Packing does not work with deterministic (and sound) negotiations.

7 k-Layered Negotiations

In this section, we consider k-layeredness, a syntactic property that can be efficiently verified (see Section 2).

7.1   Algorithmic properties

Let k be a fixed integer. We first show that the maximum execution time can be computed in PTIME for k-layered negotiations. Let N_i be the set of nodes at layer i. We define for every layer i the set S_i of subsets of nodes $X \subseteq N_i$ which can be jointly enabled and such that for every process p, there is exactly one node $n(X, p)$ in X with $p \in n(X, p)$. An element X in S_i is a subset of nodes that can be selected by solving all non-determnism with an appropriate choice of outcomes. Formally, we define S_i inductively. We start with $S_0 = \{n_0\}$. We then define S_{i+1} from the contents of layer S_i: we have $Y \in S_{i+1}$ iff $\bigcup_{n \in Y} P_n = P$ and there exist $X \in S_i$ and an outcome $r_m \in R_m$ for every $m \in X$, such that $n \in \mathcal{X}(n(X, p), p, r_m)$ for each $n \in Y$ and $p \in P_n$.

Theorem 6. *Let $k \in \mathbb{N}^+$. Computing the maximum execution time for a k-layered acyclic negotiation $\mathcal{N}$ can be done in PTIME. More precisely, the worst-case time complexity is $O(|P| \cdot |\mathcal{N}|^{k+1})$.*

Proof (Sketch). The first step is to compute S_i layer by layer, by following its inductive definition. The set S_i is of size at most 2^k, as $|N_i| < k$ by definition of k-layeredness. Knowing S_i, it is easy to build S_{i+1} by induction. This takes time in $O(|P||\mathcal{N}|^{k+1})$: We need to consider all k-uples of outcomes for each layer. There can be $|\mathcal{N}|^k$ such tuples. We need to do that for all processes ($|P|$), and for all layers (at most $|\mathcal{N}|$).

We then keep for each subset $X \in S_i$ and each node $n \in X$, the maximal time $f_i(n, X) \in \mathbb{N}$ associated with n and X. From S_{i+1} and f_i, we inductively compute f_{i+1} in the following way: for all $X \in S_i$ with successor $Y \in S_{i+1}$ for outcomes $(r_p)_{p \in P}$, we denote $f_{i+1}(Y, n, X) = \max_{p \in P(n)} f_i(X, n(X, p)) + \gamma^+(n(X, p), r_p)$. If there are several choices of $(r_p)_{p \in P}$ leading to the same Y, we take r_p with the maximal $f_i(X, n(X, p)) + \gamma^+(n(X, p), r_p)$. We then define $f_{i+1}(Y, n) = \max_{X \in S_i} f_{i+1}(Y, n, X)$. Again, the initialization is trivial, with $f_0(\{n_0\}, n_0) = 0$. The maximal execution time of $\mathcal{N}$ is $f(\{n_f\}, n_f)$. $\qquad\square$

We can bound the complexity precisely by $O(d(\mathcal{N}) \cdot C(\mathcal{N}) \cdot ||R||^{k^*})$, with:

- $d(\mathcal{N}) \leq |\mathcal{N}|$ the depth of n_f, that is the number of layers of $\mathcal{N}$, and $||R||$ is the maximum number of outcomes of a node,
- $C(\mathcal{N}) = \max_i |S_i| \leq 2^k$, which we will call the *number of contexts of* $\mathcal{N}$, and which is often much smaller than 2^k.
- $k^* = \max_{X \in \bigcup_i S_i} |X| \leq k$. We say that $\mathcal{N}$ is k^*-*thread bounded*, meaning that there cannot be more that k^* nodes in the same context X of any layer. Usually, k^* is strictly smaller than $k = \max_i |N_i|$, as $N_i = \bigcup_{X \in S_i} X$.

Consider again the Brexit example Figure 1. We have $(k + 1) = 7$, while we have the depth $d(\mathcal{N}) = 6$, the negotiation is $k^* = 3$-thread bounded (k^* is bounded by the number of processes), $||R|| = 2$, and the number of contexts is at most $C(\mathcal{N}) = 4$ (EU chooses to enforce backstop or not, and Pa chooses to go to court or not).

7.2   Minimal Execution Time

As with sound negotiations, computing minimal time is much harder than computing the maximal time for k-layered negotiations:

Theorem 7. *Let $k \geq 6$. The Min $\leq T$ problem is NP-Complete for k-layered acyclic negotiations, even if the negotiation is sound and very weakly non-deterministic.*

Proof. One can guess in polynomial time a final run of size $\leq |\mathcal{N}|$. If the execution time of this final run is smaller than T then we have found a final run witnessing $mintime(\mathcal{N}) \leq T$. Hence the problem is in NP.

Let us now show that the problem is NP-hard. We proceed by reduction from the **Knapsack** decision problem. Let us consider a set of items $U = \{u_1, \ldots u_n\}$ of respective values $v_1, \ldots v_n$ and weight $w_1, \ldots, w_n$ and a knapsack of maximal capacity W. The knapsack problem asks, given a value V whether there exists a subset of items $U' \subseteq U$ such that $\sum_{u_i \in U'} v_i \geq V$ and such that $\sum_{u_i \in U'} w_i \leq W$.

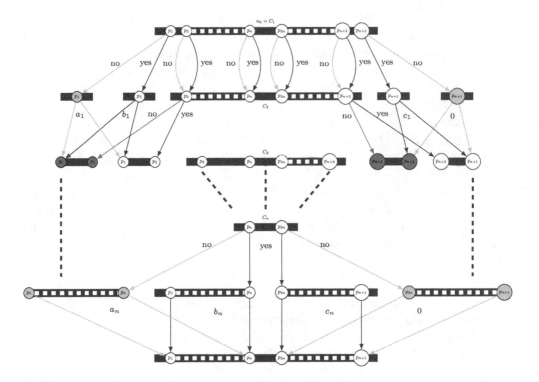

Fig. 5. The negotiation encoding Knapsack

We build a negotiation with $2n$ processes $P = \{p_1, \ldots p_{2n}\}$, as shown in Fig. 5. Intuitively, $p_i, i \leq n$ will serve to encode the value of selected items as timing, while $p_i, i > n$ will serve to encode the weight of selected items as timing.

Concerning timing constraints for outcomes we do the following: Outcomes 0, yes and no are associated with $[0, 0]$. Outcome c_i is associated with $[w_i, w_i]$, the weight of u_i. Last, outcome b_i is associated with a more complex function, such that $\sum_i b_i \leq W$ iff $\sum_i v_i \geq V$. For that, we set $\left[\frac{(v_{max} - v_i)W}{n \cdot v_{max} - V}, \frac{v_{max}W}{n \cdot v_{max} - v_i}\right]$ for outcome b_i, where v_{max} is the largest value of an item, and V is the total value we want to reach at least. Also, we set $\left[\frac{(v_{max})W}{n \cdot v_{max} - V}, \frac{v_{max}W}{n \cdot v_{max} - v_i}\right]$ for outcome a_i. We set $T = W$, the maximal weight of the knapsack.

Now, consider a final run ρ in $\mathcal{N}$. The only choices in ρ are outcomes yes or no from $C_1, \ldots, C_n$. Let I be the set of indices such that yes is the outcome from all C_i in this path. We obtain $\delta(\rho) = \max(\sum_{i \notin I} a_i + \sum_{i \in I} b_i, \sum_{i \in I} c_i)$. We have $\delta(\rho) \leq T = W$ iff $\sum_{i \in I} w_i \leq W$, that is the sum of the weights is lower than W, and $\sum_{i \notin I} \frac{(v_{max})W}{n \cdot v_{max} - V} + \sum_{i \in I} \frac{(v_{max} - v_i)W}{n \cdot v_{max} - V} \leq W$. That is, $n \cdot v_{max} - \sum_{i \in I} v_i \leq n \cdot v_{max} - V$, i.e. $\sum_{i \in I} v_i \geq V$. Hence, there exists a path ρ with $\delta(\rho) \leq T = W$ iff there exists a set of items of weight less than W and of value more than V. $\square$

It is well known that Knapsack is weakly NP-hard, that is, it is NP-hard only when weights/values are given in binary. This means that Thm. 7 shows that minimum execution time $\leq T$ is NP-hard only when T is given in binary. We can actually show that for k-layered negotiations, the $mintime(\mathcal{N}) \leq T$ problem can be decided in PTIME if T is given in unary (i.e. if T is not too large):

Theorem 8. *Let $k \in \mathbb{N}$. Given a k-layered negotiation $\mathcal{N}$ and T written in unary, one can decide in PTIME whether the minimum execution time of $\mathcal{N}$ is $\leq T$. The worst-case time complexity is $O(|\mathcal{N}| \cdot |P| \cdot (T \cdot |\mathcal{N}|)^k)$.*

Proof. We will remember for each layer i a set $\mathcal{T}_i$ of functions τ from nodes N_i of layer i to a value in $\{1, \ldots, T, \bot\}$. Basically, we have $\tau \in \mathcal{T}_i$ if there exists a path ρ reaching $X = \{n \in N_i \mid \tau(n) \neq \bot\}$, and this path reaches node $n \in X$ after $\tau(n)$ time units. As for S_i, for all p, we should have a unique node $n(\tau, p)$ such that $p \in n(\tau, p)$ and $\tau(n(\tau, p)) \neq \bot$. Again, it is easy to initialize $\mathcal{T}_0 = \{\tau_0\}$, with $\tau_0(n_0) = 0$, and $\tau_0(n) = \bot$ for all $n \neq n_0$.

Inductively, we build $\mathcal{T}_{i+1}$ in the following way: $\tau_{i+1} \in \mathcal{T}_{i+1}$ iff there exists a $\tau_i \in \mathcal{T}_i$ and $r_p \in R_{n(\tau_i, p)}$ for all $p \in P$ such that for all n with $\tau_{i+1}(n) \neq \bot$, we have $\tau_{i+1}(n) = \max_p \tau_i^-(n(\tau_i, p)) + \gamma(n(\tau_i, p), r_p)$.

We have that the minimum execution time for $\mathcal{N}$ is $\min_{\tau \in \mathcal{T}_n} \tau(n_\tau)$, for n the depth of n_f. There are at most T^k functions τ in any $\mathcal{T}_i$, and there are at most $|\mathcal{N}|$ layers to consider, giving the complexity. $\square$

As with Thm. 6, we can more accurately state the complexity as $O(d(\mathcal{N}) \cdot C(\mathcal{N}) \cdot ||R||^{k^*} \cdot T^{k^*-1})$. The $k^* - 1$ is because we only need to remember minimal functions $\tau \in \mathcal{T}_i$: if $\tau'(n) \geq \tau(n)$ for all n, then we do not need to keep τ' in $\mathcal{T}_i$. In particular, for the knapsack encoding in the proof of Thm. 7, we have $k^* = 3$, $||R|| = 2$ and $C(\mathcal{N}) = 4$. Notice that if k is part of the input, then the problem is strongly NP-hard, even if T is given in unary, as e.g. encoding bin packing with ℓ bins result to a $2\ell + 1$-layered negotiations.

8   Conclusion

In this paper, we considered timed negotiations. We believe that time is of the essence in negotiations, as examplified by the Brexit negotiation. It is thus important to be able to compute in a tractable way the minimal and maximal execution time of negotiations. We showed that we can compute in PTIME the maximal execution time for acyclic negotiations that are either sound or k-layered, for k fixed. We showed that we cannot compute in PTIME the maximal execution time for negotiations that are not sound nor k-layered, even if they are deterministic and acyclic (unless NP=PTIME). We also showed that surprisingly, computing the minimal execution time is much harder, with strong NP-hardness results in most of the classes of negotiations, contradicting a claim in [10]. We came up with a new reasonable class of negotiations, namely k-layered negotiations, which enjoys a pseudo PTIME algorithm to compute the minimal execution time. That is, the algorithm is PTIME when the timing constants are given in unary. We showed that this restriction is necessary, as the problem becomes NP-hard for constants given in binary, even when the negotiation is sound and very weakly non-deterministic. The problem to know whether the minimal execution time can be computed in PTIME for deterministic and sound negotiation remains open.

References

1. S. Akshay, B. Genest, L. Hélouët, and S. Mital. Timed Negotiations (extended version). In *Research report, https://hal.inria.fr/hal-02337887*, 2020.

2. J. Desel. Reduction and Design of Well-behaved Concurrent Systems. In *CONCUR '90, Theories of Concurrency: Unification and Extension, Amsterdam, The Netherlands, August 27-30, 1990, Proceedings*, volume 458 of *Lecture Notes in Computer Science*, pages 166–181. Springer, 1990.

3. J. Desel, J. Esparza, and P. Hoffmann. Negotiation as Concurrency Primitive. *Acta Inf.*, 56(2):93–159, 2019.

4. J. Esparza. Decidability and Complexity of Petri Net Problems - An Introduction. In *Lectures on Petri Nets I: Basic Models, Advances in Petri Nets, Dagstuhl, September 1996*, volume 1491 of *Lecture Notes in Computer Science*, pages 374–428. Springer, 1998.

5. J. Esparza and J. Desel. *Free Choice Petri Nets*. Cambridge University Press, 1995.

6. J. Esparza and J. Desel. On Negotiation as Concurrency Primitive. In *CONCUR 2013 - Concurrency Theory - 24th International Conference, CONCUR 2013, Buenos Aires, Argentina, August 27-30, 2013. Proceedings*, volume 8052 of *Lecture Notes in Computer Science*, pages 440–454. Springer, 2013.

7. J. Esparza and J. Desel. On Negotiation as Concurrency Primitive II: Deterministic Cyclic Negotiations. In *FOSSACS'14*, volume 8412 of *Lecture Notes in Computer Science*, pages 258–273. Springer, 2014.

8. J. Esparza and P. Hoffmann. Reduction Rules for Colored Workflow Nets. In *Fundamental Approaches to Software Engineering - 19th International Conference, FASE 2016, Held as Part of the European Joint Conferences on Theory and Practice of Software, ETAPS 2016, Eindhoven, The Netherlands, April 2-8, 2016, Proceedings*, volume 9633 of *Lecture Notes in Computer Science*, pages 342–358. Springer, 2016.

9. J. Esparza, D. Kuperberg, A. Muscholl, and I. Walukiewicz. Soundness in Negotiations. *Logical Methods in Computer Science*, 14(1), 2018.

10. J. Esparza, A. Muscholl, and I. Walukiewicz. Static Analysis of Deterministic Negotiations. In *32nd Annual ACM/IEEE Symposium on Logic in Computer Science, LICS 2017, Reykjavik, Iceland, June 20-23, 2017*, pages 1–12, 2017.

11. S. Haddad. A Reduction Theory for Coloured Nets. In *Advances in Petri Nets 1989*, volume 424 of *Lecture Notes in Computer Science*, pages 209–235. Springer, 1990.

12. P. Hoffmann. Negotiation Games. In Javier Esparza and Enrico Tronci, editors, *Proceedings Sixth International Symposium on Games, Automata, Logics and Formal Verification, GandALF 2015, Genoa, Italy, 21-22nd September 2015.*, volume 193 of *EPTCS*, pages 31–42, 2015.

13. M. W. Krentel. The Complexity of Optimization Problems. *Journal of computer and system sciences*, 36(3):490–509, 1988.

14. P.M. Merlin. *A Study of the Recoverability of Computing Systems*. PhD thesis, University of California, Irvine, CA, USA, 1974.

15. C. H. Papadimitriou and M. Yannakakis. The Complexity of Facets (and Some Facets of Complexity). In *Proceedings of the Fourteenth Annual ACM Symposium on Theory of Computing*, STOC '82, pages 255–260, New York, NY, USA, 1982. ACM.

16. R.H. Sloan and U.A. Buy. Reduction Rules for Time Petri Nets. *Acta Inf.*, 33(7):687–706, 1996.

Ambiguity, Weakness and Regularity in Probabilistic Büchi Automata

Christof Löding and Anton Pirogov(✉) (iD) *

RWTH Aachen University, Templergraben 55, 52062 Aachen, Germany
{loeding,pirogov}@cs.rwth-aachen.de

Abstract. Probabilistic Büchi automata are a natural generalization of PFA to infinite words, but have been studied in-depth only rather recently and many interesting questions are still open. PBA are known to accept, in general, a class of languages that goes beyond the regular languages. In this work we extend the known classes of restricted PBA which are still regular, strongly relying on notions concerning ambiguity in classical ω-automata. Furthermore, we investigate the expressivity of the not yet considered but natural class of weak PBA, and we also show that the regularity problem for weak PBA is undecidable.

Keywords: probabilistic · Büchi · automata · ambiguity · weak

1 Introduction

Probabilistic finite automata (PFA) are defined similarly to nondeterministic finite automata (NFA) with the difference that each transition is equipped with a probability (a value between 0 and 1), such that for each pair of state and letter, the probabilities of the corresponding outgoing transitions sum up to 1. PFA have been investigated already in the 1960ies in the seminal paper of Rabin [18]. But while the development of the theory of automata on infinite words also started around the same time [7], the model of probabilistic automata on infinite words has first been studied systematically in [3]. The central model in this theory is the one of probabilistic Büchi automata (PBA), which are syntactically the same as PFA. The acceptance condition for runs is defined as for standard nondeterministic Büchi automata (NBA): a run on an infinite word is accepting if it visits an accepting state infinitely often (see [23,24] for an introduction to the theory of automata on infinite words). In general, for probabilistic automata one distinguishes different criteria of when a word is accepted. In the positive semantics, it is required that the probability of the set of accepting runs is greater than 0, in the almost-sure semantics it has to be 1, and in the threshold semantics it has to be greater than a given value λ between 0 and 1. It is easy to see that PFA with positive or almost-sure semantics can only accept regular languages, because these conditions correspond to the fact that there is an accepting run or that all runs are accepting. For infinite words the situation is different, because single runs on infinite words can have probability 0. Therefore, the existence of an accepting run is not the same as the set of accepting runs having probability greater than 0 (similarly, almost-sure semantics is not equivalent to all runs being accepting). And in fact, it turns out that PBA with positive (or almost-sure) semantics can accept non-regular languages [3]. This naturally raises the question under which conditions a PBA accepts a regular language.

In [3] a subclass of PBA that accept only regular languages (under positive semantics) is introduced, called uniform PBA. The definition uses a semantic condition on the acceptance probabilities in end components of the PBA. A syntactic class of PBA that accepts only regular languages (under positive and almost-sure semantics) are the hierarchical PBA (HPBA) introduced in [8]. The state space of HPBA is partitioned into a sequence of layers such that for each pair of state and letter there is at most one transition that does not increase the layer. Decidability and expressiveness questions for HPBA have been studied in more detail in [11,10]. While HPBA accept only regular languages for positive and almost-sure semantics, it is not very hard to come up with HPBA that accept non-regular languages under the threshold semantics [8,11] (see also the example in Figure 2(a) on page 10). Restricting HPBA further such that there are only two layers and all accepting states are on the first layer leads to a class of PBA (called simple PBA, SPBA) that accept only regular languages even under threshold semantics [9].

In this paper, we are also interested in the question under which conditions PBA accept only regular languages. We identify syntactical patterns in the transition structure of PBA whose absence guarantees regularity of the accepted language. These patterns have been used before for the classification of the degree of ambiguity of NFA and NBA [25,19,16]. The degree of ambiguity of a nondeterministic automaton corresponds to the maximal number of accepting runs that a single input word can have. For NBA, the ambiguity can (roughly) be uncountable, countable, or finite. For positive semantics, we show that PBA whose transition structure corresponds to at most countably ambiguous NBA, accept only regular languages. For almost-sure semantics, we need a slightly stronger condition for ensuring regularity. But both classes that we identify are easily seen to strictly subsume the class of HPBA. For the emptiness and universality problems for these classes we obtain the same complexities as the ones for HPBA. In the case of threshold semantics, we show that finite ambiguity is a sufficient condition for regularity of the accepted language, generalizing a corresponding result for PFA from [12]. The class of finitely ambiguous PBA strictly subsumes the class of SPBA.

Besides the relation between regularity and ambiguity in PBA, we also investigate the class of weak PBA (abbreviated PWA). In weak Büchi automata, the set of accepting states is a union of strongly connected components of the automaton. We show that PWA with almost-sure semantics define the same class of languages as PBA with almost-sure semantics (which implies that with positive semantics PWA define the same class as probabilistic co-Büchi automata).

This is in correspondence to results for non-probabilistic automata: weak automata with universal semantics (a word is accepted if all runs are accepting) define the same class as Büchi automata with universal semantics, and nondeterministic weak automata correspond to nondeterministic co-Büchi automata (see, e.g., [17], where weak automata are called weak parity automata). Furthermore, it is known that universal Büchi automata, respectively nondeterministic co-Büchi automata, can be transformed into equivalent deterministic automata (with the same acceptance condition). An analogue of deterministic automata in the probabilistic setting are the so-called 0/1 automata, in which each word is either accepted with probability 0 or with probability 1. It is known that almost-sure PBA can be transformed into equivalent 0/1 PBA (see the proof of Theorem 4.13 in [4]). Concerning weak automata, a language can be accepted by a deterministic weak automaton (DWA) if, and only if, it can be accepted by a deterministic Büchi and by a deterministic co-Büchi automaton (this follows from results in [14], see [6] for a more direct construction). We show an analogous result in the probabilistic setting: The class of languages defined by 0/1 PWA corresponds to the intersection of the two classes defined by PWA with almost-sure semantics and with positive semantics, respectively. It turns out that this class contains only regular languages, that is, 0/1 PWA define the same class as DWA.

We also show that the regularity problem for PBA is undecidable (the problem of deciding for a given PBA whether its language is regular). For PBA with positive semantics this is not surprising, as for those already the emptiness problem is undecidable [4]. However, for PBA with almost-sure semantics the emptiness and universality problems are decidable [1,2,8]. We show that regularity is undecidable already for PWA with almost-sure or with positive semantics. The proof also yields that it is undecidable for a fixed regular language whether a given PWA accepts this language.

This work is organized as follows. After introducing basic notations in Section 2 we first characterize various regular subclasses of PBA that we derive from ambiguity patterns in Section 3 and then we derive some related complexity results in Section 4. In Section 5 we present our results concerning weak probabilistic automata and in Section 6 we conclude.

2   Preliminaries

First we briefly review some basic definitions.

If Σ is a finite alphabet, then Σ^* is the set of all finite and Σ^ω is the set of all infinite *words* $w = w_0 w_1 \ldots$ with $w_i \in \Sigma$. For a word w we denote by $w(i)$ the i-th symbol w_i.

Classical automata used in this work have usually the shape $(Q, \Sigma, \Delta, Q_0, F)$, where Q is a finite set of states, Σ a finite alphabet, $\Delta \subseteq Q \times \Sigma \times Q$ is the transition relation and $Q_0, F \subseteq Q$ are the sets of initial and final states, respectively.

We write $\Delta(p, a) := \{q \in Q \mid (p, a, q) \in \Delta\}$ to denote the set of *successors* of $p \in Q$ on symbol $a \in \Sigma$, and $\Delta(P, w)$ for $P \subseteq Q, w \in \Sigma^*$ with the usual meaning, i.e., states reachable on word w from any state in P.

A *run* of an automaton on a word $w \in \Sigma^\omega$ is an infinite sequence of states $q_0, q_1, \ldots$ starting in some $q_0 \in Q_0$ such that $(q_i, w(i), q_{i+1}) \in \Delta$ for all $i \geq 0$. We say that a set of runs is *separated (at time i)* when the prefixes of length i of those runs are pairwise different.

As usual, an automaton is *deterministic* if $|Q_0| = 1$ and $|\Delta(p, a)| \leq 1$ for all $p \in Q, a \in \Sigma$, and *nondeterministic* otherwise. For deterministic automata we may use a transition function $\delta : Q \times \Sigma \to Q$ instead of a relation.

Probabilistic automata we consider have the shape $(Q, \Sigma, \delta, \mu_0, F)$, i.e., the transition relation is replaced by a function $\delta : Q \times \Sigma \times Q \to [0, 1]$ which for each state and symbol assigns a probability distribution on successor states (i.e. $\sum_{q \in Q} \delta(p, a, q) = 1$ for all $p \in Q, a \in \Sigma$), and $\mu_0 : Q \to [0, 1]$ with $\sum_{q \in Q} \mu_0(q) = 1$ is the initial probability distribution on states. The *support* of a distribution μ is the set $\mathsf{supp}(\mu) := \{x \mid \mu(x) > 0\}$. Similarly as above, we may write $\delta(\mu, w)$ and mean the resulting probability distribution after reading $w \in \Sigma^*$, when starting with probability distribution μ.

For a probabilistic automaton $\mathcal{A}$ the *underlying automaton* $\mathcal{A}^\lhd$ is given by recovering the transition relation $\Delta := \{(p, x, q) \mid \delta(p, x, q) > 0\}$ of positively reachable states and the initial state set $Q_0 := \mathsf{supp}(\mu_0)$.

As usual, a run of an automaton for finite words is *accepting* if it ends in a final state. For automata on infinite words, run acceptance is determined by the Büchi (run visits infinitely many final states) or Co-Büchi (run visits finitely many final states) conditions.

We write $p \xrightarrow{x} q$ if there exists a path from p to q labelled by $x \in \Sigma^+$ and $p \to q$ if there exists some x such that $p \xrightarrow{x} q$. The *strongly connected component (SCC)* of $p \in Q$ is $\mathsf{scc}(p) := \{q \in Q \mid p = q \text{ or } p \to q \text{ and } q \to p\}$. The set $\mathsf{SCCs}(\mathcal{A}) := \{\mathsf{scc}(q) \mid q \in Q\}$ is the set of all SCCs and partitions Q. An SCC is *accepting (rejecting)* if all (no) runs that stay there forever are accepting. An SCC is *useless* if no accepting run can continue from there. An automaton is *weak*, if the set of final states is a union of its SCCs. In this case, Büchi and Co-Büchi acceptance are equivalent and we treat weak automata as Büchi automata.

A classical automaton is *trim* if it has no useless SCCs, whereas a probabilistic automaton is trim if it has at most one useless SCC, which is a rejecting sink that we canonically call q_{rej}. We assume w.l.o.g. that all considered automata are trim, which also means that in an underlying automaton the sink q_{rej} is removed.

We call transitions of probabilistic automata that have probability 1 *deterministic* and otherwise *branching*. If there are transitions $p \xrightarrow{a} q$ and $p \xrightarrow{a} q'$ with $q \neq q'$, we call this pattern a *fork*. Every branching transition clearly has at least one fork. We call a (p, q, q') fork *intra-SCC*, if p, q, q' are all in the same SCC, otherwise it is an *inter-SCC* fork. A run of an automaton is *deterministic* if it never goes through forks, and *limit-deterministic* if it goes only through finitely many forks. We say that two deterministic runs *merge* when they reach the same state simultaneously. For a finite run prefix ρ, we call all valid runs with this prefix *continuations* of ρ.

A classical automaton $\mathcal{A}$ *accepts* $w \in \Sigma^\omega$ if there exists an accepting run on w, and the language $L(\mathcal{A})$ *recognized* by $\mathcal{A}$ is the set of all accepted words. If P is a set of states of an automaton, we write $L(P)$ for the language accepted by this automaton with initial state set P. For sets consisting of one state q, we write $L(q)$ instead of $L(\{q\})$.

For a probabilistic automaton $\mathcal{A}$ and an input word w (finite or infinite), the transition structure of $\mathcal{A}$ induces a probability space on the set of runs of $\mathcal{A}$ on w in the usual way. We do not provide the details here but rather refer the reader not familiar with these concepts to [4]. In general, we write $\Pr(E)$ for the probability of a measurable event E in a probability space. For probabilistic automata, we consider *positive, almost-sure* and *threshold* semantics, i.e., an automaton accepts w if the probability of the set of accepting runs on w is > 0, $=1$ or $>\lambda$ (for some fixed $\lambda \in]0, 1[$), respectively. For an automaton $\mathcal{A}$ these languages are denoted by $L^{>0}(\mathcal{A}), L^{=1}(\mathcal{A})$ and $L^{>\lambda}(\mathcal{A})$, respectively, whereas $L(\mathcal{A}) := L(\mathcal{A}^{\lhd})$ is the language of the underlying automaton. A probabilistic automaton is $0/1$ if all words are accepted with either probability 0 or 1 (in this case the languages with the different probabilistic semantics coincide).

To denote the type of an automaton, we use abbreviations of the form $\text{XYA}^{(\gamma)}$ where the type of transition structure is denoted by $\text{X} \in \{$ D (det.), N (nondet.), P (prob.) $\}$, the acceptance condition is specified by $\text{Y} \in \{$ F (finite word), B (Büchi), C (Co-Büchi), W (Weak) $\}$, and for probabilistic transitions the semantics for acceptance is given by $\gamma \in \{>0, =1, >\lambda, 0/1\}$.

By $\mathbb{L}^{(\gamma)}(\text{XYA})$ we denote the whole class of languages accepted by the corresponding type of automaton. If $\mathbb{L}$ is a set of languages, then $\overline{\mathbb{L}}$ denotes the set of all complement languages (similarly, for a language L, we denote by $\overline{L}$ its complement), and $\text{BCl}(\mathbb{L})$ the set of all finite boolean combinations of languages in $\mathbb{L}$. We use the notion of *regular language* for finite words and for infinite words (the type of words is always clear from the context).

3 Ambiguity of PBA

Ambiguity of automata refers to the number of different accepting runs on a word or on all words. An automaton is *finitely ambiguous* (on w) if there are at most k different accepting runs (on w) for some fixed $k \in \mathbb{N}$, and in case of at most one accepting run it is called *unambiguous*. If on each word there are only finitely many accepting runs, but no constant upper bound over all words, then it is *polynomially ambiguous* if the number of different run prefixes that are possible for any word prefix of length n can be bounded by a polynomial in n, and otherwise *exponentially ambiguous*. Finally, if if there exist words that have infinitely many runs, but no word on which there are uncountably many accepting runs, then it is *countably ambiguous*, and otherwise it is *uncountably ambiguous*.

In [16] (see also [19]), a syntactic characterization of those classes is presented for NBA by simple patterns of states and transitions. We define those patterns here and refer to [16] for further details. An automaton $\mathcal{A}$ has an *IDA pattern* if there exist two states $p \neq q$ and a word $v \in \Sigma^*$ such that $p \overset{v}{\to} p$, $p \overset{v}{\to} q$ and $q \overset{v}{\to} q$. If additionally $q \in F$, then this is also an IDA_F pattern. Finally, $\mathcal{A}$ has an *EDA pattern* if there exists a state p and $v \in \Sigma^*$ such that there are two different paths $p \overset{v}{\to} p$, and if additionally $p \in F$, this is also an EDA_F pattern. If a PBA has no EDA pattern, we call it *flat*, reflecting the naming of a similar concept in other kinds of transition systems (e.g. [15]). The names IDA and EDA abbreviate "infinite/exponential degree of ambiguity", which they indicated in the original NFA setting, and we keep those names for consistency.

By k-NBA, n^k-NBA, 2^n-NBA, $\aleph_0$-NBA we denote the subsets of at most finitely, polynomially, exponentially and countably ambiguous NBA (and similarly for other types of automata). When speaking about ambiguity of some PBA $\mathcal{A}$, we mean the ambiguity of the trimmed underlying NBA $\mathcal{A}^\lhd$.

In [8], hierarchical PBA (HPBA) were identified as a syntactic restriction on PBA which ensures regularity under positive and almost-sure semantics. A PBA with a unique initial state is hierarchical, if it admits a ranking on the states such that at most one successor on a symbol has the same rank, and no successor has a smaller rank. A HPBA has k levels if it can be ranked with only k different values. Simple PBA (SPBA) were introduced in [9] and are restricted HPBA with two levels such that all accepting states are on level 0.

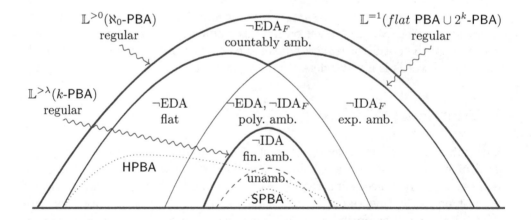

Fig. 1: Illustration of the automata classes with restricted ambiguity as presented for NBA in [16], which are characterized by the absence of the state patterns IDA, IDA_F, EDA, and EDA_F and their relation to the restricted classes called "Hierarchical PBA" (HPBA) [8] and "Simple PBA" (SPBA) [9]. We identify classes in this hierarchy which can be seen as extensions "in spirit" of respectively SPBA and HPBA, subsuming them while also preserving their good properties, as e.g. definition by syntactic means, regularity under different semantics and several complexity results.

First, we show how HPBA relate to the ambiguity hierarchy, which can easily be derived by inspection of the definitions. A visual illustration is given in Figure 1.

Proposition 1 (Relation of HPBA and the ambiguity hierarchy).

1. HPBA $\subset$ *flat PBA* $\subset \aleph_0$-PBA.
2. k-PBA $\nsubseteq$ HPBA *and* HPBA $\nsubseteq k$-PBA.
3. SPBA $\subset$ *unambiguous PBA* $\subset k$-PBA.

Starting from these observations, this work was motivated by the question whether the ambiguity restrictions, which were only implicit in HPBA and SPBA, can be used explicitly to get larger classes with good properties. In the following we will positively answer this question.

3.1   From classical to probabilistic automata

First, we observe that probabilistic automata can recognize regular languages even under severe ambiguity restrictions.

Proposition 2. *Let $\mathcal{A}$ be a DBA. Then there exists an unambiguous PBA $\mathcal{B}$ such that $L^{>0}(\mathcal{B}) = L^{=1}(\mathcal{B}) = L(\mathcal{A})$.*

Proof. As $\mathcal{A}$ is a (w.l.o.g. complete) DBA, there exists exactly one run on each word and all transitions when seen as PBA must have probability 1. Clearly this unique natural $0/1$ PBA obtained from $\mathcal{A}$ accepts the same language under both probable and almost-sure semantics and it is trivially unambiguous.   □

Limit-deterministic NBA (LDBA) are NBA which are deterministic in all non-rejecting SCCs. The natural mapping of LDBA into PBA [4, Lemma 4.2] already trivially yields countably ambiguous automata (because the deterministic part of the LDBA cannot contain an EDA_F pattern, which implies uncountable ambiguity [16]). The following result shows that already unambiguous PBA under positive semantics suffice for all regular languages.

Theorem 1. *Let $L \subseteq \Sigma^\omega$ be a regular language.*
Then there exists an unambiguous PBA $\mathcal{B}$ such that $L^{>0}(\mathcal{B}) = L$.

Proof (sketch). Let $\mathcal{A} = (Q, \Sigma, \delta, q_0, c)$ be a deterministic parity automaton accepting L, i.e., a finite automaton with priority function $c : Q \to \{1, \ldots, m\}$ such that $w \in L(\mathcal{A})$ iff the smallest priority assigned to a state on the unique run of $\mathcal{A}$ on w which is seen infinitely often is even.

We construct an unambiguous LDBA for L, which then easily yields a PBA$^{>0}$ by assigning arbitrary probabilities ([4, Lemma 4.2]) without influencing the ambiguity. If the parity automaton $\mathcal{A}$ has m priorities, the LDBA $\mathcal{B}$ can be obtained by taking $m+1$ copies, where m of them are responsible for one priority each, and one is modified to guess which priority i on the input word is the most important one appearing infinitely often along the run of $\mathcal{A}$, and correspondingly switch into the correct copy. This switching is done unambiguously for the first position after which no priority more important than i appears.   □

3.2   From probabilistic to classical automata

First we establish a result for flat PBA, i.e. PBA that have no EDA pattern. In automata without EDA pattern there are no states which are part of two different cycles labeled by the same finite word. Even though we defined flat PBA by using an ambiguity pattern, the set of flat PBA does not correspond to an ambiguity class, but it is useful for our purposes due to the following property:

Lemma 1. *If $\mathcal{A}$ is a flat PBA and $w \in \Sigma^\omega$, then the probability of a run of $\mathcal{A}$ on w to be limit-deterministic is 1.*

Proof. Let $\mathsf{Runs}(\mathcal{A}, w)$ denote the set of all runs of $\mathcal{A}$ on w and $\mathsf{nldRuns}(\mathcal{A}, w)$ denote the subset containing all such runs that are not limit-deterministic. As $\mathcal{A}$ is flat, it has no EDA and thus also no EDA_F pattern, hence $\mathcal{A}$ is at most countably ambiguous (by [16]). Moreover, there are not only at most countably many accepting runs on any word, but also countably many rejecting runs (which can be seen by a simple generalization of [16, Lemma 4]). But as all runs are disjoint events, each run ρ that uses infinitely many forks has probability 0, and the total number of runs is countable, we can see that

$$\Pr(\mathsf{Runs}(\mathcal{A}, w) \setminus \mathsf{nldRuns}(\mathcal{A}, w)) = \sum_{\rho \in \mathsf{Runs}(\mathcal{A}, w)} \Pr(\rho) \quad - \sum_{\rho \in \mathsf{nldRuns}(\mathcal{A}, w)} \Pr(\rho) = 1 - 0 = 1. \qquad \square$$

The following lemma characterizes acceptance of PBA under extremal semantics with restricted ambiguity and is crucial for the constructions in the following sections:

Lemma 2 (Characterizations for extremal semantics).
Let $\mathcal{A}$ be a PBA.

1. *If $\mathcal{A}$ is at most countably ambiguous, then*
   $w \in L^{>0}(\mathcal{A}) \Leftrightarrow$ there exists an accepting run on w that is limit-deterministic.
2. *If there are finitely many accepting runs of $\mathcal{A}$ on w, then*
   $w \in L^{=1}(\mathcal{A}) \Leftrightarrow$ all runs on w are accepting and limit-deterministic.
3. *If $\mathcal{A}$ is flat, then*
   $w \in L^{=1}(\mathcal{A}) \Leftrightarrow$ there is no limit-deterministic rejecting run on w.

Proof. (1.) : For contradiction, assume that every accepting run on w goes through forks infinitely often. But then the probability of every individual accepting run on w is 0. Each run is a measurable event (it is a countable intersection of finite prefixes) and clearly disjoint from other runs, as two different runs must eventually differ after a finite prefix. But as the number of accepting runs is countable by assumption, by σ-additivity it follows that the probability of all accepting runs is also 0, contradicting the fact that $w \in L^{>0}(\mathcal{A})$.

For the other direction, pick a limit-deterministic accepting run ρ of $\mathcal{A}$ on w and let $uv = w$ and $q \in Q$ such that the state of ρ after reading u is q and there are no forks visited on v. Clearly, the probability to be in q after u in a run of $\mathcal{A}$ is positive (because u is finite), and the probability that $\mathcal{A}$ continues like ρ from q on v is 1. Hence, the probability of ρ is positive.

(2.) : The ($\Leftarrow$) direction is obvious. We now proceed to show ($\Rightarrow$). Take some time t after which all accepting runs on w separated. Assume that some accepting run ρ is not limit-deterministic. But then ρ goes through infinitely many forks after t which with positive probability lead to a successor from which the probability to accept is 0, and the probability of following ρ is also 0. As the probability to follow ρ until time t is positive, but after that the probability to accept is 0, this implies that there is a positive probability that $\mathcal{A}$ rejects w. Therefore, all accepting runs on w must be limit-deterministic. Now assume that some run ρ on w is rejecting. Following this run until the time at which ρ is separated from all accepting runs has positive probability and all continuations must be also rejecting, so $\mathcal{A}$ must reject w.

(3.) : Clearly ($\Rightarrow$) holds, because a limit-deterministic rejecting run has positive probability, i.e., if such a run exists on w, then $\mathcal{A}$ cannot accept almost surely. For ($\Leftarrow$), observe that because $\mathcal{A}$ is flat, we know by Lemma 1 that with probability 1 runs are limit-deterministic. Hence, if there exists no limit-deterministic rejecting run on w (which would have positive probability), then with probability 1 runs are limit-deterministic and accepting. □

Using these characterizations, we can provide simple constructions from probabilistic to classical automata.

Theorem 2. *Let $\mathcal{A}$ be a PBA that is at most countably ambiguous.*
  Then $L^{>0}(\mathcal{A})$ is a regular language.

Proof (sketch). An NBA construction taking two copies of the PBA, where in the first copy no state is accepting and the second copy has no forks, with the purpose of guessing a limit-deterministic accepting run. □

Corollary 1. *If $L^{>0}(\mathcal{A})$ is not regular, then it contains an EDA_F pattern.*

Theorem 3. *Let $\mathcal{A}$ be a PBA that is at most exponentially ambiguous or flat.*
  Then $L^{=1}(\mathcal{A})$ is regular and recognizable by DBA.

Proof (sketch). Both cases (exp. ambiguous or flat) shown using a deterministic breakpoint construction resulting in a DBA. In one case it checks whether all runs are accepting, in the other it checks that there are no limit-deterministic rejecting runs. □

Corollary 2. *If $L^{=1}(\mathcal{A})$ is not regular,*
then $\mathcal{A}$ contains both an EDA and an IDA_F pattern.

The corollaries above follow directly from the theorems and the syntactic characterization of ambiguity classes [16]. The following proposition states that these characterizations of regularity in terms of the ambiguity patterns are tight.

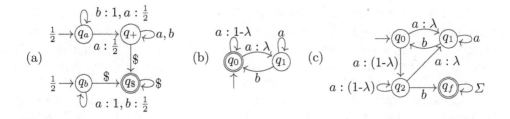

Fig. 2: (a) Some PWA which accepts the non-regular language $\{\, w = (a+b)^*\$^\omega \mid$ $\#_a(w) > \#_b(w) \,\}$ with a threshold of $\frac{1}{2}$, where $\#_x(w)$ denotes the number of occurrences of $x \in \Sigma$ in $w \in \Sigma^\omega$. (b) A family of PBA $\mathcal{P}_\lambda$ from [4] such that $\mathbb{L}^{>0}(\mathcal{P}_\lambda)$ is not regular for any $\lambda \in \mathbb{R}$. (c) A family of PWA $\tilde{\mathcal{P}}_\lambda$ (closely related to [4, Fig. 6]) such that $\mathbb{L}^{=1}(\tilde{\mathcal{P}}_\lambda)$ is not regular for any $\lambda \in \mathbb{R}$.

Proposition 3.   *There exist PBA...*

1. *...with* EDA_F *pattern (i.e. uncountably ambiguous) that accept non-regular languages under positive semantics.*
2. *...with no* EDA_F *pattern (i.e. countably ambiguous) that accept non-regular languages under almost-sure semantics.*

Proof. (1.) Note that this statement just means that there are PBA accepting non-regular languages, which is well known. For example, the automata family from [4, Fig. 3], depicted in Figure 2(b), accepts non-regular languages under positive semantics and clearly contains an EDA_F pattern, e.g. there are two different paths from p_0 to p_0 on the word aab.

(2.) The automata family depicted in Figure 2(c) is a simple modification of the PBA family depicted in [4, Fig. 6] and recognizes the same non-regular languages under almost-sure semantics. It does not contain an EDA_F pattern, because the accepting state is a sink, but it does contain an IDA_F and an EDA pattern (both e.g. on aab), so it is countably ambiguous and not flat.   □

This completes our classification of regular subclasses of PBA under extremal semantics that are defined by ambiguity patterns, showing that going beyond the restricted classes presented above (by allowing more patterns) in general leads to a loss of regularity.

Notice that the presented constructions do not track exact probabilities, just whether transitions have a probability > 0 or $= 1$. This is a noteworthy observation, as in general, the probabilities do matter for PBA, as shown in [4, Thm. 4.7, Thm. 4.11].

Proposition 4. *Let $\mathcal{A}$ be a PBA. The exact probabilities in $\mathcal{A}$ do not influence $L^{>0}(\mathcal{A})$ if $\mathcal{A}$ is at most countably ambiguous, and $L^{=1}(\mathcal{A})$ if $\mathcal{A}$ is at most exponentially ambiguous or flat.*

3.3   Threshold Semantics

In this section we consider PBA under threshold semantics and we will see that in this setting, we lose regularity much earlier than in the case of extremal semantics, but there is still the large and natural subclass of finitely ambiguous PBA that retains regularity. Before we can show this, we need to derive a suitable characterization of such languages.

We derive it from the following simple observation, which was also used more implicitly in the proof that Simple HPBA with threshold semantics are equivalent to DBA in [9].

Lemma 3. *Let $\mathcal{A}$ be a PBA. Then for every threshold $\lambda \in]0, 1]$, there exists a finite set of probability values $V_{\geq \lambda} \subset [\lambda, 1]$ such that for every finite run prefix with probability v in $\mathcal{A}$ we have $v \geq \lambda \Rightarrow v \in V_{\geq \lambda}$.*

Proof. Observe that given a finite set of real numbers $R \subset [0, 1]$, the set $R_{\geq \lambda} := \{r \mid r = \prod_i r_i \geq \lambda, \ r_i \in R\}$ must be finite, as in any sequence $p_1 p_2 \ldots$ of $p_i \in R$, only at most $m = \lceil \log_\lambda(\max R) \rceil$ values can be < 1 and such that the product of the sequence remains $\geq \lambda$. In our case, let R be the set of distinct probabilities assigned to edges (including the initial edges) in $\mathcal{A}$. As every finite run prefix by definition has the probability given by the product of the edge probabilities, this implies the statement.   □

If there is just one accepting run (i.e., the automaton is unambiguous), one can easily construct a nondeterministic automaton that guesses an accepting run and tracks it along with its probability value, of which there are only finitely many above the threshold. In the case that there are multiple accepting runs, for acceptance only the sum of their probabilities matters. As individual runs can in principle have arbitrarily small probability values, it is not obvious that the same approach (tracking a set of runs) can work. Determining a suitable cut-off point is not as simple, because it is not apparent when a single run becomes so improbable that it does not matter among the others. However, we will now show that such a cut-off point must exist:

Lemma 4. *Let $\mathcal{A}$ be a PBA, $\lambda \in]0, 1]$ a threshold and $k \in \mathbb{N}$. There exists $\varepsilon_k \in]0, \lambda[$ such that for all sets $R^t = \{\rho_i^t\}_{i=1}^j$ of at most $j \leq k$ different run prefixes in $\mathcal{A}$ of the same length $t \in \mathbb{N}$, $\mathsf{Pr}(R^t) = \sum_{i=1}^j \mathsf{Pr}(\rho_i^t) < \lambda$ implies that $\mathsf{Pr}(R^t) < \lambda - \varepsilon_k$.*

Proof. We prove this by induction on the number of runs k. For $k = 1$, i.e. a single run prefix, let $V_{\geq \lambda}$ be the finite (by Lemma 3) set of different probability values $\geq \lambda$ and let E be the set of distinct probabilities in the automaton $\mathcal{A}$. Then clearly $v_{\max, <\lambda} := \max\{a \cdot b \mid a \cdot b < \lambda, a \in V_{\geq \lambda}, b \in E\}$ is the largest probability value $< \lambda$ that can correspond to a finite run prefix in $\mathcal{A}$. Hence, we can just pick an $\varepsilon_1 < \lambda - v_{\max, <\lambda}$ and immediately get that for any run prefix with probability $v < \lambda$, we have that $v \leq v_{\max, <\lambda} < \lambda - \varepsilon_1$.

Now assume the statement holds for all sets with at most k run prefixes. Let R^t be a set of $k + 1$ of different run prefixes of the same length such that

$\Pr(R^t) < \lambda$ and let $\varepsilon := \varepsilon_k$. Then we know that for every subset S of at most k runs of R^t we have $\Pr(S) < \lambda - \varepsilon$. Also, every single run prefix can by Lemma 3 have one of only finitely many probability values in $V_{\geq \varepsilon}$ that are $\geq \varepsilon$ and there exists a value $v_{\max,<\varepsilon}$ denoting the largest possible probability value $< \varepsilon$ that a single run prefix can have.

If there exists a run prefix $\rho \in R^t$ with probability value $v < \varepsilon$, then we know that $\Pr(R^t) = \Pr(R^t \setminus \{\rho\}) + v < (\lambda - \varepsilon) + v_{\max,<\varepsilon} < \lambda$. If every run in R^t has a probability value $\geq \varepsilon$, then every run prefix in R^t has as probability one of the values in $V_{\geq \varepsilon}$. Consider all sums of k values from $V_{\geq \varepsilon}$, which are finitely many, and pick the largest sum s which is $< \lambda$. Choose ε_{k+1} such that $\varepsilon_{k+1} < \min(\varepsilon - v_{\max,<\varepsilon}, \lambda - s)$ to account for both cases. $\qquad\square$

From this we can derive the following characterization of languages accepted by finitely ambiguous PBA under threshold semantics:

Lemma 5. *Let $\mathcal{A}$ be a k-ambiguous PBA and $\lambda \in\,]0,1]$ a threshold. There exists an $\varepsilon \in\,]0,\lambda]$ such that for all $w \in \Sigma^\omega$: $w \in L^{>\lambda}(\mathcal{A})$ iff there exists a set R of limit-deterministic accepting runs of $\mathcal{A}$ on w with $\Pr(R) > \lambda$, $\Pr(S) \leq \lambda$ for all $S \subset R$ and at most one run $\rho \in R$ with $\Pr(\rho) < \varepsilon$.*

Proof. Clearly ($\Leftarrow$) holds, as then w is accepted with probability $\geq \Pr(R) > \lambda$. We now show ($\Rightarrow$). In a finitely ambiguous PBA there are only finitely many different accepting runs on each word. Furthermore, as after finite time all accepting runs have separated and each accepting run that visits forks infinitely often has probability 0, accepting runs that visit forks infinitely often do not contribute positively to the acceptance probability and thus can be ignored. Hence, if $w \in L^{>\lambda}(\mathcal{A})$, there is a number of accepting runs that eventually all become deterministic and each such run has a positive probability, which must in total be $> \lambda$.

Let R be a set of different limit-deterministic accepting runs of $\mathcal{A}$ on w such that $\Pr(R) > \lambda$ and $\Pr(S) \leq \lambda$ for all $S \subset R$. As there are only finitely many accepting runs, such a set R must exist. Furthermore, notice that each limit-deterministic run has a finite prefix which has the same probability as the whole run, so there exists a time t such that the probability of the set of all different prefixes of runs in R of length t is exactly $\Pr(R)$, so that Lemma 4 applies.

Now pick an $\varepsilon := \varepsilon_k$ given by Lemma 4. We claim that at most one run $\rho \in R$ can have a probability less than ε. If there is no such run in R, we are done. Otherwise let ρ be a run with $\Pr(\rho) =: p < \varepsilon$ and notice that by choice of R, we have that $\Pr(R \setminus \{\rho\}) =: s \leq \lambda$. It cannot be the case that $s < \lambda$, as then by Lemma 4 we have $s < \lambda - \varepsilon$, which implies that $\Pr(R) = s + p < \lambda$, which is a contradiction. Hence, now assume that $s = \lambda$. But then, if there is any $\rho' \neq \rho \in R$ such that $\Pr(\rho') =: p' < \varepsilon$, by the same argument we get the contradiction that $s - p' < \lambda - \varepsilon$ and hence $s < \lambda$. Therefore, no other run in R can have a probability $< \varepsilon$. $\qquad\square$

Now we can perform the intended automaton construction to show:

Theorem 4. $L^{>\lambda}(\mathcal{A})$ *is regular for each k-ambiguous PBA $\mathcal{A}$ and $\lambda \in\,]0,1[$.*

Proof (sketch). We use the characterization of Lemma 5 to construct a generalized Büchi automaton accepting $L^{>\lambda}(\mathcal{A})$. Intuitively, the new automaton just guesses at most k different runs of $\mathcal{A}$ and verifies that the guessed runs are limit-deterministic and accepting. The automaton additionally tracks the probability of the runs over time, to determine whether the individual runs and their sum have enough "weight". The automaton rejects when the total probability of the guessed runs is $\leq \lambda$, one of the runs goes into the rejecting sink q_{rej} or a run does not see accepting states infinitely often.

By Lemma 5 we only need to consider sets of runs with at most one run that has a probability $< \varepsilon$, where $\varepsilon := \varepsilon_k$ is given by Lemma 4. For this single run we also do not need to track the exact probability value, as its only purpose is to witness that the acceptance probability is strictly greater than λ, whereas all other runs must have one of the finitely many different probabilities which are $\geq \varepsilon$ and must sum to λ. □

This generalizes the corresponding result for PFA [12, Theorem 3]. The proof in [12] uses similar concepts, though a rather different presentation. In the setting of infinite words we additionally have to deal with a single run that has arbitrarily low probability, and we have to ensure that this probability remains positive.

After seeing that finitely ambiguous PBA retain regularity, we show that this is the best we can do under threshold semantics:

Corollary 3. *There are polynomially ambiguous PBA $\mathcal{A}$, that is, with an IDA pattern and no EDA, IDA_F patterns, such that $L^{>\lambda}(\mathcal{A})$ is not regular even for rational thresholds $\lambda \in]0, 1[$.*

Proof. Follows from the fact that the PWA $\mathcal{A}$ from Figure 2(a), which recognizes a non-regular language (and is used to show Proposition 6), has just an IDA pattern in the underlying NBA, but no EDA or IDA_F patterns. □

This completes our characterization of languages which are recognized by PBA that are restricted by forbidden ambiguity patterns, so that we can state our main result of this section (see Figure 1 for a visualization):

Theorem 5. *The following results hold about PBA with restricted ambiguity:*

- $\mathbb{L}^{>0}(k\text{-PBA}) = \mathbb{L}^{>0}(\aleph_0\text{-PBA}) = \mathbb{L}(\text{NBA})$
- $\mathbb{L}^{=1}(k\text{-PBA}) = \mathbb{L}^{=1}(2^k\text{-PBA}) = \mathbb{L}^{=1}(\textit{flat} \text{ PBA}) = \mathbb{L}(\text{DBA}) \subset \mathbb{L}^{=1}(\aleph_0\text{-PBA})$
- $\mathbb{L}^{>\lambda}(k\text{-PBA}) = \mathbb{L}(\text{NBA}) \subset \mathbb{L}^{>\lambda}(n^k\text{-PBA})$

Proof. The statements follow from the following inclusion chains:

$$\mathbb{L}(\text{NBA}) \overset{(1.)}{\subseteq} \mathbb{L}^{>0}(k\text{-PBA}) \overset{def.}{\subseteq} \mathbb{L}^{>0}(\aleph_0\text{-PBA}) \overset{(2.)}{\subseteq} \mathbb{L}(\text{NBA})$$

$$\mathbb{L}(\text{DBA}) \overset{(3.)}{\subseteq} \mathbb{L}^{=1}(k\text{-PBA}) \overset{def.}{\subseteq} \mathbb{L}^{=1}(2^k\text{-PBA} \cup \textit{flat PBA}) \overset{(4.)}{\subseteq} \mathbb{L}(\text{DBA}) \overset{(5.)}{\subset} \mathbb{L}^{=1}(\aleph_0\text{-PBA})$$

$$\mathbb{L}(\text{NBA}) \overset{(1.)}{\subseteq} \mathbb{L}^{>0}(k\text{-PBA}) \overset{(6.)}{\subseteq} \mathbb{L}^{>\lambda}(k\text{-PBA}) \overset{(7.)}{\subseteq} \mathbb{L}(\text{NBA}) \overset{(8.)}{\subset} \mathbb{L}^{>\lambda}(n^k\text{-PBA})$$

Where the marked relationships hold due to: (1.) Theorem 1, (2.) Theorem 2, (3.) Proposition 2, (4.) Theorem 3, (5.) Proposition 3, (6.) Simple transformation by adding a new accepting sink q_{acc} and modifying the initial distribution μ_0 [4, Lemma 4.16], (7.) Theorem 4, (8.) Corollary 3, and (def.) by definition of the ambiguity-restricted automata classes. □

4 Complexity results

In this section, we state some upper and lower bounds on the complexity for deciding emptiness and universality for PBA with restricted ambiguity, derived from the characterizations and constructions presented above.

Theorem 6.

1. *the emptiness problem for* $\aleph_0\text{-}PBA^{>0}$ *is in* NL
2. *the universality problem for* $\aleph_0\text{-}PBA^{>0}$ *is in* PSPACE
3. *the universality problem for at most exp. ambiguous or flat* $PBA^{=1}$ *is in* NL

Proof. $(1.+2.)$: By Theorem 2 the languages of $\aleph_0\text{-}PBA^{>0}$ are regular. The construction of an NBA just uses two copies of the given PBA. For emptiness, it thus suffices to guess an accepted ultimately periodic word and verify that it is accepted by the NBA, which can be done in NL. Since universality for NBA in in PSPACE [21], we also obtain (2.).

(3.): If the automaton is at most exponentially ambiguous, there are only finitely many accepting runs on each word and as we know by Lemma 2 that $w \in L^{=1}(\mathcal{A})$ iff all runs are accepting, it suffices to guess a rejecting run in $\mathcal{A}^{\lhd}$, which implies that the ultimately periodic word w labelling that run can not be in $L^{=1}(\mathcal{A})$. If the automaton is flat, then we know that for each rejected word there must exist a limit-deterministic rejecting run in the underlying NBA, which we also can guess. □

Type	regular?		Emptiness		Universality	
	$>0=1$	$>\lambda$	>0	$=1$	>0	$=1$
k-PBA						
n^k-PBA			$\in$ NL	$\in$ PSPACE	$\in$ PSPACE	$\in$ NL
2^n-PBA	✓	✗				
flat PBA			$\in$ NL c.	$\in$ PSPACE c.	$\in$ PSPACE c.	$\in$ NL c.
$\aleph_0$-PBA						$\in$ PSPACE

Table 1: Summary of main results from Theorems 5 and 6 concerning PBA with ambiguity restrictions. The completeness results follow from the hardness results for HPBA (which are subsumed by flat PBA) from [8, Section 5], the PSPACE inclusion of universality for almost-sure $\aleph_0$-PBA follows from [8, Theorem 4.4].

Observe that $\aleph_0\text{-}PBA^{>0}$ subsume $HPBA^{>0}$ and the union of flat $PBA^{=1}$ and exp. ambiguous $PBA^{=1}$ subsumes $HPBA^{=1}$, while preserving the same complexity of the emptiness and universality problems. A summary of the main results from Theorem 5 and Theorem 6 is presented in Table 1.

We conclude with an observation relevant to the question about feasibility of PBA with restricted ambiguity for the purpose of application in e.g. model-checking or synthesis.

Proposition 5 (Relationship to classical formalisms).

- *There is a doubly-exponential lower bound for translation from LTL formula to countably ambiguous PBA with positive semantics.*
- *There is an exponential lower bound for conversion from NBA to countably ambiguous PBA with positive semantics.*

Proof. It is known [20, Theorem 2] that there is a doubly-exponential lower bound from LTL to LDBA. It is also known that LTL to NBA has an exponential lower bound (e.g. [5, Theorem 5.42]), which implies an exponential lower bound from NBA to LDBA.

By Theorem 2 there is a polynomial transformation from countably ambiguous PBA with positive semantics into LDBA, which together with the aforementioned bounds implies the claimed lower bounds. $\square$

5   Weakness in Probabilistic Büchi Automata

In this section we investigate the class of probabilistic weak automata (PWA), establishing the relation between different classes defined by PWA as shown in Figure 3 (see also the description of our contribution in the introduction).

As a first remark, notice that PWA can be "complemented" by inverting accepting and rejecting states and switching between dual semantics, e.g., for a PWA $\mathcal{A}$ we have $\overline{L^{>0}(\mathcal{A})} = L^{=1}(\overline{\mathcal{A}})$, where $\overline{\mathcal{A}}$ is just $\mathcal{A}$ with inverted accepting state set $F' = Q \setminus F$.

Since the overarching theme of this paper is trying to find regular subclasses of PBA, we will next establish the following result, showing that there is no hope to find a complete syntactical characterization of regularity in PBA:

Theorem 7. *The regularity of PWA (and therefore of PBA) under positive, almost-sure and threshold semantics is an undecidable problem.*

Proof (sketch). Since $\mathbb{L}^{>\lambda}(\text{PWA}) \supseteq \mathbb{L}^{>0}(\text{PWA})$ (see Theorem 10), $\mathbb{L}^{>0}(\text{PWA}) = \overline{\mathbb{L}^{=1}(\text{PWA})}$, and the class of regular ω-languages is closed under complement, it suffices to show the statement for $\text{PWA}^{=1}$. We do this by reduction from the value 1 problem for PFA, which is the question whether for each $\varepsilon > 0$ there exists a word accepted by the PFA with probability $> 1 - \varepsilon$. This problem is known to be undecidable [13]. We consider a slightly modified version of the problem by assuming that no word is accepted with probability 1 by the given PFA. The problem remains undecidable under this assumption, because one can check if a PFA accepts a finite word with probability 1 by a simple subset construction.

Given some PFA $\mathcal{A}$, we construct a $\text{PWA}^{=1}$ $\mathcal{B}$ by taking a copy of $\mathcal{A}$ and extending it with a new symbol # such that from accepting states of $\mathcal{A}$ the automaton is "restarted" on #, while from non-accepting states # leads into a

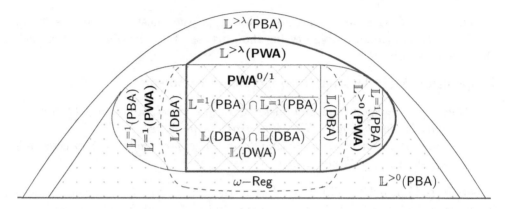

Fig. 3: Illustration of relationships between the class of languages accepted by weak probabilistic automata under various semantics with other already known classes. The overlapping patterns indicate intersection of classes, where dots mark $\mathbb{L}^{>0}(\text{PBA})$, and different diagonal lines respectively $\mathbb{L}^{=1}(\text{PBA})$ and $\overline{\mathbb{L}}^{=1}(\text{PBA})$. The dashed line indicates intersections with different subclasses of regular languages. The class $\mathbb{L}^{>\lambda}(\text{PBA})$ contains all the other depicted classes, $\mathbb{L}^{>\lambda}(\text{PWA})$ contains the area inside the thick line. The depicted fact that $\mathbb{L}^{>0}(\text{PWA}) = \mathbb{L}^{>\lambda}(\text{PWA}) \cap \mathbb{L}^{>0}(\text{PBA})$ is a conjecture, one direction is shown in Theorem 10.

new part which ensures that infinitely many # are seen and contains the only accepting state of $\mathcal{B}$. We show that $L^{=1}(\mathcal{B}) = (\Sigma^* \#)^\omega \setminus R$, where $R = \emptyset$ if $\mathcal{A}$ does not have value 1, and R is non-empty but does not contain an ultimately periodic word, otherwise. This implies that $L^{=1}(\mathcal{B})$ is regular iff $\mathcal{A}$ does not have value 1.   □

We will now show that PWA with almost-sure semantics are as expressive as PBA, and with positive semantics as expressive as PCA.

Theorem 8. $\mathbb{L}^{>0}(\text{PWA}) = \mathbb{L}^{>0}(\text{PCA})$ *and* $\mathbb{L}^{=1}(\text{PWA}) = \mathbb{L}^{=1}(\text{PBA})$.

Proof (sketch). It suffices to show the first statement. The second then follows by duality, i.e., we can interpret a $\text{PBA}^{=1}$ $\mathcal{A}$ recognizing L as a $\text{PCA}^{>0}$ recognizing $\overline{L}$ and just apply the construction to get a $\text{PWA}^{>0}$ $\mathcal{B}$ for $\overline{L}$, such that $\overline{\mathcal{B}}$ (with inverted accepting and rejecting states) is a $\text{PWA}^{=1}$ for L. In the first statement the $\subseteq$ inclusion is trivial, hence we only need to show that $\mathbb{L}^{>0}(\text{PCA}) \subseteq \mathbb{L}^{>0}(\text{PWA})$.

We construct a $\text{PWA}^{>0}$ consisting of two copies of the original $\text{PCA}^{>0}$, a *guess* copy and a *verify* copy. In the first copy, the automaton can guess that no final states will be visited anymore and switch to the verify copy, which is accepting, but where all transitions into final states are redirected to a rejecting sink.   □

Next, we show that languages that can be accepted by both, a PWA with almost-sure semantics, and by a PWA with positive semantics, are regular and can be accepted by a DWA. For the proof, we rely on a characterization of DWA languages in terms of the Myhill-Nerode equivalence relation from [22]. So we first define this equivalence, and show that languages defined by PBA with positive semantics have only finitely many equivalence classes. Then we come back to the result for PWA.

For $L \subseteq \Sigma^\omega$, define the Myhill-Nerode equivalence relation $\sim_L \subseteq \Sigma^* \times \Sigma^*$ by $u \sim_L v$ iff $uw \in L \Leftrightarrow vw \in L$ for all $w \in \Sigma^\omega$. Then the following holds:

Lemma 6 (Finitely many Myhill-Nerode classes).
Languages in $\mathbb{L}^{>0}(\mathrm{PBA})$ have finitely many Myhill-Nerode equivalence classes.

Proof. Let $\mathcal{A} = (Q, \Sigma, \delta, \mu_0, F)$ be some $\mathrm{PBA}^{>0}$ and $u \in \Sigma^*$ some word and let $\mu_u := \delta^*(\mu_0, u)$ be the probability distribution on states of $\mathcal{A}$ after reading u. Pick any $w \in \Sigma^\omega$ and notice that $uw \in L = L^{>0}(\mathcal{A})$ iff there exists some state q such that $\mu_u(q) > 0$ and the probability to accept w from q is also > 0, as the product of two positive numbers clearly still is positive. But then, for any two $u, v \in \Sigma^*$ we have that whenever $\mu_u(q) > 0 \Leftrightarrow \mu_v(q) > 0$ for all q, then we have $uw \in L \Leftrightarrow vw \in L$ for all $w \in \Sigma^\omega$ by the reasoning above, as the exact value does not matter for acceptance, and therefore $u \sim_L v$. But as there are only at most $2^{|Q|}$ different possibilities how values in a distribution μ over Q are either equal to or greater than 0, this is an upper bound on the number of different equivalence classes. $\square$

Theorem 9. $\mathbb{L}^{>0}(\mathrm{PWA}) \cap \mathbb{L}^{=1}(\mathrm{PWA}) = \mathbb{L}(\mathrm{DWA}) = \mathbb{L}(\mathrm{PWA}^{0/1})$

Proof. The inclusions $\mathbb{L}(\mathrm{DWA}) \subseteq \mathbb{L}(\mathrm{PWA}^{0/1}) \subseteq \mathbb{L}^{>0}(\mathrm{PWA}) \cap \mathbb{L}^{=1}(\mathrm{PWA})$ are trivial, hence it remains to show $\mathbb{L}^{>0}(\mathrm{PWA}) \cap \mathbb{L}^{=1}(\mathrm{PWA}) \subseteq \mathbb{L}(\mathrm{DWA})$.

So let L be a language from $\mathbb{L}^{>0}(\mathrm{PWA}) \cap \mathbb{L}^{=1}(\mathrm{PWA})$. We want to show that L can be accepted by a DWA. We use the following characterization of DWA languages [22, Theorem 21]: The DWA languages are precisely the languages with finitely many Myhill-Nerode classes in the class $G_\delta \cap F_\sigma$ in the Borel hierarchy. The classes G_δ and F_σ of the Borel hierarchy are often also referred to as Π_2 and Σ_2. We do not introduce the details of this hierarchy here, but rather refer the reader not familiar with these concepts to [22] and [8].

We already know that L has finitely many Myhill-Nerode classes by Lemma 6 (as PWA are special cases of PBA). It remains to show that L is in the class $G_\delta \cap F_\sigma$. It is known that PBA with almost-sure semantics define languages in G_δ [8, Lemma 3.2]. Hence L is in G_δ. Since L is accepted by a PWA with positive semantics, the complement of L is accepted by a PWA with almost-sure semantics (as noted at the beginning of this section). We obtain that the complement of L is also in G_δ again by [8, Lemma 3.2]. This means that L is in F_σ, which by definition consists of the complements of languages from G_δ. $\square$

Concluding this section, we show a result about weak automata with threshold semantics, which (not surprisingly) turn out to be even more expressive. A careful analysis of the PWA $\mathcal{A}$ in Fig. 2(a) shows the following result:

Proposition 6. *For all thresholds $\lambda \in\ ]0, 1[$ there exists a PWA $\mathcal{A}$ such that $L^{>\lambda}(\mathcal{A})$ is not regular and not $PBA^{>0}$ recognizable.*

Putting things together, we can say the following about threshold PWA, establishing the relation of $\mathbb{L}^{>\lambda}(\text{PWA})$ to the other classes in Figure 3:

Theorem 10 (Expressive power of threshold PWA).

1. $\mathbb{L}^{>0}(\text{PWA}) \subseteq \mathbb{L}^{>\lambda}(\text{PWA}) \cap \mathbb{L}^{>0}(\text{PBA})$.
2. $\mathbb{L}^{>\lambda}(\text{PWA})$ *and* $\mathbb{L}^{>0}(\text{PBA})$ *are incomparable (wrt. set inclusion).*
3. $\mathbb{L}^{>0}(\text{PWA}) \subset \mathbb{L}^{>\lambda}(\text{PWA}) \subset \mathbb{L}^{>\lambda}(\text{PBA})$.

Proof. (1.) $\mathbb{L}^{>0}(\text{PWA}) \subseteq \mathbb{L}^{>0}(\text{PBA})$ by definition and $\mathbb{L}^{>0}(\text{PWA}) \subseteq \mathbb{L}^{>\lambda}(\text{PWA})$, as any $\text{PWA}^{>0}$ can be modified to a $\text{PWA}^{>\lambda}$ recognizing the same language by just adding an additional accepting sink and modifying the initial distribution, just as described in [4, Lemma 4.16] for general PBA.

(2.) By Proposition 6, there are languages recognized by $\text{PWA}^{>\lambda}$ that cannot be recognized with $\text{PBA}^{>0}$. To show that there are languages accepted by $\text{PBA}^{>0}$ that cannot be accepted by $\text{PWA}^{>\lambda}$ we can give a topological characterization of languages accepted by PWA by a simple adaptation of [8, Lemma 3.2] and combine it with other results shown in [8] to show that there are $\text{PBA}^{>0}$ that accept languages that cannot be accepted by $\text{PWA}^{>\lambda}$.

(3.) The first inclusion was discussed in (1.), the strictness follows from Proposition 6 and the fact that $\mathbb{L}^{>0}(\text{PWA}) = \mathbb{L}^{=1}(\text{PBA}) \subset \text{BCl}(\mathbb{L}^{=1}(\text{PBA})) = \mathbb{L}^{>0}(\text{PBA})$, where the first equality is Theorem 8 and the second is shown in [8]. The second inclusion of the statement follows from (2.) and the fact from [4] that $\mathbb{L}^{>0}(\text{PBA}) \subset \mathbb{L}^{>\lambda}(\text{PBA})$.   □

For the dual class $\mathbb{L}^{\geq\lambda}(\text{PWA})$ one can show symmetric results that correspond to statements (1.) and (2.) above, for statement (3.) however there is no proof yet for the strictness of the inclusions (especially the second one), whereas the statement $\mathbb{L}^{=1}(\text{PWA}) \subseteq \mathbb{L}^{\geq\lambda}(\text{PWA}) \subseteq \mathbb{L}^{\geq\lambda}(\text{PBA})$ is obvious. We leave this issue as an open question. Another interesting question is whether $> \lambda$ is equivalent to $< \lambda$ (or dually for $\geq$ / $\leq$).

6   Conclusion

By using notions from ambiguity in classical Büchi automata, we were able to extend the set of easily (syntactically) checkable PBA which are regular under some or all of the usual semantics. As a consequence, ambiguity appears to be an even more interesting notion in the probabilistic setting, as here it in fact has consequences for the expressive power of automata, whereas in the classical setting there is no such effect. Our results also indicate that to get non-regularity, one requires the use of certain structural patterns which at least imply the existence of the ambiguity patterns that we used. It is an open question whether it is possible to identify more fine-grained syntactic characterizations, patterns or easily checkable properties which are just over-approximated by the ambiguity patterns and are required for non-regularity.

References

1. Baier, C., Bertrand, N., Größer, M.: On decision problems for probabilistic büchi automata. In: Foundations of Software Science and Computational Structures, 11th International Conference, FOSSACS 2008. Lecture Notes in Computer Science, vol. 4962, pp. 287–301. Springer (2008), https://doi.org/10.1007/978-3-540-78499-9

2. Baier, C., Bertrand, N., Größer, M.: Probabilistic automata over infinite words: Expressiveness, efficiency, and decidability. In: Proceedings Eleventh International Workshop on Descriptional Complexity of Formal Systems, DCFS 2009. EPTCS, vol. 3, pp. 3–16 (2009), https://doi.org/10.4204/EPTCS.3

3. Baier, C., Größer, M.: Recognizing omega-regular languages with probabilistic automata. In: 20th IEEE Symposium on Logic in Computer Science (LICS 2005), 26-29 June 2005, Chicago, IL, USA, Proceedings. pp. 137–146 (2005)

4. Baier, C., Größer, M., Bertrand, N.: Probabilistic ω-automata. Journal of the ACM (JACM) **59**(1), 1 (2012)

5. Baier, C., Katoen, J.: Principles of model checking. MIT Press (2008)

6. Boigelot, B., Jodogne, S., Wolper, P.: An effective decision procedure for linear arithmetic over the integers and reals. ACM Trans. Comput. Log. **6**(3), 614–633 (2005), https://doi.org/10.1145/1071596.1071601

7. Büchi, J.R.: On a decision method in restricted second order arithmetic. In: Studies in Logic and the Foundations of Mathematics, vol. 44, pp. 1–11. Elsevier (1966)

8. Chadha, R., Sistla, A.P., Viswanathan, M.: Power of randomization in automata on infinite strings. Logical Methods in Computer Science **7** (2011)

9. Chadha, R., Sistla, A.P., Viswanathan, M.: Probabilistic Büchi automata with non-extremal acceptance thresholds. In: International Workshop on Verification, Model Checking, and Abstract Interpretation. pp. 103–117. Springer (2011)

10. Chadha, R., Sistla, A.P., Viswanathan, M.: Emptiness under isolation and the value problem for hierarchical probabilistic automata. In: FOSSACS 2017. LNCS, vol. 10203, pp. 231–247 (2017), https://doi.org/10.1007/978-3-662-54458-7

11. Chadha, R., Sistla, A.P., Viswanathan, M., Ben, Y.: Decidable and expressive classes of probabilistic automata. In: FoSSaCS 2015. LNCS, vol. 9034, pp. 200–214. Springer (2015), https://doi.org/10.1007/978-3-662-46678-0

12. Fijalkow, N., Riveros, C., Worrell, J.: Probabilistic automata of bounded ambiguity. In: 28th International Conference on Concurrency Theory (CONCUR 2017). Schloss Dagstuhl-Leibniz-Zentrum fuer Informatik (2017)

13. Gimbert, H., Oualhadj, Y.: Probabilistic automata on finite words: Decidable and undecidable problems. In: International Colloquium on Automata, Languages, and Programming. pp. 527–538. Springer (2010)

14. Landweber, L.H.: Decision problems for ω-automata. Mathematical Systems Theory **3**, 376–384 (1969)

15. Leroux, J., Sutre, G.: On flatness for 2-dimensional vector addition systems with states. In: International Conference on Concurrency Theory. pp. 402–416. Springer (2004)

16. Löding, C., Pirogov, A.: On finitely ambiguous Büchi automata. In: Developments in Language Theory - 22nd International Conference, DLT 2018, Tokyo, Japan, September 10-14, 2018, Proceedings. pp. 503–515 (2018)

17. Löding, C., Thomas, W.: Alternating automata and logics over infinite words. In: Proceedings of the IFIP International Conference on Theoretical Computer Science, IFIP TCS2000. LNCS, vol. 1872, pp. 521–535. Springer (2000)

18. Rabin, M.O.: Probabilistic automata. Information and control **6**(3), 230–245 (1963)
19. Rabinovich, A.: Complementation of finitely ambiguous Büchi automata. In: Developments in Language Theory - 22nd International Conference, DLT 2018, Tokyo, Japan, September 10-14, 2018, Proceedings. pp. 541–552 (2018)
20. Sickert, S., Esparza, J., Jaax, S., Křetínský, J.: Limit-deterministic Büchi automata for linear temporal logic. In: Chaudhuri, S., Farzan, A. (eds.) Computer Aided Verification. pp. 312–332. Springer International Publishing, Cham (2016)
21. Sistla, A.P., Vardi, M.Y., Wolper, P.: The complementation problem for Büchi automata with applications to temporal logic (extended abstract). In: ICALP 1985. LNCS, vol. 194, pp. 465–474. Springer (1985), https://doi.org/10.1007/BFb0015725
22. Staiger, L.: Finite-state ω-languages. Journal of Computer and System Sciences **27**(3), 434–448 (1983)
23. Thomas, W.: Automata on infinite objects. In: Handbook of Theoretical Computer Science, vol. B: Formal Models and Semantics, pp. 133–192. Elsevier Science Publishers, Amsterdam (1990)
24. Thomas, W.: Languages, automata, and logic. In: Rozenberg, G., Salomaa, A. (eds.) Handbook of Formal Language Theory, vol. III, pp. 389–455. Springer (1997)
25. Weber, A., Seidl, H.: On the degree of ambiguity of finite automata. Theoretical Computer Science **88**(2), 325–349 (1991)

The Polynomial Complexity of Vector Addition Systems with States

Florian Zuleger (✉)
zuleger@forsyte.tuwien.ac.at

TU Wien

Abstract. Vector addition systems are an important model in theoretical computer science and have been used in a variety of areas. In this paper, we consider vector addition systems with states over a parameterized initial configuration. For these systems, we are interested in the standard notion of computational time complexity, i.e., we want to understand the length of the longest trace for a fixed vector addition system with states depending on the size of the initial configuration. We show that the asymptotic complexity of a given vector addition system with states is either $\Theta(N^k)$ for some computable integer k, where N is the size of the initial configuration, or at least exponential. We further show that k can be computed in polynomial time in the size of the considered vector addition system. Finally, we show that $1 \leq k \leq 2^n$, where n is the dimension of the considered vector addition system.

1 Introduction

Vector addition systems (VASs) [13], which are equivalent to Petri nets, are a popular model for the analysis of parallel processes [7]. Vector addition systems with states (VASSs) [10] are an extension of VASs with a finite control and are a popular model for the analysis of concurrent systems, because the finite control can for example be used to model shared global memory [12]. In this paper, we consider VASSs over a parameterized initial configuration. For these systems, we are interested in the standard notion of computational time complexity, i.e., we want to understand the length of the longest execution for a fixed VASS depending on the size of the initial configuration. VASSs over a parameterized initial configuration naturally arise in two areas: 1) *The parameterized verification problem.* For concurrent systems the number of system processes is often not known in advance, and thus the system is designed such that a template process can be instantiated an arbitrary number of times. The problem of analyzing the concurrent system for all possible system sizes is a common theme in the literature [9, 8, 1, 11, 4, 2, 3]. 2) *Automated complexity analysis of programs.* VASSs (and generalizations) have been used as backend in program analysis tools for automated complexity analysis [18–20]. The VASS considered by these tools are naturally parameterized over the initial configuration, modelling the dependency of the program complexity on the program input. The cited papers have proposed practical techniques but did not give complete algorithms.

Two recent papers have considered the computational time complexity of VASSs over a parameterized initial configuration. [15] presents a PTIME procedure for deciding whether a VASS is polynomial or at least exponential, but does not give a precise analysis in case of polynomial complexity. [5] establishes the precise asymptotic complexity for the special case of VASSs whose configurations are linearly bounded in the size of the initial configuration. In this paper, we generalize both results and fully characterize the asymptotic behaviour of VASSs with polynomial complexity: We show that the asymptotic complexity of a given VASS is either $\Theta(N^k)$ for some computable integer k, where N is the size of the initial configuration, or at least exponential. We further show that k can be computed in PTIME in the size of the considered VASS. Finally, we show that $1 \leq k \leq 2^n$, where n is the dimension of the considered VASS.

1.1   Overview and Illustration of Results

We discuss our approach on the VASS $\mathcal{V}_{run}$, stated in Figure 1, which will serve as running example. The VASS has dimension 3 (i.e., the vectors annotating the transitions have dimension 3) and four states s_1, s_2, s_3, s_4. In this paper we will always represent vectors using a set of variables Var, whose cardinality equals the dimension of the VASS. For $\mathcal{V}_{run}$ we choose $Var = \{x, y, z\}$ and use x, y, z as indices for the first, second and third component of 3-dimensional vectors. The configurations of a VASS are pairs of states and valuations of the variables to non-negative integers. A step of a VASS moves along a transition from the current state to a successor state, and adds the vector labelling the transition to the current valuation; a step can only be taken if the resulting valuation is non-negative. For the computational time complexity analysis of VASSs, we consider traces (sequences of steps) whose initial configurations consist of a valuation whose maximal value is bounded by N (the parameter used for bounding the size of the initial configuration). The computational time complexity is then the length of the longest trace whose initial configuration is bounded by N. For ease of exposition, we will in this paper only consider VASSs whose control-flow graph is *connected*. (For the general case, we remark that one needs to decompose a VASS into its strongly-connected components (SCCs), which can then be analyzed in isolation, following the DAG-order of the SCC decomposition; for this, one slightly needs to generalize the analysis in this paper to initial configurations with values $\Theta(N^{k_x})$ for every variable $x \in Var$, where $k_x \in \mathbb{Z}$.) For ease of exposition, we further consider traces over arbitrary initial states (instead of some fixed initial state); this is justified because for a fixed initial state one can always restrict the control-flow graph to the reachable states, and then the two options result in the same notion of computational complexity (up to a constant offset, which is not relevant for our asymptotic analysis).

In order to analyze the computational time complexity of a considered VASS, our approach computes *variable bounds* and *transition bounds*. A variable bound is the maximal value of a variable reachable by any trace whose initial configuration is bounded by N. A transition bound is the maximal number of times a transition appears in any trace whose initial configuration is bounded by N. For

$\mathcal{V}_{run}$, our approach establishes the linear variable bound $\Theta(N)$ for x and y, and the quadratic bound $\Theta(N^2)$ for z. We note that because the variable bound of z is quadratic and not linear, $\mathcal{V}_{run}$ cannot be analyzed by the procedure of [5]. Our approach establishes the bound $\Theta(N)$ for the transitions $s_1 \to s_3$ and $s_4 \to s_2$, the bound $\Theta(N^2)$ for transitions $s_1 \to s_2$, $s_2 \to s_1$, $s_3 \to s_4$, $s_4 \to s_3$, and the bound $\Theta(N^3)$ for all self-loops. The computational complexity of $\mathcal{V}_{run}$ is then the maximum of all transition bounds, i.e., $\Theta(N^3)$. In general, our main algorithm (Algorithm 1 presented in Section 4) either establishes that the VASS under analysis has at least exponential complexity or computes asymptotically precise variable and transition bounds $\Theta(N^k)$, with k computable in PTIME and $1 \le k \le 2^n$, where n is the dimension of the considered VASS. We note that our upper bound 2^n also improves the analysis of [15], which reports an exponential dependence on the number of transitions (and not only on the dimension).

We further state a family $\mathcal{V}_n$ of VASSs, which illustrate that k can indeed be exponential in the dimension (the example can be skipped on first reading). $\mathcal{V}_n$ uses variables $x_{i,j}$ and consists of states $s_{i,j}$, for $1 \le i \le n$ and $j = 1, 2$. We note that $\mathcal{V}_n$ has dimension $2n$. $\mathcal{V}_n$ consists of the transitions

- $s_{i,1} \xrightarrow{d} s_{i,2}$, for $1 \le i \le n$, with $d(x_{i,1}) = -1$ and $d(x) = 0$ for all $x \ne x_{i,1}$,
- $s_{i,2} \xrightarrow{d} s_{i,1}$, for $1 \le i \le n$, with $d(x) = 0$ for all x,
- $s_{i,1} \xrightarrow{d} s_{i,1}$, for $1 \le i \le n$, with $d(x_{i,1}) = -1$, $d(x_{i,2}) = 1$, $d(x_{i+1,1}) = d(x_{i+1,2}) = 1$ in case $i < n$, and $d(x) = 0$ for all other x,
- $s_{i,2} \xrightarrow{d} s_{i,2}$, for $1 \le i \le n$, with $d(x_{i,1}) = 1$, $d(x_{i,2}) = -1$, and $d(x) = 0$ for all other x,
- $s_{i,1} \xrightarrow{d} s_{i+1,1}$, for $1 \le i < n$, with $d(x_{i,1}) = -1$ and $d(x) = 0$ for all $x \ne x_{i,1}$,
- $s_{i+1,2} \xrightarrow{d} s_{i,2}$, for $1 \le i < n$, with $d(x) = 0$ for all x.

$\mathcal{V}_{exp}$ in Figure 1 depicts $\mathcal{V}_n$ for $n = 3$, where the vector components are stated in the order $x_{1,1}, x_{1,2}, x_{2,1}, x_{2,2}, x_{3,1}, x_{3,2}$. It is not hard to verify for all $1 \le i \le n$ that $\Theta(N^{2^{i-1}})$ is the precise asymptotic variable bound for $x_{i,1}$ and $x_{i,2}$, that $s_{i,1} \to s_{i,2}$, $s_{i,2} \to s_{i,1}$ and $s_{i,1} \to s_{i+1,1}$, $s_{i+1,2} \to s_{i,2}$ in case $i < n$, and that $\Theta(N^{2^i})$ is the precise asymptotic transition bound for $s_{i,1} \to s_{i,1}$, $s_{i,2} \to s_{i,2}$ (Algorithm 1 can be used to find these bounds).

1.2 Related Work

A celebrated result on VASs is the EXPSPACE-completeness [16, 17] of the boundedness problem. Deciding termination for a VAS with a *fixed* initial configuration can be reduced to the boundedness problem, and is therefore also EXPSPACE-complete; this also applies to VASSs, whose termination problem can be reduced to the VAS termination problem. In contrast, deciding the termination of VASSs for *all* initial configurations is in PTIME. It is not hard to see that non-termination over all initial configurations is equivalent to the existence of non-negative cycles (e.g., using Dickson's Lemma [6]). Kosaraju and Sullivan have given a PTIME procedure for the detection of zero-cycles [14], which can be easily be adapted to non-negative cycles. The existence of zero-cycles is decided

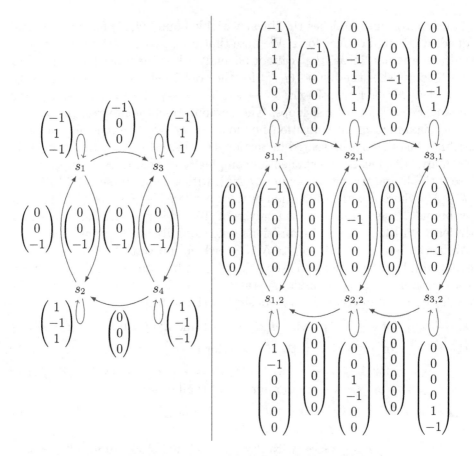

Fig. 1. VASS $\mathcal{V}_{run}$ (left) and VASS $\mathcal{V}_{exp}$ (right)

by the repeated use of a constraint system in order to remove transitions that can definitely not be part of a zero-cycle. The algorithm of Kosaraju and Sullivan forms the basis for both cited papers [15, 5], as well as the present paper.

A line of work [18–20] has used VASSs (and their generalizations) as backends for the automated complexity analysis of C programs. These algorithms have been designed for practical applicability, but are not complete and no theoretical analysis of their precision has been given. We point out, however, that these papers have inspired the Bound Proof Principle in Section 5.

2   Preliminaries

Basic Notation. For a set X we denote by $|X|$ the number of elements of X. Let $\mathbb{S}$ be either $\mathbb{N}$ or $\mathbb{Z}$. We write $\mathbb{S}^I$ for the set of vectors over $\mathbb{S}$ indexed by some set I. We write $\mathbb{S}^{I \times J}$ for the set of matrices over $\mathbb{S}$ indexed by I and J. We write $\mathbf{1}$ for the vector which has entry 1 in every component. Given $a \in \mathbb{S}^I$, we write $a(i) \in \mathbb{S}$ for the entry at line $i \in I$ of a, and $\|a\| = \max_{i \in I} |a(i)|$ for the maximum absolute value of a. Given $a \in \mathbb{S}^I$ and $J \subseteq I$, we denote by $a|_J \in \mathbb{S}^J$ the restriction of a to J, i.e., we set $a|_J(i) = a(i)$ for all $i \in J$. Given $A \in \mathbb{S}^{I \times J}$, we write $A(j)$ for the vector in column $j \in J$ of A and $A(i,j) \in \mathbb{S}$ for the entry in column $i \in I$ and row $j \in J$ of A. Given $A \in \mathbb{S}^{I \times J}$ and $K \subseteq J$, we denote by $A|_K \in \mathbb{S}^{I \times K}$ the restriction of A to K, i.e., we set $A|_K(i,j) = A(i,j)$ for all $(i,j) \in I \times K$. We write **Id** for the square matrix which has entries 1 on the diagonal and 0 otherwise. Given $a, b \in \mathbb{S}^I$ we write $a + b \in \mathbb{S}^I$ for component-wise addition, $c \cdot a \in \mathbb{S}^I$ for multiplying every component of a by some $c \in \mathbb{S}$ and $a \geq b$ for component-wise comparison. Given $A \in \mathbb{S}^{I \times J}$, $B \in \mathbb{S}^{J \times K}$ and $x \in \mathbb{S}^J$, we write $AB \in \mathbb{S}^{I \times K}$ for the standard matrix multiplication, $Ax \in \mathbb{S}^I$ for the standard matrix-vector multiplication, $A^T \in \mathbb{S}^{J \times I}$ for the transposed matrix of A and $x^T \in \mathbb{S}^{1 \times J}$ for the transposed vector of x.

Vector Addition System with States (VASS). Let *Var* be a finite set of variables. A vector addition system with states (VASS) $\mathcal{V} = (St(\mathcal{V}), Trns(\mathcal{V}))$ consists of a finite set of *states* $St(\mathcal{V})$ and a finite set of *transitions* $Trns(\mathcal{V})$, where $Trns(\mathcal{V}) \subseteq St(\mathcal{V}) \times \mathbb{Z}^{Var} \times St(\mathcal{V})$; we call $n = |Var|$ the *dimension* of $\mathcal{V}$. We write $s_1 \xrightarrow{d} s_2$ to denote a transition $(s_1, d, s_2) \in Trns(\mathcal{V})$; we call the vector d the *update* of transition $s_1 \xrightarrow{d} s_2$. A *path* π of $\mathcal{V}$ is a finite sequence $s_0 \xrightarrow{d_1} s_1 \xrightarrow{d_2} \cdots s_k$ with $s_i \xrightarrow{d_{i+1}} s_{i+1} \in Trns(\mathcal{V})$ for all $0 \leq i < k$. We define the *length* of π by $length(\pi) = k$ and the *value* of π by $val(\pi) = \sum_{i \in [1,k]} d_i$. Let $\texttt{instance}(\pi, t)$ be the number of times π contains the transition t, i.e., the number of indices i such that $t = s_i \xrightarrow{d_i} s_{i+1}$. We remark that $length(\pi) = \sum_{t \in Trns(\mathcal{V})} \texttt{instance}(\pi, t)$ for every path π of $\mathcal{V}$. Given a finite path π_1 and a path π_2 such that the last state of π_1 equals the first state of π_2, we write $\pi = \pi_1 \pi_2$ for the path obtained by joining the last state of π_1 with the first state of π_2; we call π the *concatenation* of π_1 and π_2, and $\pi_1 \pi_2$ a *decomposition* of π. We say π' is a *sub-path* of π, if there is a decomposition $\pi = \pi_1 \pi' \pi_2$ for some π_1, π_2. A *cycle* is a path that has the same start- and end-state. A *multi-cycle* is a finite set of cycles. The value $val(M)$ of a multi-cycle M is the sum of the values of its cycles. $\mathcal{V}$ is *connected*, if for all $s, s' \in St(\mathcal{V})$ there is a path from s to s'. VASS $\mathcal{V}'$ is a *sub-VASS* of $\mathcal{V}$, if $St(\mathcal{V}') \subseteq St(\mathcal{V})$ and $Trns(\mathcal{V}') \subseteq Trns(\mathcal{V})$. Sub-VASSs $\mathcal{V}_1$ and $\mathcal{V}_2$ are *disjoint*, if $St(\mathcal{V}_1) \cap St(\mathcal{V}_2) = \emptyset$. A *strongly-connected component (SCC)* of a VASS $\mathcal{V}$ is a maximal sub-VASS S of $\mathcal{V}$ such that S is connected and $Trns(S) \neq \emptyset$.

Let $\mathcal{V}$ be a VASS. The set of *valuations* $Val(\mathcal{V}) = \mathbb{N}^{Var}$ consists of *Var*-vectors over the natural numbers (we assume $\mathbb{N}$ includes 0). The set of *configurations* $Cfg(\mathcal{V}) = St(\mathcal{V}) \times Val(\mathcal{V})$ consists of pairs of states and valuations. A *step* is a triple $((s_1, \nu_1), d, (s_2, \nu_2)) \in Cfg(\mathcal{V}) \times \mathbb{Z}^{dim(\mathcal{V})} \times Cfg(\mathcal{V})$ such that $\nu_2 = \nu_1 + d$ and $s_1 \xrightarrow{d} s_2 \in Trns(\mathcal{V})$. We write $(s_1, \nu_1) \xrightarrow{d} (s_2, \nu_2)$ to denote a step $((s_1, \nu_1), d, (s_2, \nu_2))$ of $\mathcal{V}$. A *trace* of $\mathcal{V}$ is a finite sequence $\zeta = (s_0, \nu_0) \xrightarrow{d_1} (s_1, \nu_1) \xrightarrow{d_2} \cdots (s_k, \nu_k)$ of steps. We lift the notions of length and instances from paths to traces in the obvious way: we consider the path $\pi = s_0 \xrightarrow{d_1} s_1 \xrightarrow{d_2} \cdots s_k$ that consists of the transitions used by ζ, and set $length(\zeta) := length(\pi)$ and $\texttt{instance}(\zeta, t) = \texttt{instance}(\pi, t)$, for all $t \in Trns(\mathcal{V})$. We denote by $\texttt{init}(\zeta) = \|\nu_0\|$ the maximum absolute value of the starting valuation ν_0 of ζ. We say that ζ *reaches* a valuation ν, if $\nu = \nu_k$. The *complexity* of $\mathcal{V}$ is the function $comp_{\mathcal{V}}(N) = \sup_{\text{trace } \zeta \text{ of } \mathcal{V}, \text{init}(\zeta) \leq N} length(\zeta)$, which returns for every $N \geq 0$ the supremum over the lengths of the traces ζ with $\text{init}(\zeta) \leq N$. The *variable bound* of a variable $x \in Var$ is the function $\text{vbound}_x(N) = \sup_{\text{trace } \zeta \text{ of } \mathcal{V}, \text{init}(\zeta) \leq N, \zeta \text{ reaches valuation } \nu} \nu(x)$, which returns for every $N \geq 0$ the supremum over the the values of x reachable by traces ζ with $\text{init}(\zeta) \leq N$. The *transition bound* of a transition $t \in Trns(\mathcal{V})$ is the function $\text{tbound}_t(N) = \sup_{\text{trace } \zeta \text{ of } \mathcal{V}, \text{init}(\zeta) \leq N} \text{instance}(\zeta, t)$, which returns for every $N \geq 0$ the supremum over the number of instances of t in traces ζ with $\text{init}(\zeta) \leq N$.

Rooted Tree. A *rooted tree* is a connected undirected acyclic graph in which one node has been designated as the root. We will usually denote the root by ι. We note that for every node η in a rooted tree there is a unique path of η to the root. The *parent* of a node $\eta \neq \iota$ is the node connected to η on the path to the root. Node η is a *child* of a node η', if η' is the parent of η. η' is a *descendent* of η, if η lies on the path from η' to the root; η' is a *strict* descendent, if furthermore $\eta \neq \eta'$. η is an *ancestor* of η', if η a descendent of η; η is a *strict* ancestor, if furthermore $\eta \neq \eta'$. The *distance* of a node η to the root, is the number of nodes $\neq \eta$ on the path from η to the root. We denote by $\text{layer}(l)$ the set of all nodes with the same distance l to the root; we remark that $\text{layer}(0) = \{\iota\}$.

All proofs are presented in the extended version [21] for space reasons.

3   A Dichotomy Result

We will make use of the following matrices associated to a VASS throughout the paper: Let $\mathcal{V}$ be a VASS. We define the *update matrix* $D \in \mathbb{Z}^{Var \times Trns(\mathcal{V})}$ by setting $D(t) = d$ for all transitions $t = (s, d, s') \in Trns(\mathcal{V})$. We define the *flow matrix* $F \in \mathbb{Z}^{St(\mathcal{V}) \times Trns(\mathcal{V})}$ by setting $F(s, t) = -1$, $F(s', t) = 1$ for transitions $t = (s, d, s')$ with $s' \neq s$, and $F(s, t) = F(s', t) = 0$ for transitions $t = (s, d, s')$ with $s' = s$; in both cases we further set $F(s'', t) = 0$ for all states s'' with $s'' \neq s$ and $s'' \neq s'$. We note that every column t of F either contains exactly one -1 and 1 entry (in case the source and target of transition t are different) or only 0 entries (in case the source and target of transition t are the same).

Example 1. We state the update and flow matrix for $\mathcal{V}_{run}$ from Section 1:

$$D = \begin{pmatrix} -1 & 1 & -1 & 1 & 0 & 0 & 0 & 0 & -1 & 0 \\ 1 & -1 & 1 & -1 & 0 & 0 & 0 & 0 & 0 & 0 \\ -1 & 1 & 1 & -1 & -1 & -1 & -1 & -1 & 0 & 0 \end{pmatrix}, F = \begin{pmatrix} 0 & 0 & 0 & 0 & 1 & -1 & 0 & 0 & -1 & 0 \\ 0 & 0 & 0 & 0 & -1 & 1 & 0 & 0 & 0 & 1 \\ 0 & 0 & 0 & 0 & 0 & 0 & 1 & -1 & 1 & 0 \\ 0 & 0 & 0 & 0 & 0 & 0 & -1 & 1 & 0 & -1 \end{pmatrix},$$

with column order $s_1 \to s_1$, $s_2 \to s_2$, $s_3 \to s_3$, $s_4 \to s_4$, $s_2 \to s_1$, $s_1 \to s_2$, $s_4 \to s_3$, $s_3 \to s_4$, $s_1 \to s_3$, $s_4 \to s_2$ (from left to right) and row order x, y, z for D resp. s_1, s_2, s_3, s_4 for F (from top to bottom).

We now consider the constraint systems (P) and (Q), stated below, which have maximization objectives. The constraint systems will be used by our main algorithm in Section 4. We observe that both constraint systems are always satisfiable (set all coefficients to zero) and that the solutions of both constraint systems are closed under addition. Hence, the number of inequalities for which the maximization objective is satisfied is unique for optimal solutions of both constraint systems. The maximization objectives can be implemented by suitable linear objective functions. Hence, both constraint systems can be solved in PTIME over the integers, because we can use linear programming over the rationales and then scale rational solutions to the integers by multiplying with the least common multiple of the denominators.

constraint system (P):	constraint system (Q):
there exists $\mu \in \mathbb{Z}^{Trns(\mathcal{V})}$ with	there exist $r \in \mathbb{Z}^{Var}, z \in \mathbb{Z}^{St(\mathcal{V})}$ with
$$D\mu \geq 0$$ $$\mu \geq 0$$ $$F\mu = 0$$	$$r \geq 0$$ $$z \geq 0$$ $$D^T r + F^T z \leq 0$$
Maximization Objective: Maximize the number of inequalities with $(D\mu)(x) > 0$ and $\mu(t) > 0$	Maximization Objective: Maximize the number of inequalities with $r(x) > 0$ and $(D^T r + F^T z)(t) < 0$

The solutions of (P) and (Q) are characterized by the following two lemmata:

Lemma 2 (Cited from [14]). $\mu \in \mathbb{Z}^{Trns(\mathcal{V})}$ *is a solution to constraint system (P) iff there exists a multi-cycle M with $val(M) \geq 0$ and $\mu(t)$ instances of transition t for every $t \in Trns(\mathcal{V})$.*

Lemma 3 (Cited from [5][1]). *Let r, z be a solution to constraint system (Q). Let $rank(r, z) : Cfg(\mathcal{V}) \to \mathbb{N}$ be the function defined by $rank(r, z)(s, \nu) = r^T \nu + z(s)$. Then, $rank(r, z)$ is a quasi-ranking function for $\mathcal{V}$, i.e., we have*

1. *for all $(s, \nu) \in Cfg(\mathcal{V})$ that $rank(r, z)(s, \nu) \geq 0$;*

2. *for all transitions $t = s_1 \xrightarrow{d} s_2 \in Trns(\mathcal{V})$ and valuations $\nu_1, \nu_2 \in Val(\mathcal{V})$ with $\nu_2 = \nu_1 + d$ that $rank(r, z)(s_1, \nu_1) \geq rank(r, z)(s_2, \nu_2)$; moreover, the inequality is strict for every t with $(D^T r + F^T z)(t) < 0$.*

We now state a dichotomy between optimal solutions to constraint systems (P) and (Q), which is obtained by an application of Farkas' Lemma. This dichotomy is the main reason why we are able to compute the precise asymptotic complexity of VASSs with polynomial bounds.

---

[1] There is no explicit lemma with this statement in [5], however the lemma is implicit in the exposition of Section 4 in [5]. We further note that [5] does not include the constraint $z \geq 0$. However, this difference is minor and was added in order to ensure that ranking functions always return non-negative values, which is more standard than the choice of [5]. A proof of the lemma can be found in the extended version [21].

Lemma 4. *Let r and z be an optimal solution to constraint system (Q) and let μ be an optimal solution to constraint system (P). Then, for all variables $x \in Var$ we either have $r(x) > 0$ or $(D\mu)(x) \geq 1$, and for all transitions $t \in Trns(\mathcal{V})$ we either have $(D^T r + F^T z)(t) < 0$ or $\mu(t) \geq 1$.*

Example 5. Our main algorithm, Algorithm 1 presented in Section 4, will directly use constraint systems (P) and (Q) in its first loop iteration, and adjusted versions in later loop iterations. Here, we illustrate the first loop iteration. We consider the running example $\mathcal{V}_{run}$, whose update and flow matrices we have stated in Example 1. An optimal solution to constraint systems (P) and (Q) is given by $\mu = (1441111100)^T$ and $r = (220)^T$, $z = (0011)^T$. The quasi-ranking function $rank(r, z)$ immediately establishes that $\mathtt{tbound}_t(N) \in O(N)$ for $t = s_1 \to s_3$ and $t = s_4 \to s_2$, because 1) $rank(r, z)$ decreases for these two transitions and does not increase for other transitions (by Lemma 3), and because 2) the initial value of $rank(r, z)$ is bounded by $O(N)$, i.e., we have $rank(r, z)(s, \nu) \in O(N)$ for every state $s \in St(\mathcal{V}_{run})$ and every valuation ν with $\|\nu\| \leq N$. By a similar argument we get $\mathtt{vbound}_x(N) \in O(N)$ and $\mathtt{vbound}_y(N) \in O(N)$. The exact reasoning for deriving upper bounds is given in Section 5. From μ we can, by Lemma 2, obtain the cycles $C_1 = s_1 \to s_2 \to s_2 \to s_2 \to s_2 \to s_2 \to s_1 \to s_1$ and $C_2 = s_3 \to s_4 \to s_4 \to s_4 \to s_4 \to s_4 \to s_4 \to s_4$ with $\nu(C_1) + \nu(C_2) \geq (001)^T$ (*). We will later show that the cycles C_1 and C_2 give rise to a family of traces that establish $\mathtt{tbound}_t(N) \in \Omega(N^2)$ for all transitions $t \in Trns(\mathcal{V}_{run})$ with $t \neq s_1 \to s_3$ and $t \neq s_4 \to s_2$. Here we give an intuition on the construction: We consider a cycle C of $\mathcal{V}_{run}$ that visits all states at least once. By (*), the updates along the cycles C_1 and C_2 cancel each other out. However, the two cycles are not connected. Hence, we execute the cycle C_1 some $\Omega(N)$ times, then (a part of) the cycle C, then execute C_2 as often as C_1, and finally the remaining part of C; this we repeat $\Omega(N)$ times. This construction also establishes the bound $\mathtt{vbound}_z(N) \in \Omega(N^2)$ because, by (*), we increase z with every joint execution of C_1 and C_2. The precise lower bound construction is given in Section 6.

4   Main Algorithm

Our main algorithm – Algorithm 1 – computes the complexity as well as variable and transition bounds of an input VASS $\mathcal{V}$, either detecting that $\mathcal{V}$ has at least exponential complexity or reporting precise asymptotic bounds for the transitions and variables of $\mathcal{V}$ (up to a constant factor): Algorithm 1 will compute values $\mathtt{vExp}(x) \in \mathbb{N}$ such that $\mathtt{vbound}_N(x) \in \Theta(N^{\mathtt{vExp}(x)})$ for every $x \in Var$ and values $\mathtt{tExp}(t) \in \mathbb{N}$ such that $\mathtt{tbound}_N(t) \in \Theta(N^{\mathtt{tExp}(t)})$ for every $t \in Trns(\mathcal{V})$.

Data Structures. The algorithm maintains a rooted tree T. Every node η of T will always be labelled by a sub-VASSs $\mathtt{VASS}(\eta)$ of $\mathcal{V}$. The nodes in the same layer of T will always be labelled by disjoint sub-VASS of $\mathcal{V}$. The main loop of Algorithm 1 will extend T by one layer per loop iteration. The variable l always contains the next layer that is going to be added to T. For computing variable and transition bounds, Algorithm 1 maintains the functions $\mathtt{vExp} : Var \to \mathbb{N} \cup \{\infty\}$ and $\mathtt{tExp} : Trns(\mathcal{V}) \to \mathbb{N} \cup \{\infty\}$.

Initialization. We assume D to be the update matrix and F to be the flow matrix associated to $\mathcal{V}$ as discussed in Section 3. At initialization, T consists of the root node ι and we set $\mathtt{VASS}(\iota) = \mathcal{V}$, i.e., the root is labelled by the input $\mathcal{V}$. We initialize $l = 1$ as Algorithm 1 is going to add layer 1 to T in the first loop iteration. We initialize $\mathtt{vExp}(x) = \infty$ for all variables $x \in \mathit{Var}$ and $\mathtt{tExp}(t) = \infty$ for all transitions $t \in \mathit{Trns}(\mathcal{V})$.

The constraint systems solved during each loop iteration. In loop iteration l, Algorithm 1 will set $\mathtt{tExp}(t) := l$ for some transitions t and $\mathtt{vExp}(x) := l$ for some variables x. In order to determine those transitions and variables, Algorithm 1 instantiates constraint systems (P) and (Q) from Section 3 over the set of transitions $U = \bigcup_{\eta \in \mathtt{layer}(l-1)} \mathit{Trns}(\mathtt{VASS}(\eta))$, which contains all transitions associated to nodes in layer $l-1$ of T. However, instead of a direct instantiation using $D|_U$ and $F|_U$ (i.e., the restriction of D and F to the transitions U), we need to work with an extended set of variables and an extended update matrix. We set $\mathit{Var}_{ext} := \{(x, \eta) \mid \eta \in \mathtt{layer}(l - \mathtt{vExp}(x))\}$, where we set $n - \infty = 0$ for all $n \in \mathbb{N}$. This means that we use a different copy of variable x for every node η in layer $l - \mathtt{vExp}(x)$. We note that for a variable x with $\mathtt{vExp}(x) = \infty$ there is only a single copy of x in Var_{ext} because $\iota \in \mathtt{layer}(0)$ is the only node in layer 0. We define the extended update matrix $D_{ext} \in \mathbb{Z}^{\mathit{Var}_{ext} \times U}$ by setting

$$D_{ext}((x, \eta), t) := \begin{cases} D(x, t), & \text{if } t \in \mathit{Trns}(\mathtt{VASS}(\eta)), \\ 0, & \text{otherwise.} \end{cases}$$

Constraint systems (I) and (II) stated in Figure 2 can be recognized as instantiation of constraint systems (P) and (Q) with matrices D_{ext} and $F|_U$ and variables Var_{ext}, and hence the dichotomy stated in Lemma 4 holds.

We comment on the choice of Var_{ext}: Setting $\mathit{Var}_{ext} = \{(x, \eta) \mid \eta \in \mathtt{layer}(i)\}$ for any $i \leq l - \mathtt{vExp}(x)$ would result in correct upper bounds (while $i > l - \mathtt{vExp}(x)$ would not). However, choosing $i < l - \mathtt{vExp}(x)$ does in general result in sub-optimal bounds because fewer variables make constraint system (I) easier and constraint system (II) harder to satisfy (in terms of their maximization objectives). In fact, $i = l - \mathtt{vExp}(x)$ is the optimal choice, because this choice allows us to prove corresponding lower bounds in Section 6. We will further comment on key properties of constraint systems (I) and (II) in Sections 5 and 6, when we outline the proofs of the upper resp. lower bound.

We note that Algorithm 1 does not use the optimal solution μ to constraint system (I) for the computation of the $\mathtt{vExp}(x)$ and $\mathtt{tExp}(t)$, and hence the computation of the optimal solution μ could be removed from the algorithm. The solution μ is however needed for the extraction of lower bounds in Sections 6 and 8, and this is the reason why it is stated here. The extraction of lower bounds is not explicitly added to the algorithm in order to not clutter the presentation.

Discovering transition bounds. After an optimal solution r, z to constraint system (II) has been found, Algorithm 1 collects all transitions t with $(D_{ext}^T r + F|_U^T z)(t) < 0$ in the set R (note that the optimization criterion in constraint system (II) tries to find as many such t as possible). Algorithm 1 then sets $\mathtt{tExp}(t) := l$ for all $t \in R$. The transitions in R will not be part of layer l of T.

Input: a connected VASS $\mathcal{V}$ with update matrix D and flow matrix F
$T :=$ single root node ι with $\text{VASS}(\iota) = \mathcal{V}$;
$l := 1$;
$\text{vExp}(x) := \infty$ for all variables $x \in \text{Var}$;
$\text{tExp}(t) := \infty$ for all transitions $t \in \text{Trns}(\mathcal{V})$;
repeat
    let $U := \bigcup_{\eta \in \text{layer}(l-1)} \text{Trns}(\text{VASS}(\eta))$;
    let $\text{Var}_{ext} := \{(x, \eta) \mid \eta \in \text{layer}(l - \text{vExp}(x))\}$, where $n - \infty = 0$ for $n \in \mathbb{N}$;
    let $D_{ext} \in \mathbb{Z}^{\text{Var}_{ext} \times U}$ be the matrix defined by
$$D_{ext}((x, \eta), t) = \begin{cases} D(x, t), & \text{if } t \in \text{Trns}(\text{VASS}(\eta)) \\ 0, & \text{otherwise} \end{cases};$$
    find optimal solutions μ and r, z to constraint systems (I) and (II);
    let $R := \{t \in U \mid (D_{ext}^T r + F|_U^T z)(t) < 0\}$;
    set $\text{tExp}(t) := l$ for all $t \in R$;
    foreach $\eta \in \text{layer}(l-1)$ **do**
        let $\mathcal{V}' := \text{VASS}(\eta)$ be the VASS associated to η;
        decompose $(St(\mathcal{V}'), \text{Trns}(\mathcal{V}') \setminus R)$ into SCCs;
        foreach SCC S of $(St(\mathcal{V}'), \text{Trns}(\mathcal{V}') \setminus R)$ **do**
            create a child η' of η with $\text{VASS}(\eta') = S$;
    foreach $x \in \text{Var}$ with $\text{vExp}(x) = \infty$ **do**
        if $r(x, \iota) > 0$ **then** set $\text{vExp}(x) := l$;
    if there are no $x \in \text{Var}$, $t \in \text{Trns}(\mathcal{V})$ with $l < \text{vExp}(x) + \text{tExp}(t) < \infty$ **then**
        return "$\mathcal{V}$ has at least exponential complexity"
    $l := l + 1$;
until $\text{vExp}(x) \neq \infty$ and $\text{tExp}(t) \neq \infty$ for all $x \in \text{Var}$ and $t \in \text{Trns}(\mathcal{V})$;

Algorithm 1: Computes transition and variable bounds for a VASS $\mathcal{V}$

constraint system (I):	constraint system (II):
there exists $\mu \in \mathbb{Z}^U$ with	there exist $r \in \mathbb{Z}^{\text{Var}_{ext}}, z \in \mathbb{Z}^{St(\mathcal{V})}$ with
$D_{ext}\mu \geq 0$	$r \geq 0$
$\mu \geq 0$	$z \geq 0$
$F\|_U \mu = 0$	$D_{ext}^T r + F\|_U^T z \leq 0$
Maximization Objective:	Maximization Objective:
Maximize the number of inequalities with $(D_{ext}\mu)(x) > 0$ and $\mu(t) > 0$	Maximize the number of inequalities with $r(x, \eta) > 0$ and $(D_{ext}^T r + F\|_U^T z)(t) < 0$

Fig. 2. Constraint Systems (I) and (II) used by Algorithm 1

Construction of the next layer in T. For each node η in layer $l - 1$, Algorithm 1 will create children by removing the transitions in R. This is done as follows: Given a node η in layer $l - 1$, Algorithm 1 considers the VASS $\mathcal{V}' = \text{VASS}(\eta)$ associated to η. Then, $(St(\mathcal{V}'), \text{Trns}(\mathcal{V}')\setminus R)$ is decomposed into its SCCs. Finally, for each SCC S of $(St(\mathcal{V}'), Trns(\mathcal{V}') \setminus R)$ a child η' of η is created with $\text{VASS}(\eta') = S$. Clearly, the new nodes in layer l are labelled by disjoint sub-VASS of $\mathcal{V}$.

The transitions of the next layer. The following lemma states that the new layer l of T contains all transitions of layer $l-1$ except for the transitions R; the lemma is due to the fact that every transition in $U \setminus R$ belongs to a cycle and hence to some SCC that is part of the new layer l.

Lemma 6. *We consider the new layer constructed during loop iteration l of Algorithm 1: we have $U \setminus R = \bigcup_{\eta \in \text{layer}(l)} Trns(\text{VASS}(\eta))$.*

Discovering variable bounds. For each $x \in Var$ with $\text{vExp}(x) = \infty$, Algorithm 1 checks whether $r(x, \iota) > 0$ (we point out that the optimization criterion in constraint systems (II) tries to find as many such x with $r(x, \iota) > 0$ as possible). Algorithm 1 then sets $\text{vExp}(x) := l$ for all those variables.

The check for exponential complexity. In each loop iteration, Algorithm 1 checks whether there are $x \in Var$, $t \in Trns(\mathcal{V})$ with $l < \text{vExp}(x) + \text{tExp}(t) < \infty$. If this is not the case, then we can conclude that $\mathcal{V}$ is at least exponential (see Theorem 9 below). If the check fails, Algorithm 1 increments l and continues with the construction of the next layer in the next loop iteration.

Termination criterion. The algorithm proceeds until either exponential complexity has been detected or until $\text{vExp}(x) \neq \infty$ and $\text{tExp}(t) \neq \infty$ for all $x \in Var$ and $t \in Trns(\mathcal{V})$ (i.e., bounds have been computed for all variables and transitions).

Invariants. We now state some simple invariants maintained by Algorithm 1, which are easy to verify:

- For every node η that is a descendent of some node η' we have that $\text{VASS}(\eta)$ is a sub-VASS of $\text{VASS}(\eta')$.
- The value of vExp and tExp is changed at most once for each input; when the value is changed, it is changed from ∞ to some value $\neq \infty$.
- For every transition $t \in Trns(\mathcal{V})$ and layer l of T, we have that either $\text{tExp}(t) \leq l$ or there is a node $\eta \in \text{layer}(l)$ such that $t \in Trns(\text{VASS}(\eta))$.
- We have $\text{tExp}(t) = l$ for $t \in Trns(\mathcal{V})$ if and only if there is a $\eta \in \text{layer}(l-1)$ with $t \in Trns(\text{VASS}(\eta))$ and there is no $\eta \in \text{layer}(l)$ with $t \in Trns(\text{VASS}(\eta))$.

Example 7. We sketch the execution of Algorithm 1 on $\mathcal{V}_{run}$. In iteration $l = 1$, we have $Var_{ext} = \{(x, \iota), (y, \iota), (z, \iota)\}$, and thus matrix D_{ext} is identical to the matrix D. Hence, constraint systems (I) and (II) are identical to constraint systems (P) and (Q), whose optimal solutions $\mu = (1441111100)^T$ and $r = (220)^T$, $z = (0011)^T$ we have discussed in Example 5. Algorithm 1 then sets $\text{tExp}(s_1 \rightarrow s_3) = 1$ and $\text{tExp}(s_4 \rightarrow s_2) = 1$, creates two children η_A and η_B of ι labeled by $\mathcal{V}_A = (\{s_1, s_2\}, \{s_1 \rightarrow s_1, s_1 \rightarrow s_2, s_2 \rightarrow s_2, s_2 \rightarrow s_1\})$ and $\mathcal{V}_B = (\{s_3, s_4\}, \{s_3 \rightarrow s_3, s_3 \rightarrow s_4, s_4 \rightarrow s_4, s_4 \rightarrow s_3\})$, and sets $\text{vExp}(x) = 1$ and $\text{vExp}(y) = 1$. In iteration $l = 2$, we have $Var_{ext} = \{(x, \eta_A), (y, \eta_A), (x, \eta_B), (y, \eta_B), (z, \iota)\}$ and the matrix D_{ext} stated in Figure 3. Algorithm 1 obtains $\mu = (11110000)^T$ and $r = (12211)^T$, $z = (0000)^T$ as optimal solutions to (I) and (II). Algorithm 1 then

$$D_{ext} = \begin{pmatrix} -1 & 1 & 0 & 0 & 0 & 0 & 0 & 0 \\ 1 & -1 & 0 & 0 & 0 & 0 & 0 & 0 \\ 0 & 0 & -1 & 1 & 0 & 0 & 0 & 0 \\ 0 & 0 & 1 & -1 & 0 & 0 & 0 & 0 \\ -1 & 1 & 1 & -1 & -1 & -1 & -1 & -1 \end{pmatrix}$$

with column order $s_1 \to s_1$, $s_2 \to s_2$, $s_3 \to s_3$, $s_4 \to s_4$, $s_2 \to s_1$, $s_1 \to s_2$, $s_4 \to s_3$, $s_3 \to s_4$ (from left to right) and row order $(x, \eta_A), (y, \eta_A), (x, \eta_B)$, $(y, \eta_B), (z, \iota)$ (from top to bottom)

$$D_{ext} = \begin{pmatrix} -1 & 0 & 0 & 0 \\ 1 & 0 & 0 & 0 \\ 0 & 1 & 0 & 0 \\ 0 & -1 & 0 & 0 \\ 0 & 0 & -1 & 0 \\ 0 & 0 & 1 & 0 \\ 0 & 0 & 0 & 1 \\ 0 & 0 & 0 & -1 \\ -1 & 1 & 0 & 0 \\ 0 & 0 & 1 & -1 \end{pmatrix}$$

with column order $s_1 \to s_1$, $s_2 \to s_2$, $s_3 \to s_3$, $s_4 \to s_4$, (from left to right) and row order $(x, \eta_1), (y, \eta_1), (x, \eta_2)$, $(y, \eta_2), (x, \eta_3), (y, \eta_3)$, $(x, \eta_4), (y, \eta_4), (z, \eta_A)$, (z, η_B) (from top to bottom)

Fig. 3. The extended update matrices during iteration $l = 2$ (left) and $l = 3$ (right) of Algorithm 1 on the running example $\mathcal{V}_{run}$ from Section 1.

sets $\texttt{tExp}(s_1 \to s_2) = \texttt{tExp}(s_2 \to s_1) = \texttt{tExp}(s_3 \to s_4) = \texttt{tExp}(s_4 \to s_3) = 2$, creates the children η_1, η_2 resp. η_3, η_4 of η_A resp. η_B with η_i labelled by $\mathcal{V}_i = (\{s_i\}, \{s_i \to s_i\})$, and sets $\texttt{vExp}(z) = 2$. In iteration $l = 3$, we have $Var_{ext} = \{(x, \eta_1), (y, \eta_1), (x, \eta_2), (y, \eta_2), (x, \eta_3), (y, \eta_3), (x, \eta_4), (y, \eta_4), (z, \eta_A), (z, \eta_B)\}$ and the matrix D_{ext} stated in Figure 3. Algorithm 1 obtains $\mu = (0000)^T$ and $r = (1113311111)^T$, $z = (0000)^T$ as optimal solutions to (I) and (II). Algorithm 1 then sets $\texttt{tExp}(s_i \to s_i) = 3$, for all i, and terminates.

We now state the main properties of Algorithm 1:

Lemma 8. *Algorithm 1 always terminates.*

Theorem 9. *If Algorithm 1 returns "$\mathcal{V}$ has at least exponential complexity", then $comp_{\mathcal{V}}(N) \in 2^{\Omega(N)}$, and we have $\texttt{tbound}_t(N) \in 2^{\Omega(N)}$ for all $t \in Trns(\mathcal{V})$ with $\texttt{tExp}(t) = \infty$ and $\texttt{vbound}_t(N) \in 2^{\Omega(N)}$ for all $x \in Var$ with $\texttt{vExp}(x) = \infty$.*

The proof of Theorem 9 is stated in Section 8. We now assume that Algorithm 1 does not return "$\mathcal{V}$ has at least exponential complexity". Then, Algorithm 1 must terminate with $\texttt{tExp}(t) \neq \infty$ and $\texttt{vExp}(x) \neq \infty$ for all $t \in Trns(\mathcal{V})$ and $x \in Var$. The following result states that $\texttt{tExp}$ and $\texttt{vExp}$ contain the precise exponents of the asymptotic transition and variable bounds of $\mathcal{V}$:

Theorem 10. $\texttt{vbound}_N(x) \in \Theta(N^{\texttt{vExp}(x)})$ *for all $x \in Var$ and $\texttt{tbound}_N(t) \in \Theta(N^{\texttt{tExp}(t)})$ for all $t \in Trns(\mathcal{V})$.*

The upper bounds of Theorem 10 will be proved in Section 5 (Theorem 16) and the lower bounds in Section 6 (Corollary 20).

We will prove in Section 7 that the exponents of the variable and transition bounds are bounded exponentially in the dimension of $\mathcal{V}$:

Theorem 11. *We have $\texttt{vExp}(x) \leq 2^{|Var|}$ for all $x \in Var$ and $\texttt{tExp}(t) \leq 2^{|Var|}$ for all $t \in Trns(\mathcal{V})$.*

Finally, we obtain the following corollary from Theorems 10 and 11:

Corollary 12. *Let $\mathcal{V}$ be a connected VASS. Then, either $comp_{\mathcal{V}}(N) \in 2^{\Omega(N)}$ or $comp_{\mathcal{V}}(N) \in \Theta(N^i)$ for some computable $1 \leq i \leq 2^{|Var|}$.*

4.1   Complexity of Algorithm 1

In the remainder of this section we will establish the following result:

Theorem 13. *Algorithm 1 (with the below stated optimization) can be implemented in polynomial time with regard to the size of the input VASS $\mathcal{V}$.*

We will argue that A) every loop iteration of Algorithm 1 only takes polynomial time, and B) that polynomially many loop iterations are sufficient (this only holds for the optimization of the algorithm discussed below).

Let $\mathcal{V}$ be a VASS, let $m = |\mathit{Trns}(\mathcal{V})|$ be the number of transitions of $\mathcal{V}$, and let $n = |\mathit{Var}|$ be the dimension of $\mathcal{V}$. We note that $|\mathtt{layer}(l)| \leq m$ for every layer l of T, because the VASSs of the nodes in the same layer are disjoint.

A) Clearly, removing the decreasing transitions and computing the strongly connected components can be done in polynomial time. It remains to argue about constraint systems (I) and (II). We observe that $|\mathit{Var}_{ext}| = |\{(x, \eta) \mid \eta \in \mathtt{layer}(l - \mathtt{vExp}(x))\}| \leq n \cdot m$ and $|U| \leq m$. Hence the size of constraint systems (I) and (II) is polynomial in the size of $\mathcal{V}$. Moreover, constraint systems (I) and (II) can be solved in PTIME as noted in Section 3.

B) We do not a-priori have a bound on the number of iterations of the main loop of Algorithm 1. (Theorem 11 implies that the number of iterations is at most exponential; however, we do not use this result here). We will shortly state an improvement of Algorithm 1 that ensures that polynomially many iterations are sufficient. The underlying insight is that certain layers of the tree do not need to be constructed explicitly. This insight is stated in the lemma below:

Lemma 14. *We consider the point in time when the execution of Algorithm 1 reaches line $l := l + 1$ during some loop iteration $l \geq 1$. Let $RelevantLayers = \{\mathtt{tExp}(t) + \mathtt{vExp}(x) \mid x \in \mathit{Var}, t \in \mathit{Trns}(\mathcal{V})\}$ and let $l' = \min\{l' \mid l' > l, l' \in RelevantLayers\}$. Then, $\mathtt{vExp}(x) \neq i$ and $\mathtt{tExp}(t) \neq i$ for all $x \in \mathit{Var}$, $t \in \mathit{Trns}(\mathcal{V})$ and $l < i < l'$.*

We now present the optimization that achieves polynomially many loop iterations. We replace the line $l := l + 1$ by the two lines $RelevantLayers := \{\mathtt{tExp}(t) + \mathtt{vExp}(x) \mid x \in \mathit{Var}, t \in \mathit{Trns}(\mathcal{V})\}$ and $l := \min\{l' \mid l' > l, l' \in RelevantLayers\}$. The effect of these two lines is that Algorithm 1 directly skips to the next relevant layer. Lemma 14, stated above, justifies this optimization: First, no new variable or transition bound is discovered in the intermediate layers $l < i < l'$. Second, each intermediate layer $l < i < l'$ has the same number of nodes as layer l, which are labelled by the same sub-VASSs as the nodes in l (otherwise there would be a transition with transition bound $l < i < l'$); hence, whenever needed, Algorithm 1 can construct a missing layer $l < i < l'$ on-the-fly from layer l.

We now analyze the number of loop iterations of the optimized algorithm. We recall that the value of each $\mathtt{vExp}(x)$ and $\mathtt{tExp}(t)$ is changed at most once from ∞ to some value $\neq \infty$. Hence, Algorithm 1 encounters at most $n \cdot m$ different values in the set $RelevantLayers = \{\mathtt{tExp}(t) + \mathtt{vExp}(x) \mid x \in \mathit{Var}, t \in \mathit{Trns}(\mathcal{V})\}$ during execution. Thus, the number of loop iterations is bounded by $n \cdot m$.

5   Proof of the Upper Bound Theorem

We begin by stating a proof principle for obtaining upper bounds.

Proposition 15 (Bound Proof Principle). *Let $\mathcal{V}$ be a VASS. Let $U \subseteq Trns(\mathcal{V})$ be a subset of the transitions of $\mathcal{V}$. Let $w : Cfg(\mathcal{V}) \to \mathbb{N}$ and $\mathrm{inc}_t :$ $\mathbb{N} \to \mathbb{N}$, for every $t \in Trns(\mathcal{V}) \setminus U$, be functions such that for every trace $\zeta = (s_0, \nu_0) \xrightarrow{d_1} (s_1, \nu_1) \xrightarrow{d_2} \cdots$ of $\mathcal{V}$ with $\mathrm{init}(\zeta) \leq N$ we have for every $i \geq 0$ that*

1) $s_i \xrightarrow{d_i} s_{i+1} \in U$ implies $w(s_i, \nu_i) \geq w(s_{i+1}, \nu_{i+1})$, and

2) $s_i \xrightarrow{d_i} s_{i+1} \in Trns(\mathcal{V}) \setminus U$ implies $w(s_i, \nu_i) + \mathrm{inc}_t(N) \geq w(s_{i+1}, \nu_{i+1})$.

We call such a function w a complexity witness *and the associated inc_t functions the* increase certificates.

Let $t \in U$ be a transition on which w decreases, i.e., we have $w(s_1, \nu_1) \geq w(s_2, \nu_2) - 1$ for every step $(s_1, \nu_1) \xrightarrow{d} (s_2, \nu_2)$ of $\mathcal{V}$ with $t = s_1 \xrightarrow{d} s_2$. Then,

$$\mathrm{tbound}_t(N) \leq \max_{(s,\nu) \in Cfg(\mathcal{V}), \|\nu\| \leq N} w(s, \nu) + \sum_{t' \in Trns(\mathcal{V}) \setminus U} \mathrm{tbound}_{t'}(N) \cdot \mathrm{inc}_{t'}(N).$$

Further, let $x \in Var$ be a variable such that $\nu(x) \leq w(s, \nu)$ for all $(s, \nu) \in Cfg(\mathcal{V})$. Then,

$$\mathrm{vbound}_x(N) \leq \max_{(s,\nu) \in Cfg(\mathcal{V}), \|\nu\| \leq N} w(s, \nu) + \sum_{t' \in Trns(\mathcal{V}) \setminus U} \mathrm{tbound}_{t'}(N) \cdot \mathrm{inc}_{t'}(N).$$

Proof Outline of the Upper Bound Theorem. Let $\mathcal{V}$ be a VASS for which Algorithm 1 does not report exponential complexity. We will prove by induction on loop iteration l that $\mathrm{vbound}_N(x) \in O(N^l)$ for every $x \in Var$ with $\mathrm{vExp}(x) = l$ and that $\mathrm{tbound}_N(t) \in O(N^l)$ for every $t \in Trns(\mathcal{V})$ with $\mathrm{tExp}(t) = l$.

We now consider some loop iteration $l \geq 1$. Let $U = \bigcup_{\eta \in \mathrm{layer}(l-1)} Trns(\mathrm{VASS}(\eta))$ be the transitions, Var_{ext} be the set of extended variables and $D_{ext} \in \mathbb{Z}^{Var_{ext} \times U}$ be the update matrix considered by Algorithm 1 during loop iteration l. Let r, z be some optimal solution to constraint system (II) computed by Algorithm 1 during loop iteration l. The main idea for the upper bound proof is to use the quasi-ranking function from Lemma 3 as witness function for the Bound Proof Principle. In order to apply Lemma 3 we need to consider the VASS associated to the matrices in constraint system (II): Let $\mathcal{V}_{ext}$ be the VASS over variables Var_{ext} associated to update matrix D_{ext} and flow matrix $F|_U$. From Lemma 3 we get that $rank(r, z) : Cfg(\mathcal{V}_{ext}) \to \mathbb{N}$ is a quasi-ranking function for $\mathcal{V}_{ext}$. We now need to relate $\mathcal{V}$ to the extended VASS $\mathcal{V}_{ext}$ in order to be able to use this quasi-ranking function. We do so by extending valuations over Var to valuations over Var_{ext}. For every state $s \in St(\mathcal{V})$ and valuation $\nu : Var \to \mathbb{N}$, we define the *extended valuation* $\mathrm{ext}_s(\nu) : Var_{ext} \to \mathbb{N}$ by setting

$$\mathrm{ext}_s(\nu)(x, \eta) = \begin{cases} \nu(x), & \text{if } s \in St(\mathrm{VASS}(\eta)), \\ 0, & \text{otherwise.} \end{cases}$$

As a direct consequence from the definition of extended valuations, we have that $(s, \text{ext}_s(\nu)) \in Cfg(\mathcal{V}_{ext})$ for all $(s, \nu) \in Cfg(\mathcal{V})$, and that $(s_1, \text{ext}_{s_1}(\nu_1)) \xrightarrow{D_{ext}(t)} (s_2, \text{ext}_{s_2}(\nu_2))$ is a step of $\mathcal{V}_{ext}$ for every step $(s_1, \nu_1) \xrightarrow{d} (s_2, \nu_2)$ of $\mathcal{V}$ with $s_1 \xrightarrow{d} s_2 \in U$. We now define the witness function w by setting

$$w(s, \nu) = rank(r, z)(s, \text{ext}_s(\nu)) \qquad \text{for all } (s, \nu) \in Cfg(\mathcal{V}).$$

We immediately get from Lemma 3 that w maps configurations to the non-negative integers and that condition 1) of the Bound Proof Principle is satisfied. Indeed, we get from the first item of Lemma 3 that $w(s, \nu) \geq 0$ for all $(s, \nu) \in Cfg(\mathcal{V})$, and from the second item that $w(s_1, \nu_1) \geq w(s_2, \nu_2)$ for every step $(s_1, \nu_1) \xrightarrow{d} (s_2, \nu_2)$ of $\mathcal{V}$ with $t = s_1 \xrightarrow{d} s_2 \in U$; moreover, the inequality is strict if $(D_{ext}^T r + F|_U^T z)(t) < 0$, i.e., the witness function w decreases for transitions t with $\text{tExp}(t) = l$. It remains to establish condition 2) of the Bound Proof Principle. We will argue that we can find increase certificates $\text{inc}_t(N) \in O(N^{l-\text{tExp}(t)})$ for all $t \in Trns(\mathcal{V}) \setminus U$. We note that $\text{tExp}(t) < l$ for all $t \in Trns(\mathcal{V}) \setminus U$, and hence the induction assumption can be applied for such t. We can then derive the desired bounds from the Bound Proof Principle because of $\sum_{t \in Trns(\mathcal{V}) \setminus U} \text{tbound}_t(N) \cdot \text{inc}_t(N) = \sum_{t \in Trns(\mathcal{V}) \setminus U} O(N^{\text{tExp}(t)}) \cdot O(N^{l-\text{tExp}(t)}) = O(N^l)$.

Theorem 16. $\text{vbound}_N(x) \in O(N^{\text{vExp}(x)})$ for all $x \in Var$ and $\text{tbound}_N(t) \in O(N^{\text{tExp}(t)})$ for all $t \in Trns(\mathcal{V})$.

6 Proof of the Lower Bound Theorem

The following lemma will allow us to consider traces ζ_N with $\text{init}(\zeta_N) \in O(N)$ instead of $\text{init}(\zeta_N) \leq N$ when proving asymptotic lower bounds.

Lemma 17. Let $\mathcal{V}$ be a VASS, let $t \in Trns(\mathcal{V})$ be a transition and let $x \in Var$ be a variable. If there are traces ζ_N with $\text{init}(\zeta_N) \in O(N)$ and $\text{instance}(\zeta_N, t) \geq N^i$, then $\text{tbound}_N(t) \in \Omega(N^i)$. If there are traces ζ_N with $\text{init}(\zeta_N) \in O(N)$ that reach a final valuation ν with $\nu(x) \geq N^i$, then $\text{vbound}_N(x) \in \Omega(N^i)$.

The lower bound proof uses the notion of a *pre-path*, which relaxes the notion of a path: A pre-path $\sigma = t_1 \cdots t_k$ is a finite sequence of transitions $t_i = s_i \xrightarrow{d_i} s'_i$. Note that we do not require for subsequent transitions that the end state of one transition is the start state of the next transition, i.e., we do not require $s'_i = s_{i+1}$. We generalize notions from paths to pre-paths in the obvious way, e.g., we set $val(\sigma) = \sum_{i \in [1,k]} d_i$ and denote by $\text{instance}(\sigma, t)$, for $t \in Trns(\mathcal{V})$, the number of times σ contains the transition t. We say the pre-path σ *can be executed from valuation* ν, if there are valuations $\nu_i \geq 0$ with $\nu_{i+1} = \nu_i + d_{i+1}$ for all $0 \leq i < k$ and $\nu = \nu_0$; we further say that σ *reaches* valuation ν', if $\nu' = \nu_k$. We will need the following relationship between execution and traces: in case a pre-path σ is actually a path, σ can be executed from valuation ν, if and only if there is a trace with initial valuation ν that uses the same sequence of transitions as σ. Two pre-paths $\sigma = t_1 \cdots t_k$ and $\sigma' = t'_1 \cdots t'_l$ can be *shuffled* into a pre-path $\sigma'' = t''_1 \cdots t''_{k+l}$, if σ'' is an order-preserving interleaving of σ and σ'; formally, there are injective monotone functions $f : [1, k] \to [1, k + l]$ and $g : [1, l] \to [1, k + l]$ with $f([1, k]) \cap g([1, l]) = \emptyset$ such that $t''_{f(i)} = t_i$ for all $i \in [1, k]$ and $t''_{g(i)} = t'_i$ for all $i \in [1, l]$. Further, for $d \geq 1$ and pre-path σ, we denote by $\sigma^d = \underbrace{\sigma\sigma \cdots \sigma}_{d}$ the pre-path that consists of d subsequent copies of σ.

For the remainder of this section, we fix a VASS $\mathcal{V}$ for which Algorithm 1 does not report exponential complexity and we fix the computed tree T and bounds vExp, tExp. We further need to use the solutions to constraint system (I) computed during the run of Algorithm 1: For every layer $l \geq 1$ and node $\eta \in \texttt{layer}(l)$, we fix a cycle $C(\eta)$ that contains $\mu(t)$ instances of every $t \in \textit{Trns}(\texttt{VASS}(\eta))$, where μ is an optimal solution to constraint system (I) during loop iteration l. The existence of such cycles is stated in Lemma 18 below. We note that this definition ensures $val(C(\eta)) = \sum_{t \in \textit{Trns}(\texttt{VASS}(\eta))} D(t) \cdot \mu(t)$. Further, for the root node ι, we fix an arbitrary cycle $C(\iota)$ that uses all transitions of $\mathcal{V}$ at least once.

Lemma 18. *Let μ be an optimal solution to constraint system (I) during loop iteration l of Algorithm 1. Then there is a cycle $C(\eta)$ for every $\eta \in \texttt{layer}(l)$ that contains exactly $\mu(t)$ instances of every transition $t \in \textit{Trns}(\texttt{VASS}(\eta))$.*

Proof Outline of the Lower Bound Theorem.
  Step I) We define a pre-path τ_l, for every $l \geq 1$, with the following properties:

1) $\texttt{instance}(\tau_l, t) \geq N^{l+1}$ for all transitions $t \in \bigcup_{\eta \in \texttt{layer}(l)} \textit{Trns}(\texttt{VASS}(\eta))$.
2) $val(\tau_l) = N^{l+1} \sum_{\eta \in \texttt{layer}(l)} val(C(\eta))$.
3) $val(\tau_l)(x) \geq 0$ for every $x \in \textit{Var}$ with $\texttt{vExp}(x) \leq l$.
4) $val(\tau_l)(x) \geq N^{l+1}$ for every $x \in \textit{Var}$ with $\texttt{vExp}(x) \geq l + 1$.
5) τ_l is executable from some valuation ν with
    a) $\nu(x) \in O(N^{\texttt{vExp}(x)})$ for $x \in \textit{Var}$ with $\texttt{vExp}(x) \leq l$, and
    b) $\nu(x) \in O(N^l)$ for $x \in \textit{Var}$ with $\texttt{vExp}(x) \geq l + 1$.

The difficulty in the construction of the pre-paths τ_l lies in ensuring Property 5). The construction of the τ_l proceeds along the tree T using that the cycles $C(\eta)$ have been obtained according to solutions of constraint system (I).

  Step II) It is now a direct consequence of Properties 3)-5) stated above that we can choose a sufficiently large $k > 0$ such that for every $l \geq 0$ the pre-path $\rho_l = \tau_0^k \tau_1^k \cdots \tau_l^k$ (the concatenation of k copies of each τ_i, setting $\tau_0 = C(\iota)^N$), can be executed from some valuation ν and reaches a valuation ν' with

1) $\|\nu\| \in O(N)$,
2) $\nu'(x) \geq kN^{\texttt{vExp}(x)}$ for all $x \in \textit{Var}$ with $\texttt{vExp}(x) \leq l$, and
3) $\nu'(x) \geq kN^{l+1}$ for all $x \in \textit{Var}$ with $\texttt{vExp}(x) \geq l + 1$.

The above stated properties for the pre-path $\rho_{l_{\max}}$, where $l_{\max}$ is the maximal layer of T, would be sufficient to conclude the lower bound proof except that we need to extend the proof from pre-paths to proper paths.

Step III) In order to extend the proof from pre-paths to paths we make use of the concept of shuffling. For all $l \geq 0$, we will define paths γ_l that can be obtained by shuffling the pre-paths $\rho_0, \rho_1, \ldots, \rho_l$. The path $\gamma_{l_{\max}}$, where $l_{\max}$ is the maximal layer of T, then has the desired properties and allows to conclude the lower bound proof with the following result:

Theorem 19. *There are traces ζ_N with $\mathtt{init}(\zeta_N) \in O(N)$ such that ζ_N ends in configuration (s_N, ν_N) with $\nu_N(x) \geq N^{\mathtt{vExp}(x)}$ for all variables $x \in Var$ and we have $\mathtt{instance}(\zeta_N, t) \geq N^{\mathtt{tExp}(t)}$ for all transitions $t \in Trns(\mathcal{V})$.*

With Lemma 17 we get the desired lower bounds from Theorem 19:

Corollary 20. $\mathtt{vbound}_N(x) \in \Omega(N^{\mathtt{vExp}(x)})$ *for all $x \in Var$ and $\mathtt{tbound}_N(t) \in \Omega(N^{\mathtt{tExp}(t)})$ for all $t \in Trns(\mathcal{V})$.*

7 The Size of the Exponents

For the remainder of this section, we fix a VASS $\mathcal{V}$ for which Algorithm 1 does not report exponential complexity and we fix the computed tree T and bounds vExp, tExp. Additionally, we fix a vector $z_l \in \mathbb{Z}^{St(\mathcal{V})}$ for every layer l of T and a vector $r_\eta \in \mathbb{Z}^{Var}$ for every node $\eta \in \mathtt{layer}(l)$ as follows: Let r, z be an optimal solution to constraint system (II) in iteration $l+1$ of Algorithm 1. We then set $z_l = z$. For every $\eta \in \mathtt{layer}(l)$ we define r_η by setting $r_\eta(x) = r(x, \eta')$, where $\eta' \in \mathtt{layer}(l - \mathtt{vExp}(x))$ is the unique ancestor of η in layer $l - \mathtt{vExp}(x)$. The following properties are immediate from the definition:

Proposition 21. *For every layer l of T and node $\eta \in \mathtt{layer}(l)$ we have:*

1) $z_l \geq 0$ and $r_\eta \geq 0$.
2) $r_\eta^T d + z_l(s_2) - z_l(s_1) \leq 0$ for every transition $s_1 \xrightarrow{d} s_2 \in Trns(\mathtt{VASS}(\eta))$; moreover, the inequality is strict for all transitions t with $\mathtt{tExp}(t) = l+1$.
3) Let $\eta' \in \mathtt{layer}(i)$ be a strict ancestor of η. Then, $r_{\eta'}^T d + z_i(s_2) - z_i(s_1) = 0$ for every transition $s_1 \xrightarrow{d} s_2 \in Trns(\mathtt{VASS}(\eta))$.
4) For every $x \in Var$ with $\mathtt{vExp}(x) = l+1$ we have $r_\eta(x) > 0$ and $r_\eta(x) = r_{\eta'}(x)$ for all $\eta' \in \mathtt{layer}(l)$.
5) For every $x \in Var$ with $\mathtt{vExp}(x) > l+1$ we have $r_\eta(x) = 0$.
6) For every $x \in Var$ with $\mathtt{vExp}(x) \leq l$ there is an ancestor $\eta' \in \mathtt{layer}(i)$ of η such that $r_{\eta'}(x) > 0$ and $r_{\eta'}(x') = 0$ for all x' with $\mathtt{vExp}(x') > \mathtt{vExp}(x)$.

For a vector $r \in \mathbb{Z}^{Var}$, we define the *potential* of r by setting $\mathtt{pot}(r) = \max\{\mathtt{vExp}(x) \mid x \in Var, r(x) \neq 0\}$, where we set $\max \emptyset = 0$. The motivation for this definition is that we have $r^T \nu \in O(N^{\mathtt{pot}(r)})$ for every valuation ν reachable by a trace ζ with $\mathtt{init}(\zeta) \leq N$. We will now define the *potential* of a set of vectors $Z \subseteq \mathbb{Z}^{Var}$. Let M be a matrix whose columns are the vectors of Z and whose rows are ordered according to the variable bounds, i.e., if the row associated to variable x' is above the row associated to variable x, then we have

$\text{vExp}(x') \geq \text{vExp}(x)$. Let L be some lower triangular matrix obtained from M by elementary column operations. We now define $\text{pot}(Z) = \sum_{\text{column } r \text{ of } L} \text{pot}(r)$, where we set $\sum \emptyset = 0$. We note that $\text{pot}(Z)$ is well-defined, because the value $\text{pot}(Z)$ does not depend on the choice of M and L.

We next state an upper bound on potentials. Let $l \geq 0$ and let $B_l = \{\text{vExp}(x) \mid x \in Var, \text{vExp}(x) < l\}$ be the set of variable bounds below l. We set $\text{varsum}(l) = 1$, for $B_l = \emptyset$, and $\text{varsum}(l) = \sum B_l$, otherwise. The following statement is a direct consequence of the definitions:

Proposition 22. *Let $Z \subseteq \mathbb{Z}^{Var}$ be a set of vectors such that $r(x) = 0$ for all $r \in Z$ and $x \in Var$ with $\text{vExp}(x) > l$. Then, we have $\text{pot}(Z) \leq \text{varsum}(l+1)$.*

We define $\text{pot}(\eta) = \text{pot}(\{r_{\eta'} \mid \eta' \text{ is a strict ancestor of } \eta\})$ as the *potential* of a node η. We note that $\text{pot}(\eta) \leq \text{varsum}(l+1)$ for every node $\eta \in \text{layer}(l)$ by Proposition 22. Now, we are able to state the main results of this section:

Lemma 23. *Let η be a node in T. Then, every trace ζ with $\text{init}(\zeta) \leq N$ enters $\text{VASS}(\eta)$ at most $O(N^{\text{pot}(\eta)})$ times, i.e., ζ contains at most $O(N^{\text{pot}(\eta)})$ transitions $s \xrightarrow{d} s'$ with $s \notin St(\text{VASS}(\eta))$ and $s' \in St(\text{VASS}(\eta))$.*

Lemma 24. *For every layer l, we have that $\text{vExp}(x) = l$ resp. $\text{tExp}(t) = l$ implies $\text{vExp}(x) \leq \text{varsum}(l)$ resp. $\text{tExp}(t) \leq \text{varsum}(l)$.*

The next result follows from Lemma 24 only by arithmetic manipulations and induction on l:

Lemma 25. *Let l be some layer. Let k be the number of variables $x \in Var$ with $\text{vExp}(x) < l$. Then, $\text{varsum}(l) \leq 2^k$.*

Theorem 11 is then a direct consequence of Lemma 24 and 25 (using $k \leq |Var|$).

8　Exponential Witness

The following lemma from [15] states a condition that is sufficient for a VASS to have exponential complexity[2]. We will use this lemma to prove Theorem 9:

Lemma 26 (Lemma 10 of [15]). *Let $\mathcal{V}$ be a connected VASS, let U, W be a partitioning of Var and let $C_1, \ldots, C_m$ be cycles such that a) $val(C_i)(x) \geq 0$ for all $x \in U$ and $1 \leq i \leq m$, and b) $\sum_i val(C_i)(x) \geq 1$ for all $x \in W$. Then, there is a $c > 1$ and paths π_N such that 1) π_N can be executed from initial valuation $N \cdot 1$, 2) π_N reaches a valuation ν with $\nu(x) \geq c^N$ for all $x \in W$ and 3) $(C_i)^{c^N}$ is a sub-path of π_N for each $1 \leq i \leq m$.*

We now outline the proof of Theorem 9: We assume that Algorithm 1 returned "$\mathcal{V}$ has at least exponential complexity" in loop iteration l. According to Lemma 18, there are cycles $C(\eta)$, for every node $\eta \in \text{layer}(l)$, that contain $\mu(t)$ instances of every transition $t \in Trns(\text{VASS}(\eta))$. One can then show that the cycles $C(\eta)$ and the sets $U = \{x \in Var \mid \text{vExp}(x) \leq l\}$, $W = \{x \in Var \mid \text{vExp}(x) > l\}$ satisfy the requirements of Lemma 26, which establishes Theorem 9.

---

[2] Our formalization differs from[15], but it is easy to verify that our conditions a) and
　b) are equivalent to the conditions on the cycles in the 'iteration schemes' of [15].

References

1. Parosh Aziz Abdulla, Giorgio Delzanno, and Laurent van Begin. A language-based comparison of extensions of Petri nets with and without whole-place operations. In *LATA*, pages 71–82, 2009.
2. Benjamin Aminof, Sasha Rubin, and Florian Zuleger. On the expressive power of communication primitives in parameterised systems. In *LPAR*, pages 313–328, 2015.
3. Benjamin Aminof, Sasha Rubin, Florian Zuleger, and Francesco Spegni. Liveness of parameterized timed networks. In *ICALP*, pages 375–387, 2015.
4. Roderick Bloem, Swen Jacobs, Ayrat Khalimov, Igor Konnov, Sasha Rubin, Helmut Veith, and Josef Widder. Decidability in parameterized verification. *SIGACT News*, 47(2):53–64, 2016.
5. Tomás Brázdil, Krishnendu Chatterjee, Antonín Kucera, Petr Novotný, Dominik Velan, and Florian Zuleger. Efficient algorithms for asymptotic bounds on termination time in VASS. In *LICS*, pages 185–194, 2018.
6. Leonard Dickson. Finiteness of the odd perfect and primitive abundant numbers with n distinct prime factors. *Am. J. Math*, 35:413—-422, 1913.
7. Javier Esparza and Mogens Nielsen. Decidability issues for Petri nets - a survey. *Elektronische Informationsverarbeitung und Kybernetik*, 30(3):143–160, 1994.
8. Alain Finkel, Gilles Geeraerts, Jean-François Raskin, and Laurent van Begin. On the *omega*-language expressive power of extended Petri nets. *TCS*, 356(3):374–386, 2006.
9. Steven M. German and A. Prasad Sistla. Reasoning about systems with many processes. *J. ACM*, 39(3):675–735, 1992.
10. John E. Hopcroft and Jean-Jacques Pansiot. On the reachability problem for 5-dimensional vector addition systems. *TCS*, 8:135–159, 1979.
11. Annu John, Igor Konnov, Ulrich Schmid, Helmut Veith, and Josef Widder. Parameterized model checking of fault-tolerant distributed algorithms by abstraction. In *FMCAD*, pages 201–209, 2013.
12. Alexander Kaiser, Daniel Kroening, and Thomas Wahl. A widening approach to multithreaded program verification. *TOPLAS*, 36(4):14:1–14:29, 2014.
13. Richard M. Karp and Raymond E. Miller. Parallel program schemata. *J. Comput. Syst. Sci.*, 3(2):147–195, 1969.
14. S. Rao Kosaraju and Gregory F. Sullivan. Detecting cycles in dynamic graphs in polynomial time (preliminary version). In *STOC*, pages 398–406, 1988.
15. Jérôme Leroux. Polynomial vector addition systems with states. In *ICALP*, pages 134:1–134:13, 2018.
16. Richard J. Lipton. *The Reachability Problem Requires Exponential space*. Research report 62. Department of Computer Science, Yale University, 1976.
17. Charles Rackoff. The covering and boundedness problems for vector addition systems. *TCS*, 6:223–231, 1978.
18. Moritz Sinn, Florian Zuleger, and Helmut Veith. A simple and scalable static analysis for bound analysis and amortized complexity analysis. In *CAV*, pages 745–761, 2014.
19. Moritz Sinn, Florian Zuleger, and Helmut Veith. Difference constraints: An adequate abstraction for complexity analysis of imperative programs. In *FMCAD*, pages 144–151, 2015.
20. Moritz Sinn, Florian Zuleger, and Helmut Veith. Complexity and resource bound analysis of imperative programs using difference constraints. *JAR*, 59:3–45, 2017.
21. Florian Zuleger. The polynomial complexity of vector addition systems with states. *CoRR*, abs/1907.01076, 2019.

Permissions

The contributors of this book come from diverse backgrounds, making this book a truly international effort. This book will bring forth new frontiers with its revolutionizing research information and detailed analysis of the nascent developments around the world.

We would like to thank all the contributing authors for lending their expertise to make the book truly unique. They have played a crucial role in the development of this book. Without their invaluable contributions this book wouldn't have been possible. They have made vital efforts to compile up to date information on the varied aspects of this subject to make this book a valuable addition to the collection of many professionals and students.

This book was conceptualized with the vision of imparting up-to-date information and advanced data in this field. To ensure the same, a matchless editorial board was set up. Every individual on the board went through rigorous rounds of assessment to prove their worth. After which they invested a large part of their time researching and compiling the most relevant data for our readers.

The editorial board has been involved in producing this book since its inception. They have spent rigorous hours researching and exploring the diverse topics which have resulted in the successful publishing of this book. They have passed on their knowledge of decades through this book. To expedite this challenging task, the publisher supported the team at every step. A small team of assistant editors was also appointed to further simplify the editing procedure and attain best results for the readers.

Apart from the editorial board, the designing team has also invested a significant amount of their time in understanding the subject and creating the most relevant covers. They scrutinized every image to scout for the most suitable representation of the subject and create an appropriate cover for the book.

The publishing team has been an ardent support to the editorial, designing and production team. Their endless efforts to recruit the best for this project, has resulted in the accomplishment of this book. They are a veteran in the field of academics and their pool of knowledge is as vast as their experience in printing. Their expertise and guidance has proved useful at every step. Their uncompromising quality standards have made this book an exceptional effort. Their encouragement from time to time has been an inspiration for everyone.

The publisher and the editorial board hope that this book will prove to be a valuable piece of knowledge for researchers, students, practitioners and scholars across the globe.

List of Contributors

Thomas Colcombet
Université de Paris, IRIF, CNRS, Paris, France

Nathanaël Fijalkow
CNRS, LaBRI, Bordeaux, France
The Alan Turing Institute of data science, London, United Kingdom

Pierre Ohlmann
Université de Paris, IRIF, CNRS, Paris, France

Jiří Adámek
Czech Technical University, Prague, Czech Republic

Stefan Milius
Friedrich-Alexander-Universität Erlangen-Nürnberg, Germany

Lawrence S. Moss
Indiana University, Bloomington, IN, USA

S. Akshay
IIT Bombay, Mumbai, India

Blaise Genest
Univ Rennes, CNRS, IRISA, Rennes, France

Loïc Hélouët
Univ Rennes, Inria, Rennes, France

Sharvik Mital
IIT Bombay, Mumbai, India

Usama Mehmood
Stony Brook University, Stony Brook NY, USA

Shouvik Roy
Stony Brook University, Stony Brook NY, USA

Radu Grosu
Technische Universitat Wien, Wien, Austria

Scott A. Smolka
Stony Brook University, Stony Brook NY, USA

Scott D. Stoller
Stony Brook University, Stony Brook NY, USA

Ashish Tiwari
Microsoft Research, San Francisco CA, USA

Ivan Lanese
Focus Team, University of Bologna/INRIA, Italy

Iain Phillips
Imperial College London, England

Irek Ulidowski
University of Leicester, England

Thomas Neele
Eindhoven University of Technology, Eindhoven, The Netherlands

Antti Valmari
University of Jyväskylä, Jyväskylä, Finland

Tim A.C. Willemse
Eindhoven University of Technology, Eindhoven, The Netherlands

Brigitte Pientka
McGill University, Montreal, Canada

Ulrich Schöpp
fortiss GmbH, Munich, Germany

Miriam Polzer and Sergey Goncharov
FAU Erlangen-Nürnberg, Erlangen, Germany

Christof Löding and Anton Pirogov
RWTH Aachen University, Templergraben 55, 52062 Aachen, Germany

David Sherratt
Friedrich-Schiller-Universität Jena, Germany

Willem Heijltjes
University of Bath, United Kingdom

Tom Gundersen
Red Hat, Inc. Norway

Michel Parigot
Institut de Recherche en Informatique
Fondamentale, CNRS, Université de Paris
France

Romain Péchoux
Université de Lorraine, CNRS, Inria, LORIA,
F 54000 Nancy, France

Simon Perdrix
Université de Lorraine, CNRS, Inria, LORIA,
F 54000 Nancy, France

Mathys Rennela
Leiden University, Leiden, The Netherlands

Vladimir Zamdzhiev
Université de Lorraine, CNRS, Inria, LORIA,
F 54000 Nancy, France

Florian Zuleger
TU Wien, University of Vienna, Austria

Index

A

Abstract Syntax, 38-40, 42, 45, 55-56
Algebra Morphism, 60, 64-65, 71, 107-108
Atomic Propositions, 119, 129-130, 132, 135
Axiomatic Approach, 18, 36, 56

B

Basic Flocking, 139, 141-149
Bi-algebras, 99, 107, 113
Bi-hyperdoctrine, 98-100, 107-109, 113, 115
Binary Relation, 21, 32, 124
Bound Variables, 78-80, 82, 84, 87, 91
Büchi Automata, 193-196, 207, 210-212

C

Categorical Semantics, 98, 172
Category-theoretic Semantics, 38-39
Causal Liveness, 18-20, 24, 27-28, 34
Causal Safety, 18-20, 24, 26-30, 33-34
Causal-consistent Reversibility, 19-20, 35-36
Classical Automata, 195, 200-201
Coalgebra, 58-62, 64-76
Commutative Monoid, 98, 108
Concurrent System, 18, 213
Contextual Modal Type, 38-39, 47, 55-56
Contextual Objects, 38, 46-48, 52, 57
Contextual Types, 38-39, 42-43, 46-48, 51-53, 55
Convex Sums, 165, 170

D

Deep Inference, 78, 95-96
Deep Neural Network, 138-139, 146
Director Strings, 80, 96-97
Distributed Computing, 2, 16
Distributed Neural Controller, 138-139, 144
Dynamic Memory Allocation, 98, 115

E

Exptime-complete, 1, 175

F

Final Configuration, 174-175, 178
Flocking Controllers, 138, 140, 144-145
Flow Matrix, 218, 221-222, 226
Free Variables, 43, 46, 83-84, 92
Full Ground Store, 98-100, 102, 106, 109, 115

G

General Recursion Theorem, 58-60, 64, 70, 75, 77

H

Higher-order Abstract, 38, 40, 42, 45, 55-56

I

Inconsistent Labelling Problem, 118-119, 123, 125-128, 134-135
Induction, 11, 39, 53, 58, 64, 71-72, 76-77, 91, 103, 132, 155, 160, 166, 168-170, 187, 189, 203, 226-227, 230
Inductive Datatypes, 154-155, 164, 166, 171
Inductive Types, 154
Infinite Reverse Computation, 23
Initial Algebra, 58, 60, 64, 70, 72-74, 166

L

Labelled Transition Systems, 19, 21, 66
Lambda-calculus, 40-41, 55, 78, 96-97

M

Markov Decision Process, 1, 3
Model Predictive Control, 138, 152-153
Modelling Biological Systems, 2, 16
Morphisms, 41-42, 44-45, 54, 62-63, 71-73, 75-76, 104-105, 164-165, 168-169

N

Natural Numbers, 58, 63, 102-103, 154-155, 158, 217
Neural Flocking, 138-139, 143-145, 151

O

Open Deduction, 80-82, 95

Operational Semantics, 157, 159, 165, 170

Optimal Reduction, 79, 84, 95

P

Parameterised Control, 2, 15

Parameterised Systems, 1, 231

Parameterized Verification, 16, 213, 231

Partial-order Reduction, 118, 136

Petri Nets, 3, 17, 19-20, 36, 119, 128, 132, 134-137, 174-175, 180, 192, 213, 231

Phantom-abstraction, 83, 85

Polynomial Complexity, 213-214, 231

Probabilistic Automata, 2-3, 16-17, 193, 195-197, 199, 208, 211-212

Probabilistic Büchi Automata, 193, 207, 211

Process Calculi, 18-19, 37

Programming Language, 37-38, 154-155, 171-173

Proof Theory, 78, 81, 95, 98

Pspace-complete, 175, 179

Q

Quantum Computing, 154-155, 165, 173

Quantum Programming, 154-155, 171-173

R

Recursive Coalgebras, 58-59, 64, 71, 76

Reversible Computation, 18-19, 36

S

Self-loops, 129, 215

Semantical Analysis, 38, 56

Semantics, 2, 13, 33-34, 36, 38-39, 55-58, 66, 76, 96-102, 106, 113-116, 119, 154-155, 157, 159-160, 165-166, 168, 170-173, 176, 178, 180, 193-195, 197-200, 202-205, 207-210, 212

Separation Logic, 99-100, 108-109, 111-112, 116

Sharing Calculus, 81, 83

State-action Pairs, 138-139, 144

Stochastic Control Problem, 1-4, 6-11, 15-16

Supervised Learning, 138-139, 144, 151

Syntactic Structures, 38-39

Syntax, 13, 38-42, 44-45, 48, 55-56, 79, 83, 96, 102, 155-156, 171

T

Target Seeking, 138, 140, 142-146, 151

Timed Negotiations, 174, 176, 178, 180, 183, 191-192

Timed Valuation, 180

U

Upper Bound Theorem, 226

V

Vector Addition Systems, 211, 213, 231